*Russia, the Soviet Union,
and the United States:
An Interpretive History*

# Russia, the Soviet Union, and the United States:

## An Interpretive History

Second Edition

JOHN LEWIS GADDIS
*Ohio University*

**McGraw-Hill Publishing Company**
New York  St. Louis  San Francisco  Auckland
Bogotá  Caracas  Hamburg  Lisbon  London  Madrid
Mexico  Milan  Montreal  New Delhi  Oklahoma City  Paris
San Juan  São Paulo  Singapore  Sydney  Tokyo  Toronto

This book was set in Palatino by the College Composition Unit
in cooperation with Monotype Composition Company.
The editors were Christopher J. Rogers and Ira C. Roberts;
the production supervisor was Louise Karam.
The cover was designed by John Hite.
R. R. Donnelley & Sons Company was printer and binder.

RUSSIA, THE SOVIET UNION,
AND THE UNITED STATES
An Interpretive History

1 2 3 4 5 6 7 8 9 0   DOC   DOC   9 5 4 3 2 1 0

ISBN   0-07-557258-3

Library of Congress Cataloging-in-Publication Data

Gaddis, John Lewis.
    Russia, the Soviet Union, and the United States: an interpretive history/
    John Lewis Gaddis.    2nd ed.
    p.    cm.
    Includes bibliographical references (p.    )
    ISBN 0-07-557258-3
    1. United States—Foreign relations—Soviet Union.    2. Soviet
Union—Foreign relations—United States.    3. United States—Foreign
relations—20th century.    I. Title
E183.8.S65G34        1990
327.73047—dc20                                                89-28784

# About the Author

John Lewis Gaddis is Distinguished Professor of History and Director of the Contemporary History Institute at Ohio University. He received his B. A., M. A., and Ph. D. degrees from the University of Texas at Austin; his other publications include *The United States and the Origins of the Cold War, 1941-1947* (Columbia University Press, 1972); *Strategies of Containment: A Critical Appraisal of Postwar American National Security Policy* (Oxford University Press, 1982); and *The Long Peace: Inquiries into the History of the Cold War* (Oxford University Press, 1987).

Professor Gaddis has served as Visiting Professor of Strategy at the United States Naval War College (1975-1977), Bicentennial Professor of American Studies at the University of Helsinki (1980-1981), and Visiting Professor of War and Peace at Princeton University (1987). He is a member of the American Historial Association, the Organization of American Historians, the Society for Historians of American Foreign Relations, the Council on Foreign Relations, and is co-chair of the History, Social Sciences, and International Security Affairs Workshop of the American Academy of Arts and Sciences.

*For the Grandparents*
*of Michael and David*

# Contents

# Foreword

IT IS DIFFICULT TO CONCEIVE OF A MORE SIGNIFICANT TOPIC in twentieth-century American diplomacy than our relations with the Soviet Union. Ever since Lenin's accession to power in 1917, Russian leaders and their enigmatic behavior, from Stalin's brutal purges and sphinxlike demeanor to Khrushchev's peasant charm and outrageous tirades to Gorbachev's mastery of public relations and efforts at sweeping reforms, have engrossed American policymakers and the American public alike. Yet, as John Lewis Gaddis makes clear in these pages, our relationship with Russia goes back yet another century. Since the American Revolution, United States diplomats have borne the indignities that Russians have heaped on foreigners, have searched for ways to permit mutual interests to triumph over conflicting ideologies, and have sought to win the favor of such capricious rulers as Catherine the Great and Tsar Alexander I. The stakes became much greater in the Cold War years, but the essential outline of Russian-American relations remained unchanged—oscillation between friendship and enmity as diplomats succeeded only occasionally in balancing interests against principles.

Against the backdrop of these nineteenth-century beginnings, Professor Gaddis focuses his attention on the more recent experience with the Soviet regime, tracing the uneven course of relations from the Bolshevik Revolution down to the Gorbachev era of *glasnost* and *perestroika*. He treats the varied aspects of Soviet-American diplomacy: repeated efforts to stimulate trade, attempts to lessen Soviet internal repression, negotiations to ease the arms race, and, above all, the constant search for stability in Europe. The continental balance of power remains the focal point from the time Russia leaves World War I in 1918 through the Helsinki

accords that ratified the de facto post-World War II division of
Germany, and thus of all Europe, between the East and the West.
He even suggests that this acceptance of political reality may indicate that the Cold War is ending just as George Kennan predicted it would—with the mellowing of the Soviet system.

Professor Gaddis has written a comprehensive account that
transcends the historiographical disputes over the Cold War to
achieve a balanced and perceptive understanding of how these
two great nations, so alike in some ways and so different in others, have survived more than two centuries of mutual distrust.

ROBERT A. DIVINE

# Preface to the Second Edition

GIVEN THE POTENTIAL FOR CATACLYSM THAT IS INHERENT IN ITS SUBJECT, I find it more than usually gratifying to be in a position to prepare a second edition of this book. For it, I have added a new chapter on the Carter and Reagan administrations, substantially rewritten portions of Chapters VII, VIII, and IX, made minor modifications elsewhere in the text, added maps, and updated footnote and bibliographical references throughout. I am grateful to Karin Wright for research assistance; to James K. Libbey for pointing out a shaky translation from the Russian in the first edition; to Christopher Rogers and Ira Roberts at McGraw-Hill for seeing this new edition through the necessary editorial and publication processes; and, of course, to Bob Divine for his suggestions and encouragement at all points along the way.

Barbara Gaddis read the new material with her usual sharp eye for oversimplification and error, and pitched in at a busy time to do most of the revised index. My son Michael, who has already encountered the first edition of this book as required reading in a college course, has not hesitated to make clear where he did and did not get his money's worth; David's views on this subject will, I trust, follow soon enough.

JOHN LEWIS GADDIS

# Preface to the First Edition

"THERE ARE NOW TWO GREAT NATIONS IN THE WORLD which, starting from different points, seem to be advancing toward the same goal: the Russians and the Anglo-Americans. ...Each seems called by some secret design of Providence one day to hold in its hands the destinies of half the world."[1] It is almost obligatory to begin any history of Russian-American relations with a reference to this famous prophecy, put forward by Alexis de Tocqueville in 1835. In fact, however, there was nothing foreordained about the circumstances that nearly brought its fulfillment more than a century later. The division of most of the post-1945 world into Russian and American spheres was not the result of those two countries' expanding population and territory, as Tocqueville had thought it would be, but rather of the suicidal instincts of the Europeans, whose wars opened opportunities for the simultaneous extension of influence by the United States and the Soviet Union. Nor was this bipolar configuration of power either as absolute or as lasting as Tocqueville had anticipated: the ability of Russians and Americans to control their respective halves of the world was never complete and has, in recent years, substantially declined.

A more fruitful approach to the history of Russian-American relations is to examine the interplay, in the foreign policies of both countries, between interests and ideologies. "Interests" are here understood to mean those conditions a state considers necessary in order to maintain its authority in the world; "ideologies" are the justifications advanced for the exercise of that au-

---

[1] Alexis de Tocqueville, *Democracy in America*, J. P. Mayer and Max Lerner, eds., translated by George Lawrence (New York: 1966), pp. 378–379.

thority. These admittedly oversimplified definitions are not mutually exclusive; ideologies can become interests, and interests can become ideologies. Even so, this interpretive framework contributes more to an understanding of the topic at hand than does Tocqueville's doctrine of "inevitability," and, for this reason, I have chosen to employ it in the discussion to follow.

This is a work of both synthesis and original scholarship. Where satisfactory secondary accounts exist, I have generally followed them and hereby express my indebtedness to their authors. Where they do not (and there are a surprising number of areas in the history of Russian-American relations where this is the case), I have had recourse to such primary sources as are available. Detailed examinations of historiographical disputes seemed inappropriate in a book of this nature; my accounts of such controversial subjects as the Bolshevik Revolution and the origins of the Cold War should be taken as reflecting my own best judgment, and nothing more.

I should like to express my appreciation to Robert A. Divine for suggesting that I undertake this volume and for the helpful advice he provided while it was being written. For reading and commenting on preliminary drafts, I am grateful to James A. Field, Jr., Alonzo L. Hamby, David Schoenbaum, Thomas H. Etzold, Alan T. Isaacson, and Akira Iriye. An Ohio University Research Council fellowship helped to defray photoduplication expenses. My wife, Barbara, calmly tolerated the tantrums, scowls, and brooding silences which go with authorship. My sons, Michael and David, kindly refrained (most of the time) from scribbling on their father's manuscript.

Portions of Chapters VI and VII appeared originally as an essay in Frank Merli and Theodore A. Wilson, eds., *Makers of American Diplomacy* (New York: 1974), and are reprinted by permission of Charles Scribner's Sons. Before it was abolished in 1918, the Russian calendar was thirteen days behind that of the West for the twentieth century, twelve days for the nineteenth, and eleven days for the eighteenth. All dates cited in this book are according to the Western, or "New Style" calendar.

JOHN LEWIS GADDIS

CHAPTER I

# A Heritage of Harmony: 1781–1867

*I*T WOULD BE BEST FOR US TO WAIVE ALL DISCUSSION upon abstract principles....we must endeavor to settle the differences between our Governments on the basis [of] our *mutual interests.*"[1] It was the kind of statement that might have been made at any one of the Nixon-Brezhnev summits of 1972–1974, but in fact it dates from 1824, when Count Karl Robert Nesselrode, foreign minister to the Tsar Alexander I, opened negotiations with American minister Henry Middleton on boundary problems in the Pacific Northwest. Nesselrode, who served as foreign minister from 1816 to 1856, was more noted for his stamina than his sagacity, but in this statement he neatly characterized the early Russian-American relationship. Profound ideological differences existed between the young American republic, in many ways the most revolutionary government of its day, and the ancient tsarist autocracy, which had sworn hostility to revolutions everywhere. But they also shared common interests, and because both states, at this time, gave more weight to interests than ideology in their diplomacy, the basis was established for the most consistently friendly relationship the United States would have with a major European power in the nineteenth century.

I

Americans knew from the beginning that their struggle for independence from Great Britain could not succeed without for-

---

[1] Henry Middleton to John Quincy Adams, April 19, 1824, in U.S. Congress, Senate (58th Cong., 2nd Sess.), *Alaska Boundary Tribunal, Appendix* (Washington: 1903), pp. 71–72.

eign assistance. Such aid would not be difficult to obtain, they believed, because independence would open the hitherto-forbidden North American trade to Britain's rivals. In holding this view, the colonists exaggerated the importance of economic considerations in the minds of Old World diplomats, a mistake they would repeat frequently in the next two centuries.[2] France, Spain, and several other powers were prepared to grant the colonists varying degrees of help—and to risk war with Britain in order to do so. But they acted from considerations of power politics; the lure of trade was, for them, a distinctly secondary consideration.

Catherine the Great's Russia was no exception. The chief goal of the Russian monarch at the time of the American Revolution was to maintain a balance of power on the European continent. Her principal instrument for doing this was the so-called "Northern system," a loose alignment with Britain, the Scandinavian and Baltic countries designed to balance the land power of France and Austria. At the same time, Catherine was wary of Britain's becoming too powerful, because that nation could control, through its domination of trade in the Baltic, much of Russia's commerce with the rest of the world.[3] It is within this context that Catherine's response to the American Revolution must be viewed.

Catherine seemed, at first, sympathetic. She made clear her opinion that the British could not suppress the revolt in North America and refused requests from George III for military assistance. In 1780, Catherine formed a League of Armed Neutrality, based on the principle, dear to the Americans, that "free ships make free goods." Her foreign minister, Nikita Panin, originated a plan for mediating the Anglo-French war sparked by the Revolution on a basis that would have confirmed the independence of most, if not all, of the American colonies.[4] These hopeful signs encouraged the Continental Congress, late in 1780, to send Francis Dana, a Massachusetts lawyer then in

---

[2]Felix Gilbert, *To the Farewell Address: Ideas of Early American Foreign Policy* (Princeton: 1961), pp. 54–56. See also Jonathan R. Dull, *A Diplomatic History of the American Revolution* (New Haven: 1985), pp. 53–54.

[3]David M. Griffiths, "Nikita Panin, Russian Diplomacy, and the American Revolution," *Slavic Review*, XXVIII (March, 1969), 4–7.

[4]Ibid., pp. 1–24.

Europe as John Adams' secretary, to St. Petersburg in an effort "to engage Her Imperial Majesty to favor and support the sovereignty and independence of the United States, and to lay a foundation for a good understanding and friendly intercourse between the subjects of Her Imperial Majesty and the citizens of these United States, to the mutual advantage of both nations."[5]

Dana's reception in Russia was, to say the least, disappointing. Catherine studiously ignored the American envoy's presence, on the grounds that she could not acknowledge American independence until the British had done so. When Dana, following the Congress' instructions, tried to associate the United States with the League of Armed Neutrality, Catherine's ministers rebuffed him on the irrefutable ground that the United States could hardly qualify as a neutral in the existing conflict. Efforts to hold out trade as an inducement to recognition proved equally futile: nonrecognition did not preclude such trade as did exist, nor were the Russians, at that time, very interested in expanding it.[6] Embittered by his treatment, Dana left the Russian capital after two ineffectual and frustrating years. It was not an auspicious beginning for the Russian-American relationship.

The failure of Dana's mission has been variously explained as the result of Catherine's ideological antipathy toward the American revolutionaries, the inability of a stuffy Puritan diplomat to engage in boudoir politics, and France's cynical attempts to undercut its American ally.[7] None of these explanations has much merit. In fact, both the Russian government's initial sympathy for the American Revolution and its subsequent indifference to it can best be understood as the product of realistic considerations, on the part of Catherine and her ministers, of Russian national interests.

Neither Catherine nor her advisers saw any particular ideological challenge in the Americans' revolt against Britain: George III, the empress believed, had brought on his own difficulties through inept administration. She did see a threat to

---

[5]Worthington C. Ford, et al., eds., *Journals of the Continental Congress* (Washington: 1904–1937), XVIII, 1168–1169.

[6]David M. Griffiths, "American Commercial Diplomacy in Russia, 1780 to 1783," *William and Mary Quarterly*, XXVII (July, 1970), 390–400.

[7]Ibid., pp. 379–380.

the European balance of power, though, if Britain, an important counterweight to France and Austria, should get bogged down in a lengthy colonial war in North America. It was this consideration that caused Catherine to reject British requests for troops and naval supplies to help put down the rebellion. The eruption of war between Britain and France in 1778, and between Britain and Spain in 1779, lent urgency to the situation: these events moved Panin to propose mediation. Russian interest in American independence stemmed, therefore, from a calculated assessment of what was necessary to maintain equilibrium in Europe, not from any abstract infatuation on the part of the empress or her ministers for republican principles.[8]

Nor did the Americans understand the distinction between mediation and recognition—the first did not necessarily imply the second. Catherine's chief interest was to settle the war between Britain and its enemies. Recognition of American independence before the British had acknowledged it would have impaired her ability to achieve such a settlement. And, by the end of 1781, even mediation had become a remote prospect: the Americans had defeated Cornwallis at Yorktown and were insisting on direct negotiations with the British. Catherine, meanwhile, had turned her attention toward the Turkish Empire, a move requiring reconciliation with Austria and, more than in the past, the benevolent sympathy of Great Britain. The congruence of interests that caused the Continental Congress to send Dana to St. Petersburg was deceptive, therefore; although Russians and Americans took similar positions on several of the great issues of the day, they arrived at those positions from wholly different perspectives, which provided little basis for mutual cooperation.

## II

A firmer basis for cooperation developed as a result of trade between Russia and the United States during the first decade of the nineteenth century. Commercial contacts between Russians

---

[8]Griffiths, "Panin, Russian Diplomacy, and the American Revolution," pp. 1–18; Frank A. Golder, "Catherine II and the American Revolution," *American Historical Review*, XXI (1915), 92–96; Nikolai N. Bolkhovitinov, *The Beginnings of Russian-American Relations, 1775–1815*, translated by Elena Levin (Cambridge, Massachusetts: 1975), pp. 28–29.

and Americans were nothing new. Virginia tobacco had found its way to Russia, by way of England, in the late seventeenth century, and by 1763 Boston merchants had begun a profitable direct trade with St. Petersburg, in violation of British maritime regulations. It was not until after 1800, however, that the volume of commerce became considerable. Carried on almost exclusively in American ships, it involved the sale of such commodities as sugar, rice, indigo, and, later, cotton, from the United States and the West Indies, in return for Russian hemp, iron, and sailcloth, all highly prized for their use on sailing vessels. Britain remained, of course, Russia's largest trading partner during this period, but the Russian government did attach sufficient importance to direct commerce with the United States to encourage it as a means of escaping London's domination of trade in the Baltic.[9]

But commerce could not be kept aloof from politics: by 1807 the Napoleonic wars had seriously constricted Russian-American trade. The British, through their Orders in Council, severely limited neutral trade with the Continent, while Napoleon responded by threatening to confiscate ships found complying with the British regulations. This "damned if you do, damned if you don't" situation led President Jefferson, late that year, to impose an embargo on all American trade with foreign countries. The embargo hit Russia especially hard because she had just gone to war with her major commercial partner, Britain, following the reconciliation with Napoleon at Tilsit. It was this common predicament of being denied access to trade that caused Alexander I and Jefferson, apparently independently of each other, to decide in 1808 to establish formal diplomatic relations between their two countries.[10]

"It cannot be unimportant to have, in a party so powerful and influential as Russia, a good will and wakeful attention to

---

[9]Norman E. Saul, "The Beginnings of American-Russian Trade, 1763–1766," *William and Mary Quarterly*, XXVI(October, 1969), 596–600; Alfred W. Crosby, Jr., *America, Russia, Hemp and Napoleon: American Trade with Russia and the Baltic, 1783–1812* (Columbus: 1965), pp. 14–39; Aa. Rasch, "American Trade in the Baltic, 1783–1807," *Scandinavian Economic History Review*, XIII(1965), 63–64; N.N. Bolkhovitinov, "Novye raboty o russko-amerikanskoi torgovle v XVII-nachale XIX veka," *Novaia i noveishaia istoriia*, 1967, #4, 122–126.

[10]Bolkhovitinov, *The Beginnings of Russian-American Relations*, pp. 187–193; John C. Hildt, *Early Diplomatic Relations of the United States with Russia* (Baltimore: 1906), pp. 35–43.

the just rights and interests of the United States," wrote Secretary of State James Madison to William Short, the new minister-designate to St. Petersburg. Alexander I was more blunt. "I seek in the United States a kind of rival to England," he told his new minister to Washington, Count Pahlen. "I believe that it is in their own interest...at least to moderate, if not to limit, the baneful despotism which Great Britain exerts over the sea."[11]

When the Senate refused to confirm Short, Madison, who by then had become president, nominated in his place John Quincy Adams. It was not Adams' first exposure to Russia: as a boy, he had spent two years in the Russian capital serving as Francis Dana's secretary. An astute diplomat and an accomplished linguist (in French—Russian was little used at the emperor's court), the crusty New Englander was an excellent choice. The four years he spent in St. Petersburg laid the foundation for what became a tradition of good relations between the United States and Russia.[12]

The common interest the two countries had in asserting maritime rights led both into war in June 1812, although with different enemies. The alliance between France and Russia had, from the first, rested on a fragile base. It was stretched even further when the British, in 1809, agreed to allow neutral trade with Russia. This action stimulated a great increase in American commerce, freed by repeal of the embargo that same year, to the point that by 1810, American vessels were carrying 20% of all exports out of St. Petersburg.[13] Napoleon's efforts to stop this trade, which he rightly suspected the British of using to undercut his Continental System, contributed in part to the worsening of Franco-Russian relations and to the French invasion of Russia in the summer of 1812.

Meanwhile, United States relations with Great Britain had deteriorated with the refusal of the British to modify their Or-

[11]Madison to Short, September 8, 1808, U.S. Department of State Records, National Archives [hereafter DSR], microfilm M-77, roll 2; Alexander to Pahlen, January 8, 1810, Ministerstvo inostrannykh del SSSR, *Vneshniaia politika Rossii XIX i nachala XX veka* (Moscow: 1967), V, 338.

[12]Samuel Flagg Bemis, *John Quincy Adams and the Foundations of American Foreign Policy* (New York: 1949), pp. 156–189.

[13]Norman E. Saul, "Jonathan Russell, *President Adams*, and Europe in 1810," *American Neptune*, XXX(October, 1970), 287–289.

ders in Council in the face of economic coercion. Both the British and the French violated American neutral rights, but the British violations, involving impressment as well as the searching of ships and the seizure of cargoes, were more humiliating. Furthermore, in Canada the Americans had a convenient place to attack the British; there was no such contiguous territory under French control. As a result, Congress on June 18, 1812, declared war, not knowing that only two days earlier the British government had announced its intention to repeal the offending Orders in Council.

Britain's involvement in war with the Americans posed problems for the Russians, just as some three and a half decades earlier, George III's determination to crush the American Revolution had worried Catherine II. Alexander's response was much the same as his grandmother's: he sought to arrange mediation of the Anglo-American war so that Britain would be free to concentrate its resources against the French in Europe. The tsar proposed mediation in September, 1812, and by April of the following year President Madison, without waiting to see whether the British would accept, had dispatched Albert Gallatin and James A. Bayard to join Adams in St. Petersburg for the purpose of negotiating a peace under the benevolent supervision of the Russian emperor.

This proved to be a mistake, for the British refused to discuss peace under Russian mediation. They did propose separate bilateral negotiations with the Americans, however, and these, after much delay, got underway at Ghent in the summer of 1814. By Christmas of that year, a treaty had been signed ending the conflict on the basis of a return to the status quo before the war. Alexander, who by this time had defeated Napoleon at the head of the victorious Fourth Coalition, took little interest in the talks at Ghent, now overshadowed by more dramatic developments at the Congress of Vienna. But the Russian mediation offer had prodded the British into beginning negotiations, and the Americans could at least be grateful for that.[14]

---

[14]Frank A. Golder, "The Russian Offer of Mediation in the War of 1812," *Political Science Quarterly*, XXXI(1916), 380–391; J. C. A. Stagg, *Mr. Madison's War: Politics, Diplomacy, and Warfare in the Early American Republic, 1783–1830* (Princeton: 1983), pp. 298–303.

## III

The developing congruence of interests between Russia and the United States during the Napoleonic wars obscured, for the moment, potential areas of conflict, but the return of peace made it clear that antagonisms did exist. The task of resolving these differences amicably provided the first real test of the habit of cooperation that had grown up between the two nations.

One such conflict was territorial. Early in the eighteenth century Russian explorers had laid claim to what is today Alaska, and in 1799 the Russian-America Company had been organized to exploit this area. Almost immediately the company's remote possessions became subject to incursions from American trappers and traders; one reason why the Russians were anxious to establish diplomatic relations in 1808 was their desire to lodge an official protest.[15] Not until 1821, however, did the matter become serious: in September of that year, Alexander I issued a *ukase* denying foreigners access to Russian-America and asserting control of its adjoining seas for a distance of more than one hundred miles from the shore.[16]

This order, signed at the instigation of the Russian-America Company, aroused concern in Washington not only because of its restrictions on maritime commerce, but also because the conviction had begun to form in the minds of many Americans that the United States was destined to dominate the Western Hemisphere and should therefore oppose further attempts by European powers to establish colonies there. Secretary of State John Quincy Adams put the argument forcefully to the Russian minister in Washington in July 1823:

> I told him specially that we should contest the right of Russia to *any* territorial establishment on this continent, and that we should assume distinctly the principle that the American continents are no longer subjects for *any* new European colonial establishments.[17]

---

[15]Rumiantsev to Levett Harris, May 29, 1808, *Vneshniaia politika Rossii*, IV, 267.

[16]Howard I. Kushner, *Conflict on the Northwest Coast: American-Russian Rivalry in the Pacific Northwest, 1790–1867* (Westport, Connecticut: 1975), pp. 11–12.

[17]Charles Francis Adams, ed., *The Memoirs of John Quincy Adams* (Philadelphia: 1875), VI, 163.

In a somewhat less direct form, this noncolonization principle was incorporated into President Monroe's message to Congress in December of that year, thus forming part of what came to be known as the Monroe Doctrine.

The Emperor Alexander had long since decided not to enforce the 1821 *ukase*, which he had apparently signed without much thought. Confronted with protests from both the American and British ministers, he agreed to initiate joint discussions with them in an effort to establish, once and for all, territorial limits in the Pacific Northwest. These talks resulted, in 1824, in separate Russian-American and Anglo-Russian treaties setting the southern boundary of Russian-America at the latitude fifty-four degrees, forty minutes.[18]

More serious than the territorial question in the Pacific Northwest was the issue of whether Spanish rule was to be restored in Latin America. Independence movements in that part of the world had grown out of Spain's weakness resulting largely from the Napoleonic wars, but it was not until after Napoleon's defeat that the European powers were able to give serious thought to what should be done about these insurgencies. Except for the British, who saw trade opportunities in an independent Latin America, the European monarchies could hardly welcome the establishment of republics throughout most of Spain's New World empire. But without the cooperation of the British navy there was little the European monarchs could do to suppress these movements and restore Spanish authority.

Alexander I made clear his antipathy for the Latin American rebels and gave official support to the Spanish government's efforts to suppress them. At the same time, he was realistic enough to recognize that he could do little in the absence of British support and that, by pressing the point too hard, he might alienate the Americans, to whom he still looked as a counterweight to London. And in 1820, revolution broke out in Spain itself, forcing plans for the reestablishment of Spanish control in the New World to be put off. Accordingly, when the

---

[18]Irby C. Nichols, Jr., "The Russian Ukase and the Monroe Doctrine: A Re-Evaluation," *Pacific Historical Review*, XXXV(February, 1967), 23–25; N. N. Bolkhovitinov, "Russia and the Declaration of the Non-Colonization Principle: New Archival Evidence," *Oregon Historical Quarterly*, LXXII(June, 1971), 110–114.

United States announced its intention to recognize the Latin American republics in 1822, the Russian government expressed no immediate objections.[19]

The events of 1823, however, altered the situation. That year saw the successful suppression by the French of the Spanish uprising and the development of so strong a fear that the European monarchs might now try to send troops to Latin America that the British foreign secretary, George Canning, proposed to the Americans a joint declaration opposing any such action. Just as the Monroe administration was debating this suggestion, two messages arrived from the Russian government expressing its determination not to recognize the Latin American republics and celebrating the crushing of revolutions in Europe.[20] These messages provoked the statement of the other two principles of the Monroe Doctrine: that although the United States would abstain from interference in European affairs, it would oppose any effort by a European power to extend its political system to the Western Hemisphere.

Because Russian activities in the Pacific Northwest and in Latin America provided the occasion for the Monroe Doctrine, that proclamation has often been interpreted as an anti-Russian measure. This is an inaccurate view. At no point were United States officials seriously worried about Russian intervention in the Western Hemisphere; their concern was directed toward Britain and France.[21] The Russians simply had the bad luck to provide the excuse, through several carelessly worded pronouncements, for a declaration that was really directed against their continental rivals. Indeed, the decision to proclaim the Monroe Doctrine independently of Great Britain was made, at

---

[19]Dexter Perkins, "Russia and the Spanish Colonies, 1817–1818," *American Historical Review*, XXVIII(July, 1923), 671–672; William Spence Robertson, "Russia and the Emancipation of Spanish America, 1816–1826," *Hispanic American Historical Review*, XXI(May, 1941), 207–211.

[20]Worthington C. Ford, "John Quincy Adams and the Monroe Doctrine," *American Historical Review*, VII(July, 1902), 685–686, and VIII(October, 1902), 30–32.

[21]Bolkhovitinov, "Russia and the Non-Colonization Principle," pp. 125–126; Nichols, "The Russian Ukase and the Monroe Doctrine," pp. 18–21; Irby C. Nichols, Jr., and Richard A. Ward, "Anglo-American Relations and the Russian Ukase: A Reassessment," *Pacific Historical Review* XLI(November, 1972), 458–459.

least in part, to avoid giving the Russians the impression that London and Washington were acting together.[22]

It cannot be said that Russian foreign policy during this period was noninterventionist: as one historian has noted, the tsarist government "allowed little distinction or discrimination between international relations proper and the internal affairs of...states."[23] But this was true only in Europe; in both Latin America and the Pacific Northwest, the Russians showed a realistic sense of their own limitations and a cautious deference to the power of others. "It may be that our frank & consistent conduct impresses respect," American minister Henry Middleton commented in 1824, "but our *maritime force*, & the consequent *impossibility of dictation* towards us must also be taken into account."[24] If one amends this statement to include British as well as American maritime force, it is not an inaccurate assessment of the situation.

## IV

One of the more puzzling aspects of early Russian-American relations is how two such ideologically disparate states could get along with each other as well as they did. The United States, since independence, had been strongly and self-consciously committed to republicanism: to the right of each nation, as John Quincy Adams put it, to have a government "founded upon the consent, and by the agreement of those that are governed." Russia, after 1815, seemed pledged to precisely the opposite principle. Sworn to uphold legitimacy everywhere, its implacable opposition to revolutions had earned it, by mid-century, the epithet "gendarme of Europe." "Russia occupies, and will continue to occupy, a commanding position in every struggle against popular rights," the American minister in St. Petersburg noted in 1852. "[It is] impelled by a hostility to free

---

[22]On this point, see James Monroe to Thomas Jefferson, December, 1823, printed in Ford, "Adams and the Monroe Doctrine," p. 51.

[23]Nicholas V. Riasanovsky, *Nicholas I and Official Nationality in Russia, 1825–1855* (Berkeley: 1959), p. 236.

[24]Middleton to Adams, March 8, 1824, DSR, M-35:10. See also Ernest R. May, *The Making of the Monroe Doctrine* (Cambridge, Massachusetts: 1975), p. 250.

institutions, that admits of no compromise and yields to no relaxation."[25]

Certainly Americans were aware of the ideological gulf that separated them from the Russians. The reactionary nature of the tsarist government was the subject of frequent comment in the press and in dispatches from American ministers in St. Petersburg. "In the direction of public affairs here," George Washington Campbell observed in 1819, "the Emperor is, in fact, *everything*, and his Ministers *nothing*." James Buchanan reported to President Jackson in 1832 that "here there is no freedom of the Press, no public opinion, ... but little political conversation, and that very much guarded. In short, we live in the calm of despotism." The Emperor Nicholas I might be "one of the best of despots," Buchanan added, "*but he is still a despot.*"[26]

Moreover, the difficulties of serving in St. Petersburg furnished constant irritants. The climate was harsh—"this Hyperborean Prison," William Pinkney called it. George Washington Campbell lost three of his children to illness there within a week in 1819. John Randolph fumed about "innumerable files gigantick as the Empire they inhabit." The diplomatic establishment was expensive to keep up; bribery seemed required to get any information of value. "I am certain," John Randolph Clay wrote in 1831, "that with a little tact and more bribery, I could at this time buy nearly every thing which has taken place with regard to these affairs." Interference with the mails was a constant problem, which the Russians' clumsy efforts to forge the American official seal could not conceal. "The Post Office American eagle here is a sorry bird," Buchanan noted in 1833. Neill Brown summed up the feelings of a steady procession of ministers, past and future, when he observed in 1852 that "this government possesses in an exquisite degree, the art of worry-

[25]Ford, "Adams and the Monroe Doctrine," p. 41; Neill Brown to Daniel Webster, January 28, 1852, DSR, M-35:15.

[26]Campbell to John Quincy Adams, February 18, 1819, DSR, M-35: 7; Buchanan to Jackson, June 22, 1832, John Bassett Moore, ed., *The Works of James Buchanan* (New York: 1908–1911), II, 199. See also Thomas A. Bailey, *America Faces Russia: Russian-American Relations from Early Times to Our Own Day* (Ithaca: 1954), pp. 8–11, 20–21, 27–31, 39–44, and 52–55.

ing a foreign representative, without giving him the consolation of an insult."[27]

But there were mitigating factors. One was the belief that Russia was too backward to be governed by anything other than despotism. Henry Middleton commented in 1826 that "the opinion is perhaps not erroneous which holds [absolutism] to be the only principle which can bind together so heterogeneous a mass as is aggregated under the Sceptre of the Russian autocrat." James Buchanan wrote Andrew Jackson in 1833: "The most ardent republican, after having resided here for one year, would be clearly convinced that the mass of the people, composed as it is of ignorant and superstitious barbarians who are also slaves, is not fit for political freedom. Besides they are perfectly contented." Because they saw autocracy as the only form of government suited to Russia, American representatives could even rationalize it into a crude form of self-determination. Charles Todd noted in 1841:

It is a gratifying fact to see the Imperial Autocrat frequently walking the Streets as a private citizen altogether unattended...; and it is rather a singular coincidence that the most absolute Monarch ruling the most powerful Empire, of Europe should be the only Chief Magistrate in Europe or America, with the exception of the President of the United States, who can thus mingle with his fellow citizens or subjects.... The fact affords curious matter for the contemplation of the political philosopher.[28]

Even if Americans had viewed Russia as ripe for republicanism, they would have felt serious inhibitions about trying to propagate that ideology there. While Americans believed as firmly in the eventual triumph of their system as Lenin and

---

[27]Pinckney to Adams, October 9, 1817, DSR, M-35:6; Campbell to Adams, May 3, 1819, ibid., M-35: 7; Randolph to Martin Van Buren, August 19, 1830, ibid., M-35: 12; Clay to Edward Livingston, October 7, 1831, ibid.; Buchanan to Livingston, February 22, 1833, ibid.; Brown to Webster, May 27, 1852, ibid., M-35:15.

[28]Middleton to Clay, February 11, 1826, ibid., M-35: 10; Buchanan to Jackson, May 29, 1833, Moore, ed., *Buchanan Works*, II, 339; Todd to Webster, December 22, 1841, DSR, M-35: 14. See also Marc Raeff, "An American View of the Decembrist Revolt," *Journal of Modern History*, XXV(September, 1953), 286–293.

Trotsky did in theirs a century later, they were sensitive to the fragility of republican institutions and to the danger that they might be corrupted by constant involvement in war. Hence, it was perfectly possible for John Quincy Adams to proclaim, on the one hand, that

> The influence of our example has unsettled all the ancient governments of Europe. It will overthrow them all without a single exception. I hold this revolution to be as infallible as that the earth will perform a revolution around the sun in a year.

and to state, with equal fervor, on the other, that there would be an "'inevitable tendency of a direct interference in foreign wars, even wars for freedom, to change the very foundations of our own government from *liberty to power.*" Therefore, "though Republican to the last drop of blood in their veins, [Americans] have thought it no sacrifice of their principles to cultivate with sincerity and assiduity Peace and Friendship even with the most absolute Monarchies and their Sovereigns."[29]

The Russians too were well aware of the ideological differences which separated them from the Americans. Count Pahlen, the first Russian minister to the United States, commented upon his arrival in Washington in 1810: "The republican simplicity makes a considerable impression on one accustomed to the pomp of European courts." Count Nesselrode, the Russian foreign minister, found it necessary to warn Pahlen's successor in 1818 that in the United States, "governed by democratic institutions, the political prejudices of the government are all the more difficult to eradicate as those usually common. And however plausible the argument, . . . it always ends by reinforcing the opinions which it sought to reverse." The Russians viewed the Americans as avaricious, contentious, violent, and, above all, saddled with an inefficient form of government. The Russian *chargé* in 1854 described it as the "principle of anarchy, which prevails here under the pseudonym of 'self-

---

[29]Adams to Charles Jared Ingersoll, June 19, 1823, W.C. Ford, ed., *The Writings of John Quincy Adams* (New York: 1913–1917), VII, 488; Adams to Edward Everett, January 31, 1822, ibid., p. 201; Adams draft, Monroe presidential address, November 27, 1823, quoted in Ford, "Adams and the Monroe Doctrine," p. 42. See also Adams' famous Independence Day address, July 4, 1821, quoted in E.H. Tatum, *The United States and Europe, 1815–1823: A Study in the Background of the Monroe Doctrine* (Berkeley: 1936), pp. 241–245.

government.'" "What can be expected," Russian minister Edouard de Stoeckl complained at the height of the Civil War,

from a country where men of humble origin are elevated to the highest positions, where honest men refuse to vote and dishonest ones cast their ballots at the bidding of shameless politicians? This is democracy in practice, the democracy that European theorists rave about. If they could only see it at work they would cease their agitation and thank God for the government which they are enjoying.[30]

Extremely sensitive to revolution, the Russian government had reason to fear the ideological precedent the Americans had set. As Alexander I noted in 1823, "Too many examples demonstrate that the contagion of revolutionary principles is arrested neither by distance nor by physical obstacles." Moreover, the influence of the American Revolution was not lost on Russian radicals—it played an important part in the Decembrist revolt of 1825, as if in confirmation of Alexander's fears. "I do not mean to state that the Russian government are unfriendly to the people of the United States," Buchanan wrote in 1832, "but yet they must attribute to our example the existence of those liberal principles in Europe which give them so much trouble."[31]

But the Russian government generally made a distinction between the American Revolution and its more violent French and Latin American successors. Catherine the Great took strong ideological exception to the French Revolution; she did not to the American. Alexander I, in 1809, could refer to the United

---

[30]Pahlen to Rumiantsev, June 30, 1810, *Vneshniaia politika Rossii*, V, 472; Nesselrode to Poletica, November 21, 1818, "Correspondence of the Russian Ministers in Washington, 1818–1825," *American Historical Review*, XVIII (April, 1913), 316; Frank A. Golder, *Guide to Materials for American History in Russian Archives* (Washington: 1917, 1937), I, 37, 46, 52, 68, 74, II, 1; Dexter Perkins, *The Monroe Doctrine, 1823–1826* (Cambridge, Massachusetts: 1927), pp. 172–173; Frank A. Golder, "The American Civil War through the Eyes of a Russian Diplomat," *American Historical Review*, XXVI(April, 1921), 457.

[31]Alexander I to Chateaubriand, quoted in Perkins, *The Monroe Doctrine, 1823–1826*, p. 131; Buchanan to Jackson, June 22, 1832, Moore, ed., *Buchanan Works*, II, 200. See also Max Laserson, *The American Impact on Russia: Diplomatic and Ideological, 1784–1817* (New York: 1950), pp. 115–138; George Vernadsky, "Reforms Under Alexander I: French and American Influence," *Review of Politics*, IX(January, 1947), 47–64; and N. N. Bolkhovitinov, "Dekabristy i Amerika," *Voprosy istorii*, 1974, #4, 91–104.

States, "so wise and so well-governed," and in 1823 asked, "Where are the Franklins, the Washingtons, and the Jeffersons of southern [Latin] America?" The Russians were well aware of the American noninterventionist tradition: "Our rule of not interfering with the affairs of other Powers has certainly contributed much towards rendering us acceptable to Russia," John Randolph Clay noted in 1833. Neill Brown observed in 1851 that "Americans rank as high here, if not more so [,] than any other people; and though republicans, they are known and acknowledged not to be propagandists." Finally, Russians tended to distinguish between the American nation, whose potential power they respected, and its government, which they could view as a transitory phenomenon.[32] As a result, what seemed on the surface to be a fundamental ideological antipathy did not seriously affect relations between the two countries during the first half of the nineteenth century.

## V

A mutual interest in preserving the European balance of power also contributed to the amicable nature of the nineteenth century Russian-American relationship. Russia's stake in maintaining the delicate equilibrium established at Vienna in 1815 against nationalism and liberalism is well known. Less well known is the fact that the United States, though committed to a policy of nonintervention in European affairs, did not expect to be able to keep the Western Hemisphere wholly insulated from European quarrels: the balance of power in the New World depended, in part, on what happened in the Old.[33] Thus, Americans looked to Russia, during the first half of the nine-

---

[32]Bolkhovitinov, *Beginnings of Russian-American Relations*, p. 30; Alexander I to P. K. Sukhtelen, November 9, 1809, *Vneshniaia politika Rossii*, V, 278; Golder, *Guide to Russian Archives*, I, 22; Patricia Kennedy Grimsted, *The Foreign Ministers of Alexander I: Political Attitudes and the Conduct of Russian Diplomacy, 1801–1825* (Berkeley: 1969), p. 51; Alexander I conversation with La Ferronays, November 28, 1823, quoted in Robertson, "Russia and the Emancipation of Spanish America," p. 215; Clay to Louis McLane, August 16, 1833, DSR, M-35: 12; Brown to Webster, November 6, 1851, ibid., M-35: 15; E. A. Adamov, "Russia and the United States at the Time of the Civil War," *Journal of Modern History*, II(December, 1930), 593.

[33]On this point, see the analysis in Alan Dowty, *The Limits of American Isolation: The United States and the Crimean War* (New York: 1971), pp. 18–27.

teenth century, as a counterweight to those powers most capable of upsetting the New World balance—Great Britain and France.

Francis Dana's mission to St. Petersburg in 1781 can be seen in that context, as can the decision to establish diplomatic relations with Russia in 1808 and acceptance of the tsar's mediation during the War of 1812. Even after proclamation of the Monroe Doctrine, there remained a pervasive fear that Britain and France might try to establish new centers of power in the Western Hemisphere, thereby impairing what Americans saw as their God-given right to dominate the continent.[34] The crushing of revolutions of 1848 seemed to increase this danger, as did the revolution in naval technology brought about by the use of steam power. "Those who believe...that the United States can long escape difficulties with Europe have more faith in the future than I have," United States minister Neill Brown noted in 1852. Ten years later another American minister in St. Petersburg, Cassius M. Clay, made the same point:

It is useless to deceive ourselves with the idea that we can isolate ourselves from European interventions. We become in spite of ourselves—the Monroe Doctrine—Washington's Farewell Address—and all that—a part of the "balance of power."[35]

Since Russia had fewer bases for conflict with the United States than any other European power, Americans saw it throughout the early nineteenth century as a country worth cultivating good relations with to the end that Britain and France not become too powerful in Europe and hence capable of threatening the balance of power in the New World.

The Russians were, if anything, more interested in maintaining this relationship than the Americans. It was not that they expected military assistance if war broke out in Europe; Alexander I's abortive effort to recruit the United States into the Holy Alliance had taught the Russians something about the

---

[34]Frederick Merk, *The Monroe Doctrine and American Expansionism, 1843–1849* (New York: 1966); David M. Pletcher, *The Diplomacy of Annexation: Texas, Oregon, and the Mexican War* (Columbia, Missouri: 1973); and Dowty, *Limits of American Isolation,* all emphasize this sense of vulnerability. See also Thomas R. Hietala *Manifest Design: Anxious Aggrandizement in Late Jacksonian America* (Ithaca: 1985).

[35]Brown to Webster, May 27, 1852, DSR, M-35: 15; Clay to William H. Seward, April 13, 1862, ibid., M-35; 19.

Americans' aversion to formal commitments.[36] But they did see good relations with the United States as a means of avoiding excessive reliance on Great Britain in the two crucial areas of trade and technology. Having no substantial merchant fleet of their own, the Russians had looked, since the turn of the century, to trade in American bottoms as a way to ensure access to world markets should the Empire's much larger commerce through Great Britain be cut off.[37] Later, under Nicholas I, Americans were enlisted to build railways, telegraph lines, and naval vessels, again to avoid too much dependence on the British.[38] The theme of seeking good relations with Washington as a counterweight to London recurred frequently in Russian diplomatic correspondence from the 1820s through the 1850s.[39] The idea bore fruit, for both sides, during the Crimean War and the American Civil War.

The war in the Crimea brought to an end almost a half-century in which Russia had played a decisive role in maintaining the European balance of power. Involvement in war simultaneously with Britain, France, and Turkey ruined Russia's ability to play off its antagonists against one another. The ignominious defeat the Russians suffered at the hands of the Allies also destroyed the myth of massive and invulnerable Russian armies, poised for intervention in European affairs. Confronted with a hostile Europe, the tsar's government hoped that its friendly relationship with Washington might counterbalance, however modestly, the position of its enemies.

The Russians sought to accomplish this objective in three ways: by encouraging Washington to insist upon the rights of neutrals, in the expectation that such action might bring the Americans into conflict with the British; by securing the right to fit out privateers in American ports to prey on British and French commerce; and by attempting to protect the Pacific

---

[36]Benjamin Platt Thomas, *Russo-American Relations, 1815-1867* (Baltimore: 1930, pp. 27–33.

[37]Tatum, *The United States and Europe*, pp. 25, 116–118.

[38]Albert Parry, *Whistler's Father* (New York: 1939), *passim.*; Frederick M. Binder, "American Shipbuilding and Russian Naval Power, 1837–1846," *Military Affairs*, XXI(Summer, 1957), 79–84; Charles Vevier, "The Collins Overland Line and American Continentalism," *Pacific Historical Review*, XXVIII(August, 1959), 237–253.

[39]Golder, *Guide to Russian Archives*, I, 32, 52, 54, 58, 62, 63.

Northwest by arranging a fictitious sale of the Russian-America Company's interests to a group of San Francisco businessmen. None of these schemes worked out as planned. The British showed no inclination to interfere with neutral trade. The Russians gave up the effort to fit out privateers for fear of violating American neutrality laws. The sale of Russian-America became unnecessary when the Russian-American Company negotiated its own truce with the Hudson's Bay Company, thereby exempting their respective territories from the war. But the hopes the Russians entertained do indicate the extent to which they saw the United States, in this period, as an element of some significance in the world balance of power.[40]

For Americans, the Crimean War, as United States minister Thomas Seymour put it, presented "no redeeming features. ... The peace of the world is broken, by the cutthroat nations of Europe, who care infinitely less for 'holy places' or 'the integrity of the Sultan' than for their own selfish aggrandizement." But the war did offer advantages from the point of view of power politics. It tied down Britain and France at a time when relations between the two were close, and when prospects for their intervention in the Caribbean appeared considerable. It provided opportunities for a new definition of neutral rights in wartime and for increased trade with Russia. "Whatever we may think of Russia in its character of a despotic power," Seymour observed, "here is a government which has been uniformly friendly to that of the States, and we can continue our trade with her and improve it if we please, without either endorsing her policy or compromising our republican principles."[41]

Washington's sympathy for the Russians during the Crimean War had no direct effect on the outcome of that struggle. It did demonstrate to the British, though, that Europe and North

---

[40]Frank A. Golder, "Russian-American Relations During the Crimean War," *American Historical Review*, XXXI(1926), 462–471; Dowty, *Limits of American Isolation*, pp. 73–83; Norman E. Saul, "Beverly C. Sanders and the Expansion of American Trade with Russia, 1853–1855," *Maryland Historical Magazine*, LXVI(Summer, 1972), 160-168; Eufrosina Dvoichenko-Markov, "Americans in the Crimean War," *Russian Review*, XIII(April, 1954), 137–145.

[41]Seymour to William L. Marcy, July 24 and May 8, 1854, DSR, M–35: 16. For the situation in the Caribbean, see Dowty, *Limits of American Isolation*, pp. 133–167; and Kenneth Bourne, *Britain and the Balance of Power in North America, 1815–1908* (Berkeley: 1967), pp. 170-205.

America could no longer be considered as separate spheres; that events in one could affect the balance of power in the other. The Palmerston government seems to have concluded form this experience that while Britain should not encourage the expansion of United States influence in North America, there was now little it could do to prevent it, since Washington could expect to have friends in Europe in any future conflict with London.[42] This realization would pay important dividends for the Americans in their own Civil War, which was soon to follow.

Within five years of the Crimean War's termination, the United States itself was involved in a bloody civil conflict which involved the prospect of European intervention. Alone among the major European powers, Russia maintained a position of sympathetic neutrality toward the North. There was, at the time, and has been since, much confusion as to why the Russians did this. The half-century tradition of Russian-American friendship was often cited as the explanation, as was the fact that both countries were then going through the process of ending involuntary servitude. But the real reason was that Russia continued to see the United States as a vital element in the international balance of power. As Prince Gorchakov, the Russian foreign minister, put it in 1861, the United States was "the only commercial counterpoise in the world...to Great Britain, and Russia would do nothing, therefore, to diminish its just power and influence."[43]

Russian sympathy for the North played a larger role in the diplomacy of the war than is often realized. Late in 1862 France proposed joint mediation, with Britain and Russia, on a basis that probably would have confirmed Southern independence. Timely Union military victories and the Emancipation Proclamation usually have been credited with forestalling this move, but recent research indicates that, while not without their long-

---

[42]Ibid., pp. 204–205; Charles S. Campbell, *From Revolution to Rapprochement: The United States and Great Britain, 1783–1900* (New York: 1974), pp. 89–90.

[43]John Appleton to Seward, April 20, 1861, U.S. Department of State, *Foreign Relations of the United States,* [hereafter *FR*] 1861, p. 299. See also Edouard de Stoeckl to Gorchakov, February 24, 1862, and Gorchakov to Stoeckl, October 22, 1863, both quoted in Adamov, "Russia and the United States at the Time of the Civil War," pp. 595, 601–602.

range effects, these events had little immediate impact in Europe. The mediation proposal failed mainly because Britain was unwilling to go to war to enforce it, and because the Russians, whose cooperation was deemed vital to secure the Union's acquiescence without war, refused to go along. It was not that the Russians opposed a negotiated settlement; indeed, they repeatedly urged this course upon Union leaders. But the tsar's government was willing to let Washington choose the proper time for negotiations, and this policy, given the intransigence of both sides, ensured that they would never take place.[44]

Failure of the 1862 mediation proposal by no means removed the danger of European intervention; British and French recognition of the Confederacy remained a possibility throughout the first half of 1863. Once again, though, the interrelation of events in Europe with those in America worked to Washington's advantage. An uprising against Russian rule in Poland broke out in January, and as prospects of British and French intervention in that crisis increased, chances diminished that Paris and London would seek to impose a settlement in America. Secretary of State William H. Seward, though sympathetic to the Poles, quickly rejected a French invitation to join remonstrances on their behalf on the grounds that such a move would be inconsistent with the American noninterventionist tradition. Cassius M. Clay, in a dispatch from St. Petersburg, put the reason more bluntly: "Why should Americans take part against an avowed friend, in behalf of the ally of avowed enemies?"[45]

The Russians, grateful to the Americans for their friendly attitude, sent both their Atlantic and Pacific fleets to winter in United States ports late in 1863. Many in both Europe and America took these unannounced visits as a sign of Russian

---

[44]D. P. Crook, *The North, the South, and the Powers*, 1861–1865 (New York: 1974), pp. 221–225; Daniel B. Carroll, *Henri Mercier and the American Civil War* (Princeton: 1971), pp. 234–241.

[45] Clay to Seward, August 5, 1863, DSR, M-35: 20. See also Carroll, *Henri Mercier*, pp. 315–319; John Kutolowski, "The Effect of the Polish Insurrection of 1863 on American Civil War Diplomacy," *The Historian*, XXVII(August, 1965), 560–577; and Harold E. Blinn, "Seward and the Polish Rebellion of 1863," *American Historical Review*, XLV(July, 1940), 828–833.

support for the Union, and they were warmly welcomed in the North. But the real reasons for the visits did not escape sophisticated observers at the time. Concerned about the possibility of war over Poland, the Russian government, perhaps with excessive optimism, hoped to use its ramshackle fleet to harass British and French commerce on the high seas. Sending the ships to the United States would keep them from being bottled up in Russian ports and would give them convenient bases from which to operate. The Lincoln administration was well aware of the Russians' motives, but Seward was not above conveying the false impression that a Russian-American defensive alliance had been formed, thereby further discouraging whatever chances still remained of British and French intervention on behalf of the Confederacy.[46]

It is, of course, impossible to say with precision what effect Russian-American cooperation had in inhibiting intervention by those countries, either in Poland or in the American Civil War. Certainly it was not the decisive factor in either case. But as early as March, 1863, long before the Russian fleet's visit to the United States, Lord John Russell, the British foreign secretary, had speculated privately on the possibility of a Russian-American agreement that might lead to a new balance of power in the world.[47] Given the potential power of these two great states, given the surface appearances of cooperation in their relationship, this possibility could not be without its effect upon the calculations of European statesmen.

## VI

An apparent consequence of the cordial relationship between St. Petersburg and Washington during the Civil War was the

---

[46] Howard I. Kushner, "The Russian Fleet and the American Civil War: Another View," *The Historian*, XXXIV(August, 1972), 633–649. See also Frank A. Golder, "The Russian Fleet and the Civil War," *American Historical Review*, XX(July, 1915), 801–812; Thomas A. Bailey, "The Russian Fleet Myth Re-Examined," *Mississippi Valley Historical Review*, XXXVIII(June, 1951), 81–90; and I. Ia. Levitas, "Russkie eskadry v Amerike," *Istoriia SSSR*, 1968, #5, 135–141.

[47] Russell to Lord Lyons, March 7, 1863, quoted in Kutolowski, "Polish Insurrection," p. 565. See also Crook, *The North, the South and the Powers*, pp. 284–286; and, for evidence that this kind of thinking was widespread in Europe in the mid-nineteenth century, Geoffrey Barraclough, "Europa, Amerika and Russland in Vorstellung und Denken des 19. Jahrhunderts," *Historische Zeitschrift*, CCIII(1966), 280–315.

tsar's decision to sell Alaska, or Russian-America, as it was then known, to the United States in 1867. One needs to be careful in assessing the motives on both sides, though, for what appears on the surface to have been the fruit of an amicable relationship was in fact a sophisticated recognition by the Russians of where power lay along the desolate but strategically important shores of the northern Pacific.

The establishment of mutually recognized boundaries for Russian-America in 1824 had not stopped United States citizens from fishing in its waters or trading with its natives. Despite repeated efforts to achieve self-sufficiency, the Russian-America Company had been forced, by 1854, to arrange with a group of San Francisco businessmen to furnish its forlorn northern outposts with supplies and markets. The company's abortive attempt to "sell" its interests to this group during the Crimean War had not been forgotten, and in succeeding years, California and New England commercial interests pushed energetically for the acquisition of Russian-America, an idea they found consistent with the conveniently malleable principles of Manifest Destiny. Among the most persistent advocates of this point of view was the senator from New York, William H. Seward, who as Secretary of State would later be in an excellent position to realize this vision.[48]

Increasing American interest in Russian-America coincided with a growing conviction among the tsar's advisers that it would be unwise, even futile, to try to retain the territory. Plagued by distance and mismanagement, the Russian-America Company had never made money on its colony. By 1860 the acquisition of Vladivostok and the mouth of the Amur had given Russia a firmer foothold on the Pacific; Russian-America, as a result, became strategically less significant. The most important reason for St. Petersburg's pessimism regarding Russian-America, though, was the belief that if the territory was not soon sold, the Americans would simply take it. As Admiral Ivan Popov, commander of the Russian Pacific fleet, noted in 1860:

Whatever they may say in Europe about... the "Monroe Doctrine," or the doctrine of "manifest destiny," anyone who has lived in [North

[48]Saul, "Sanders and American Trade with Russia," pp. 162–163; Howard I. Kushner, "Visions of the Northwest Coast: Gwin and Seward in the 1850's," *Western Historical Quarterly*, IV(July, 1973), 295–306.

America] cannot fail to understand instinctively that this principle is entering more and more into the blood of the people, and that new generations are sucking it in with their mothers' milk....[Cede Russian-America, the Aleutians and the islands of the Bering Sea,]...but let us retain the Commander Islands so as not to have the Yankees too near us.[49]

The sale of Russian-America might have been arranged as early as 1861 had not the Civil War intervened.[50] By the time that conflict was over, the Russian government was all the more eager to unload its unprofitable colony, and early in 1867, Russian minister Stoeckl, in secret negotiations with Secretary of State Seward, negotiated its sale for $7,200,000, some $2,200,000 more than the price at which Stoeckl had been authorized to sell. Senate approval came quickly, but the House of Representatives delayed appropriating the necessary funds for more than a year.

The history of the Alaskan purchase has become encrusted with more than the usual number of myths unsupported by evidence. Public opinion was not overwhelmingly against the acquisition, and Seward had little difficulty demonstrating that the territory contained more than just walruses and polar bears. Both Russians and Americans were aware of the presence of gold—indeed, one reason the Russians wanted to sell was their fear that the territory would become another California—but fisheries, for the Americans, were probably the more important attraction. The Russian minister did bribe lobbyists, journalists, and possibly even key members of the House of Representatives, but this was done to discourage the attachment of crippling amendments to the appropriations bill; it was not necessary to secure approval of the purchase itself. Finally, the sale of Alaska was the result, not so much of Russian-American friendship, as of a recognition by the Russians of the realities of power. As Stoeckl noted in one of his last dispatches from Washington, if they had not been sold "our possessions, menaced by the proximity of the Americans, would have dragged us into serious disputes with the Federal Government and

---

[49]Quoted in Kushner, *Conflict on the Northwest Coast*, p. 138. See also Ronald J. Jensen, *The Alaska Purchase and Russian-American Relations* (Seattle: 1975), pp. 9–22.

[50]Ibid., pp. 23–24.

would have wound up by becoming booty of the Americans."[51]

The cordiality that developed between Russia and the United States during the first half of the nineteenth century was not, therefore, the product of genuine friendship; relations between nations rarely are. It did reflect a peculiar congruence of interests, brought about by the existence of common antagonists, the absence of direct points of conflict, a realistic awareness, particularly on the Russians' part, of the limits of national power, and, probably most important, a determination on the part of both nations to keep diplomacy insulated from ideology. That these components of the early Russian-American relationship resulted from the comparatively marginal position which that relationship assumed most of the time in the concerns of Washington and St. Petersburg seems unarguable; events of the late nineteenth and early twentieth centuries would prove that they were decidedly transitory as well.

---

[51]Stoeckl to Gorchakov, July 24, 1867, printed in Hunter Miller, "Russian Opinion on the Cession of Alaska," *American Historical Review*, XLVIII(April, 1943), 526–531. See also Thomas A. Bailey, "Why the United States Purchased Alaska," *Pacific Historical Review*, III (March, 1934), 39–48; Anatole G. Mazour, "The Prelude to Russia's Departure from Alaska," ibid., X(September, 1941), 317–318; Jensen, *The Alaska Purchase*, pp. 138–141; Kushner, *Conflict on the Northwest Coast*, pp. 156–158; and, for allegations of Russian bribery, Paul S. Holbo, *Tarnished Expansion: The Alaska Scandal, the Press, and Congress, 1867–1871* (Knoxville: 1983).

CHAPTER II

# Diverging Interests: 1867–1917

THE PURCHASE OF ALASKA MARKED A HIGH POINT in Russian-American cordiality. From then on, a gradual deterioration set in, so that when the tsar was overthrown a half-century later, Americans expressed little regret. The good relations that existed in the first half of the nineteenth century had been based on the absence of conflicting interests and, to an extent, on the presence of a mutual antipathy—the suspicion both nations felt toward Great Britain. During the late nineteenth and early twentieth centuries, all this changed: Russia and the United States clashed directly over Manchuria, and a new alignment of powers made Washington a tacit ally of Britain and Japan, another nation whose growing strength the Russians had reason to fear. But this international realignment was not the only reason Russian-American relations worsened. Even before that happened, the United States had begun to take Russia's internal structure as well as external policies into account in shaping its official attitude toward that country. Ideology began to make a difference; questions began to be raised as to whether a democracy could, or should, maintain friendly relations with the most autocratic nation in Europe. This preoccupation with Russian internal conditions was, in the long run, a more lasting cause of tension than East Asian rivalries because it made reconciliation dependent upon reform. It is an indication of the resulting bitterness that relations between the two countries remained frigid right up to the onset of the revolution in 1917— despite the development, during the first three years of World War I, of an economic relationship of considerable importance to both countries.

I

"The American eagle should not strain his naturally fine voice by shrill and prolonged screaming on small occasions," Secretary of State Frederick Frelinghuysen commented in 1881.[1] It was an elegant restatement of the nonintervention principle upon which, in large part, the amicable nineteenth-century relationship between Russia and the United States had been based. But nonintervention had never been wholly without challenge. Throughout their history, Americans had reserved and frequently exercised the right to intervene in foreign countries to protect their own citizens. There also existed a proclivity for rhetorical, though rarely actual, intervention on behalf of foreigners for humanitarian reasons.[2] Both traditions began, in the 1870s, to erode traditional noninterventionism as it had been applied to Russia.

Americans long had been aware of the tsarist autocracy's repressive nature, but ideological differences generally had not been seen as an impediment to diplomatic cordiality. This situation changed after the Civil War. The Russian government, under increasing attack from revolutionaries, was becoming more repressive than it had been at a time when Americans, who were traveling and reading more widely than in the past about events in the rest of the world, were becoming more aware than they had been of internal conditions in Russia. Also, adherence to nonintervention in the past had been based on the realistic judgment that, whatever it might think of them, the United States lacked the capacity to influence events in most of the rest of the world. The gradual emergence of the United States as a world power toward the end of the century tended to blur the distinction, in the eyes of many Americans, between what they could only condemn and what they could reasonably expect to change.

Emancipation of the serfs and the other reforms of the 1860s had not solved Russia's problems, and in the following decade the liberalism of Alexander II began to wane. As this happened,

---

[1] Quoted in Milton Plesur, *America's Outward Thrust: Approaches to Foreign Affairs, 1865–1890* (De Kalb, Illinois: 1971), p. 6.

[2] D. A. Graber, *Crisis Diplomacy: A History of U.S. Intervention Policies and Practices* (Washington: 1959), p. 324.

revolutionary activity increased, culminating in the assassination of the tsar in March 1881, after several previously unsuccessful attempts. Americans had little sympathy with the Russian revolutionary movement at this time and certainly none with assassination, but they could not help but object to some of the measures the Russian government took to restore order.

Officially sanctioned anti-Semitism caused the greatest concern. Persecution of Jews in Russia was nothing new, but their suspected involvement in revolutionary activity led, after the tsar's murder, to renewed enforcement of laws forcing Jews to live in the so-called "Pale," a strip of territory along the western border of the Empire, and to pogroms directed against inhabitants of that region which the government made no serious attempt to stop.

These moves offended American sensibilities in two ways. By singling out a whole class for suspicion, the Russian government made American citizens who happened to be Jews subject to discrimination when traveling or residing in Russia. United States diplomats generally succeeded in protecting the interests of American Jews, but only through persistent intervention on a case-by-case basis. Efforts to convince the Russians that an American passport entitled its holder to equal protection regardless of religious belief proved frustratingly futile.[3] But despite the great volume of diplomatic correspondence relating to their affairs, the number of American Jews in Russia was never large. Russian anti-Semitism shocked most Americans, not as a violation of a few of their fellow citizens' rights, but as an outrage against humanity. The problem was to find a basis upon which to protest Russia's treatment of its own citizens without calling into question the generally acknowledged right of a sovereign nation to frame its own laws.

Efforts were made to persuade the Russian government that better treatment of the Jews would be in its own best interests. "Our experience," Secretary of State Hamilton Fish pointed out

---

[3] Cyrus Adler and Aaron M. Margalith, *With Firmness in the Right: American Diplomatic Action Affecting Jews, 1840–1945* (New York: 1946), pp. 171–207; Alice Felt Tyler, *The Foreign Policy of James G. Blaine* (Minneapolis: 1927), pp. 271–277; Edward J. Carroll, "The Foreign Relations of the United States with Tsarist Russia, 1867–1900" (Ph. D. Dissertation, Georgetown University, 1953), pp. 121–159.

gently in 1870, "shows that the removal of restrictions of a sectarian character elevates the class relieved and advances the common good and social organization." Ten years later, his successor, William M. Evarts, told the American minister in St. Petersburg that while the United States could not intervene in Russian internal affairs, his attitude in communications with the Russian government should be "wholly consistent with the theory [of religious freedom] upon which this government is founded." Russian officials politely rejected these suggestions, however, on the grounds that Russian Jews were not of the same character as American Jews, and that since the United States had not seen fit to treat Orientals (not to mention blacks) equally, there seemed little reason why the Russian government should be expected to accord equal treatment to its minorities. Following the 1890 census, American officials were able to show that the emigration of Russian Jews to the United States had greatly increased, thereby demonstrating a direct connection between Russian anti-Semitism and American interests.[4] But the Harrison administration did not press the point, perhaps because of the obvious counterargument that if the United States regarded Russian Jews as undesirable immigrants, it could exclude them, as it did Orientals. There appeared, in short, to be no very effective basis upon which the United States could prevail upon the Russians to improve their treatment of Jews.

But it was not just Jews who suffered in Russia: Americans gradually became aware that arbitrary arrest, imprisonment, and exile to Siberia were common features of life under tsarism. No one did more to impress this view upon the public than George Kennan, indefatigible traveler, writer, and lecturer, whose book,

---

[4] Fish to Curtin, February 4, 1870, DSR, M-77: 137; Evarts to Foster, April 14, 1880, *FR: 1880*, p. 873; Foster to Evarts, December 30, 1880, *FR: 1881*, pp. 996–1004; Blaine to Smith, February 18, 1891, *FR: 1891*, pp. 737–739. See also Adler and Margalith, *With Firmness in the Right*, pp. 215–225; Ann E. Healy, "Tsarist Anti-Semitism and Russian-American Relations," *Slavic Review*, XLII(Fall, 1983), especially pp. 408–415; Stephen M. Berk, *Year of Crisis, Year of Hope: Russian Jewry and the Pogroms of 1881–1882* (Westport, Connecticut: 1985), especially pp. 141–178; and Ronald J. Jensen, "The Politics of Discrimination: America, Russia and the Jewish Question, 1869–1872," *American Jewish History*, LXXV(March, 1986), 280–295. On the overall increase in Russian emigration to the United States during this period, see G. P. Kuropiatnik, *Rossiia i SShA: ekonomicheskie, kul'turnye i diplomaticheskie sviazi, 1867–1881* (Moscow: 1981), pp. 84–93.

*Siberia and the Exile System*, was published in 1891. Kennan awed audiences all over the country with his vivid accounts of Russian prisons, often delivered in convict garb to the accompaniment of clanking chains. His prolific writings evoked outrage throughout much of the world, including Russia itself, where they circulated surreptitiously in an early form of *samizdat*. Organizations were formed to protest conditions in Russia, and exiled Russian radicals, their way prepared by Kennan's work, toured the United States, attracting large and sympathetic responses.[5]

Kennan's writings had little direct effect on Russian-American diplomatic relations, which remained correct though not as cordial as in the past. But they did do much to change public attitudes toward Russia, and, in an age when public opinion was having an increasingly important influence on diplomacy, this shift eventually had its effect. When famine broke out in Russia in 1891–1892, the response of individual Americans was generous, but a considerable debate broke out in Congress over whether United States citizens should be aiding a repressive autocracy. Two years later, the Senate's approval of a treaty providing for the extradition of Russian political refugees provoked surprisingly widespread criticism. "I am more and more convinced," United States minister Clifton Breckinridge reported from St. Petersburg late in 1895, "that... to protect our own sense of dignity and right, we need to let [the Russians] know that, however regretful it may be to us, it is possible to cool our ardor by persistently trampling in matters concerning us, upon principles we hold most dear."[6]

---

[5] Taylor Stults, "Imperial Russia through American Eyes, 1894–1904" (Ph. D. Dissertation, University of Missouri, 1970), pp. 10–20, 45–46; Louis J. Budd, "Twain, Howells, and the Boston Nihilists," *New England Quarterly*, XXXII(September, 1959), 351–371. See also the only full biography of Kennan, Frederick F. Travis, *George Kennan and the American-Russian Relationship, 1865–1924* (Athens, Ohio: 1989); and a shorter Soviet account, E. I. Melamed, *Dzhordzh Kennan protiv tsarisma* (Moscow: 1981).

[6] Breckinridge to Olney, December 24, 1895, DSR, M-35: 48. See also Bailey, *America Faces Russia*, pp. 150–160; Carroll, "Foreign Relations of the United States with Tsarist Russia," pp. 196–228; George S. Queen, "American Relief in the Russian Famine of 1891–1892," *Russian Review*, XIV(April, 1955), 140–150; Harold F. Smith, "Bread for the Russians: William C. Edgar and the Relief Campaign of 1892," *Minnesota History*, XLII(Summer, 1970), 54–62; and Allan Spetter, "The United States, the Russian Jews and the Russian Famine of 1891–1892," *American Jewish Historical Quarterly*, LXIV(March, 1975), 236–244.

The change in public attitudes toward Russia between 1875 and 1895 marked the end of the friendly relationship that had persisted throughout most of the nineteenth century. It was not that Russia had done anything directly harmful to American interests, though what seemed like a direct challenge would come, soon enough, in East Asia. What had happened was that the American people had come to regard ideological differences as important in their relations with the tsarist empire. As a later George Kennan (and distant relative of the first) has noted:

The rise of the institution of what we might call popular nationalism in the nineteenth century...brought new qualities into the conduct of diplomacy everywhere. Not the least of these was a tendency on the part of statesmen to conduct foreign policy histrionically, as on a stage, bearing prominently in mind at all times the reaction of a domestic public opinion, which constituted the audience, rather than the bare requirements of the situation from the standpoint of national interest. What you did, in these circumstances, became less important than how you looked doing it.[7]

The tendency of professional diplomats is to eschew ideology, to base relationships solely on interests. But an aroused public can limit their ability to do this, and, while the attention devoted to Russia was never large in the nineteenth century, it did expand significantly in the late 1880s and the 1890s.[8] This development altered the tone, and eventually the substance, of United States policy.

## II

Neither Russian nor American interest in East Asia originated in the 1890s. The tsar's empire had made extensive territorial gains there at China's expense in 1858 and 1860, while the United States had been working during the same period to open Japan and China to trade with the West. But in the mid-nineteenth century, St. Petersburg and Washington had seen each other's activities in East Asia as complementary. Both wor-

---

[7] George F. Kennan, "Arbitration and Conciliation in American Diplomacy," *Arbitration Journal*, XXVI(1971), 29.
[8] Stults, "Imperial Russia," pp. 8–10.

ried about the pretensions of Great Britain; both had been willing to cooperate to keep London from gaining a dominant position in the Pacific.

The situation in the 1890s was very different. Russia and the United States again were looking to East Asia, but this time they came to see their interests there as mutually antagonistic. Two unrelated events that occurred in 1895 helped to produce this change: China's defeat by Japan demonstrated for all to see the extreme vulnerability of the Middle Kingdom and set off a scramble for concessions that quickly appeared to threaten that country's continued existence as an independent state. Meanwhile, the Venezuelan crisis sparked a slow but steady improvement in the long-touchy relationship between the United States and Great Britain. Russian-American cordiality, based as it had been on the absence of direct conflicts and the existence of shared antipathies, did not survive these developments. Russia would henceforth see the United States as associating itself with Great Britain in East Asia to the detriment of its own interests. The United States, convinced of Britain's good intentions, would now see Russia as the chief threat to the East Asian balance of power, at a time when American interests increasingly demanded that that balance be maintained.

The Russian stake in East Asia was both strategic and economic. Construction of the Trans-Siberian Railroad in the 1890s promised access to the area; with it came opportunities to improve Russia's military position on the Pacific and to exploit the "great China market," a myth as believable to Russians as to Americans.[9] The Russians' immediate problem was to obtain transit rights for the railroad across Manchuria, which, though Chinese territory, offered the easiest and shortest route, and to secure an ice-free port. For this purpose the Russians negotiated a treaty with the Chinese in 1896 giving them permission to build the Trans-Siberian through Manchuria (this section would be known as the Chinese Eastern Railroad). Two years later, following the example Germany had set at Kiaochow (Jiaozhou) Bay, Russia obtained leases from China to the ice-free Manchurian harbors of Port Arthur (Lushun) and

---

[9] Andrew Malozemoff, *Russian Far Eastern Policy*, 1881–1904 (Berkeley: 1958), pp. 20–68.

*East Asia, 1889–1914.*

Talienwan (Dalian), together with the right to connect these to existing rail lines by a branch to be known as the South Manchurian Railroad.

Americans did not immediately see Russian activities in Manchuria as a threat. There was as yet no indication that United States trade would be discriminated against, and the Russian government, perhaps seeking to reinforce this impression, placed large orders with American firms for railroad equipment to be used there. Private American investors in China at this time saw the Russian presence as an asset rather than a liability in extracting concessions from the Chinese government. Nor were the Russians alone in their imperial enterprises: the Germans had preceded them, the British and French were soon to follow, and the United States was on the verge of taking the Philippines, a move to which the Russian government pointedly made no objection.[10]

But concerns were quick to develop. As early as January, 1898, Charles Denby, the United States minister in Peking, raised the possibility that Russia might try to shut American influence out of Manchuria. Such an event, Denby thought, might well justify modifying the nonintervention principle that had guided American foreign policy since Washington's Farewell Address. Such worries increased in 1899 when Secretary of State John Hay had difficulty in securing Russian endorsement of the first Open Door note, designed to ensure equal commercial access within spheres of influence in China. Hay in the end was reduced to announcing the Powers' general acquiescence, knowing full well that the Russians had no intention of applying the Open Door policy in Manchuria but gambling, successfully as it turned out, that they would not publicly say so. Shortly thereafter, Russia took advantage of the Boxer Rebellion to occupy all of Manchuria. Its failure to withdraw led to the formation of the Anglo-Japanese alliance in 1902; although the United States did not formally associate itself with this new

---

[10] Marilyn Blatt Young, *The Rhetoric of Empire: American China Policy, 1895–1901* (Cambridge, Massachusetts: 1968), pp. 56, 94–95; Edward H. Zabriskie, *American-Russian Rivalry in the Far East: 1895–1914* (Philadelphia: 1946), pp. 33–34, 37–38, 44; James K. Eyre, Jr., "Russia and the American Acquisition of the Philippines," *Mississippi Valley Historical Review*, XXVIII(March, 1942) 539–562.

alignment, Russian fears that Washington's sympathies lay in that direction were, by this time, correct.[11]

American interests in Manchuria were not large—in retrospect, they hardly seem worth the diplomatic ink spilled over them. But it must be kept in mind that what was at stake were not actual but potential interests: it was this fact made them capable of indefinite extension in the minds of ambitious politicians, enterprising exporters, aggressive consuls, and gloomy geopoliticians. It is significant that Brooks Adams, Charles Conant, and Alfred Thayer Mahan all published books in 1900 warning of Russian ambitions in East Asia.[12] Or, as Henry Miller, the free-spelling United States consul in Manchuria, put it in 1901:

[Russia] will annihilate American trade here, and with her political methods will make industrial slaves of the Chinese race and soon become a serious obsticle [sic] to the extention [sic] of our trade in all the Orient, and eventually a menace to our higher civilization.[13]

Escalating rhetoric of this type could easily transform marginal interests into vital ones; Manchuria quickly became nothing less than a symbolic test of American willingness to wield power in the world. It was a test in which Russia provided the main challenge.

It is not at all clear that the Russians had anything like this in mind; indeed, the tsar's ministers took a surprisingly relaxed view of expanding American influence in East Asia. Slow to see the significance of the Anglo-American rapprochement, they welcomed the annexation of Hawaii as evidence that the United States had resolved to thwart the ambitions of Britain and Japan. Nor did American acquisition of the Philippines concern

---

[11] Denby to Sherman, January 31, 1898, DSR, M-92: 104; Tyler Dennett, *John Hay: From Poetry to Politics* (New York: 1933), pp. 292–294. See also Theodore Roosevelt to Albert Shaw, June 22, 1903, Elting R. Morison, ed., *The Letters of Theodore Roosevelt* (Cambridge, Massachusetts: 1951), III, 497.

[12] Brooks Adams, *America's Economic Supremacy* (New York: 1900); Charles A. Conant, *The United States in the Orient* (New York: 1900); Alfred Thayer Mahan, *The Problem of Asia* (Boston: 1900). For an assessment of these works and their influence, see Young, *Rhetoric of Empire*, pp. 219–231; and Michael Hunt, *Frontier Defense and the Open Door: Manchuria in Chinese-American Relations, 1895–1911* (New Haven: 1973), pp. 34–35.

[13] Miller to H. G. Squires, June 27, 1901, quoted in ibid., p. 82.

them, although Russian officials were prepared to object should the islands fall to one of their European rivals. St. Petersburg's dilatory response to the first Open Door note reflected not so much hostility as genuine puzzlement at Washington's intentions, together with the characteristic cautiousness and inertia of the Russian bureaucracy. Russian diplomats did betray some irritation at American persistence in defending the Open Door: "If it were not for the Philippines the United States... would have been... satisfied with a passive relationship to... China," one envoy complained during the Boxer Rebellion. "Now, the interference of America is spreading in wider and wider circles."[14] But generally Russian officials saw no reason for American and Russian interests in East Asia to clash: they appear to have been surprised at the hostile response Russian actions in Manchuria provoked.

By 1903 this hostility had reached the highest levels of the Roosevelt administration. President Roosevelt and his secretary of state, John Hay, had not at first seen sinister motives in the Russian occupation of Manchuria. As late as May 1902, Hay could assure Roosevelt that "no matter what happens... the United States shall not be placed in any worse position than while the country was under the unquestioned domination of China." But in April, 1903, the Russians decided to prolong their occupation of Manchuria indefinitely. Hay regarded this decision as "injurious to our legitimate interests" and complained of the difficulties of dealing "with a government with whom mendacity is a science." Roosevelt agreed, writing in July:

I have not the slightest objection to the Russians knowing that I feel thoroughly aroused and irritated at their conduct in Manchuria; that I don't intend to give way and that I am year by year growing more confident that this country would back me up in going to an extreme in this matter.

---

[14] De Wollant (first secretary, Russian embassy in Washington), to the Ministry of Foreign Affairs, June 7, 1900, quoted in A. Ia. Kantorovich, *Amerika v bor'beza Kitai* (Moscow: 1935), p. 94. See also Ernest R. May, *Imperial Democracy: The Emergence of America as a Great Power* (New York: 1961), pp. 234–236; Eyre, "Russia and the American Acquisition of the Philippines," pp. 550–551; Zabriskie, *American-Russian Rivalry,* pp. 55, 57, 201; and Tower to Hay, December 11 and 28, 1899, DSR, M-35:55.

That same month he congratulated the Navy on the excellence of its plans developed in anticipation of a possible war with Russia in the Pacific.[15]

The prospect of war was never great, however, because Roosevelt was not in fact sure that the country would back him up. In January, 1904, he told a group of luncheon guests, including George Kennan, that while public opinion had coalesced into an anti-Russian attitude, there was not sufficient support for a military confrontation. But then he added, with a laugh, "If everybody regarded this thing as Mr. Kennan and I do, I know where our warships would be." There would be no Russian-American war over Manchuria, but as Kennan noted, "the sentimental 'friendship' that has long been supposed to exist between the governments of Russia and the United States is at an end—& thank the Lord for it!"[16]

The United States was not willing to fight for its interests in Manchuria, but Japan was, and in the end, Roosevelt came to rely on Tokyo to contain St. Petersburg's East Asian ambitions. The Japanese would have tolerated Russian control of the Manchurian railroads, but when the Russians made it clear that they would keep a permanent military force in Manchuria and refuse to allow the Japanese a comparable sphere of influence in Korea, the Tokyo government responded violently. On the night of February 8–9, 1904, Japanese naval forces suddenly attacked the Russian Far Eastern fleet at Port Arthur, and the Russo-Japanese War was on. Roosevelt could scarcely contain his glee. "For several years Russia has behaved very badly in the Far East," he wrote to his son. "I was thoroughly well pleased with the Japanese victory, for Japan is playing our game."[17]

---

[15] Hay to Roosevelt, May 1, 1902, quoted in Tyler Dennett, *Roosevelt and the Russo-Japanese War* (New York: 1925), pp. 135–136; Hay to McCormick, April 25, 1903, DSR, M-77: 140; Hay to Roosevelt, May 12, 1903, quoted in Alfred L. P. Dennis, *Adventures in American Diplomacy, 1896–1906* (New York: 1928), p. 357; Roosevelt to Hay, July 18, 1903, Morison, ed., *Roosevelt Letters*, III, 520; Stults, "Imperial Russia," p. 218n. See also Howard K. Beale, *Theodore Roosevelt and the Rise of America to World Power* (Baltimore: 1956), pp. 229–233; and Kenton J. Clymer, *John Hay: The Gentleman as Diplomat* (Ann Arbor: 1975); pp. 148–149.

[16] Kennan to Lyman Abbott, January 4, 1904, quoted in Stults, "Imperial Russia," pp. 222–223, 225.

[17] Roosevelt to Theodore Roosevelt, Jr., February 10, 1904, Morison, ed., *Roosevelt Letters*, IV, 724. See also John Albert White, *The Diplomacy of the Russo-Japanese War* (Princeton: 1964), pp. 95–131.

The Russians were bitter about the attitude of the American government and came to believe that the Japanese would not have acted so freely had they not had the tacit support of Britain and the United States. "How dare you to pretend to be our friends while you were knifing us all the time in the back?" the wife of the Russian ambassador in Tokyo complained to her husband's American colleague there. On the day of the Japanese attack, *Novoe Vremiia,* a leading St. Petersburg newspaper, speculated that "were the Panama Canal ready, were the powerful fleet of America in existence, were the Americans and the English in possession of [an] organized army..., peace would stand very little chance in general and the Russian in particular." A year later, the same newspaper published a report from its London correspondent charging that "America, uniting the European Powers and Japan by means of the doctrine of 'The Open Door, ' commenced to instigate Japan to war with Russia." Another St. Petersburg newspaper, the semiofficial *Journal de St. Petersbourg,* commented self-pityingly on the "painful spectacle of what human inconstancy can do" and ran a long series of documents reminding Americans of the help Russia had provided them during the Civil War.[18]

Roosevelt's lack of sympathy for such arguments became clear in the summer of 1904 when the Russian Navy, operating under a vague definition of contraband, sank a British merchant ship and seized one from Germany, both of which had been carrying American-owned cargo. The State Department, coordinating its actions with those of the British, lodged stiff protests; but Roosevelt was prepared to go even further. Worried about what might happen if the Russians acted directly against an American ship, he wrote Hay: "My own inclination is to notify them immediately that we will not stand it and to move our

---

[18] Lloyd Griscom, *Diplomatically Speaking* (Boston: 1940), p. 242; *Novoe Vremiia,* February 8, 1904, and April 11, 1905, translations enclosed in McCormick to Hay, February 9, 1904, and Meyer to Hay, April 18, 1905, DSR, M-35: 60, 62; *Journal de St. Petersbourg,* June 17 and 18, 1904, translation enclosed in McCormick to Hay, June 25, 1904, DSR, M-35: 61. Soviet historiography still reflects bitterness over the American attitude in 1904. See, for example, L. I. Zubok, *Ekspansionistskaia politika SShA v nachale XX veka* (Moscow: 1969), especially pp. 211–215.

Asiatic Squadron northward....I should do it with the intention of having our squadron bottle up the Vladivostok fleet." That same day the president ordered the Navy to prepare plans for just such a contingency.[19]

Despite his fulminations about "the literally fathomless mendacity" of the Russians, however, Roosevelt did not in fact oppose their continued presence in East Asia. When, by 1905, an unbroken series of Japanese victories appeared to threaten Russia with expulsion from that region, the president began working energetically to arrange a settlement. "While Russia's triumph would have been a blow to civilization," he wrote, "her destruction as an eastern Asiatic power would also in my opinion be unfortunate. It is best that she should be left face to face with Japan so that each may have a moderative action on the other." Through skillful diplomacy, Roosevelt managed to bring Russian and Japanese emissaries together at Portsmouth, New Hampshire, in August, 1905. There, under his careful but discreet supervision, they negotiated a settlement that gave Japan control of southern Manchuria, but left Russian interests in northern Manchuria substantially intact.[20]

Following successful mediation of the Russo-Japanese War, the crucial question for the United States was whether its interests would better be served by continuing Roosevelt's policy of "balanced antagonisms"—a policy that would keep Manchuria from falling under the domination of any one power but do little to preserve the principle of the Open Door—or by trying to challenge Russian and Japanese influence in Manchuria in the name of the Open Door. Roosevelt's balance of power instincts led him in the first direction, but he did not supervise East Asian policy as closely as he might have during his last years in office. Overzealous subordinates in the State Department pushed the idea of challenging both Japan and Russia, in coop-

---

[19] Roosevelt to Hay, July 29, 1904, Morison, ed., *Roosevelt Letters*, IV, 869. For an account of this incident, see John W. Coogan, *The End of Neutrality: The United States, Britain, and Maritime Rights, 1899–1915* (Ithaca: 1981), pp. 44–48.

[20] Roosevelt to George Von Lengerke Meyer, December 16, 1904, Morison, ed., *Roosevelt Letters*, IV, 1079; Roosevelt to Henry Cabot Lodge, June 16, 1905, ibid., p. 1230. See also White, *Diplomacy of the Russo-Japanese War*, pp. 206–309; Eugene P. Trani, *The Treaty of Portsmouth: An Adventure in American Diplomacy* (Lexington: 1969); and Raymond A. Esthus, *Double Eagle and Rising Sun: The Russians and Japanese at Portsmouth in 1905* (Durham, North Carolina: 1988).

eration with China, and during the Taft administration they put this policy into effect.[21]

Taft's secretary of state, Philander C. Knox, hoped to pry open Manchuria by encouraging American investment there. Two approaches were tried: a project to lend China sufficient money to purchase all foreign-owned railroads in Manchuria, thereby neutralizing them, and, failing that, the construction by China of parallel lines there, with Western financing, in hope of competing with the Russians and the Japanese. Neither project succeeded. American investors were reluctant to risk scarce capital on politically motivated projects whose economic potential seemed questionable. European investors had capital available but were not likely to sink it in projects like this without the approval of their governments. And with Britain allied to Japan, France allied to Russia, and Russo-Japanese and Anglo-French rapprochements well underway, the diplomatic climate was distinctly unfavorable to Knox's schemes. "When the United States put the Manchuria proposal forward..., it primarily wished to separate Russia and Japan," the Chinese foreign ministry commented with some asperity early in 1910. "Now they have on the contrary joined together. If the United States has some remedy, what then is it?"[22]

The United States in fact had no remedy other than to retreat to pious but impotent invocations of the Open Door. Knox's Manchurian policy had been a classic case of projecting interests beyond capabilities: it sought to break up, through nonforcible means, spheres of influence which both Russians and Japanese were prepared to use force to maintain. Far from balancing antagonisms, it only served to unite them in opposition to Washington's ineffectual intrusions. But the Russians too would soon be cut out of the Manchurian market. World War I, and the turmoil of revolution and civil war that followed, would win Japan dominance in East Asia by default. Russian

---

[21] Hunt, *Frontier Defense and the Open Door*, pp. 142–178; Raymond A. Esthus, *Theodore Roosevelt and Japan* (Seattle: 1966), pp. 229–245; Charles E. Neu, *An Uncertain Friendship: Theodore Roosevelt and Japan, 1906–1909* (Cambridge, Massachusetts: 1967), pp. 260–268, 319.

[22] Wai-wu Pu to Chang Yin-t'ang, February 7, 1910, quoted in Hunt, *Frontier Defense and the Open Door*, pp. 215–216. See also ibid., pp. 181–244; Zabriskie, *American-Russian Rivalry*, pp. 144–189; and Walter V. and Marie V. Scholes, *The Foreign Policies of the Taft Administration* (Columbia, Missouri: 1970), pp. 109–248.

and American dreams of empire in that part of the world proved, in the end, to be equally illusory.

It is interesting to speculate on why the United States did not make a greater effort to cooperate with the Russians in East Asia. Certainly the Russians, despite lingering suspicions over the role the United States had played in the Russo-Japanese War, considered the idea and even made tentative approaches to Washington at several points.[23] Both nations should have realized, it would seem, that Japan was the real threat to the China market, and that if either of them was to have any significant influence in the Orient in the future, they would have to work together.

There would appear to be several reasons why this cooperation did not take place. Professionalization and bureaucratization in the State Department, symbolized by the formation, in 1908, of a separate Division of Far Eastern Affairs, drained authority from the White House, reducing the kind of close control over foreign policy that would have been required to implement Roosevelt's balance of power strategy. Moreover, Taft and his advisers had little understanding of this policy to begin with; their approach placed far more emphasis on the defense of abstract principle than had Roosevelt's. But even Roosevelt would have found it difficult to cooperate with the Russians, not because they were autocratic, but because they were "so corrupt, so treacherous and shifty, and so incompetent."[24] This, in the end, may have been tsarist Russia's greatest sin in the eyes of progressive Americans: not its despotic government, not its imperialism, but its inefficiency.

## III

East Asia was not the only area of controversy in Russian-American relations; by the turn of the century the Jewish question had again begun to attract attention. This time, Jewish or-

---

[23] On this point, see Hunt, *Frontier Defense and the Open Door*, p. 206; Scholes, *Foreign Policies of the Taft Administration*, pp. 151–152; Zabriskie, *American-Russian Rivalry*, pp. 148–153; and William Appleman Williams, *American Russian Relations, 1781–1947* (New York: 1952), pp. 52–80.

[24] Roosevelt to Lodge, June 16, 1905, Morison, ed., *Roosevelt Letters*, IV, 1230. See also Jerry Israel, "A Diplomatic Machine: Scientific Management in the Department of State, 1906–1924," in Israel, ed., *Building the Organizational Society* (New York: 1972), pp. 185–187; and Richard Hume Werking, *The Master Architects: Building the United States Foreign Service, 1890–1913* (Lexington: 1977), pp. 129–137, 166–170.

ganizations within the United States succeeded in applying sufficient pressure on the White House to bring about official protests to St. Petersburg and, in 1911, unilateral abrogation of a seventy-nine-year-old Russian-American commercial treaty. The United States thus took its stand on behalf of suffering humanity; unfortunately, as in East Asia, American concern was projected into an area beyond the influence of American power. The result was a further deterioration in relations between Russia and the United States, with no discernible improvement in the situation of the protested persecution's victims.

It was news of the Kishinev pogrom of April, 1903, in which some 45 Jews were killed, between 400 and 600 injured, and at least 10,000 made homeless, [25] that again brought the issue of Russian anti-Semitism into the public eye. Neither the State Department nor President Roosevelt condoned this outrage, of course, but their initial inclination, upon being assured that Americans had not been involved, was to do nothing. This approach was consistent with the policy of the past thirty years, in which protests against Russian anti-Semitism had been confined to cases directly involving American interests. As Secretary of State John Hay wrote to Jacob Schiff, the wealthy Jewish financier, "What possible advantage would it be to the United States, and what possible advantage to the Jews of Russia, if we should make a protest against these fiendish cruelties and be told that it was none of our business?"[26]

But when public protests continued to mount, Roosevelt reversed himself, received a delegation of Jewish leaders, and promised to forward to St. Petersburg a petition the group was putting together. The Russian government refused to receive this document on the grounds that "the Emperor whose will is the sole law of this land had no need of information from outside sources as to what is taking place within his dominions." It was not the kind of reply likely to improve Russian-American relations, especially since it came just as Roosevelt had been

---

[25] Taylor Stults, "Roosevelt, Russian Persecution of Jews, and American Public Opinion," *Jewish Social Studies*, XXXIII(January, 1971), 14; Philip Ernest Schoenberg, "The American Reaction to the Kishinev Pogrom of 1903," *American Jewish Historical Quarterly*, LXIII(March, 1974), 262–263.

[26] Hay to Schiff, May 10, 1903, quoted in Stults, "Roosevelt, Russian Persecution," p. 17.

threatening to "go to extremes" over Manchuria. "What inept asses they are, these Kalmucks!" Hay fumed, in a letter to the Chief Executive. "They would have scored by receiving the petition & pigeonholing it. I think *you* have scored, as it is!"[27] But Roosevelt's action in transmitting the appeal had been significant: for the first time the United States government had associated itself with a protest against Russian anti-Semitism, not on the grounds that American interests were directly involved, but in the name of humanity at large.

It is ironic that this happened in the administration of Theodore Roosevelt, one of the few American presidents in recent history to recognize the need to keep rhetoric in line with capabilities. There is no doubt that the plight of the Jews genuinely moved Roosevelt, and that the way the Russians treated them confirmed his view of the tsarist empire as an incompetent, reactionary autocracy. But Roosevelt's political interests were also involved: leading Jews such as Schiff and Oscar Straus had called his attention to the favorable impact this protest would have on his reelection prospects, and Roosevelt himself suggested that "it will be a good thing to recite [in the campaign literature] what has been done in the Kishineff matter." It is only fair to note that Roosevelt continued his efforts on behalf of Russian Jews after the election: during the Portsmouth peace negotiations in 1905 he approached the Russian delegate, Count Witte, on the subject, at Straus's request. But he retained reservations about the effectiveness of this kind of diplomacy. "For the Jews in Russia," he acknowledged, "we were able to accomplish a little, *a very* little, toward temporarily ameliorating their conditions." But he added that "out in the west we always used to consider it a cardinal crime to draw a revolver and brandish it about unless the man meant to shoot. And it is apt to turn out to be sheer cruelty to encourage men by words and then not back up the words by deeds."[28]

---

[27] Riddle to Hay, July 16, 1903, DSR, M-35: 60; Hay to Roosevelt, July 16, 1903, quoted in Dennett, *John Hay*, p. 400. See also Clymer, *John Hay*, pp. 78–81; and Frederick W. Marks III, *Velvet on Iron: The Diplomacy of Theodore Roosevelt* (Lincoln, Nebraska: 1979), pp. 150–151.

[28] Roosevelt to Elihu Root, June 2, 1904, Morison, ed., *Roosevelt Letters*, IV, 810; Roosevelt to George Otto Trevelyan, May 13, 1905, ibid., pp. 1174–1175. See also Stults, "Roosevelt, Russian Persecution," pp. 21–22; and Naomi W. Cohen, "The Abrogation of the Russo-American Treaty of 1832," *Jewish Social Studies*, XXV(January, 1963), 5.

The Russian government's treatment of the Jews had a direct effect on its ability to finance the Russo-Japanese War. Schiff, senior partner in the firm of Kuhn, Loeb & Company, had been one of the leaders in the protest against the Kishinev pogrom. Unlike many other Jews, he was in a position to do something about Russian anti-Semitism. Schiff worked to discourage loans to Russia by the Rothschilds and other European banking firms and, once the Russo-Japanese War got underway, helped arrange the extremely successful Japanese financing effort. Schiff's motives were quite frankly those of the Russian revolutionaries of 1905: to work for a Russian defeat at the hands of Japan, in the belief that this would hasten the revolution which, Schiff thought, would improve the condition of the Jews.[29]

But, as it turned out, the revolutionary violence of 1905 resulted, in November, in the worst pogroms yet. These attacks attracted considerable attention in the United States, and again protest meetings were held and relief campaigns organized. But this time, despite persistent efforts, Straus and Schiff were unable to secure an official protest from the White House. Though privately sympathetic to the plight of Russian Jews, Secretary of State Elihu Root opposed public action on the grounds that this would only worsen their conditions. Roosevelt agreed, telling Schiff with some irritation that "we could do nothing, and where we can do nothing I have a horror of saying anything. We have never taken—and while I am President we will never take—any action which we cannot make good." But of course the United States had done precisely that two years earlier, at the time of Kishinev. It may be uncharitable, but probably not inaccurate, to suggest that what was different this time was the fact that Roosevelt was not running for reelection.[30]

---

[29] Gary Dean Best, "Financing A Foreign War: Jacob H. Schiff and Japan, 1904–1905," *American Jewish Historical Quarterly*, LXI(June, 1972), 313–324; C. C. Aronsfield, "Jewish Bankers and the Tsar," *Jewish Social Studies*, XXXV(April, 1973, 99–102; Cyrus Adler, *Jacob Schiff: His Life and Letters* (Garden City, New York: 1928), II, 120–128; White, *Diplomacy of the Russo-Japanese War*, pp. 169–170, 260–261, 290.

[30] Roosevelt to Schiff, December 14, 1905, Morison, ed., *Roosevelt Letters*, V, 113. See also Arthur W. Thompson and Robert W. Hart, *The Uncertain Crusade: America and the Russian Revolution of 1905* (Amherst, Massachusetts: 1970), pp. 103–117; Philip C. Jessup, *Elihu Root* (New York: 1938), II, 65–66; Dennett, *John Hay*, p. 401; and Adler, *Jacob Schiff*, II, 133–140.

When, in spite of everything, the Russian government remained adamant on the Jewish question, pressure began to develop among Jewish groups in the United States for direct retaliation through abrogation of a commercial treaty James Buchanan had negotiated with Russia almost eight decades earlier. This 1832 treaty provided that Russians and Americans should

mutually have liberty to enter the ports, places and rivers of the territories of each party, wherever foreign commerce is permitted. They shall be at liberty to sojourn and reside in all parts whatsoever of said territories, in order to attend to their affairs, and they shall enjoy, to that effect, the same security and protection as natives of the country wherein they reside, on condition of their submitting to the laws and ordinances there prevailing, and particularly to the regulations in force concerning commerce.

The Russians had violated this treaty, the argument ran, by refusing to honor passports to Russia held by American Jews and by prohibiting American Jews residing in Russia from living where they wanted. United States officials as early as 1873 had seen such discrimination as contrary to the treaty, but the clause conditioning freedom of residence on adherence to domestic laws complicated the matter, since there could be no denying that a large body of laws existed in Russia imposing restrictions on Jews.[31]

As far as American Jewish organizations were concerned, though, the issue was not simply those few Jews who wanted to travel to or reside in Russia. Their concern was the treatment of Russian Jews generally; their belief was that by forcing the Russians to abandon discrimination against American Jews, they would soon have to do the same thing for all Jews. Hence, following the Russo-Japanese War, these groups concentrated on having the United States threaten to abrogate the 1832 commercial treaty—a threat which, it was thought, would carry weight with the Russians because of the increasing volume of Russian-American trade.[32]

---

[31] Hamilton Fish to Marshall Jewell, November 20, 1873, and May 22, 1874, DSR, M-77: 137. For the 1832 treaty, see Hunter Miller, ed., *Treaties and Other International Acts of the United States of America* (Washington: 1931–1948), III, 723–734.

[32] Cohen, "Abrogation of the Russo-American Treaty," pp. 7–8; Healy, "Tsarist Anti-Semitism and Russian-American Relations," pp. 417–419.

These arguments did not impress the Taft administration, which considered the legal reasoning dubious (the United States itself still reserved the right to deny citizenship to Japanese and Chinese) and believed that abrogation would have no effect. Moreover, State Department officials argued that making an issue of the treaty would harm growing commercial ties with Russia and endanger American efforts to maintain a balance against increasing Japanese influence in East Asia. Undeterred by these arguments, the Jewish organizations launched a public campaign for abrogation, and by the end of 1911 had succeeded in getting through the House of Representatives, by a 301–1 vote, a resolution unilaterally abrogating the treaty. Confronted with the likelihood of a similar vote in the Senate, the administration quickly gave the Russians notice of termination in a year's time; shortly thereafter the Senate unanimously approved this action.[33]

Abrogation of the commercial treaty failed to have the effect its supporters had anticipated. St. Petersburg officials saw it as an attempt to interfere in Russian internal affairs, and a strong anti-American backlash developed, especially among right-wing elements in the capital. The Jews' condition actually worsened as the government subjected them to new reprisals. United States diplomats, who had opposed abrogation, quickly worked out an informal *modus vivendi* with the Russians which prevented any significant disruption of trade relations. The action of Congress accomplished little other than to increase the already considerable sense of bitterness educated Russians felt toward the United States. The joke, Taft is said to have chuckled, was on the Jews.[34]

The treaty episode was important, however, because it indicated a growing susceptibility on the part of Washington officials to the influence of pressure groups on foreign policy—

---

[33] Ibid., pp. 419–422; Cohen, "Abrogation of the Russian-American Treaty," pp. 8–37; Clifford L. Egan, "Pressure Groups, the Department of State, and the Abrogation of the Russian-American Treaty of 1832," American Philosophical Society *Proceedings*, CXV(August, 1971), 329–333; Gilbert C. Kohlenberg, "Russian-American Economic Relations, 1906–1917" (Ph.D. Dissertation, University of Illinois, 1951), pp. 182–188.

[34] Cohen, "Abrogation of the Russo-American Treaty," pp. 38–41; Egan, "Pressure Groups," pp. 333–334; Laserson, *American Impact on Russia*, pp. 359–361; Kohlenberg, "Russian-American Economic Relations," pp. 75–82.

Taft, like Roosevelt in 1903, had not been unmindful of the fact that an election was coming up. It is significant that although the United States was in no way unique in having its Jewish citizens discriminated against in Russia, no other country followed the American example in launching a protest.[35] The American people, Ambassador Curtis Guild explained to the Russian foreign minister, were "more easily appealed to by questions of sentiment when the appeal was made on the ground of humanity and civilization than any other nation in the world."[36] Unfortunately in this case, as in the case of Knox's Manchurian policy, Americans lost sight of the relationship between objectives and capabilities; economic diplomacy, in both situations, had little effect in altering policies the Russian government considered to be in its vital national interests.

## IV

Economic relations between the United States and Russia had, until 1911, remained more or less insulated from political difficulties. Although by no means oblivious to the advantages of increased economic ties with the rest of the world, government officials generally refrained, until the Taft administration, from trying to direct foreign trade and investment in such a way as to reinforce diplomatic policies.[37] Nor did American businessmen depend on government to keep economic opportunities open; while the government could furnish useful information and, occasionally, help in times of crisis, those businessmen who sought trade and investment opportunities overseas—and this was by no means the majority of them[38]—normally did so on

---

[35] Zosa Szajkowski, "The European Aspect of the American-Russian Passport Question," *Publications of the American Jewish Historical Society*, XLVI (December, 1956), 86–100.

[36] Guild to Knox, December 16, 1911, *FR: 1911*, pp. 696–697.

[37] Mira Wilkins, *The Emergence of Multinational Enterprise: American Business Abroad from the Colonial Era to 1914* (Cambridge, Massachusetts: 1970), p. 67.

[38] William H. Becker, "American Manufacturers and Foreign Markets, 1870–1900," *Business History Review*, XLVII(Winter, 1973), 466–481; Paul S. Holbo, "Economics, Emotion and Expansion: An Emerging Foreign Policy," in H. Wayne Morgan, ed., *The Gilded Age*, Revised Edition (Syracuse: 1970), pp. 199–221.

their own.[39] As a result, deteriorating political relations had surprisingly little effect on economic contacts between Russia and the United States.

Trade between the United States and Russia had never been very extensive because of the similarity of exportable products produced in each country, the existence of tariff barriers, the lack of direct shipping facilities, European competition, and the persistent reluctance of American exporters to adapt their products to foreign tastes and needs.[40] Official statistics show an unremarkable increase in trade volume during the three decades preceding World War I, with exports rising from an annual average of $13 million for 1881–1885 to $20 million for 1907–1911, and imports from $2.6 million to $14.1 million during the same period. These figures do not reflect trade through third countries, however, and since most Russian-American commerce went by way of Germany, they are almost certainly too low. Reputable estimates place the actual volume of American exports to Russia in 1911 at between $65 and $70 million, or around 3.3% of total exports, and imports at $17.0 million, or 0.8% of the total. American imports as a percentage of total Russian imports were about 9% in 1911, making the United States Russia's third largest source of imports, after Germany and Great Britain.[41]

Until around the turn of the century, cotton made up the bulk of American exports to Russia. Geography and climate made it difficult for the Russians to produce this commodity, and despite official efforts to encourage its cultivation, almost

---

[39] Wilkins, *Multinational Enterprise*, pp. 74–75.

[40] Kohlenberg, "Russian-American Economic Relations," pp. 61–69; George S. Queen, "The United States and the Material Advance in Russia, 1881–1906" (Ph.D. Dissertation, University of Illinois, 1942), p. 98.

[41] Based on statistics in U.S. Treasury Department, Bureau of Statistics, *Statistical Tables Exhibiting the Commerce of the United States with European Countries from 1790 to 1890* (Washington: 1893), p. xxxviii; U.S. Department of Commerce, *Statistical Abstract, 1913* (Washington: 1914), pp. 327, 363; Gail L. Owen, "Dollar Diplomacy in Default: The Economics of Russian-American Relations, 1910–1917," *Historical Journal*, XIII(1970), 265; John V. Hogan, "Russian-American Commercial Relations," *Political Science Quarterly*, XXVII(December, 1912), 641; Margaret Miller, *The Economic Development of Russia, 1905–1914*, Second Edition (New York: 1967), pp. 66, 77.

half the raw cotton used in Russian mills still came from the United States as late as 1905. Agricultural equipment constituted another large portion of American exports: in 1911 Russia took more than one-third of all agricultural implements and machinery produced for export in the United States. Other popular American products included rails and rolling stock, mining and milling equipment, machine tools, typewriters, cash registers, and probably the most ubiquitous American export of all during this period, Singer sewing machines. Imports from Russia, consisting mainly of animal hides and raw wool, fell far behind exports, so that by 1911 the United States was running an annual credit balance of around $50 million on a total trade of approximately $85 million.[42]

American investment in Russia took two forms: investment in government securities and in privately owned businesses. Government bonds were sold on the New York Stock Exchange from time to time, but they were not popular, probably in part because of the activities of Jacob Schiff. American insurance companies operating in Russia were required to put capital generated by their Russian policies into government securities, though, so that the two major American companies active there, New York Life and Equitable, did have extensive holdings. Most American investment, however, went into private enterprises operating within the Russian Empire. Many of these were branch factories set up to produce popular export items without having to pay tariffs. Thus, by 1911, the Singer, International Harvester, Westinghouse, and New York Air Brake companies all had factories in Russia. Other investment capital went into oil, mining, chemical, tobacco, and pharmaceutical enterprises. Estimates of total American investments in Russia are difficult to make, but a rough approximation places it at

---

[42] Queen, "Material Advance," pp. 112–73; Kohlenberg, "Russian-American Economic Relations," pp. 99–129; Hogan, "Russian-American Commercial Relations," pp. 638–641; M. K. Kuz'min, "K istorii russko-amerikanskoi torgovli," *Istoricheskii Arkhiv*, 1956, #6, p. 88. See also George S. Queen, "The McCormick Harvesting Machine Company in Russia," *Russian Review*, XXIII(April, 1964), 164–181; and Fred V. Carstensen, *American Enterprise in Foreign Markets: Studies of Singer and International Harvester in Imperial Russia* (Chapel Hill: 1984).

around $160 million by 1911, or about 8% of total American investment overseas at that time.[43]

The Russian government welcomed American trade and investment. Finance Minister Sergei Witte, whose industrialization program required the importation of foreign capital, had tried, unsuccessfully, to float Russian government bonds on the New York money market in 1898 and again in 1905. He also encouraged American imports on the grounds that Americans were "honest and single-minded... not as in the case of certain other people we have to deal with, who make a treaty of commerce with us today and tomorrow we find a cannon hidden behind it!" After the Russo-Japanese War, the Russian government made several unsuccessful attempts to draw American capital into Manchurian railroad investments in hopes of creating a counterweight to growing Japanese influence there. In 1910, it invited American financier John Hays Hammond to visit Russia in an effort to facilitate the flow of American and British capital into that country. Hammond was personally welcomed by the tsar and other top officials, and left "convinced [that] I had with me the most important packet of commercial opportunities ever to be of such prospective benefit to two nations."[44]

But, by this time, deteriorating political relations had begun to affect economic ties. The Russians welcomed American investment in Manchuria only if it would strengthen their sphere of influence there; the Taft administration's encouragement of investment in Chinese-controlled Manchurian railroads seemed designed to undercut that position and hence was unacceptable. While abrogation of the commercial treaty in 1911 had no significant effect on trade, the anti-American outbursts it pro-

---

[43] Richard B. Fisher, "American Investments in Pre-Soviet Russia," *American Slavic and East European Review*, VIII(1949), 90–105; Barbara Jackson Gaddis, "American Economic Interests in Russia, August, 1914–March, 1917" (M. A. Thesis, University of Texas, 1966), pp. 8–11; Queen, "Material Advance," pp. 176–221; Wilkins, *Multinational Enterprise*, pp. 102–105, 212–213; Carstensen, *American Enterprise in Foreign Markets*, pp. 41–48, 158–194.

[44] Tower to Hay, July 3, 1901, DSR, M-35: 58; *The Autobiography of John Hays Hammond* (New York: 1935), II, 467–474. See also Theodore H. Von Laue, *Sergei Iu. Witte and the Industrialization of Russia* (New York: 1963), pp. 105–107; Paul A. Varg, *Open Door Diplomat: The Life of W. W. Rockhill* (Urbana: 1952), pp. 101–103; Zabriskie, *American-Russian Rivalry*, pp. 148–153; and the documents relating to Hammond's visit in DSR, 711.61/4 –18 (M-33: 2).

voked probably did inhibit investment prospects. Hammond claimed, in retrospect, that abrogation "utterly destroyed any hope of carrying out my plan of obtaining American capital for Russia."[45] Economics, for the moment, had fallen victim to politics, but only for the moment, for an unforeseen event—the outbreak of war in Europe—would soon drive Russian-American economic contacts to unprecedented heights.

When Russia went to war against Germany in August, 1914, it did so against a country which, in the previous year, had supplied 47.4% of its imports and had taken 31.8% of its exports. Germany had long dominated Russian foreign trade, but now, with commercial access cut off, Russia had to look elsewhere for the war supplies its own poorly developed industries could not provide. Like its allies, Britain and France, Russia soon had to turn to the United States for these materials. American businessmen were not at all hesitant to take advantage of the opportunity.[46]

During the year ending June 30, 1914, just on the eve of the war, United States exports to Russia amounted to $31.3 million, or 1.3% of total exports. Three years later, for the year ending June 30, 1917, United States exports had risen to $558.9 million, or 8.9% of total exports. These figures do not appear particularly impressive when compared to the percentage of American exports going to Great Britain during the latter year (32.5%) or to France (16.1%). But the rate of increase was striking: exports to Russia in fiscal 1917 were 1785% of what they had been in fiscal 1914, as compared with a 334% rise for exports to Britain and a 632% rise for exports to France. Exports to Germany during the same period declined from 14.6% of total exports to virtually nothing three years later. Russian-American trade had achieved such importance that by 1917 one-fourth of all American profits on foreign trade and two-thirds of all outside Russian military assistance were deriving from it.[47]

---

[45] Hammond, *Autobiography*, II, 475; Healy, "Tsarist Anti-Semitism and Russian-American Relations," pp. 423–425.

[46] Boris E. Nolde, *Russia in the Economic War* (New Haven: 1928), pp. 125–127; Miller, *Economic Development of Russia*, pp. 63–65; Gaddis, "American Economic Interests," pp. 16, 20–25, 39–40, 51–52.

[47] U.S. Department of Commerce, *Statistical Abstract, 1918* (Washington: 1919), pp. 383, 416; Gaddis, "American Economic Interests," pp. 51–52, 115; Owen, "Dollar Diplomacy," p. 266.

Financing these exports caused problems. Even after the Wilson administration overcame its objections against private loans to belligerents, American bankers remained reluctant to arrange direct loans to Russia, partly because of the absence of Russian collateral in the United States, the inadequacy of direct banking facilities, the continued objections of the Schiff group, and the general deterioration in political relations that had followed abrogation of the commercial treaty. In the end, the Russians financed their American purchases principally by borrowing from their Anglo-French allies, who in turn arranged loans in the United States to cover their resulting indebtedness. Direct American advances to Russia from August, 1914, through March, 1917, totaled $233 million; indirect advances to Russia through Britain and France, all arranged by J. P. Morgan and Company, came to $1,480 million during the same period. Since total advances to Britain and France during this period totaled $2,112 million, it is apparent that approximately 70% of the loans extended to Britain and France during the period of American neutrality went to cover Russian war orders.[48]

Hence, despite decidedly cool official relations, American financial resources played a crucial role in supporting tsarist Russia's war effort. As in the case of relations with Britain and France, the Wilson administration's political neutrality did not extend to economics. *Laissez-faire* still prevailed; "dollar diplomacy," if by this is meant efforts by government to channel private trade and investment in directions consistent with political objectives, had proven to be a distinctly transitory phenomenon.[49]

## V

Growing economic ties between Russia and the United States did little to improve political relations, which remained, in the words of a Russian newspaper, in a state of "cold indifference."

---

[48] Ibid., pp. 258–267; Benson Lee Grayson, *Russian-American Relations in World War I* (New York: 1979), pp. 47–59; Cleona Lewis, *America's Stake in International Investments* (Washington: 1938), p. 355.

[49] Owen, "Dollar Diplomacy," pp. 271–272. See also W. Bruce Lincoln, *Passage through Armageddon: The Russians in War and Revolution, 1914–1918* (New York: 1986), pp. 61, 134, 241.

Woodrow Wilson had described the Russian government in 1889 as "a belated example of those crude forms of politics which the rest of Europe has outgrown," and there is little evidence that he had modified his views significantly in the intervening years. Fully conscious of the political advantages of doing so, he had publicly supported abrogation of the commercial treaty in 1911 on the grounds that economic interests ought not to take precedence over "the maintenance of those rights of manhood which [the United States] government was set up to vindicate." Upon becoming president, Wilson demonstrated the relative unimportance he attached to Russian affairs by naming to the St. Petersburg embassy a succession of political appointees whose qualifications, even by the relaxed standards of his administration, were minimal—so much so, indeed, that the Russian government rejected the first two of them. When Wilson finally did come up with an acceptable ambassador, George Marye, in the summer of 1914, the Russians made it clear that, despite the outbreak of war, they were in no hurry for him to proceed to his post.[50]

Efforts to negotiate a new commercial treaty with Russia had met with no success. "The [Russian] Government has the firm intention," Foreign Minister Sazonov had told the Imperial Duma in 1912, "not to allow any infringements from abroad of the inalienable rights of Russia, as a sovereign state, to regulate its internal legislation." President-elect Wilson had written, several months later, "I feel it is absolutely inconsistent with either the dignity or the principles of our government to enter into any treaty relations with the government of Russia which would permit the treatment of one class of our citizens in one way and all other classes in another." The Russians did show some interest in a new treaty late in 1914, when it became apparent that the war was going to require a large volume of supplies from the United States, but the indirect financing arrange-

---

[50] *Novoe Vremiia*, January 14, 1914, translation enclosed in Charles S. Wilson to William Jennings Bryan, January 16, 1914, DSR, 711.61/2 9, M-333: 2; Arthur S. Link, et al., eds., *The Papers of Woodrow Wilson* (Princeton: 1966–), VI, 259–260; R. S. Baker and W. E. Dodd, eds., *The Public Papers of Woodrow Wilson* (New York: 1925), II, 318–322; Arthur S. Link, *Wilson* (Princeton: 1947–), I, 338, II, 102–103; George Thomas Marye, *Nearing the End in Imperial Russia* (Philadelphia: 1929), pp. 17–22.

ment for Russian war orders which the British and the French worked out through J. P. Morgan removed any need to deal directly with the United States government, and Russian interest in a new commercial treaty quickly waned. Neither Ambassador Marye nor his successor, David R. Francis, had any success in pursuing the matter.[51]

Wilson and his advisers reflected considerable ambivalence in thinking about Russia and the war. The President initially sympathized with Russian territorial aspirations on the grounds that Russia deserved better access to the sea—in January, 1915, he even endorsed the Russian acquisition of Constantinople. But Wilson shared the fear of his confidant, Colonel Edward M. House, that a complete German defeat might only substitute Russian despotism for Prussian militarism in Europe. Through his intermediary, House, Wilson was not above holding out the possibility of a separate German-Russian peace as a means of frightening the British and French into accepting less than total victory. But Russian experts like George Kennan and Samuel Harper, the nation's only academic specialist in Slavic affairs, argued that Russian autocracy was not a danger: the war, they believed, would provoke either reform or revolution in Russia. By 1917, Wilson and House had come to accept this argument. When the possibility of a postwar German-Russian-Japanese alliance was raised at a February, 1917, cabinet meeting, Wilson dismissed it with the observation that "the Russian peasant might save the world this misfortune." The overthrow of the tsar, which occurred a month later, therefore came as no great surprise to Washington officials.[52]

The March Revolution (February by the old Russian calendar, still in effect at this time) has often been seen as having fa-

---

[51] Sazonov speech to the Imperial Duma, April, 1912, quoted in Laserson, *American Impact on Russia,* p. 366; Wilson to Curtis Guild, November 30, 1912, quoted in Ray Stannard Baker, *Woodrow Wilson: His Life and Letters: Governor, 1910–1913* (Garden City, New York: 1931), p. 417; Owen, "Dollar Diplomacy," p. 260; Grayson, *Russian-American Relations in World War I,* pp. 53–59.

[52] Harley Notter, *The Origins of the Foreign Policy of Woodrow Wilson* (Baltimore: 1937), pp. 373, 614; Ernest R. May, *The World War and American Isolation, 1914–1917* (Cambridge, Massachusetts: 1959), pp. 77, 85; Charles Seymour, *The Intimate Papers of Colonel House* (Boston: 1926), II, 121, 129, 258; Christopher Lasch, *The American Liberals and the Russian Revolution* (New York: 1962), pp. 1–26.

cilitated an ideological justification for American entry into World War I. Wilson could not credibly have portrayed that struggle as a "fight to make the world safe for democracy," the argument runs, had he been forced to ally himself with the Russian tsar.[53] There is reason to believe, though, that Wilson would have justified the war in much the same way even if the Revolution had not occurred at the fortunate time that it did. His commitment to the international diffusion of democratic institutions predated the Revolution, having been most notably expressed in his "peace without victory" speech in January 1917. Nor, as that very phrase implied, was universal democracy necessarily a prerequisite for ending the war; that goal reflected rather the kind of international structure Wilson thought most likely to sustain peace once the war was over. Nor did Wilson see ideological consistency as a requirement for joint military action: he carefully depicted the United States as an "associated," not an "allied" power, and presumably could have operated on this basis even with tsarist Russia. The Revolution probably did allow Wilson to use more sweeping rhetoric than would otherwise have been the case; it also doubtless encouraged his belief in the feasibility of a league of democratic states that would integrate order with justice in the postwar world.[54] It would be a mistake, though, to see the gap between promises and performance that came to characterize Wilsonian diplomacy as necessarily, or even primarily, the result of the portentous events that occurred in St. Petersburg in March 1917.

The deterioration of Russian-American relations that took place in the fifty years separating the Alaska Purchase from the Russian Revolution occurred primarily as a result of American, not Russian, initiatives. The traditional concerns of Russian for-

---

[53] See, for example, George F. Kennan, *Russia and the West under Lenin and Stalin* (Boston: 1961), p. 18; Peter G. Filene, *Americans and the Soviet Experiment, 1917–1933* (Cambridge, Massachusetts: 1967), pp. 12–13; Bailey, *America Faces Russia*, p. 232.

[54] Notter, *Origins of the Foreign Policy of Woodrow Wilson*, pp. 648–649; Harry H. Savage, "Official Policies and Relations of the United States with the Provisional Government of Russia, March–November, 1917" (Ph. D. Dissertation, University of Minnesota, 1971), pp. 31–56.

eign policy—secure frontiers, access to open seas, ethnic and religious solidarity, and maintenance of a balance of power in Europe[55] —remained largely constant. American diplomatic objectives, however, changed drastically. The cautious noninterventionist tradition of the nineteenth century had given way to the belief that American institutions could be made secure only through their maximum possible diffusion in the world. The consequent proliferation of interests brought the United States into conflict with Russia over economic-strategic rivalries in East Asia and, on humanitarian grounds, over the very internal structure of the Russian state. Under the pressures of revolution that structure would now change, but not in a manner to the Americans' liking. The events of 1917 would produce, in the end, a government more committed to ideological imperialism than the United States had ever been. The result would be to frustrate the hopes so widely held in the United States for the improvement in relations the Russian Revolution had been expected to bring.

---

[55] Cyril E. Black, "The Pattern of Russian Objectives," in Ivo J. Lederer, ed., *Russian Foreign Policy: Essays in Historical Perspective* (New Haven: 1962), pp. 6–22.

CHAPTER III

# The Russian Revolution: 1917–1920

THE YEAR 1917 SAW THE UNITED STATES ENTER WORLD WAR I
and Russia, for all practical purposes, leave it. Wholly unrelated sets of circumstances produced these developments, but
their cumulative effects upon the course of history would be
profound. These would include the eventual migration of international political power from the center of Europe, where it had
been concentrated for several hundred years, to its periphery.
They would also include proclamation of two rival ideologies,
Wilson's versus Lenin's, which, though selective in application,
were sufficiently universal in their appeal to make them powerful influences on the behavior of men and nations for decades
to come. Finally, though somewhat anticlimactically, the events
of 1917 would, for the first time in their long history of contacts,
make the policies of Russia and the United States matters of major concern to statesmen in each country.

I

On the night of April 2, 1917, Woodrow Wilson stood before
the Congress of the United States and asked it to declare war on
Germany. In the course of his address, the president referred to
"the wonderful and heartening things that have been happening within the last few weeks in Russia." That country, Wilson
continued,

was always known by those who knew it best to have been always in
fact democratic at heart. . . . The autocracy that crowned the summit of
her political structure, long as it had stood and terrible as was the reality of its power, was not in fact Russian in origin, character, or purpose; and now it has been shaken off and the great, generous Russian
people have been added in all their naive majesty and might to the

57

forces that are fighting for freedom in the world, for justice and for peace.[1]

It has been pointed out that none of the assumptions that lay behind this statement were correct: Russia had no democratic tradition; the tsarist autocracy had hardly been an alien regime; the Russian people did not see the war's objectives in the same way that Americans did.[2] Wilson's statement, it seems clear, reflected more what he wanted to believe than what was, in fact, the case.

It is significant, though, that Wilson made these remarks, not in relation to prosecuting the war, but in the context of what would be necessary to keep war from breaking out in the future. "A steadfast concern for peace can never be maintained except by a partnership of democratic nations," the president had proclaimed, immediately before making his observations on Russia: "No autocratic government could be trusted to keep faith with it or observe its covenants." This, for Wilson, was the chief significance of the March Revolution: not so much its effect on the war as its long-range implications for the postwar international structure. Lasting peace would require both order and justice; only a coalition of democratic states could achieve these goals. Overthrowing its autocracy made Russia a "fit partner" in this postwar "league of honor."[3]

But this very conviction that peace and autocracy were incompatible had the ironic effect of rendering Wilson insensitive to the requirements for democracy's survival in Russia. It is clear in retrospect, although admittedly it was not at the time, that three years of bloody and mismanaged conflict had so demoralized that country as to render its new government capable of remaining in authority only by ending active participation in the war. But Wilson, by this time, had accepted the view of his Anglo-French allies: that the only guarantee of lasting peace would be vigorous prosecution of the war to total victory, an enterprise in which continued Russian belligerency would be essential.[4] Hence, the short-range problem of keeping Russia in

---

[1] R. S. Baker and W. E. Dodd, eds., *The Public Papers of Woodrow Wilson: War and Peace* (New York: 1927), I, 12–13.

[2] Kennan, *Russia and West*, p. 19.

[3] Savage, "Official Policies," pp. 35–39.

[4] Arno J. Mayer, *Political Origins of the New Diplomacy, 1917–1918* (New Haven: 1958), pp. 182–183.

the war came to overshadow Wilson's long-range hopes for the March Revolution.

Most American experts on Russia (and the number who qualified in this respect could have been counted on the fingers of one hand) expected that the overthrow of the tsar would enable Russia to fight more effectively. The upheaval in Petrograd had been a political, not a social, phenomenon, they believed; while discontented elements doubtless existed in Russia, the Provisional Government would, it was thought, be able to keep them well in hand. Wilson, interestingly, was one of the few Americans to question this judgment. He is said to have suggested, in a conversation on April 14, that "in setting up their new form of Government and in working out domestic reforms [the Russians might] find the war an intolerable evil and would desire to get out of it on any reasonable terms. It would be a serious blow to the Allies if that took place."[5]

Events soon confirmed Wilson's fears. Although the Provisional Government formally assured its allies of Russia's continued commitment to the war, that government, it quickly became clear, possessed only the trappings of political authority. Real power rested with the Petrograd Soviet, or council, an amorphous and unruly body of several thousand elected workers' and soldiers' representatives which, through its Executive Committee, controlled the factories and garrisons of Petrograd. This confused situation gave the Soviet, made up of Social Revolutionaries and the two mutually antagonistic factions of the Social Democratic Party, the Mensheviks and the Bolsheviks, a veto over the Provisional Government's policies. Similar Soviets were formed in urban centers and military units throughout the country. The Soviet did not, it is important to note, call for a separate peace. It did view the war as an "imperialist" struggle, though, and appealed to "all the peoples, in our Allies' countries as well as in the countries at war with Russia, to exert pressure on their governments to renounce their programs of conquest."[6]

---

[5] Link, *Wilson*, V, 410n. See also Savage, "Official Policies," pp. 30–31; and R.Sh. Ganelin, *Rossiia i SShA, 1914–1917: Ocherki istorii russko-amerikanskich otnoshenii* (Leningrad: 1969), pp. 160–161.

[6] Robert Paul Browder and Alexander F. Kerensky, eds., *The Russian Provisional Government, 1917* (Stanford: 1961), II, 1084.

On the surface, this formula was not all that different from
Wilson's "peace without victory" concept, enunciated several
months earlier. But there were important incongruities. The Soviet's peace appeal proclaimed the war to be unjust almost exactly at the time Wilson had convinced himself of its justice. It
implied revolutionary action to end the war if diplomatic negotiations failed, a prospect no established government could welcome. It threatened, by increasing the disarray which already
existed within the Russian Army, to bring an end to military operations on the eastern front, thereby permitting Germany to
transfer large numbers of troops to the west. For these reasons,
the Soviet's call for a peace based on "no annexations, no indemnities" met with as little sympathy in Washington as it did
in London and Paris.[7]

The appeal of the Petrograd formula might have been neu-
tralized by clarifying the objectives for which the Allies were
fighting, but Wilson adamantly refused to allow public discussion of war aims at this time. When the Soviet called for an international conference of socialists to meet at Stockholm to discuss peace prospects, Wilson denied passports to the American
delegates who wanted to attend and encouraged the British and
French to do the same. Shortly thereafter, he dismissed Pope
Benedict's appeal for a statement of war aims on the grounds
that there could be no negotiation with "the present rulers of
Germany." Requirements of coalition warfare dictated these positions: although Wilson himself did not object to the "no annexations, no indemnities" formula, he knew that his allies did.
Public discussion of war aims would only provoke disagreements, thereby weakening the war effort. "When the war is
over we can force them [Britain and France] to our way of thinking," Wilson wrote House, "because by that time they will,
among other things, be financially in our hands; but we cannot
force them now."[8] Maintenance of Allied unity took prece-

---

[7] Mayer, *Political Origins*, pp. 182–183.

[8] Wilson to House, July 21, 1917, quoted in Ray Stannard Baker, *Woodrow
Wilson: Life and Letters: War Leader* (New York: 1939), p. 180. See also Mayer,
*Political Origins*, pp. 225–229, 233–236; and David F. Trask, *The United States in
the Supreme War Council: American War Aims and Inter-Allied Strategy, 1917–1918*
(Middletown, Connecticut: 1961), pp. 6–8.

dence, in the White House view, over satisfying the demands of the Petrograd Soviet.

There would thus be no revision of war aims, but there were other means of trying to keep Russia in the war, and the Wilson administration was quick to use them. Official expressions of sympathy for the Revolution had been generous, and widely publicized, from the beginning; indeed, the United States had been the first nation to extend formal recognition to the Provisional Government, on March 22. Economic assistance would be more useful, though, and on this the Wilson administration held back until it had clear assurances from Petrograd that Russia would not quit the war. In the end some $450 million was set aside for Russia, but only $188 million had actually been used by the time the Provisional Government was overthrown in November.[9] The Wilson administration's chief initiative, however, involved the dispatch of a series of official "missions" to Russia, designed to welcome that country into the ranks of democratic states and to investigate ways in which the United States could aid the Russian war effort.

The most elaborate of these was the delegation headed by Elihu Root, staunch conservative Republican and former secretary of state, which arrived in Petrograd in June. The Root Mission had been selected in a leisurely manner, with more care being taken to choose members who would reflect the diversity of American life than to find experts on Russia capable of explaining developments there to Washington. To say that the delegation was ill-prepared for what it found would be a considerable understatement. The American warship on which it was traveling sailed into Vladivostok harbor unnoticed, an unusual occurrence, the members noted, in the middle of a war. During the long trip across Siberia the mission frequently encountered loaded troop trains headed away from the front. At Novo-Nikolaevsk, Cyrus McCormick, president of the International Harvester Company and a member of the delegation, was disconcerted to learn that despite a 45% wage increase, half his company's employees in the area had quit. One customer had written that since he "supposed all machines belonged to the government... that would release him from paying the note he

[9] Savage, "Official Policies," pp. 27, 336n.

owed." On arriving in Petrograd, the mission found that political power had shifted dramatically to the left, with the formation of a new coalition government including six members of the Soviet, so that the carefully balanced delegation put together in Washington now bore little relevance to the actual configuration of power in the Russian capital.[10]

Despite all of this, the delegation remained surprisingly optimistic. Root confined himself to contacts with business and government officials, in one case solemnly explaining the advantages of constitutional guarantees of private property to the members of the Moscow bourse. General Hugh L. Scott, chief of staff of the United States Army, managed to visit the front just as the ill-fated July offensive was getting underway. The sight of troops advancing convinced him that the Russian army would be able to hold its own; news of their disastrous reverses several days later did little to shake his optimism. Admiral James H. Glennon, the Navy's representative, twice encountered situations in which local Soviets had superseded the authority of Russian naval officers, but neglected to mention these in his report. Charles Edward Russell, the lone Socialist on the delegation, did address the All-Russian Congress of Soviets, but his efforts to achieve rapport by wearing a red tie and waving membership cards in the American Socialist Party and the International Typographical Union had little effect. Russell was one of the few members of the mission who perceived the power of the Soviets and the strength of antiwar sentiment in Russia, yet he too made no effort to evaluate these factors in his report to the State Department.[11]

The Root Mission concluded that its visit had materially strengthened the Provisional Government. While the Russians would need aid, particularly in the area of war supplies and transportation equipment, "we have little doubt that they will be able to establish and maintain successfully free self-government on a grand scale." Almost as an afterthought, the mission recommended that a propaganda agency be set up in Russia to "sell" the war, and that representatives of the Young Men's Christian Association be sent out to help improve morale

[10] Alton Earl Ingrams, "The Root Mission to Russia, 1917" (Ph.D. Dissertation, Louisiana State University, 1970), pp. 38–64.

[11] Ibid., pp. 157, 206, 214–216, 220–223, 225–227, 239–241, 251–252.

in the Russian Army. "I am astounded at their optimism," Secretary of State Robert Lansing wrote in his diary after reading the mission's report. "I cannot see upon what it is founded....I hope they are right and I presume they know more about it than I do, and yet in spite of what they say I am very skeptical."[12] Other "missions" soon followed. A group of railroad experts under John F. Stevens arrived in Russia at the same time as the Root Mission for the purpose of recommending improvements in the Russian transportation system, particularly the vital Trans-Siberian Railroad. A Red Cross commission, operating as a military unit but financed largely from private sources, arrived in August. Shortly thereafter the Committee on Public Information opened its propaganda office in Russia, and the YMCA's "morale boosters" arrived. These groups coexisted alongside the regular representatives of the State, War, Navy, and Treasury departments, as well as a considerable number of well-intentioned individuals who came to Russia on their own, often under the impression that they were to "report" their findings directly to the president.[13]

There is no evidence that any of these missions, official or unofficial, had any significant effect on the Russian war effort. Expressions of sympathy were of but limited utility, and the Provisional Government was overthrown before more tangible forms of assistance had begun to arrive. The missions could have been useful in gathering information on conditions in Russia, but their members were rarely selected for this purpose. Instead, the optimism they were supposed to impart to the Russians colored their own reporting, particularly on military affairs. Few of the Americans who went to Russia in 1917 understood the importance of the Soviets; confusing legitimacy with authority, they assumed that power resided in the Provisional Government, and, with rare exceptions, confined their attention to it.[14] And, because their activities were not coordinated, there was

---

[12] Ibid., pp. 288–300.

[13] George F. Kennan, *Russia Leaves the War* (Princeton: 1956), pp. 41–70, 78; Claude E. Fike, "The Influence of the Creel Committee and the American Red Cross on Russian-American Relations, 1917–1919," *Journal of Modern History*, XXXI(June, 1959), 93–109; W. B. Fowler, *British-American Relations, 1917–1918: The Role of Sir William Wiseman* (Princeton: 1969), pp. 108–118.

[14] Ganelin, *Rossiia i SShA*, pp. 177–178.

no mechanism by which the members of one mission could compare their findings with those of the others. The result, as can be imagined, was more confusion than enlightenment.

Meanwhile, the Provisional Government's authority was crumbling. The failure of the July offensive set off rioting in Petrograd which the government managed to suppress only by locking up prominent Bolsheviks and driving others into exile. But less than two months later, the government of Premier Alexander Kerensky had to seek help from the Bolsheviks in order to repel a right-wing coup led by General Lavr Kornilov. Kerensky was successful once more, but the price was a further erosion of his power. The Kornilov affair gave the Bolsheviks a majority in the Soviet, and from this point it was only a matter of time until the Provisional Government fell. The event occurred on the night of November 7, 1917; the next morning Vladimir Ilich Lenin mounted the rostrum of the Congress of Soviets to announce construction of the Socialist order.

There appears to be, in retrospect, painfully little that the Wilson administration, or any of the Allies, for that matter, could have done to alter this course of events. It may be, as a distinguished student of Russian affairs has argued, that the Bolshevik Revolution, and the consequent alienation of Russia from the West, was part of the price the Allies had to pay for insisting on military victory over Germany.[15] But there is little evidence that the German government was prepared to accept anything like reasonable terms in the summer of 1917.[16] Nor is it fair to blame the Provisional Government's suicidal July offensive on the Allies' "no fight, no credits" policy: that ill considered operation was at least as much the product of a strange belief on the part of Kerensky and his associates that the best way to restore army morale and increase Russian influence at the peace table was to launch an attack.[17] The revolution in Russia, like the one in China some thirty years later, grew largely out of internal conditions not susceptible to manipulation or modification from the outside.

---

[15] Kennan, *Russia and the West*, p. 32.

[16] On this point, see Gordon A. Craig, *The Politics of the Prussian Army, 1640–1945* (New York: 1956), pp. 326–337; and Fritz Fischer, *Germany's Aims in the First World War* (New York: 1967), pp. 327–443.

[17] Savage, "Official Policies," pp. 216–217.

What was inexcusable was not Wilson's policy of trying to keep Russia in the war, a matter in which, given the circumstances, he had little choice, but rather his failure to send experts to Russia capable of assessing realistically the prospects for continued belligerency. Nor did Wilson rely as much as he might have on the regular American diplomatic establishment in Russia: while Ambassador David R. Francis was ill-equipped to interpret events there (it was once said of him that he would not have known a Left Social Revolutionary from a potato[18]), subordinates such as Consuls North Winship in Petrograd and Maddin Summers in Moscow regularly forwarded to Washington detailed and, on the whole, perceptive accounts of what was going on. Unfortunately, these usually went by pouch instead of cable, and so arrived from four to six weeks after the events they described. It seems unlikely that Wilson ever saw them, or acted on the basis of the information they contained.[19] Instead, the president relied on the reports of the various "missions" he had dispatched to Russia; these left him with the comfortable but inaccurate impression that time still existed for the Provisional Government to pull itself together. In fact, the events of 1917 had produced an unprecedented acceleration in the process of political evolution.[20] Neither Wilson, nor his Allied counterparts, ever quite caught up.

## II

"Extreme socialist or anarchist named Lenin making violent speeches and thereby threatening Government; designedly giving him leeway and will deport opportunely."[21] This cryptic and misleading cable from Ambassador Francis gave the State Department the first news it had of the arrival in Russia, in April, 1917, of the man who would overthrow the Provisional Government and establish the first Socialist state in history. American observers badly underestimated Lenin and the Bolsheviks in the months that followed, but they were hardly

---

[18] R. H. Bruce Lockhart, *British Agent* (Garden City, New York: 1933), p. 279.
[19] These reports are printed in *FR: 1918: Russia*, I, 1–186. See also Ganelin, *Rossiia i SShA*, pp. 178–179.
[20] See, on this point, Mayer, *Political Origins*, pp. 8–9.
[21] Francis to Lansing, April 21, 1917, *FR: 1918: Russia*, I, 27.

alone in this. Few foreigners perceived the depth of antiwar sentiment in Russia; most assumed that, since Lenin had been forced to seek German help in returning, the Bolsheviks would be seen as agents of the Kaiser and would hence be incapable of winning popular support. But popular support was not the crucial determinant of events at this time. Organization and discipline were, and these the tightly controlled Bolsheviks, who were as far from being anarchists as it is possible to imagine, alone were able to provide.[22]

The sudden overthrow of the Provisional Government in November, 1917, thus came as a shock to the Americans and their allies; there was little in their own experience to guide them in dealing with the new regime, which immediately proclaimed its intention of withdrawing from the war and abolishing the private ownership of land. Nonetheless, first reactions in the West were to do nothing, partly because there was nothing that could be done immediately, partly because the Allies still clung to the belief that the Russian people supported the war and would soon rise up in wrath to expel the tiny band of outrageous revolutionaries who had seized power in Petrograd.[23] When this did not happen, when it became clear, as it did by December, that the Bolsheviks were in earnest about taking Russia out of the war, the Allies had to begin thinking seriously about what their response would be.

One thing was clear at the outset: the Allies would not join the Bolshevik government in negotiating a peace settlement with Germany. Lenin and Trotsky had never envisaged making a separate peace; with a degree of naivete wholly inconsistent with their usual realism, they had assumed that the simple proclamation of a proletarian government in Russia would spark revolutions elsewhere, forcing bourgeois governments on both sides of the conflict to seek an end to it on the basis of "no annexations, no indemnities." Much to their chagrin, Europe remained as calm as could be expected under the circumstances

---

[22] See Alexander Rabinowitch, *The Bolsheviks Come to Power: The Revolution of 1917 in Petrograd* (New York: 1978).

[23] Isaac Deutscher, *The Prophet Armed: Trotsky, 1879–1921* (New York: 1954), p. 347; Robert D. Warth, *The Allies and the Russian Revolution: From the Fall of the Monarchy to the Peace of Brest-Litovsk* (Durham: 1954), pp. 162–167.

of total war, and the Bolsheviks found themselves facing Germany alone at the peace table at Brest-Litovsk.[24]

Nor was diplomatic recognition seriously considered. The Bolsheviks, seeking legitimacy, encouraged contacts with foreign governments, but their position on the war inhibited official relations, as did their forcible dissolution of the freely elected Constituent Assembly in January 1918. Moreover, their ideological appeal was characterized, as Secretary of State Lansing noted, by a "determination, frankly avowed, to overthrow all existing governments and establish on the ruins a despotism of the proletariat in every country." The revolutionary proclamations to the masses, which Lenin and Trotsky had hoped would force bourgeois governments into official relations with the Bolsheviks, turned out to be one of the major impediments that prevented them.[25]

In the absence of formal recognition or participation in the peace talks at Brest-Litovsk, there remained three separate courses of action open to the Allies and their American associates in dealing with the Bolshevik Revolution. All were designed to keep Russia in the war, one way or another; all were pursued, at one time or another, during the winter of 1917–1918.

The first of these involved finding some way to aid anti-Bolshevik forces in Russia, in the hope that they would be able to overthrow the Bolsheviks and continue the war. Early in December, President Wilson approved clandestine financial aid through the British and French to General Kaledin in South Russia, but it quickly became apparent that Kaledin's Cossacks did not constitute an effective fighting force, and no aid was actually sent. Another possibility was direct military intervention in Siberia, a course of action strongly supported by the French and the Japanese, somewhat less so by the British. Wilson firmly rejected intervention, though, partly because he feared it would only win sympathy for the Bolsheviks, partly because he distrusted the motives of those proposing intervention, partic-

---

[24] Kennan, *Russia Leaves the War*, p. 194; Edward Hallett Carr, *The Bolshevik Revolution, 1917–1923* (New York: 1951–1953), III, 6–7.

[25] Lansing memorandum, early December, 1917, quoted in *The War Memoirs of Robert Lansing* (New York: 1935), p. 340. See also Deutscher, *The Prophet Armed*, pp. 348–352.

ularly the Japanese. As long as the negotiations at Brest-Litovsk continued, there remained the possibility, however faint, that the Bolsheviks might yet reject a separate peace and resume the struggle against Germany. Intervention, or even aid to opponents of Bolshevism in any quantity, risked foreclosing that possibility and hence was, for the moment, rejected.[26]

The second course of action open to the Americans and their allies involved informal diplomatic contacts with the Bolshevik authorities in the hope of influencing the peace negotiations. Allied diplomats had remained in Petrograd following the November revolution, but had refrained from official relations with the new Soviet government. On December 1, 1917, however, General William V. Judson, the American military attaché, saw Trotsky on his own initiative to urge that the Bolsheviks try to prevent the Germans from transferring troops to the western front. Somewhat surprisingly, Trotsky agreed, and the Bolsheviks did make energetic, if ultimately futile, efforts at Brest-Litovsk to prevent German redeployments. Judson was recalled for breaking the ban on contacts, but Washington officials soon came to see the advantages of informal relations as a means of monitoring and possibly influencing the peace negotiations, and tacitly allowed them to continue.[27]

But there were definite limitations on the effectiveness of this kind of diplomacy. Ambassador Francis proved wholly unable to coordinate the activities of his enthusiastic but mutually antagonistic subordinates, notably the dynamic head of the American Red Cross mission, Raymond Robins, who soon developed a remarkably cordial working relationship with Lenin and Trotsky. Communications with Washington were poor, leaving the Americans in Petrograd in the dark much of the time regarding the Wilson administration's intentions, and giving officials of that administration only the fuzziest impression of what was going on in the Russian capital. The American dip-

---

[26] Kennan, *Russia Leaves the War*, pp. 160–190, 291–330; Warth, *The Allies and the Russian Revolution*, pp. 189–195; Trask, *The United States and the Supreme War Council*, pp. 101–111; Betty Miller Unterberger, "President Wilson and the Decision to Send American Troops to Siberia," *Pacific Historical Review*, XXIV (February, 1955), 63–68; and "Woodrow Wilson and the Bolsheviks: The 'Acid Test' of Soviet-American Relations," *Diplomatic History*, XI (Spring, 1987), 72–78.

[27] Kennan, *Russia Leaves the War*, pp. 107–130, 230–233.

lomatic establishment simply was not equipped, at this relatively early stage in its development, to conduct diplomacy efficiently outside of official channels.[28] Yet the Bolsheviks, conspiracy theorists that they were, assumed a greater degree of coordination among the Americans than actually existed: Robins's sympathetic attitude may well have led them to expect some kind of aid from the United States and its allies in case their negotiations with the Germans at Brest-Litovsk broke down.[29]

Wilson did have aid of sorts in mind, but it was in the form, not of guns and ammunition, but of a belated public reformulation of war aims: this was the third early Allied approach to the Bolshevik Revolution. The events of November had caused Wilson to develop second thoughts about his policy of not discussing war aims while the fighting was going on. Had the Allies made their objectives clear from the outset, the president speculated in a message to Congress in December, then "the sympathy and enthusiasm of the Russian people might have been once for all enlisted on the side of the Allies, [and]...the sad reverses which have recently marked the progress of their affairs...might have been avoided."[30] Following the start of German-Russian negotiations at Brest-Litovsk, a reconsideration of this question got underway within the Allied camp. Efforts to agree on a joint redefinition of war aims failed, because of the reluctance of the French and Italians to repudiate annexations, but in January 1918, both Wilson and Lloyd George made important unilateral statements designed largely as a reply to the Bolsheviks.[31]

---

[28] Ibid., pp. 32–70, 99–100; Fike, "Influence of the Creel Committee," pp. 108–109. See also Linda Killen, *The Russian Bureau: A Case Study in Wilsonian Diplomacy* (Lexington: 1983), pp. 154–155.

[29] Soviet historiography still attaches considerable importance to these early informal contacts between Americans in Russia and the new Bolshevik government. See I. M. Krasnov, "Neizvestnye Leninskie dokumenty o Sovetsko-Amerikanskikh otnosheniiakh," *Voprosy istorii*, July, 1969, #7; Liudmila Gvishiani, *Sovetskaia Rossiia i SShA (1917–1920)* (Moscow: 1970), pp. 36–40, 62–71.

[30] Baker and Dodd, eds., *Wilson Public Papers: War and Peace*, I, 134.

[31] Kennan, *Russia Leaves the War*, pp. 131–140; Mayer, *Political Origins*, pp. 286–290; Lloyd C. Gardner, *Safe for Democracy: The Anglo-American Response to Revolution, 1913–1921* (New York: 1984), pp. 158–162.

Wilson's was his famous Fourteen Points address. In it he praised the Russian people, without referring directly to the Bolshevik government, for stating their war aims "with frankness, a largeness of view, a generosity of spirit, and a universal human sympathy which must challenge the admiration of every friend of mankind." Somewhat surprisingly, Wilson argued that the Russians had "refused to compound their ideals or desert others that they themselves would be safe":

They call to us to say what it is that we desire, in what, if anything, our purpose and our spirit differ from theirs; and I believe that the people of the United States would wish me to respond, with utter simplicity and frankness. Whether their present leaders believe it or not, it is our heartfelt desire and hope that some way may be opened whereby we may be privileged to assist the people of Russia to attain their utmost hope of liberty and ordered peace.

Within this context, Wilson went on to outline his fourteen points, the sixth of which called for the "evacuation of all Russian territory and such a settlement of all questions affecting Russia as will...[obtain] for her the independent determination of her own political development and national policy." The treatment accorded Russia by her sister nations, Wilson added, would be "the acid test of their goodwill, of their comprehension of her needs as distinguished from their own interest and of their intelligent and unselfish sympathy."[32]

There was much in the Fourteen Points that coincided with the public peace program of the Bolsheviks, notably the emphasis on self-determination, open diplomacy, and a nonpunitive war settlement. Lenin and Trotsky welcomed it with moderate enthusiasm and even facilitated efforts by American officials to have copies distributed widely in Russia and behind the lines in Germany.[33] Yet it seems clear that that the Bolsheviks' relatively friendly response reflected certain tactical advantages they saw deriving from the speech, not any fundamental agreement with Wilson on the shape of the postwar world. Wilson's open endorsement of what seemed to be important portions of the Bolshevik peace program could not help but strengthen the

---

[32] Baker and Dodd, eds., *Wilson Public Papers: War and Peace*, I, 157–160.

[33] Mayer, *Political Origins*, pp. 372–373; Kennan, *Russia Leaves the War*, pp. 260–264.

Soviet government's position in Russia, nor could Lenin and Trotsky object to Wilson's attempt to sow dissension behind German lines, since they had been trying to do the same thing themselves. The speech may have also further encouraged the Soviet leaders to believe that the United States might send aid should the Brest-Litovsk negotiations break down and Russia be forced to resume the war: indeed Lenin and Trotsky forwarded a written inquiry regarding this possibility through Robins on March 5. Through a bureaucratic mix-up, however, the message did not reach Washington until March 16, the very day the All-Russian Congress of Soviets ratified the peace.[34]

It probably did not make any difference. Lenin was not above giving the Allies the impression that their aid might have kept Russia in the war, but it seems unlikely that he ever counted on getting such assistance in any significant way. Only massive and immediate aid could have sustained the Bolsheviks against the German onslaught in March, 1918, and Lenin knew that there was no way to provide this, given transportation difficulties and the priorities of the western front. Moreover, the Bolshevik government depended for its survival on the support, or at least the toleration, of the peasantry: in securing it the promise of peace was at least as important as the promise of land. In the end, Lenin attached the highest importance to remaining in power, no matter how small his power base was.[35] The only way he could realistically expect to accomplish this was to make peace, even if it meant, as it did, the loss of one-third of Russia's population, one-third of its cultivable lands, including the rich Ukraine, and one-half of its heavy industry.[36]

But the Bolsheviks did receive help from the United States in another, less direct way. The conclusion of the Brest-Litovsk negotiations coincided with the launching of the German spring offensive in the west. An almost immediate effect was to weaken German pressure on Russia, a trend which grew far more pronounced in the summer when the Allies, bolstered by the arrival of fresh American troops, began their successful

---

[34] Ibid., pp. 497–498, 516.
[35] Carr, *The Bolshevik Revolution*, III, 33–35, 52.
[36] Warth, *The Allies and the Russian Revolution*, p. 233.

counteroffensive.[37] It is unclear to what extent Lenin had anticipated, in March, 1918, the quick impact American participation in the fighting would have in hastening Germany's defeat. Certainly he did not hesitate to take credit for such foresight at the time of the armistice, though characteristically he attributed the German surrender to revolutionary pressures, not battlefield reverses.[38] Yet it seems clear that at least "objectively," to use a term popular with Marxist historians, the United States played a major role in freeing Russia from the onerous terms imposed by the Germans at Brest-Litovsk.

## III

The Americans and their allies received no credit, however, because during the spring and summer of 1918 they had reversed their policy on intervention and dispatched troops to Russia. The reasons are both complex and simple: complex in that an involved set of circumstances related to pursuit of the war, compounded by confusion and preoccupation on the part of policymakers, provided the immediate occasion for intervention; simple because behind it all was a loathing for Bolshevism so strong that it could cause honest men to put forward and possibly even believe flimsy excuses for involving themselves in the internal affairs of another nation. At both levels, however, the means employed corrupted the end envisaged. The result was unnecessarily to poison relations between Russia and the West for years to come.

Conclusion of the Brest-Litovsk treaty created a kind of panic in Allied capitals, since it coincided almost exactly with the launching of the final German offensive in the west. Many observers now assumed that Russia had become, to all intents and purposes, a satellite of Germany. Not only would this mean that the Germans could now transfer troops to the western front, but they would also have access to the vast agricultural and industrial facilities of Russia and to the huge stockpiles of unused war supplies that had accumulated in and around the ports of Murmansk, Archangel, and Vladivostok. There were, to be sure, certain inconsistencies in this view. How Germany

---

[37] Carr, *The Bolshevik Revolution*, III, 79–80.
[38] Ibid., p. 54.

could occupy Russia and still spare troops for transfer to the west was not made clear. Nor was it apparent how the Germans would be able to utilize stockpiled war supplies any more effectively than the Russians had: the problem here was the inefficiency of Russian railroads, a situation that could not be changed overnight.[39] But these considerations were not thought of in the heat of the moment. The chief inhibition that had prevented intervention up to this point had been the fear of driving the Bolsheviks into the hands of the Germans. Now that that seemed to have happened, there appeared to be little reason to hold back.

But Wilson, doubtless recalling his unhappy experiences with Mexico several years earlier,[40] remained skeptical. He would consider intervention in Russia only if some way could be found to reconcile it with the principle of self-determination to which he had committed himself, and the nation, in the Fourteen Points speech several months earlier. As was usually the case in Wilsonian diplomacy, though, there proved to be a surprising number of ways in which this integration of power and ideals could be accomplished.[41]

One way would have been for the Bolsheviks themselves to invite the Allies in. In the spring of 1918, this possibility was not as farfetched as it might sound. The Soviet leaders made no secret of their contempt for the Brest-Litovsk treaty, and had no inhibitions about violating it when they could do so with impunity. Allied representatives in Moscow had been led to believe that the Bolsheviks might yet welcome help against the Germans, and, in a moment of panic during the Brest-Litovsk negotiations, Trotsky had actually authorized the Murmansk Soviet to accept "any and all assistance" from the Allies to forestall a possible German advance against the Murmansk railway. In fact, however, the prospects for intervention by invitation were never great. Lenin viewed the Allies and the Germans with equal suspicion, half expecting them at any moment to unite in a common crusade against Bolshevism. He was pre-

---

[39] George F. Kennan, *The Decision to Intervene* (Princeton: 1958), pp. 3–4, 97–98; Trask, *The United States in the Supreme War Council*, p. 111.

[40] Fowler, *British-American Relations*, pp. 185, 196.

[41] On this point, see N. Gordon Levin, *Woodrow Wilson and World Politics: America's Response to War and Revolution* (New York: 1968), pp. 43–45, 52; also Frederick S. Calhoun, *Power and Principle: Armed Intervention in Wilsonian Foreign Policy* (Kent, Ohio: 1986), pp. 220–224.

*Intervention in Russia, 1918.*

pared to accept food and military supplies from the Allies in order to play them off against the Germans, but not armed intervention, a move which would only encourage German
countermeasures at the expense of the still-vulnerable Soviet
state. As it became clear in the months following Brest-Litovsk
that the Germans had no intention of occupying Russia or of
challenging the existence of the Soviet government, opportunities for Allied intervention by invitation quickly faded.[42]

There remained the possibility of intervention without invitation. This too could be reconciled with the principle of self-
determination if it could be shown to be vital for victory over
Germany, for without victory, it could be argued, there would
be little chance for self-determination anywhere. Wilson was
not so naive as to believe that the presence of a few thousand
American troops in Siberia or North Russia would make any
great difference in the outcome of the war. But any weakening
of Allied unity could, and Wilson proved to be very sensitive to
this possibility. In March 1918, he almost approved a British-
French request for Japanese intervention in Siberia, not from
any military advantage he saw deriving from it, but from a reluctance to go against the wishes of the Allies. Several months
later, in July, he did in fact authorize the dispatch of a small
contingent of American troops to North Russia. The possibility of
Germany's seizing the military supplies stockpiled at Murmansk
and Archangel was at least credible; moreover, as Secretary of War
Newton Baker later recalled, "the British and French were pressing it upon his [Wilson's] attention so hard and he had refused so
many of their requests that they were beginning to feel that he
was not a good associate, much less a good ally."[43]

Somewhat different considerations caused Wilson, that same

[42] Ibid., pp. 97–98; Carr, *The Bolshevik Revolution*, III, 72, 79–80; Kennan, *The Decision to Intervene*, pp. 46–48, 123–135.

[43] Baker to Ralph Hayes, December 24, 1929, quoted in R. S. Baker, *Woodrow Wilson: Life and Letters: Armistice* (New York: 1939), p. 284n. See also Kennan, *Russia Leaves the War* pp. 471–483; Kennan, *The Decision to Intervene*, pp. 376–379; Trask, *The United States in the Supreme War Council*, pp. 118–119; Betty Miller Unterberger, *America's Siberian Expedition, 1918–1920* (Durham: 1956), pp. 30, 64; John W. Long, "American Intervention in Russia: The North Russian Expedition, 1918–19," *Diplomatic History*, VI(Winter, 1982), 45–68; Benjamin D. Rhodes, *The Anglo-American Winter War with Russia, 1918–1919: A Diplomatic and Military Tragicomedy* (Westport, Connecticut: 1988).

month, to reverse his previous policy and sanction limited Japanese-American intervention in Siberia. Here, intervention could in no way credibly affect the course of the war, which was being fought some 5000 miles away. Nor was Allied unity a motive: Wilson decided on intervention in Siberia without telling the British and the French, and had not intended that they participate. The president was concerned about the ambitions of the Japanese in Manchuria and the Russian Far East, though: convinced that eventual Japanese intervention there was inevitable, he resolved to try to control it by turning it into a joint enterprise. Then, too, there had suddenly arisen the problem of the Czech Legion, a force of some 70,000 Czechoslovak exiles and prisoners-of-war who had been fighting on the side of the Russians. The Czechs had chosen to leave Russia by way of the Trans-Siberian Railroad following signing of the Brest-Litovsk treaty. Fighting with the Bolsheviks broke out along the way, however, and Wilson had come to believe by July that only by sending American troops to Siberia could the way be cleared for the Czechs to get out. This proved to be the decisive justification, in the president's mind, for intervention in Siberia.[44]

The decision to send troops to North Russia and Siberia reflects, as well as any decision in modern history, the imperfect control government leaders sometimes have over events which they themselves set in motion. The forces sent to North Russia had strict orders not to fight the Bolsheviks, but they were placed under British command and were in fact ordered to fight. The Siberian intervention, which Wilson justified mainly as an effort to remove the Czechs, turned into something more when the British, Canadians, French, Italians, and Chinese insisted on joining the operation, and when the Japanese sent 70,000 troops instead of the 7000 Wilson had expected. "The other governments are...acting upon a plan which is altogether foreign from ours and inconsistent with it," Wilson admitted in August. Nor were the Czechs themselves in any hurry to get out. They had begun fighting the Bolsheviks at the instigation

---

[44] Kennan, *The Decision to Intervene*, pp. 381–404; Unterberger, *America's Siberian Expedition*, pp. 67–88, and "Woodrow Wilson and the Bolsheviks," pp. 80–84; Levin, *Wilson and World Politics*, pp. 112–119; John Albert White, *The Siberian Intervention* (Princeton: 1950), pp. 227–255; Robert J. Maddox, *The Unknown War with Russia: Wilson's Siberian Intervention* (San Rafael, California: 1977), pp. 45–60.

of their French advisers; moreover, no one had thought to bring ships to Vladivostok with which to evacuate them should they in fact choose to leave. On top of all of this, these events coincided with the final life and death struggle on the western front, so that American and Allied officials were able to give them only fragmentary attention.[45]

It would be a mistake, though, to see Allied intervention in Russia solely as a result of bureaucratic bungling. The fact is that a fundamental loathing for Bolshevism influenced all of Wilson's actions with regard to Russia and the actions of his Allied counterparts as well. This should hardly be surprising, since the Bolsheviks made no secret of their fundamental loathing for the West. Nor did Wilson see his antipathy for Bolshevism as in any way inconsistent with his belief in self-determination: in his view, as in the view of other Allied leaders, the Bolsheviks were not representative of the Russian people. They had come to power by force, they had dissolved the Constituent Assembly, they had made a separate peace with Germany, and there were even indications, according to documents circulating in the West in the summer of 1918, that they were German agents. Hence the overthrow of Bolshevism could be seen, in Wilson's view, not as a violation of self-determination, but as an action necessary to its attainment.[46]

Wilson was, however, far more sensitive than the other Allied leaders to the counterproductive effects of a direct onslaught against Bolshevism—something which could not be un-

---

[45] Wilson to Lansing, August 23, 1918, *Foreign Relations: The Lansing Papers, 1914–1920* (Washington: 1940), II, 378–379. See also Kennan, *The Decision to Intervene*, pp. 376–380, 399–429; and Unterberger *America's Siberian Expedition*, pp. 55–59, 72–79.

[46] Levin, *Wilson and World Politics*, p. 109; Gardner, *Safe for Democracy*, pp. 180–181; Christopher Lasch, "American Intervention in Russia: A Reinterpretation," *Political Science Quarterly*, LXVII(June, 1962), 217–223; George F. Kennan, "The Sisson Documents," *Journal of Modern History*, XXVIII(June, 1956), 130–154; Robert James Maddox, "Woodrow Wilson, the Russian Embassy and Siberian Intervention," *Pacific Historical Review*, XXXVI(November, 1967), 435–448; Eugene P. Trani, "Woodrow Wilson and the Decision to Intervene in Russia: A Reconsideration," *Journal of Modern History*, XLVIII(September, 1976), 440–461; Carl J. Richard, "'The Shadow of a Plan': The Rationale behind Wilson's 1918 Siberian Intervention," *Historian*, XLIX(November, 1986), 64–84. For a Soviet assessment of the motives for intervention, see Nikolai V. Sivachev and Nikolai N. Yakovlev, *Russia and the United States*, translated by Olga Adler Titelbaum (Chicago: 1979), pp. 42–48.

dertaken in any case as long as the war was on.[47] Accordingly, he portrayed intervention variously as designed to bolster the war effort, promote Allied unity, monitor the Japanese, help the Czechs—anything, it would seem, but an openly avowed attempt to overthrow Bolshevism. Wilson hoped that the half-measures he had approved, and had sought to justify in such a nonexceptionable manner, would weaken Bolshevism without attracting sympathy for it, whether in Russia itself or among liberals and socialists in the West. It was a subtle strategy, but one dependent on keeping American motives insulated from the franker and less innocent objectives of the Allies. Given the need to cooperate with the Allies in securing sufficient manpower to make intervention effective, such insulation proved difficult to achieve. In the end, Wilson's attempt to "purify" intervention by contributing United States troops had the perverse effect of rendering unconvincing the aura of disinterestedness he considered vital to the success of his Russian policy.

## IV

The Paris Peace Conference was held, of course, chiefly for the purpose of agreeing upon and imposing a peace settlement on Germany. But during the six months it took to do this, and for a long time thereafter, the problem of what to do about Russia remained much in the minds of Western leaders. It was, Herbert Hoover later wrote, "the Banquo's ghost sitting at every Council table."[48] In the end, the Allies had no choice but to learn to live with the Bolshevik regime. They did not come to this position gracefully, however; their failure to do so would further intensify the already considerable hostility that existed between Russia and the West.

The United States had sent troops into Russia ostensibly as part of the war effort against Germany, yet those forces remained in place long after the fighting had ended. American troops did not leave North Russia until June 1919; they remained in Siberia until April 1920. Such had not been Woodrow

---

[47] Maddox, "Wilson, the Russian Embassy, and Siberian Intervention," pp. 436–437.

[48] Quoted in John M. Thompson, *Russia, Bolshevism, and the Versailles Peace* (Princeton: 1966), p. 2.

Wilson's wish: still sensitive to the counterproductive effects of intervention, he had wanted to withdraw United States forces from Russia as soon as possible after the armistice.[49] But, as in the case of the original decision to intervene, Wilson's long-range objectives fell victim to short-range preoccupations.

At no time during the Paris Peace Conference was Wilson able to give careful and sustained thought to the Russian question. It is true that the prospect of Bolshevism spreading into Europe was a major concern of the Big Four, but they sought to deal with it not so much by confronting the Russian problem directly as by attempting to construct a postwar European order capable of resisting the contagion from the East.[50] Discussions of what to do about Russia therefore had to be fitted in around the larger and more time-consuming questions of making peace with Germany and drafting the League of Nations covenant. When the Russian question did come up, it often did so at bad moments: just as Wilson was leaving for a short visit to the United States in mid-February, for example, or at the time of Clemenceau's attempted assassination a few days later, or of Wilson's sudden illness in early April. Moreover, inadequate information, always a problem in dealing with Russian affairs, was now even more of a difficulty since the Allies no longer had representatives on the Bolshevik side; virtually all of their information came from the White Russians. As a result, distraction, misinformation, and ineptitude marked deliberations at Paris on the Russian question; despite its importance at no point did it receive, either from Wilson or his colleagues, the attention it deserved.[51]

But, distracted as he was, Wilson could not simply "forget" the presence of some 14,000 American troops in Russia. There were other reasons why they remained where they did. One important one involved coalition diplomacy. Intervention had been a joint project from the beginning: Wilson had sent troops to Russia in part to promote Allied unity and in

---

[49] Ibid., pp. 49–50.

[50] Ibid., pp. 240–241; Levin, *Wilson and World Politics*, pp. 168–169, 174–182; Arno J. Mayer, *Politics and Diplomacy of Peacemaking: Containment and Counterrevolution at Versailles, 1918–1919* (New York: 1967), pp. 9–10.

[51] Kennan, *Russia and the West*, pp. 129, 147–148; Thompson, *Russia, Bolshevism, and the Versailles Peace*, pp. 381–382.

part to control Allied actions there. Both goals precluded independent initiatives. As the American ambassador to Japan noted, in a concise summary of Wilson's policy, "unity of action in Siberia is more important than the character of the action." Allied coordination remained no less vital at the peace table than it had been in war, and Wilson was loath to imperil it by a unilateral decision to withdraw American troops. He was determined to work for withdrawal but only as part of a general settlement between the Allies and the Russians.[52]

But Wilson's attitude made his Russian policy a prisoner of the mixed motives with which the Allies had embarked upon intervention. Neither the French nor the Japanese had any intention of withdrawing their troops from Russia merely because the Germans had surrendered. British policy was more ambivalent, with Lloyd George sharing Wilson's skepticism about intervention but doing little to restrain more activist members of his government like Winston Churchill, secretary of state for war, who pressed for an even more energetic use of force against the Bolsheviks.[53] This lack of agreement among the Allies frustrated two important initiatives Wilson and Lloyd George took to try to arrange a settlement of the Russian question.

The first, proposed in January, 1919, involved a conference of all contending elements in Russia, to be held on the Prinkipo Islands in the Sea of Marmara under supervision of the Allies, for the purpose of trying to resolve outstanding differences. The Bolsheviks, anxious for recognition and legitimacy, accepted the invitation, but the Whites, now under at least the nominal authority of Admiral A. V. Kolchak's government at Omsk, refused to go along. Later it became known that the French, who had agreed to the Prinkipo proposal only with the greatest reluctance, had secretly encouraged the Whites to reject participation in the conference. The conversations, had they been held, would likely have accomplished little; differ-

---

[52] Roland S. Morris to the State Department, May 3, 1919, *FR: 1919: Russia*, p. 339. See also Levin, *Wilson and World Politics*, pp. 163, 171; and Betty Miller Unterberger, "The Russian Revolution and Wilson's Far Eastern Policy," *Russian Review*, XVI(April, 1957), 45.

[53] Thompson, *Russia, Bolshevism, and the Versailles Peace*, pp. 50–60; Unterberger, *America's Siberian Expedition*, p. 231.

ences among Russians by this time were probably too great to be resolved through negotiations. Still, not much would have been lost by trying; the inability of the Allies to agree on Russia was the main reason why the effort was not made.[54]

A second major initiative occurred in March, 1919, with the dispatch of a young American diplomat, William C. Bullitt, to Moscow for the purpose of sounding out the Bolsheviks on possible bases for a cease-fire. Bullitt was not empowered to negotiate with the Bolsheviks, but he did receive from Lenin a promising offer to accept greatly constricted boundaries, pay off Russian debts, and declare a general amnesty in return for a cease-fire and the withdrawal of foreign troops. Bullitt returned to Paris eager to implement this arrangement but was astonished to find himself repudiated by Wilson and Lloyd George upon his arrival. The reasons for Bullitt's repudiation are still not wholly clear, but among the probable explanations are concern over offending the French, who had not been consulted; fear of an unfavorable public response, certainly on Lloyd George's part but possibly also on Wilson's; preoccupation with negotiations on the German question; and the distraction of Wilson's brief but sudden physical incapacity during the first week in April. Whatever the cause, an opportunity to end the Russian civil war on terms far more favorable to the Whites than would later be available was thereby lost.[55]

But perhaps the main reason for the conspicuous halfheartedness with which Wilson pursued both the Prinkipo and the Bullitt proposals is that both would have implied at least partial recognition of the Bolshevik government. Wilson had never been prepared to go that far. Although he was more sympathetic than his Allied counterparts to the goals of the Russian Revolution, the revolution he had in mind was that of March, 1917, not November. He never viewed Bolshevism as any less dangerous than did his colleagues, and at no point was he pre-

---

[54] Thompson, *Russia, Bolshevism, and the Versailles Peace,* pp. 82–130; Kennan, *Russia and the West,* pp. 126–130; Mayer, *Politics and Diplomacy of Peacemaking,* pp. 427–449.

[55] Thompson, *Russia, Bolshevism, and the Versailles Peace,* pp. 149–177, 233–247; Mayer, *Politics and Diplomacy of Peacemaking,* pp. 450–487; Beatrice Farnsworth, *William C. Bullitt and the Soviet Union* (Bloomington: 1967), pp. 32–54.

pared to acknowledge the legitimacy of the Moscow government.[56] What he sought was a way to undermine Bolshevism peacefully, without damaging the interests of the Russian people, yet without in any way recognizing the Bolshevik regime. Herbert Hoover came up with a similar policy in late March, when he proposed to the president an ambitious scheme for establishing a relief commission in Russia which would provide food impartially to Russians on both sides. The plan's aura of impartiality was deceptive, though: Hoover made it clear privately that its intent was to erode Bolshevik authority. The plan would have required a cease-fire and transfer of the entire Russian transportation network to Allied control, yet it made no provision for the evacuation of foreign troops. Not surprisingly, the Bolsheviks rejected it.[57]

Few options now remained open other than the direct use of force against Bolshevism. At several points during the Paris Peace Conference, Marshall Foch tried to win Anglo-American support for a quick peace with Germany and a subsequent attack on Bolshevik Russia, using Poland and Rumania as staging areas. Both Wilson and Lloyd George rejected this idea, partly because they thought public opinion in their respective countries would not stand for it, partly because of the astronomical expenditures which would have been involved, partly because they feared that an overt attack would only strengthen Bolshevism. But the Allies did, in June, 1919, announce partial recognition of the Kolchak government at Omsk and the dispatch of aid to it. In view of the Kolchak regime's authoritarian nature, Wilson had some difficulty squaring this decision with his commitment to self-determination, but when Kolchak promised to move toward a more democratic orientation, the president reluctantly agreed to go along. Once again, though, the Allies' timing was wrong. No sooner had they announced partial recognition than the Bolsheviks began to drive Kolchak back. Within a year, he would be captured and executed, the Bolsheviks would control most of central Russia and Siberia,

---

[56] Levin, *Wilson and World Politics*, pp. 204, 210, 212.
[57] Thompson, *Russian, Bolshevism, and the Versailles Peace*, pp. 247–267; Mayer, *Politics and Diplomacy of Peacemaking*, pp. 474–487; Killen, *The Russian Bureau*, pp. 83–85.

and the civil war would, to all intents and purposes, be over.[58]

What Wilson had hoped to do, both in the decision to intervene and in the various initiatives he took at Paris, had been to reconstitute a political arena in Russia in which anti-Bolshevik elements could compete, with some chance of success, for the allegiance of the Russian people. This was, in itself, an ambitious undertaking, since such an arena had never existed in Russia in the first place. Its success was rendered even less likely by the severe limitations which distance and cost imposed upon the Allies' ability to influence events inside that country. Nor were the Allies in agreement among themselves: Wilson and Lloyd George found their policies constantly undercut by the hard-line approach of their French and Japanese associates and sometimes by their own subordinates. Nor was Wilson himself ever completely clear on how best to achieve his objective: as was the case with his German policy, there was in his approach to the Russian question a curious tension between the tactics of repression and reintegration that made him susceptible to appeals from both points of view, but prevented the emergence of any clear and consistent policy of his own.[59]

As a consequence, the Allies fell between stools. They sent enough force to Russia to allow the Bolsheviks credibly to portray themselves as defenders of the besieged Russian fatherland, but nothing near the number of troops that would have been required actually to overthrow that regime. In the end, they were reduced to letting events in Russia take their own course. Commitments had been projected beyond capabilities; as is usually the case in such situations, the only results were bitterness, frustration, and recrimination.

## V

It is curious that in both the United States and Russia there should have been in power, in 1917–1919, leaders capable of

---

[58] Thompson, *Russia, Bolshevism, and the Versailles Peace*, pp. 178–192, 268–308; John Silverlight, *The Victors' Dilemma: Allied Intervention in the Russian Civil War* (New York: 1970), pp. 340–352.

[59] Levin, *Wilson and World Politics*, pp. 5–6; Calhoun, *Power and Principle*, pp. 232–233; Gardner, *Safe for Democracy*, p. 188.

promulgating ideologies to which much of the world would look, in the decades to come, as guides to action. There were even certain similarities in their respective points of view: both Wilson and Lenin believed in the universal applicability of their philosophies of government and in the inevitability of their eventual triumph; both sought to alter the traditional structure of international relations in such a way as to end imperialism and war; both, in their own way, looked to democracy as the ultimate objective. But here the similarities end. Where Lenin conceived of democracy only in economic terms, Wilson tended to think of it primarily in political terms; where Lenin endorsed violent social revolution as the only means of attaining this goal, Wilson favored evolution, or, at most, controlled revolution within a liberal-capitalist framework; where Lenin sought to overthrow the existing international order, Wilson sought to alter it from within—to be in it but not of it.[60]

It would appear, at first glance, that the differences between these competing ideologies would have been sufficiently great as to preclude any kind of normal diplomatic relations between the nations that espoused them. But this was not necessarily the case. Ideologies reflect aspirations more often than they shape policies; before ideas can be put into action, practical concessions to reality usually have to be made. The ease with which this can be done in turn determines the possibilities for conventional relations between ideologically disparate states.

There was nothing in Lenin's approach to government that forbade making such concessions; indeed when choices had to be made between the competing claims of ideology and national interest, the latter almost always won out. Brest-Litovsk was the first and in many ways the most striking example, but others would follow, among them acceptance of the Prinkipo summons, the proposals made through Bullitt, and, as will be seen, Lenin's persistent offers of economic cooperation with the capitalist world. None of these initiatives indicated any weakening in the ultimate aims of Leninist ideology, but they did suggest a flexibility in tactics that could tolerate, and even encourage, normal diplomatic contacts with the West.

---

[60] Levin, *Wilson and World Politics*, p. 8; Thompson, *Russia, Bolshevism, and the Versailles Peace*, p. 43.

With Wilson the situation was more complex. He too, was capable of retreating from ideological positions where necessary, as he demonstrated more than once on non-Russian issues at the Paris Peace Conference. But Wilson was also inclined toward extreme inflexibility in particular situations, especially where high hopes had, in his view, been betrayed.[61] The Russian Revolution was one such situation: although the president had difficulty in deciding whether force or cooperation would best destroy Bolshevism, he was firm in his belief that, one way or another, it would have to be destroyed. At no point was he prepared, even for tactical purposes, to acknowledge the legitimacy of the Bolshevik regime. In this respect, he showed considerably less flexibility than did Lenin, who at least was willing to deal with capitalist governments while simultaneously plotting their destruction.

But in fairness it should be recognized that Wilson had to contend, to a greater extent than did Lenin, with the problem of placating constituencies, both at home and overseas. While Lenin's government was never a monolith, and while sharp opposition to some of his ideological compromises did at times surface, the Russian leader never had to contend with an aroused public opinion or with the problem of maintaining unity among allies. These factors limited the extent to which Wilson could depart from his public ideological stance in order to arrange accommodations with his ideological rival. Moreover, the problem of Russia could never be wholly separated from the problem of Europe as a whole: Wilson, like most Allied leaders, feared that the contagion of Bolshevism would spread into a Europe that had been left extremely vulnerable to such appeals by the social and physical destruction of war.[62] Recognizing the Bolsheviks, or dealing with them in any way

---

[61] See, on this point, John Morton Blum, *Woodrow Wilson and the Politics of Morality* (Boston: 1956), pp. 23–37, 186; Patrick Devlin, *Too Proud to Fight: Woodrow Wilson's Neutrality* (New York: 1975), pp. 36–41, 50–60; and Alexander L. George, "Some Uses of Dynamic Psychology in Political Biography: Case Materials on Woodrow Wilson," in Geoffrey Cocks and Travis L. Crosby, eds., *Psycho/History: Readings in the Method of Psychology, Psychoanalysis, and History* (New Haven: 1987), pp. 145–148.

[62] Mayer, *Politics and Diplomacy of Peacemaking*, pp. 3–30.

that would acknowledge their legitimacy, might, it was felt, facilitate this process.

For the moment, therefore, the national interest, as Wilson perceived it, coincided with Wilsonian ideology. This would not always be the case in years to come. Such coincidence was even less frequent in the case of the Soviet Union: from the time of Brest-Litovsk on, there would exist in Soviet diplomacy a persistent tension between the competing requirements of ideology and national interest.[63] The future of Russian-American relations would thus be determined, in large measure, by the ease with which each nation could transcend the fundamental ideological polarities that now set them apart, and find, on the firm ground of national self-interest, some mutually acceptable basis for peacefully tolerating each other's existence.

---

[63] Carr, *The Bolshevik Revolution*, III, 57–58; Adam B. Ulam, *Expansion and Co-existence : Soviet Foreign Policy, 1917–73* (New York: 1974), p. 75.

CHAPTER IV

# Nonrecognition: 1920–1933

By 1920, THE GOVERNMENT OF BOTH SOVIET RUSSIA AND THE UNITED STATES had begun to grapple with the problem of establishing a permanent relationship toward one another. It had become clear to the Wilson administration that neither intervention nor integration had succeeded in undermining Bolshevism; the Leninist regime seemed, for the moment, defiantly entrenched. Simultaneously, Lenin and his colleagues had come to the realistic conclusion that world revolution, upon which rested their hopes for ultimate survival, was not on the immediate horizon. Normalization of relations would depend upon the ability of each side to move beyond the deep ideological antagonisms that separated them. Somewhat surprisingly, the highly ideological Soviet state showed more flexibility in this area than did the more pluralistic, and presumably nonideological, United States.

I

There was a significant ambiguity in early Bolshevik thought about relations with the capitalist world. On the one hand, it stressed the monolithic nature of capitalism and the implacable hostility states of that persuasion could be expected to direct toward the young Soviet republic. But, on the other hand, Lenin attached great importance to playing off the capitalists against one another—to encouraging "contradictions" within the capitalist camp that would prevent concerted action against the revolution and gain time for consolidation and reorganization.[1] Brest-Litovsk had been an important part of this strategy; so too

---

[1] Ulam, *Expansion and Coexistence*, p. 78.

was the promotion of a "special relationship" with the United States.

The Bolsheviks had, from the earliest days of the revolution, differentiated between the United States and other capitalist countries. Wilson's public sympathy for the revolution's ideals, together with informal contacts with Americans in Petrograd, had led Lenin and Trotsky to believe that they might get help from the United States if they resumed the struggle against Germany. Even after Brest-Litovsk, the Soviet leaders had not been able to bring themselves to believe that the United States would actually intervene against the Bolsheviks, partly for reasons of economic self-interest, partly because of the antagonism Lenin saw developing between Japan and the United States.

These considerations led to a remarkable proposal which Lenin made to Raymond Robins on the eve of the latter's departure from Russia in May, 1918. The Soviet leader handed Robins an unsigned paper, with a note that its contents had been approved in the highest councils of the Russian government. The paper called attention to the disastrous condition of the Russian economy and noted the extent to which, in the years preceding the revolution, Russia had been dependent on imports from the West, especially the United States. It then observed that although, under the Brest-Litovsk treaty, Germany would be entitled to most-favored nation treatment in Russia after the war, she would be too exhausted to take advantage of it. The real opportunities would lie with the United States, which could take over a large share of the Russian market if it were willing to advance credits. As security, Lenin proposed granting American businessmen extensive coal, lumber, and railway concessions in eastern Siberia, as well as the opportunity to participate in the construction of power stations and the development of water routes in central Russia.[2]

Lenin made no secret of his motives in making this unusual offer. In a speech to the All-Russian Central Executive Committee and the Moscow Soviet on May 14, the same day the note to Robins was delivered, he pointed out that the fledgling Soviet state was "a lone island in the stormy seas of imperialist

---

[2] Ministerstvo inostrannykh del SSSR, *Dokumenty vneshnei politiki*, SSSR (Moscow: 1967–), I, 286–294. For the circumstances surrounding delivery of this note, see Kennan, *The Decision to Intervene*, pp. 217–220.

robbery," and that its future security would depend on encouraging the "contradictions that have arisen out of the frenzied struggle between the imperialist powers." The two most important contradictions, Lenin argued, were those between Britain and Germany on the one hand and Japan and America on the other. Just as the Brest-Litovsk treaty had prevented the German conquest of Russia, so exacerbation of Japanese-American conflict would preserve Siberia from Japanese rapaciousness. "We must not forget," he concluded, "that however solid the imperialist groupings may appear to be, they can be broken up in a few days if the interests of sacred private property, the sacred right of concessions, etc., demand it."[3]

Much to Lenin's surprise, the United States made no response to this offer. Robins' close ties with the Bolsheviks had undermined his credibility, and he was ignored upon his return to Washington. Nor did Japanese-American rivalry, which was real enough, forestall intervention. But even after American troops landed in Russia, the Bolsheviks continued to make distinctions between the United States and its allies. Foreign Minister Georgii Chicherin commented in September, 1918, that although the Bolshevik government had been forced to intern British and French citizens inside Russia, "our attitude is entirely different towards American citizens, to whom these measures were not extended, because, although the United States Government also was compelled by its Allies to agree to participate in intervention,... its decision is not regarded by us as irrevocable."[4] And as it became clear that the war was ending in an Allied victory, the Russians looked to Washington as the chief agent through whom an end to intervention could be arranged.

Again, the Soviet government held out the lure of trade and concessions as an incentive. "Do the capitalists want some of the timber in the North, part of Siberia?" Lenin asked, in his instructions to Chicherin. "If so, they won't disguise it anyway. We suggest you say straight out, how much?" Chicherin did indeed make such an appeal in a note to Wilson in October, 1918, demanding "precise and businesslike replies" to the following questions:

---

[3] V.I. Lenin, *Collected Works*, (Moscow: 1960–), XXVII, 366–368.
[4] Chicherin speech of September 2, 1918, in Jane Degras, ed., *Soviet Documents on Foreign Policy* (London: 1951–1953), I, 104. For Robins' reception in the United States, see Kennan, *The Decision to Intervene*, pp. 229–232.

Will the Governments of the United States, England, and France cease demanding the blood of the Russian people and the lives of Russian citizens, if the Russian people agree to pay a ransom, such as a man who has been suddenly set upon pays to one who attacked him? If so, precisely what tribute do the Governments of the United States, England, and France demand of the Russian people? Do they demand concessions, do they want the railways, mines, gold deposits, etc., to be handed over to them on certain conditions, or do they demand territorial concessions, some part of Siberia, or the Caucasus, or perhaps the Murmansk coast?

The note could not have been better calculated to ensure that it would not be answered, and Maxim Litvinov, the Soviet assistant commissar for foreign affairs, later admitted that its sardonic tone had been a mistake. The strategy it so blatantly expressed, however, remained the basis of early Bolshevik policy toward the United States.[5]

During the Paris Peace Conference the Soviet government continued its policy of holding out promises of economic gain in return for an end to intervention. In an unofficial conversation with an American emissary in Stockholm in January, 1919, Litvinov observed that the Bolshevik regime could not survive without foreign technical and financial assistance; he promised protection of foreign enterprises and valuable concessions if intervention ceased. The following month, Foreign Minister Chicherin, in accepting the Prinkipo invitation, announced that "in view of the great inclination which foreign capital has always displayed to exploit Russia's natural resources for its own advantage, the Russian Soviet Government is disposed to grant mining, timber, and other concessions to nationals of the Entente Powers." Wilson considered these offers insulting, and did not respond to them. "I suppose because they know they have no high motives themselves," he complained, "they do not believe that anybody else has."[6]

Undeterred, Lenin continued to push for economic ties with the United States. "We are emphatically in favor of economic

---

[5] Lenin to Chicherin, October, 1918, quoted in A. Leonidov, "Lenin and the United States: Kremlin Documents," *New Times,* January 22, 1969, pp. 4–5; Chicherin to Wilson, October 24, 1918, Degras., ed., *Soviet Documents,* I, 118–119. See also Thompson, *Russia, Bolshevism, and the Versailles Peace,* p. 88n.

[6] Buckler to Lansing, January 18, 1919, *FR: 1919: Russia,* pp. 15–16; Chicherin to Entente Governments, February 4, 1919, ibid., p. 40; Joseph P. Tumulty, *Woodrow Wilson as I Know Him* (Garden City, New York: 1921), p. 374.

arrangements with America, with all countries, but *particularly* with America," he commented, in October, 1919. And, in February, 1920: "We will need American industrial goods—locomotives, automobiles, etc.—more than those of any other country." Several months later, Lenin gave what must stand as his most comprehensive statement on relations with the United States:

So long as we have not won the entire world, so long as, from the economic and military point of view, we remain weaker than the rest of the capitalist world, we must know how to exploit the contradictions and antagonisms among the imperialists. If we had not kept to that rule, we should long ago have all been hanging from the lampposts.

In Lenin's view, one of the most important of these "contradictions" was that between the United States and the remainder of world capitalism:

America is strong, everybody is now in its debt, everything depends on it, everybody hates America more and more... everything indicates that America cannot come to terms with other countries, because the most profound economic differences divide them, because America is richer than the others. Therefore we shall consider all questions about concessions from this angle.

The United States, Lenin argued, could furnish the Soviet Union with the means of production necessary to make possible the transition to socialism. But it would not do this for nothing: "To attract the Americans, we must pay them. They are business people. What shall we pay with?... We shall answer this question with the help of concessions."[7]

In October, 1920, the Soviet government announced that it had granted an American syndicate headed by Los Angeles engineer Washington B. Vanderlip exclusive coal, oil, and fisheries rights for 60 years in some 400,000 square miles of northeastern Siberia, including the entire Kamchatka peninsula. Lenin made no secret of his motives in granting this concession. Kamchatka and much of the Russian Far East were under Japanese control at this time, and Lenin hoped to involve the United States, through the lure of economic advantages, in conflict with Tokyo. "When capitalistic thieves sharpen their

---

[7] V.I. Lenin, *Polnoe sobranie sochinenii* (Moscow: 1958–1965), XXXIX, 209, XL, 152; Degras, ed., *Soviet Documents*, I, 221–224.

knives against us," he noted, "our immediate duty is to direct such knives against one another." Lenin's scheme failed to materialize, however, because of a comic-opera series of misapprehensions. First, the Russians had confused Washington Vanderlip with a distant relative, the "billionaire" financier Frank A. Vanderlip, and did not discover their mistake until it was too late. As Lenin noted ruefully, the *Cheka* (the Russian secret police) was not yet as efficiently organized in the United States as it might be. Second, Lenin labored under the misapprehension, which Vanderlip did nothing to dispel, that the syndicate had close ties to President-elect Harding, and that upon the new president's inauguration, diplomatic recognition would be forthcoming. In fact no such ties existed; the Harding administration continued and even strengthened Wilson's nonrecognition policy. The concession never went into operation, and Vanderlip, the self-styled "Khan of Kamchatka," faded into obscurity.[8]

Lenin tried again in 1922, this time with a capitalist whose ties to the Harding administration could not be doubted. Oil magnate Harry F. Sinclair signed a contract with the Far Eastern Republic, a Soviet satellite soon to be absorbed into the USSR, for the exploitation of oil reserves on the northern half of the island of Sakhalin, which, like Kamchatka, was under Japanese control at the time. As had been the case with Vanderlip, Lenin apparently hoped that Sinclair would use his influence with Washington to get the Japanese out. Sinclair tried, but his efforts produced no response from the State Department. In part, this failure resulted from the department's desire to avoid unnecessarily provoking the Japanese. Part of the difficulty also was that Sinclair's ties to the Harding administration were *too* close; after the Teapot Dome scandal broke in 1924, the succeeding Coolidge administration went out of its way to avoid supporting Sinclair's interests. Finally, the State Department resented what it considered a Soviet effort to "buy" recognition through Sinclair. In the absence of official support, Sinclair was never able to exploit his concession; in time the Russians withdrew it and gave it to the Japanese.[9]

---

[8] Albert Parry, "Washington B. Vanderlip, the 'Khan of Kamchatka'," *Pacific Historical Review*, XVII(August, 1948), 311–330.

[9] Floyd J. Fithian, "Dollars without the Flag: The Case of Sinclair and Sakhalin Oil," *Pacific Historical Review*, XXIX(May, 1970), 205–222.

The abortive Vanderlip and Sinclair concessions were early expressions of what was to become a persistent theme in Soviet diplomacy: the view that the interests of the Soviet state could be promoted by facilitating "businesslike" dealings with foreign capitalists. Based on what one American termed an "abiding faith in bourgeois venality,"[10] the policy looked to economic self-interest as a means by which the United States government (presumably the tool of capitalist "ruling circles") could be made to oppose foreign, especially Japanese, intervention, accord the new regime the legitimacy of recognition, and provide the technology necessary to build the industrial base which would, in the long run, ensure the survival of the Soviet state. It was a strategy not unlike that of the infant American republic a century and a half earlier, when it sought recognition from European powers by holding out the lure of trade. Oddly, though, of all the major capitalist states to which the Russian directed this appeal, it was the United States, under the impeccably "businesslike" Republican administrations of the 1920s, that proved to be most resistant to it.

## II

Traditional American policy would have been to enter into diplomatic relations with the Bolshevik government once it had become clear that it controlled Russia. But Wilson had departed dramatically from normal practice in 1913, when he refused to recognize the Huerta government in Mexico because it had come to power through unconstitutional means. Two years later, in a case not directly involving diplomatic recognition, Secretary of State Bryan had declined to take official cognizance of any treaty arrangements imposed by Japan on China that might threaten the principle of the Open Door.[11] Hence, by the time of the Bolshevik Revolution, there was precedent for the view that recognition was not a neutral act, that it carried with it the connotation of approval, and that where such approval did not exist, recognition should be withheld.

---

[10] DeWitt Poole to Frank Polk, February 11, 1919, FR: 1919: *Russia*, p. 52.

[11] Edward M. Bennett, *Recognition of Russia: An American Foreign Policy Dilemma* (Waltham, Massachusetts: 1970), pp. 1–14; Warren I. Cohen, *America's Response to China: An Interpretive History of Sino-American Relations* (New York: 1971), p. 94.

Nonrecognition was more of a reflex response than a calculated decision during the first two years of Bolshevik rule. Brest-Litovsk killed whatever remote possibility existed that recognition could be used to keep Germany and Russia from making a separate peace; after March, 1918, it would have meant endorsement of Russia's withdrawal from the war and was never seriously considered.[12] By the time the war ended, civil conflict and intervention had raised the real possibility that Bolshevism might be overthrown. This circumstance, together with increasing domestic hysteria over the Bolshevik "menace," made recognition an even more remote possibility. Not until 1920 did it become clear that the Soviet regime was likely to survive; only then did the Wilson administration begin working out a public rationale for nonrecognition.

This took the form of an open letter from Secretary of State Bainbridge Colby to the Italian ambassador. Drafted in large part by the staunchly anti-Bolshevik American socialist John Spargo, it was published partly for the purpose of defining, for the first time, a clear-cut and comprehensive policy toward the Soviet Union, partly also in order to make it difficult for the Republicans to reverse Wilson's policy should they gain the White House in the November election.[13]

The Colby note began with expressions of sympathy for the Russian people, specifically exonerating them of responsibility for "the disastrous surrender at Brest-Litovsk." It viewed with confidence the prospect that "a free and unified Russia will again take a leading place in the world." This could not happen, however, as long as the Bolsheviks remained in power:

The existing regime in Russia is based upon the negation of every principle of honor and good faith, and every usage and convention, underlying the whole structure of international law; the negation, in short, of every principle upon which it is possible to base harmonious and trustful relations, whether of nations or of individuals.

Specifically, Colby made three charges against the Bolshevik government: (1) that it had seized power by force and was not

---

[12] Linda Killen, "The Search for a Democratic Russia: Bakhmetev and the United States," *Diplomatic History*, II (Summer, 1978), 242.

[13] Ronald Radosh, "John Spargo and Wilson's Russian Policy, 1920," *Journal of American History*, LII(December, 1965), 548–560. See also Daniel M. Smith, *Aftermath of War: Bainbridge Colby and Wilsonian Diplomacy, 1920–1921* (Philadelphia: 1970), pp. 55–74

representative of the Russian people; (2) that it could not be trusted to carry out its international obligations; and (3) that it had sworn hostility to existing governments throughout the world, convinced that its own position would not be secure until the revolution had spread everywhere. "There cannot be any common ground," Colby noted, "upon which [the United States government] can stand with a Power whose conceptions of international relations are so alien to its own, so utterly repugnant to its moral sense." Colby concluded with an endorsement of prewar Russian territorial integrity, with the exceptions of Finland, Poland, and Armenia. "Thus only can the Bolshevist regime be deprived of its false, but effective, appeal to Russian nationalism and compelled to meet the inevitable challenges of reason and self-respect which the Russian people, secure from invasion and territorial violation, are sure to address to a social philosophy that degrades them and a tyranny that oppresses them"[14]

The interlocking arguments of the Colby note represented an intricate attempt to turn Russian nationalism against the Bolsheviks by picturing Lenin's government as an alien regime, sustained in power at the point of a gun, determined to sacrifice the national interests of the Russian state in favor of an abstract, internationalist, revolutionary ideology. There were several difficulties with this approach. Its emphasis on Bolshevik internationalism neglected Lenin's frequently demonstrated ability, where necessary, to subordinate the interests of the world revolution to those of the Soviet state. It assumed that the Russian people, given the chance to make their views known, would have honored the international obligations of the tsarist and Provisional governments, forgetting the extent to which those governments' determination to meet those commitments had contributed to their respective downfalls. Its endorsement of prewar boundaries (except for Finland, Poland, and Armenia) left a considerable number of non-Russian peoples within the Russian state, and allowed the Bolsheviks, with their highly successful nationalities policy, to pose as advocates of self-determination. Finally, it neglected the impact of foreign intervention, which had, more than anything else, conferred upon the Bolsheviks the aura of national legitimacy.

---

[14] Colby to Avezzana, August 10, 1920, FR: 1920, III, 463–468.

Yet at the same time that Washington was hardening its policy on recognition, it was relaxing its position on trade. Those parts of Russia controlled by the Bolsheviks had been placed under an Allied blockade after Brest-Litovsk, and, although the United States had not officially recognized it, Washington had cooperated by refusing to grant export licenses. As late as August, 1919, President Wilson had expressed the view that "for any government to permit [the Bolsheviks] to increase their power through commercial intercourse with its nationals would be to... invite the condemnation of all peoples desirous of restoring peace and social order." But early in 1920 the Allies lifted their blockade, and pressures began to grow for the State Department to relax its restrictions. After consultation with Wilson, the department announced in July that "restrictions which have heretofore stood in the way of trade and communication with Soviet Russia" had been removed.

The department went out of its way to insist that this action in no way constituted diplomatic recognition, and that businessmen seeking to deal with Soviet Russia would have to do so "on their own responsibility and at their own risk." Moreover, significant impediments to trade remained in the form of passport and visa restrictions, prohibitions on long-term credit, and a ban on the acceptance of Soviet gold in payment for purchases.[15] As one student of the period has noted, these restrictions apparently reflected "the Government's ambivalent desire to allow trade in theory but to make it somewhat difficult in practice in order to bring economic pressure to bear on the Soviet regime for ideological purposes."[16]

Lenin and his associates had high hopes that the new Republican administration of Warren G. Harding, presumably more "businesslike" than its predecessor, would further loosen re-

---

[15] Lansing to Ammission, August 2, 1919, *FR: 1919: Russia*, p. 156; State Department press release, July 7, 1920, *FR: 1920, III, 717*. See also Joan Hoff Wilson, *Ideology and Economics: U.S. Relations with the Soviet Union, 1918–1933* (Columbia, Missouri: 1974), pp. 35–48; and Floyd J. Fithian, "Soviet-American Economic Relations, 1918–1933: American Business in Russia during the Period of Nonrecognition" (Ph. D. Dissertation, University of Nebraska, 1964), pp. 51–59.

[16] Wilson, *Ideology and Economics*, p. 44.

strictions on trade and authorize recognition. To this end, the All-Russian Central Executive Committee sent a note to the new president and Congress in March 1921, pointing out the special attitude the Russian government had always maintained toward the United States, and expressing the hope that the new administration "will clearly understand the immense advantage which will accrue to both Republics through the restoration of commercial relations."[17] There were in the Republican party several prominent critics of Wilson's Russian policy, among them Raymond Robins and Senator William E. Borah. There is even evidence that President Harding himself shared their views.[18] But Harding left foreign policy up to his secretary of state, Charles Evans Hughes, and Hughes quickly made it clear that there would be no change in Russian policy.

There could be no resumption of trade with Russia, Hughes announced, "until the economic bases of production are securely established." That would happen only when the Soviet government provided guarantees regarding "the safety of life, the recognition by firm guarantees of private property, the sanctity of contract, and the rights of free labor." In short, establishment of a normal economic relationship with Soviet Russia would require nothing less than fundamental change in the internal organization of the Soviet state. Lenin's expectation that economic opportunities would cause a truly "businesslike" administration to forget ideological differences proved to be ill-founded. "America... is a puzzle, its relations with Russia a paradox," Foreign Minister Chicherin noted, early in 1922. "It would seem that everything should urge it towards meeting our desire for a *rapprochement* and for entering into close economic relations.... Up to the present the new American administration has not fulfilled these hopes."[19]

Hughes' policy was not as "inscrutable" as Chicherin made it appear. Like Wilson's, it was based on the assumption, increas-

---

[17] Note of March 20, 1921, Degras, ed., *Soviet Documents*, I, 244–245.

[18] On this point, see Bennett, *Recognition of Russia*, pp. 61–64; Fithian, "Soviet-American Economic Relations," pp. 60–61; and Robert K. Murray, *The Harding Era: Warren G. Harding and His Administration* (Minneapolis: 1969), pp. 348–353.

[19] Hughes to Litvinov, March 25, 1921, *FR: 1921*, II, 768; Chicherin report to Central Executive Committee, January 27, 1922, Degras, ed., *Soviet Documents*, I, 291–292.

ingly pervasive in early twentieth-century American diplomacy, that the internal ideological orientation of a state would determine its behavior in the international arena.[20] This conviction had played a major role in shaping attitudes toward tsarist Russia and imperial Germany prior to World War I; now, in the postwar era, it continued to influence decisively Washington's policies toward the new Soviet republic.

### III

Nevertheless, there was a certain ambivalence in United States policy toward Soviet Russia in the 1920s. Although, on the one hand, official Washington hoped to bring about changes in Russia by refusing to have anything to do with its government, it was, on the other hand, eager to promote overseas trade and investment opportunities for American businessmen.[21] These businessmen found it difficult to ignore the very considerable attractions of the Russian market which Lenin and his successors held out; moreover, in this period of relative *laissez-faire*, the government did not feel it proper to compel such businessmen to adjust their activities to official political positions. As a result, extensive contacts grew up in the 1920s between individual American firms and the Soviet government. And when, during the famine of 1921–1922, the issue of humanitarian aid arose, even the government stepped in, on a thinly disguised basis, to provide relief. The overall effect of United States policy during the nonrecognition period, therefore, came close to being the very opposite to what Washington had intended: the United States inadvertently played a considerable role in laying the economic foundations of Soviet power.

The first and quite possibly the most important assistance the United States provided to the new Soviet state came in response to the devastating famine that hit major food-producing areas of that country in the summer of 1921. This crisis, partly the result of weather, partly of dislocations stemming from war, civil conflict, and forced requisitions of grain by the govern-

---

[20] See, on this point, Chapter Two, above; also Lasch, *The American Liberals and the Russian Revolution*, pp. 218–220.

[21] Wilson, *Ideology and Economics*, pp. 29–30; Fithian, "Soviet-American Economic Relations" pp. 65, 145, 351.

ment, became known to the world in July when the famous author Maxim Gorky appealed for assistance. Some days later the Soviet government acknowledged the severity of the situation and officially requested aid.[22]

Much to the Russians' surprise, the quickest and most substantial response came from the United States. Herbert Hoover, secretary of commerce in the Harding cabinet, offered in his capacity as chairman of the quasi-private American Relief Administration to provide food, clothing, and medical supplies for up to a million Russian children. Hoover's motives in making this offer were the subject of much speculation, both in the United States and Russia. The ARA chief had been an outspoken opponent of the Bolshevik regime and had strongly supported Hughes' nonrecognition policy. Moreover, he had gained some notoriety during the Paris Peace Conference for advocating the use of food as a political weapon, both in withholding aid from the short-lived Bela Kun government in Hungary and in proposing the Hoover-Nansen plan for assistance to Russia, a scheme quite frankly intended to undermine Bolshevism. Finally, Hoover's organization had provided aid to the Whites during the Russian civil war. "Everything that is known of Mr. Hoover," an American liberal journal complained, "conveys ample assurance that he would use his position in Russia for political purposes; indeed that he could hardly help doing so if he tried." The Bolsheviks were even more suspicious, seeing Hoover's plan alternatively as a new form of interference in their internal affairs ("bread intervention") and as a reflection of an economic crisis brought on by agricultural overproduction in the United States.[23]

Need overcame distrust, however, and in August, 1921, Soviet representatives signed a "treaty" with ARA officials providing for the distribution of relief supplies "without regard to race, religion or social or political status." Over the next two years, the ARA furnished some 550,000 tons of food, clothing, and medicine to Russia, at a cost, primarily borne by American

---

[22] Benjamin M. Weissman, *Herbert Hoover and Famine Relief to Soviet Russia: 1921–1923* (Stanford: 1974), pp. 1–15.

[23] Ibid., pp. 17–37. See also Mayer, *Politics and Diplomacy of Peacemaking*, pp. 24–27, 474–487; and George W. Hopkins, "The Politics of Food: United States and Soviet Hungary, March–August, 1919," *Mid-America*, LV(October, 1973), 245–270.

governmental and charitable sources, of around $50 million. (The Soviet government contributed an additional $11 million to the program in the form of gold shipments, which were allowed into the United States under a special relaxation of the gold ban.) At the height of its effort, the program was sustaining not 1 million people, as had originally been promised, but 10 million. ARA officials were given considerable latitude in determining how such aid should be distributed, and were allowed to work closely with local officials with minimal interference from Moscow. Nor were the Russians ungrateful: upon conclusion of its work the ARA received the following fulsome tribute from the Soviet government:

> [T]he Council of People's Commissars, in the name of the millions who have been rescued, and of all the working-people of Soviet Russia and the Union Republics, considers it its duty, before the representatives of the entire world, to express its deepest gratitude to this organization, to its leader, Herbert Hoover,...and to declare that the people of the Union of Soviet Socialist Republics will never forget the help rendered to them through the ARA, perceiving in it a guarantee of the future friendship of the two nations.[24]

Subsequent Soviet accounts have been less generous, to the point of describing the ARA as an instrument for dumping surplus commodities and accusing its representatives in Russia of having preoccupied themselves with "espionage and the support of counter-revolutionary elements." American historians too have been skeptical of Hoover's disinterestedness; his program was, one scholar has commented, "simultaneously a self-aggrandizing, humanitarian, anti-Communist, anti-depression effort." Certainly the ARA chief would have welcomed the demise of Bolshevism, and may well have expected such an obvious demonstration of the regime's inability to feed its people to have that effect. But no evidence has been produced linking ARA personnel with anti-Bolshevik activities, and, as Hoover himself later admitted, the relief program wound up strengthening the Soviet government more than it weakened it. Doubt-

[24] Weissman, *Hoover and Famine Relief*, pp. 46–73, 177–178, 198–199. See also Benjamin M. Weissman, "Herbert Hoover's 'Treaty' with Soviet Russia: August 20, 1921," *Slavic Review*, XXVIII(1969), 276–288; and the official history of A. R. A. activities in Russia, H. Fisher, *The Famine in Soviet Russia, 1919–1923* (New York: 1927), especially pp. 553–557.

less the program benefited an American economy in which agricultural surpluses were an increasing problem; it should be recognized, however, that these surpluses were distributed in Russia at the expense of the American taxpayer. And while it is true that the operation enhanced Hoover's already considerable personal and political reputation, at the same time it is difficult to think of anyone else with the peculiar combination of organizational skills and anti-Communist credentials that the job required.[25] In the end the most satisfactory explanation, both for Hoover's actions and the support they received from the American people, may well lie in the characteristically American belief that humanitarian interests do, at times, take precedence over, and can be kept separate from, considerations of politics or ideology.

The timely aid the Bolshevik government received through the famine relief program was only one of several ways in which it benefited from economic contacts with the West, particularly the United States. Lenin's New Economic Policy, instituted early in 1921, marked the beginning of a concerted effort to harness the resources and skills of capitalism in support of the new Socialist order. Three particular areas of emphasis were concessions, trade, and technical assistance.

Following their embarrassing failures with Vanderlip and Sinclair, the Russians abandoned the use of concessions as instruments of diplomacy and concentrated on employing them to attract foreign capital for reconstruction and development. Under the typical concessions contract, of which more than 300 were signed in the 1920s, the Soviet government would make available opportunities, usually in the area of mining or manufacturing, in return for which foreign businessmen would supply capital, technical expertise, and, of course, royalties. Several important concessions went to Americans. W. Averell Harriman, later ambassador to the Soviet Union, operated a massive manganese mining concession in the Caucasus between 1925 and 1928. Two brothers, Armand and Julius Ham-

---

[25] P. M. Malakin, "Iz istorii ekonomicheskikh sviazei s SShA," *SShA: Ekonomika, Politika, Ideologiia*, 1970, #3, p. 18; Wilson, *Ideology and Economics*, p. 24; Weissmann, *Hoover and Famine Relief*, pp. 184–188. For a more charitable Soviet interpretation, see Sivachev and Yakovlev, *Russia and the United States*, pp. 68–70.

mer, held concessions for asbestos mining and pencil manufacturing. Even an American labor union, Sidney Hillman's Amalgamated Clothing Workers, formed a corporation which channeled capital into the development of the Soviet textile industry. Generally, though, American capitalists did not respond in large numbers to the opportunity to operate concessions in the Soviet Union. Bureaucratic and labor problems caused difficulties, and, except for Hammer's pencil factory, returns on investment seemed small. Many Americans still worried about the dangers of nationalization and preferred less risky forms of economic exchange. The Russians themselves eventually came to see the disadvantages of concessions and, under the First Five-Year Plan, initiated in 1928, shifted to a policy of relying on domestic capital to support industrialization.[26]

Domestic sources could not supply the technical skills needed for large-scale projects, however, and for this the Russians came to rely heavily on German and American engineers. Technical aid contracts, under which foreign firms or individuals provided engineering and managerial skills for a fixed fee, were negotiated with increasing frequency in the late 1920s. It has been estimated that as many as 1000 American engineers held individual technical aid contracts during the First Five-Year Plan, and many more were in Russia under contracts signed with American corporations. Especially noteworthy were the activities of the Albert Kahn Company, an industrial architecture firm which designed some 600 plants in Russia; the General Electric Company, which built the massive Dneiprostroy dam and provided other forms of technical assistance to the Soviet electrical industry; and the high priest of *laissez-faire*, mass-production capitalism himself, Henry Ford, whose company virtually single-handedly created the Soviet automobile and truck industry.[27]

Trade also flourished during the nonrecognition period, despite problems raised by the one-sided nature of the exchange

---

[26] Fithian, "Soviet-American Economic Relations," pp. 87–111, 183; Wilson, *Ideology and Economics*, pp. 71–73, 155–160; John P. McKay, "Foreign Enterprise in Russian and Soviet Industry: A Long Term Perspective," *Business History Review*, XLVIII(Autumn, 1974), 350–352.

[27] Fithian, "Soviet-American Economic Relations," pp. 219–348; McKay, "Foreign Enterprise," pp. 352–353.

(American products sold far better in the Soviet Union than Russian products did in the United States), the difficulty in securing credit brought about by Washington's refusal to allow the sale of Soviet securities in the United States, and the government's ban on Soviet gold shipments. Ways were found to circumvent these impediments, however, and by 1930, American exports to the Soviet Union exceeded those of any other country, constituting 25% of the total. Exports to Russia as a percentage of total American exports never exceeded 3.6% during this period (as opposed to 8.9% during the admittedly abnormal year that preceded American entry into World War I). But in certain key areas, trade with Russia was important. Cotton exports to Russia jumped from $1 million to $37 million, or from 0.1% to 3% of total cotton exports, in the single year from 1923 to 1924. In 1925, the Ford Motor Company sent 38% of its tractors manufactured for export to the Soviet Union, or about 10% of its total production that year. In 1930 and 1931, the Soviet Union was the largest single foreign purchaser for American agricultural and industrial equipment. The Soviet Union may not have been "the greatest undeveloped market in the world," as Senator William Borah extravagantly claimed in 1930, but it was important enough for both Americans and Russians, whatever their ideological differences, to make considerable efforts to promote it.[28]

Foreign technology has always been important to Russian development; and there seems little doubt that economic contacts with the United States, whether in the form of famine relief, concessions, technical aid contracts, or commerce, played a significant role in stabilizing conditions in Russia during the first years of Soviet rule. The 1921–1922 famine in particular posed a serious crisis for the Bolsheviks; given conditions in the world at that time, it is difficult to see where outside aid in any volume could have come from if not from the United States.

---

[28] Robert Paul Browder, *The Origins of Soviet-American Diplomacy* (Princeton: 1953), pp. 24–48, 224–225; *Historical Statistics of the United States, Colonial Times to 1957* (Washington: 1960), pp. 537, 546; Fithian, "Soviet-American Economic Relations," pp. 179, 193; Philip S. Gillette, "Conditions of American-Soviet Commerce: The Beginning of Direct Cotton Trade, 1923–1924," *Soviet Union*, I (1974), 74–93; James K. Libbey, "The American-Russian Chamber of Commerce," *Diplomatic History*, IX(Summer, 1985), especially pp. 238–244.

Similarly, private American technical assistance was very likely of critical importance to the success of the First Five-Year Plan.[29] All of this is not to say, of course, that the young Soviet republic could not have survived without American aid. Other sources of commerce, technology, and capital were available, notably in Great Britain and Germany, and were used. It is to say, however, that the United States possessed these commodities in sufficient variety, quality, and abundance to make the development of economic ties with America a matter of urgent priority for the Soviet government.

What is most striking about the aid the United States rendered to the Soviet Union in the 1920s is the inadvertent, almost accidental, manner in which it was provided. No one in Washington made the decision to aid Soviet economic development; indeed, to the extent that there existed any explicit official policy on this matter, it was inclined in the opposite direction. But as in the 1914–1917 period, the government found it difficult to align the nation's economic policies with its official ideological attitude. Partly, this situation arose from the fact that economic policy was still set in large part by the decisions of individual businessmen, not all of whom sought or abided by government advice. In part, too, the contradiction stemmed from an opportunistic ambivalence on the part of government officials, most of whom would not have disagreed with *Business Week's* observation in 1930 that "the common-sense proceeding seems to be to sell the misguided fanatics all they are willing to pay for—business being what it is just now."[30] Whatever the case, the way in which Americans compartmentalized political and economic relations during the years of nonrecognition seemed to provide striking confirmation for the views of Lenin (who never engaged in such compartmentalization) that capitalists would industrialize Soviet Russia because they could not resist the short-term advantages, whatever the long-term dangers.

---

[29] Fithian, "Soviet-American Economic Relations," pp. 355–356; McKay, "Foreign Enterprise," pp. 352–354; Anthony C. Sutton, *Western Technology and Soviet Economic Development, 1917 to 1930* (Stanford: 1968), pp. 346–348; and, for a Soviet view that stresses Stalin's interest in American technology, Sivachev and Yakovlev, *Russia and the United States,* pp. 88–89.

[30] Quoted in Fithian, "Soviet-American Economic Relations," p. 196.

## IV

Despite the increasingly important economic relationship between the United States and the Soviet Union, ideological antipathy remained strong. The Soviet Union constituted a unique phenomenon on the international scene in that it sought to carry on normal diplomatic relations with the capitalist world while simultaneously, and quite openly, plotting its destruction.[31] Its chief instrument for this purpose was the Third International, or Comintern, established in March, 1919, in order to coordinate and direct revolutionary movements throughout the world. At no point in their history were the Soviets more preoccupied with world revolutionary ambitions; despite an almost total lack of success, their activities in this sphere provided the single most important impediment to the normalization of relations with the United States.

American officials had, from the first, been sensitive to the dangers of an international revolutionary movement, not because, as would be the case three decades later, they feared the military power of the Soviet state, but rather because they saw Bolshevism as a disease that would spread wherever chaos and disorder existed. "The spirit of Bolshevism is lurking everywhere," Wilson had noted, in the fall of 1918. "There is grave unrest all over the world. There are symptoms of it in this country—symptoms that are apparent although not yet dangerous." Bolshevism's appeal, Secretary of State Lansing noted, was "to the unintelligent and brutish elements of mankind to take from the intellectual and successful their rights and possessions and to reduce them to a state of slavery.... Bolshevism is the most hideous and monstrous thing that the human mind has ever conceived." Concerned about the spread of Bolshevism in the wake of war, the State Department ordered its representatives "to follow closely all efforts at Bolshevik propaganda both here and abroad."[32]

It is significant that the formation of the Comintern coincided with Lenin's efforts to normalize relations with the West

---

[31] Ulam, *Expansion and Coexistence*, pp. 130–131.

[32] Thompson, *Russia, Bolshevism, and the Versailles Peace*, pp. 14–15; Lansing to Page, November 6, 1918, *FR: 1918: Russia*, I, 726. See also ibid., p. 729.

through his reply to the Prinkipo invitation and his proposals to Bullitt; the apparent duplicity involved in these initiatives must be cited as one of several reasons why they were not accepted. Nor did the outbreak of the "Red scare" at home make United States officials any less sensitive to the Bolshevik "menace": by the fall of 1919 a note of hysteria had begun to creep into the rhetoric of Wilson himself:

> Do you honestly think, my fellow citizens, that none of that poison has got in the veins of this free people?... With the tongue of the wireless and the tongue of the telegraph all the suggestions of disorder are spread through the world.... And men look you calmly in the face in America and say they are for that sort of revolution.

Apocalyptic pronouncements of this type became less frequent as it became clear that Bolshevism was not going to take root in Europe and as the domestic "Red scare" waned. But the Comintern's activities did provide a convenient justification for nonrecognition. As Secretary of State Colby noted in his August, 1920, policy statement: "We cannot recognize, hold official relations with, or give friendly reception to the agents of a government which is determined and bound to conspire against our institutions."[33] This argument, more than any other, became the basis upon which American policy toward the Soviet Union would be based for the next thirteen years.

"We recognize the right of revolution and we do not attempt to determine the internal concerns of other States," Secretary of State Hughes observed in 1923. But recognition also depended, Hughes added, upon the willingness of the state recognized to accept the "obligations inherent in international intercourse." The Soviet regime had violated these obligations by abridging personal liberties, repudiating debts, and confiscating property. But "what is most serious is that... those in control at Moscow have not given up their original purpose of destroying existing governments wherever they can do so throughout the world." To illustrate this point, Hughes took to quoting the incendiary

---

[33] Wilson Des Moines speech, September 6, 1919, quoted in *FR: 1919: Russia*, p. 120; Colby to Avezzana, August 10, 1920, *FR: 1920*, III, 468. See also Browder, *Origins of Soviet-American Diplomacy*, pp. 12–13; and Robert K. Murray, *Red Scare: A Study in National Hysteria, 1919–1920* (Minneapolis: 1955), *passim.*

proclamations of Lenin, Trotsky, and Zinoviev, in one case before the assembled members of the Women's Committee for the Recognition of Russia. And when, in President Coolidge's first annual message to Congress in December, 1923, a relatively innocuous reference to Russia elicited from Chicherin a renewed bid for recognition, Hughes torpedoed the initiative with the curt observation that "there would seem to be at this time no reason for negotiations." To add insult to injury, he had the State Department release, on the following day, intercepted instructions from the Comintern to the Communist Party of the United States, looking forward to the day, "in the not too distant future," when the party would "raise the red flag over the White House."[34]

American officials did not take Comintern activity lightly. A 1923 analysis from the United States legation in Riga, Latvia (which served, during this period, as a primary information-gathering center on Soviet affairs), reported Comintern propaganda in such diverse areas as Germany, Eastern Europe, Great Britain, Spain, Turkey, Persia, Afghanistan, India, China, and Japan. Early in 1924 Secretary of State Hughes sent the Senate Foreign Relations Committee an extensive file on Comintern activities in the United States. Secretary of State Kellogg gave extensive publicity to reports in 1927 that the Comintern had expanded its activities into Latin America; this prompted Litvinov to complain that soon "the enlightened statesmen of the great Powers [would] begin [ascribing] to the machinations of the Bolsheviks the earthquake in Japan and the floods in America." On the occasion of the Sixth Comintern Congress in Moscow in 1928, the legation staff in Riga spent months compiling a detailed account of the proceedings and a list of participants which, when forwarded to Washington, filled hundreds of pages. "It would be truly ostrichlike," the American *chargé* there warned, "not to perceive that this 'General Staff of theWorld Revolution' is entirely in earnest in its determination to overthrow every non-Communist so-

---

[34] Hughes to Samuel Gompers, July 19, 1923, *FR: 1923*, II, 760–764; State Department press releases, March 21, December 18 and 19, 1923, ibid., pp. 755–758, 788–790.

ciety and Government, and to erect a World Soviet Socialist Republic."[35]

"The Government of the United States feels no concern lest this systematic interference in our affairs...bring about the overthrow of our Government and institutions," Secretary Kellogg noted in 1928; "[it], however, does not propose to acquiesce in such interference by entering into relations with the Soviet Union." Or, as Robert F. Kelley, the influential chief of the State Department's Division of East European Affairs, put it in an internal memorandum in April, 1929:

The essential difficulty lying in the way of the recognition of the Soviet government is not certain acts of the Bolshevik regime, such as repudiation of debts, the confiscation of property, and the carrying on of propaganda in the United States; but the Bolshevik world revolutionary purpose, of which these acts are manifestations. It is this fundamental purpose of the Bolshevik leaders which precludes the observance by them of the obligations ordinarily accepted as governing relations between nations....This...is the idea underlying all our statements of policy towards the Bolshevik regime.[36]

Soviet world revolutionary activity thus became the chief justification used by the State Department, and by the government generally, in support of its nonrecognition policy.

In fact, however, the Comintern was not a conspicuously successful organization. Although Communist parties under Soviet control were established throughout much of the world during the interwar period, the only country in which one ac-

---

[35] F. W. B. Coleman to Hughes, November 8, 1923, *FR: 1923*, II, 771; Filene, *Americans and the Soviet Experiment*, pp. 91–92; Stephen John Kneeshaw, "The Kellogg-Briand Pact and American Recognition of the Soviet Union," *Mid-America*, LVI(January, 1974), 20–23; Litvinov statement of January 17, 1924, Degras, ed., *Soviet Documents*, II, 152; Sussdorff to Kellogg, October 19 and 25, 1928, and Coleman to Stimson, April 17, 1929, in DSR, 861.00—Congress, Communist International VI/1 3, 21, 36 (M-316:67). For the activities of the Riga legation, see Natalie Grant, "The Russian Section, A Window on the Soviet Union," *Diplomatic History*, II (Winter, 1978), 107–115; also George W. Baer, ed., *A Question of Trust: The Origins of U.S.–Soviet Diplomatic Relations: The Memoirs of Loy W. Henderson* (Stanford: 1986), pp. 171–198.

[36] Kellogg to Butler, February 23, 1928, *FR: 1928*, III, 823–824; Kelley memorandum of April 12, 1929, DSR, 861.01/1 415 (M-316: 76). See also Kelley to Robert Olds, February 10, 1928, quoted in Wilson, *Ideology and Economics*, pp. 99–100.

tually came to power was Outer Mongolia. Efforts to spark revolutions in more important areas either failed completely, as in the case of Germany, or saw the revolution take an anti-Communist direction, as happened in China. Some of the reasons for this failure can be seen by examining the Comintern's relations with one of its more exotic creations, the Communist movement in the United States.

American communism in its formative years was riddled with factionalism; not until 1923 was some semblance of unity achieved. Whatever their differences, however, all American Communists mechanically sought guidance from the Comintern. "If the Comintern finds itself criss-cross with my opinions," William Z. Foster, one of the more durable party leaders commented, "there is only one thing to do and that is to change my opinions to fit the policy of the Comintern."[37] But because the Comintern had, since its formation, been in turn under the rigid control of the Communist Party of the Soviet Union, this kind of tight discipline made the fortunes of communism in the United States wholly dependent upon the ability of Soviet leaders to assess revolutionary prospects in a country few of them knew anything about.

The effects were not only destructive; they were at times ludicrous. On Comintern orders, American Communists supported Senator Robert LaFollette's third-party presidential bid in 1924, only to have these instructions abruptly reversed in mid-campaign. A year later the Comintern decided that LaFollette had been right after all, but that American Communists, as loyal Comintern members, had been right to withdraw their support from him. The Comintern insisted that the American party organize itself rigidly on the Russian model, even to the point of creating party cells in factories; the fact that American workers considered the factory both an inappropriate and wholly impractical location for political activity was not allowed to stand in the way. In 1928 the Comintern ordered the American party to support formation of a separate black state in the South; this ambitious scheme represented nothing less than an effort on the part of Stalin himself to transfer his nationalities

---

[37] Quoted in Theodore Draper, *American Communism and Soviet Russia: The Formative Period* (New York: 1960), p. 149.

policy from the Caucasus and Central Asia to the far less hos-
pitable territory of Alabama and Mississippi. Party officials pa-
tiently accommodated themselves to each successive manifesta-
tion of the Soviet leadership's collective wisdom, although not
without occasional resistance on the part of the rank and file.
American workers, one party organizer complained, greeted
"the latest and most improved model" of the party line with a
bewilderment comparable to that of "the Russian *muzhik* upon
his first contact with the American tractor." "Why was the American Communist Party like the Brooklyn Bridge?" one wag asked,
in what became a classic comment on the party's relationship to
Moscow: "Because both were suspended on cables."[38]

"It would be wrong to ignore the specific peculiarities of
American capitalism," Stalin told a delegation of American
Communists in 1929:

> But it would be still more wrong to base the activities of the Commu-
> nist Party on these specific features, since the foundation of the activ-
> ities of every Communist Party, including the American Communist
> Party, on which it must base itself, must be the general features of cap-
> italism, which are the same for all countries, and not its specific fea-
> tures in any given country.[39]

This characteristically ponderous statement reveals much, not
just about the Comintern's relationship to the American Communist party, but about its general failure in the interwar period. The Soviet autocrat's insistence on viewing capitalism as a
monolith was in fact a backhanded justification for his own
monolithic control of the international Communist movement.
The resulting tactical inflexibility proved to be a major impediment to that movement's success. Communism would gain
power, in the end, only where Stalin could impose it by force,
or where it could free itself from the debilitating effects of
Stalin's control.

Ineffective as they were, the Comintern's efforts to provoke
world revolution persistently undercut efforts of the Soviet Foreign Ministry to normalize diplomatic relations with the capital-

---

[38] Ibid., pp. 96–118, 137, 192–193, 345–356, 390. See also Lowell K. Dyson,
"The Red Peasant International in America," *Journal of American History*,
LVIII(March, 1972), 958–973.

[39] Quoted in Draper, *American Communism and Soviet Russia*, p. 409.

ist world. Attempts to start a revolution in Germany in 1923 partially undid the reconciliation between the two powers that had been arranged at Rapallo a year earlier. Comintern activity was a persistent irritant in relations with Great Britain, even to the point of causing a break in diplomatic relations in 1927. In China, the Russians followed an intricate policy of plotting against both the official government in Peking and Chiang Kaishek's insurgent movement, while simultaneously attempting to carry on conventional relations with both: the result was one of the most disastrous failures in the history of Soviet foreign policy. And in the United States, the persistence of Comintern activity at home and abroad, while it posed no significant threat to the national security, provided opponents of recognition with their most persuasive arguments. As Alexander Gumberg, a close associate of Raymond Robins and one of the most tireless workers for recognition, complained, "These fellows still seem to be sitting up nights trying to think up some scheme which will get them in dutch with the rest of the world."[40]

## V

In the summer of 1929, an official in the State Department's Division of East European Affairs, provoked by a prorecognition editorial in the *New Republic*, sat down to review the reasons why United States policy toward the Soviet Union should not be changed. The presence of official representatives in Moscow would not provide Washington with any significant amount of information it did not already have, he noted, given the efficiency of the Riga legation staff and the restrictions the Russians imposed on foreign diplomats' movements. Nor would recognition give the United States additional influence over the actions of the Soviet government—Soviet foreign policy was primarily the result of internal factors and would change only in response to them. It would not significantly improve economic contacts: indeed, since there was some evi-

---

[40] Quoted in Filene, *Americans and the Soviet Experiment*, p. 90. See also Ulam, *Expansion and Coexistence*, pp. 111–182; and Theodore H. Von Laue, "Soviet Diplomacy: G. V. Chicherin, People's Commissar for Foreign Affairs, 1918–1930," in Gordon A. Craig and Felix Gilbert, eds., *The Diplomats, 1919–1939* (Princeton: 1953), I, 234–281.

dence that the Soviet government had been placing massive orders in the United States to encourage prorecognition sentiment, the volume of trade might actually decline if recognition were granted. Finally, "it may be said that to recognize the Soviet Government now would necessarily signify that our policy in the past had been erroneous."[41]

At the time it was made, not many Americans would have quarreled with this analysis. There had always been advocates of recognition, but few of them had been able to point to any concrete benefits to be derived from extending it. Political figures like Senators William Borah and Burton K. Wheeler criticized nonrecognition as a form of intervention in the internal affairs of another state, but found it difficult to explain away the Comintern's all-too-obvious efforts along the same line. Businessmen who favored recognition on the grounds that it would increase trade found trade increasing anyway; the majority of the business community was entirely comfortable with the Republican compromise of simultaneously condemning the Bolshevik regime while profiting from economic contacts with it. Radicals and intellectuals found themselves torn between admiration for the idealistic goals of the Soviet "experiment" and repugnance for its autocratic, materialistic, at times inhumane methods. Though conspicuous in their reporting and writing on Russia, their impact on the debate over recognition was minimal.[42]

Antirecognition forces had the weight of informed opinion on their side during the 1920s; what is probably more important, they had effective organizational support. The Soviet Union's official atheism alienated all religious groups, but it so happened that the denomination that suffered the most direct outrage was also the best organized. In March, 1923, the vicar-general of the Roman Catholic Church in Russia was executed for counter-revolutionary activities. From this time on, the Catholic Church in the United States became one of the most vociferous and effective opponents of recognition. The American Federation of Labor also strongly opposed recogni-

---

[41] Memorandum by E. L. Packer, August 30, 1929, DSR, 861.01/1 510½ (M-316:76).

[42] Robert James Maddox, *William E. Borah and American Foreign Policy* (Baton Rouge: 1969), pp. 49, 203–208; Filene, *American and the Soviet Experiment*, pp. 91–92, 151–154.

tion; indeed, anti-Soviet activity had become such an important badge of respectability for the nation's largest labor union that Secretary of State Henry L. Stimson could describe it in 1931 as "our chief barrier against communism." Patriotic organizations such as the American Legion and the Daughters of the American Revolution found nonrecognition a congenial issue; so, too, did major business groups like the National Association of Manufacturers, the National Civic Federation, and the United States Chamber of Commerce.[43]

But, in the end, the most effective organized opposition to recognition may well have existed among a relatively small number of key officials in the State and Commerce departments. The State Department's Division of East European Affairs was largely staffed with diplomats who had served in Russia during the traumatic years of intervention and civil war. As in the case of other Russian "experts," both before and after, proximity impaired objectivity, with effects that were to persist for years afterward in the form of hostility toward the Russian government. In the Commerce Department, resistance to recognition was very much the result of Herbert Hoover's personal impact as secretary of commerce. Despite his willingness to trade with and even feed the Bolsheviks, Hoover nursed a deep ideological aversion to the Soviet government that precluded normal diplomatic relations, and succeeded in transmitting these views to those who worked under him. As a consequence, anti-recognition sentiment became institutionalized in these two departments; in the absence of strong incentives in favor of recognition, these bureaucratic constraints played a major role in perpetuating existing policies.[44]

After Hoover became president, however, circumstances combined to provide new arguments, both for and against recognition. One such circumstance was the onset of the Great Depression. Heavy Russian orders for industrial and agricultural equipment continued as other markets declined, leading some

---

[43] Ibid., pp. 82–84, 89, 157–160; Wilson, *Ideology and Economics*, pp. 64–67, 111; Stimson memorandum of conversation with Italian foreign minister Dino Grandi, July 9, 1931, *FR: 1931*, I, 541.

[44] Wilson, *Ideology and Economics*, pp. 20–21, 85–86, 91–92, 130–132. See also Frederic L. Propas, "Creating a Hard Line toward Russia: The Training of State Department Soviet Experts, 1927–1937," *Diplomatic History*, VIII(Summer, 1984), especially pp. 209–223.

businessmen to see in Stalin's Five-Year Plan a means of bringing about economic recovery in the United States. Exports to
Russia as a percentage of total exports remained small—2.9% in
1930, 3.6% in 1931—but recognition, it was thought, might drive
the figures higher by making it easier for the Russians to get credit
in the United States. It is important to note, however, that the depression cut both ways. It also forced the Russians to try to expand their own export markets by cutting prices; this led to such
serious competition for American producers of lumber, matches,
coal, manganese, and wheat that the Treasury banned imports of
several of these commodities, charging the Russians with dumping and the use of forced labor. Recognition might therefore bring
economic opportunities, but it could also bring dangers unless
some way was found to restrict cheap Soviet imports. As a result,
although recognition was much debated among businessmen, no
clear consensus on the matter emerged.[45]

The Russians were well aware of the political leverage trade
with the United States gave them during the depression and
sought to use it to bring about recognition. As Boris E. Skvirskii,
head of the Soviet Information Bureau in Washington, noted in
1930, "Events have shown that in times of crisis Americans feel
the importance of Soviet markets and that the threat of losing
them redounds to our benefit. . . . Knowing our decisive position,
we should be prepared to use it." The Soviet government accepted Skvirskii's advice and, in the fall of 1931, cut back sharply
on American orders. Nikolai N. Krestinskii, deputy commissar for
foreign affairs, explained the strategy in a report to the Politburo:

The maximum contraction and eventual full cessation of our purchases
will be our most important and convincing instrument for putting
pressure on America. The loss of Soviet markets, the importance of
which for some parts of American industry has grown tremendously
during the period of crisis, will more quickly impel American business
and political circles to reconsider their traditional position of not recognizing the USSR.

The trade cutback did cause concern—exports to Russia came to
only $12.6 million in 1932, down from $103.7 million the previous
year—and some intensification of pressure among businessmen

---

[45] Fithian, "Soviet-American Economic Relations," pp. 189–211; Wilson, *Ideology and Economics*, pp. 103–120; Browder, *Origins of Soviet-American Diplomacy*,
pp. 28–48; Filene, *Americans and the Soviet Experiment*, pp. 211–239.

for recognition. But opposition from other business leaders worried about Soviet imports, together with the lack of any firm assurance that recognition really would increase Soviet orders, prevented Skvirskii's strategy from succeeding. The American "ruling circles" remained divided, leaving the government free to do what it wanted.[46]

A clearer and more decisive argument in favor of recognition grew out of the fact that the United States was now the only major country that had not established diplomatic relations with the Soviet Union. With Moscow becoming more and more active in international diplomacy, the absence of official ties had begun to cause embarrassments. One came in 1928, when Russian adherence to the Kellogg-Briand Pact on the renunciation of war raised the alarming possibility that the United States, by signing the same document, might have inadvertently recognized the USSR. Another occurred during a brief Sino-Soviet conflict in Manchuria the following year when Secretary of State Stimson undertook to "remind" both sides of their obligations under the pact, only to receive in return a sharp "reminder" from Litvinov that the United States, not having seen fit yet to recognize the existence of the Soviet Union, was hardly in a position to be giving it advice and "instructions."[47]

The absence of official relations between Washington and Moscow became more than just an embarrassment in 1931, when Japan suddenly ejected China from Manchuria. Both the United States and the Soviet Union sought to deter Japan from further aggression, but without diplomatic relations, no concerted action was possible. Boris Skvirskii, the Russians' unofficial agent in Washington, launched a quiet campaign early in 1932 to promote American recognition of the Soviet Union as a means of impressing Tokyo. Stimson was not unreceptive. He

---

[46] Skvirskii to Soviet foreign ministry, August 13, 1930, *Dokumenty vneshnei politiki, SSSR,* XIII, 458; Krestinskii to Politburo, September 18, 1931, ibid., XIV, 527. See also Browder, *Origins of Soviet-American Diplomacy,* pp. 43–47; Filene, *American and the Soviet Experiment,* pp. 235–237; and Jonathan Haslam, *Soviet Foreign Policy, 1930–33: The Impact of the Depression* (New York: 1983), pp. 53–55.

[47] Litvinov to Stimson, December 3, 1929, Degras, ed., *Soviet Documents,* II, 408. See also Kneeshaw, "The Kellogg-Briand Pact," pp. 23–31; Pauline Tompkins, *American-Russian Relations in the Far East* (New York: 1949), pp. 220–246; and Robert H. Ferrell, *American Diplomacy in the Great Depression: Hoover-Stimson Foreign Policy, 1929–1933* (New Haven: 1957), pp. 45–67.

had already publicly abandoned Wilson's practice of recognizing only constitutionally legitimate regimes and, unlike Kellogg, generally deprecated the dangers of international communism. Gravely concerned by the failure of the League of Nations to act, he ordered subordinates in the State Department to study what impact recognition would have on the East Asian situation and even met secretly at the Geneva Disarmament Conference with Karl Radek, one of Litvinov's lieutenants, to discuss the matter. In the end, however, nothing was done. State Department officials concluded that Tokyo would interpret recognition as a hostile act; given Hoover's strong aversion to recognition and to any kind of provocative action in East Asia, this argument carried great weight. As Assistant Secretary of State James Grafton Rogers told Skvirskii in June, the Japanese military had already gone so far that recognition would not deter them from attacking the Soviet Union if they were so inclined: "from them one can expect anything."[48]

The very fact that recognition had been considered was encouraging to the Russians, however, and they anticipated action as soon as the new and more "practical" Roosevelt administration took office. Skvirskii reported that the new president's advisers were leaning toward recognition, largely on the grounds that it would strengthen the American position in dealing with Japan. Nor did the Russians hesitate to take advantage of these rumors. "In America there is an increasing number of people who recognize the mistake of not have relations with us," Deputy Commissar for Foreign Affairs Karakhan told the Japanese ambassador to Moscow in February, 1933. "Thus, if America wants to correct its mistake, then we will not prevent it, if it wants to restore relations with us, we, of course, wish to restore normal relations with America."[49]

---

[48] Skvirskii to Litvinov, January 29, 1932, and to Narkomindel, February 2 and June 4, 1932, *Dokumenty vneshnei politiki, SSSR*, XV, 69–70, 80, 351–352. See also Stimson to Borah, September 8, 1932, *Foreign Relations: The Soviet Union, 1933–1939* (Washington: 1952), pp. 1–2; Bennett, *Recognition of Russia*, pp. 74–80; and Tompkins, *American-Russian Relations*, pp. 247–263.

[49] Notes, meetings between Karakhan and Ota, February 27, 1933, *Dokumenty vneshnei politiki SSSR*, XVI, 129. See also Skvirskii to Narkomindel, July 8, December 2, 1932, January 28, February 21, April 1, 1933, ibid., XV, 403, 661–662, XVI, 60, 108, 210.

CHAPTER V

# Recognition and Disillusionment: 1933–1941

IN RETROSPECT, IT IS CLEAR THAT THE UNITED STATES AND THE SOVIET UNION HAD A COMMON INTEREST during the 1930s in resisting the growing power of Germany and Japan. With the establishment of formal diplomatic relations in 1933, opportunities would appear to have existed for joint action in pursuit of this aim. That such action did not occur must be attributed to the influence, within both countries, of internal constraints on foreign policy. In the United States, powerful nonintervention ist tendencies discouraged the Roosevelt administration from making commitments of any kind to oppose aggression. The Soviet Union openly encouraged such commitments, but continued Comintern activity, together with a series of gruesome purges, conveyed to the outside world the impression that the USSR was an abnormal state, not to be dealt with through the instruments of conventional diplomacy. The result was an absence of collaboration between Washington and Moscow until common enemies forced Russians and Americans into a reluctant alliance in the interests of self-preservation.

I

The question of whether or not to recognize the Soviet Union had attracted considerable public attention during the year preceding Roosevelt's inauguration, but not in such a way as to restrict the new president's freedom of action. To the extent that its opinions can be reconstructed, given the rudimentary polling techniques of the day, the general public appears to have favored recognition by a considerable margin. Organized opposition existed among business, labor, and religious communities, but prorecognition sentiment within those same groups tended to neutralize it. As a consequence, Roosevelt was free to follow his own inclinations, knowing he would meet neither unanimous support nor overwhelming opposition to whatever course he chose.[1]

Several considerations caused Roosevelt to favor establishing diplomatic ties. One was the simple fact that nonrecognition had not achieved its objectives: it had changed neither the internal configuration nor the external behavior of the Soviet state. Given Roosevelt's impatience with ineffective policies, given the low priority he attached to such things as ideological consistency, it was as easy for him to give up nonrecognition as it was to abandon Prohibition, another outdated policy that quickly fell victim to the new administration's affinity for the practical.

An equally important consideration, in Roosevelt's mind, was the fact that the world confronted several major problems that could be solved only with the Russians' active cooperation. One of these was the global economic crisis. Efforts to stabilize world wheat prices in the summer of 1933 brought about the first open contacts between American and Soviet officials since the Russian Revolution. Soon thereafter, negotiations began on the extension of Reconstruction Finance Corporation credits to support Soviet purchases of American cotton. Roosevelt did not expect recognition to bring dramatic improvements in either the international or domestic economic situations, but he did regard the USSR as too important an element in the world economy to justify a continued policy of aloofness.[2]

Nor could the Russians easily be excluded from efforts to maintain peace at a time when the World War I settlement seemed to be coming apart. Japan had already successfully challenged the League of Nations in Manchuria; the organization would soon be under attack in Europe as well. Isolationism kept Roosevelt from contemplating direct action against the aggressors, but he had no intention of remaining completely neutral. Instead he sought ways, however subtle, to increase the

---

[1] Thomas R. Maddux, *Years of Estrangement: American Relations with the Soviet Union, 1933–1941* (Tallahassee: 1980), pp. 4–10; Browder, *Origins of Soviet-American Diplomacy*, pp. 85–86.

[2] Ibid, pp. 90–95. See also Robert E. Bowers, "American Diplomacy, the 1933 Wheat Conference, and Recognition of the Soviet Union," *Agricultural History*, XL(January, 1966), 39–52.

strain and uncertainty under which Germany and Japan would have to operate, without at the same time committing the United States to specific measures of any kind. A diplomatic opening to Moscow fitted in well with this strategy.[3]

On May 16, 1933, Roosevelt included Soviet President Mikhail Kalinin among recipients of a public message, sent to fifty-two heads of state, appealing for the success of the Geneva Disarmament Conference and proposing a global nonaggression pact. The president denied that Kalinin's inclusion had any special meaning, but the significance of this first formal communication to the Soviet government could hardly be overlooked. Five months later, on October 10, Roosevelt sent a second letter to Kalinin proposing discussions with a view toward ending "the present abnormal relations between the hundred and twenty-five million people of the United States and the hundred and sixty million people of Russia." The Russians accepted with alacrity, and announced that Soviet Foreign Minister Maxim Litvinov would come to the United States himself to conduct the negotiations.[4]

Press and public reactions were generally favorable, but there were centers of resistance that worried the president. Working skillfully through personal contacts, he sought to blunt opposition among religious and labor groups by assuring them that recognition would not be granted without a price: "Leave it to me, Father," he told one Catholic critic, "I am a good horse trader." Roosevelt took the same position with the State Department, which he suspected of harboring reservations about recognition, and insisted on handling the negotiations personally. This does not mean that Roosevelt ignored his diplomats' advice: he accepted the department's recommendation that preconditions for recognition include acknowledgment of the Provisional Government's debts, a pledge of noninterference in American domestic affairs, and a promise to respect the religious freedom of Americans inside the Soviet Union. But the president rejected State's suggestion that secret preliminary discussions be held to establish areas of agreement and disagreement. Nor did he pay attention to the concern of

---

[3] Farnsworth, *Bullitt*, p. 91.

[4] Edgar B. Nixon, ed., *Franklin D. Roosevelt and Foreign Affairs: 1933–1937* (Cambridge, Massachusetts: 1967), I, 126–129; FR: *Soviet Union*, pp. 17–19.

some elements within the department over Comintern activity in Cuba.[5]

Litvinov arrived in Washington in early November, expecting immediate recognition. He was surprised, and somewhat offended, to find that commitments were expected in advance on debts, religious rights, and communist activity inside the United States. The Soviet foreign minister regarded these conditions largely as gestures intended to placate American critics of recognition: "My general impression," he reported to Moscow, "is that Roosevelt doubtlessly is striving for the establishment of the best relations, but that he is really frightened of the opponents of recognition." The agreement on religious rights for Americans in the Soviet Union was not difficult to achieve, but Litvinov balked at promising an end to communist activities in the United States, on the grounds that the Soviet government had no authority over the Comintern. He also resisted an ingenious suggestion from Roosevelt that Comintern headquarters be transferred from Moscow to that other center of international activity, Geneva. In the end, Litvinov signed a statement, drafted by the State Department, promising that the Soviet Union would not

permit the formation or residence on its territory of any organization or group ... which has as an aim the overthrow or the preparation for the overthrow of, or the bringing about by force of a change in, the political or social order of the whole or any part of the United States, its territories or possessions.

By design, however, the pledge said nothing about the Comintern, in the belief that if it were mentioned specifically the Russians could evade the agreement by simply changing the organization's name. Litvinov, in turn, made it clear that he did not regard the Comintern as covered by the agreement in the first place.[6]

---

[5] Maddux, *Years of Estrangement*, pp. 16–20; Browder, *Origins of Soviet-American Diplomacy*, pp. 106–107, 112–115, 125; Robert E. Bowers, "Hull, Russian Subversion in Cuba, and Recognition of the U.S.S.R.," *Journal of American History*, LIII(December, 1966), 542–554.

[6] Litvinov to Soviet foreign ministry, November 8, 1933, *Dokumenty uneshnei politiki SSSR*, XVI, 609–610; Litvinov to Roosevelt, November 16, 1933, FR: *Soviet Union*, p. 29. See also Donald G. Bishop, *The Roosevelt-Litvinov Agreements: The American View* (Syracuse: 1965), pp. 27–31.

Roosevelt and Litvinov reached no final agreement on the touchy question of debts, but they did arrive at an understanding whereby the Russians would pay no less than $75 million (as against a total debt of $188 million), in the form of extra interest on a loan extended to finance Soviet purchases in the United States. Roosevelt and the State Department viewed this arrangement as a "credit" which would allow Washington to control purchases made, but through careless drafting the word "loan" crept into the document the president and Litvinov signed. The Americans also failed to specify that the Russians would be expected to pay interest on the Kerensky government debt, another misunderstanding that would cause problems later on. On this less than precise basis, the agreement establishing formal diplomatic relations was signed on November 17, 1933.[7]

Despite the acrimonious nature of the negotiations, Litvinov did have reason to expect positive diplomatic benefits from them. He reported to Moscow that Roosevelt had referred specifically to Germany and Japan as sources of military danger in the world, and had raised the possibility that the United States and the Soviet Union, acting together, might be able to "stave them off." The president made it clear that the United States could not go to war, but he expressed the hope that both Germany and Japan would exhaust themselves, and that no war would be necessary. In the meantime, the United States was prepared to give the Soviet Union "100% moral and diplomatic support." Roosevelt then suggested the possibility of a triangular nonaggression pact between the United States, the Soviet Union, and Japan, and gave Litvinov the impression that, if Japan refused to sign, the United States would conclude such a pact with the Soviet Union alone.[8]

For the moment, it appeared as if the basis for cordial relations had been laid. Litvinov departed Washington in a cloud of

---

[7] For negotiation of the Roosevelt-Litvinov agreements, see Browder, *Origins of Soviet-American Diplomacy*, pp. 127–141, 181–183; and Bishop, *The Roosevelt-Litvinov Agreements*, pp. 148–152.

[8] Litvinov to Soviet foreign ministry, November 8, 17, 1933, *Dokumenty uneshnei politiki SSSR*, XVI, 609, 658–659. See also Edward M. Bennett, *Franklin D. Roosevelt and the Search for Security: American-Soviet Relations, 1933–1939* (Wilmington, Delaware: 1985), pp. 23–24.

friendly rhetoric, and Roosevelt impressed the Russians by naming as the first American ambassador to the Soviet Union William C. Bullitt, Wilson's secret emissary to Lenin and Trotsky in 1919 and a long-standing advocate of Soviet recognition. Bullitt's reception in Moscow the following month did nothing to disappoint him. President Kalinin solemnly assured the new envoy of the Russians' realization that President Roosevelt "really cared about the welfare of the laboring men and the farmers and was not engaged in protecting the vested rights of property." Stalin did Bullitt the unprecedented courtesy of attending a lavish feast in his honor, accompanied by innumerable toasts, which ended with the Soviet dictator planting a wet kiss on the cheek of the astonished diplomat. Stalin also agreed to the construction of an American embassy modeled on Jefferson's Monticello, to be built on a bluff overlooking the Russian capital. ("I like the idea of planting Thomas Jefferson in Moscow," Roosevelt later noted.) "It is obvious," Bullitt reported to the president, "that our representatives in the Soviet Union today can have a really immense influence."[9]

## II

Disillusionment soon crept into the new Soviet-American relationship, however, as it became clear that both sides had misunderstood what the other had expected from the Roosevelt-Litvinov agreements. This occurred first with respect to the question of Japan. Since no records were kept on the American side, it is impossible to confirm Litvinov's account of what Roosevelt had said to him on this subject. While the president may well have talked about an East Asian nonaggression pact, it seems doubtful that he regarded these discussions as anything other than "brainstorming." The Russians, however, took them seriously. Moscow press commentaries contained considerable speculation about joint Soviet-American cooperation against Japan, and Bullitt found his first days in the Russian capital filled with rumors of war in East Asia, together with hints of what the

---

[9] Bullitt to Roosevelt, January 1, 1934, in Orville H. Bullitt, ed., *For the President: Personal and Secret: Correspondence between Franklin D. Roosevelt and William C. Bullitt* (Boston: 1972), pp. 63–70; Roosevelt to Cordell Hull, February 16, 1934, Nixon, ed., *F. D. R. and Foreign Affairs*, I, 647.

United States could do to help. Stalin himself suggested the immediate shipment of 250,000 tons of steel rails to reequip the Trans-Siberian Railroad, while V. M. Molotov, chairman of the Council of People's Commissars, publicly observed that "the most reactionary Japanese militarists fear that such countries as the USSR, the United States, and China, may work together against the instigators of a new Far-Eastern war."[10]

In fact, public and Congressional opposition to foreign commitments made any form of active United States cooperation with the Soviet Union against Japan virtually impossible. The Roosevelt administration viewed the East Asian situation with extreme caution, and although the president himself clearly hoped that the normalization of Soviet-American relations might inhibit the Japanese, he was at no point in a position to take more positive action.[11] The Russians' failure to see this fact must be attributed in part to wishful thinking, in part to their chronic lack of sophistication in analyzing American politics, and in part to a tendency, shared by many others, to confuse Rooseveltian banter with national policy.

Ideological blinders compounded the confusion. Long-anticipated "contradictions of capitalism" had, Russian officials believed, forced the non-fascist West into seeking cooperation with the Soviet Union. The United States, *Izvestiia* noted at the time of recognition, had been "compelled" to deal with the USSR in order to ward off the twin dangers of global depression and fascist aggression.[12] But in the view of the Roosevelt administration, it was the Soviet Union that was acting under compulsion and should be willing to pay whatever price was necessary to achieve such limited cooperation as American opinion might allow. As Bullitt put it in a letter to the president, "It is obvious that the Soviet Government values so highly the moral support it may receive from the United States in the mat-

---

[10] Bullitt to Roosevelt, January 1, 1934, in Bullitt, ed., *For the President,* pp. 67–68; Molotov speech of December 28, 1933, Degras, ed., *Soviet Documents,* III, 46–47. See also Browder, *Origins of Soviet-American Diplomacy,* pp. 153–156.

[11] See, on Roosevelt's general foreign policy position during this period, Robert Dallek, *Franklin D. Roosevelt and American Foreign Policy, 1932–1945* (New York: 1979), p. 20; and Wayne S. Cole, *Roosevelt and the Isolationists, 1932–45* (Lincoln, Nebraska: 1983), p. 243.

[12] *Izvestiia,* November 20, 1933, quoted in *FR: Soviet Union,* p. 44.

ter of preventing war with Japan that there is almost nothing we may not ask for and obtain at the present time."[13]

Once Bullitt made it clear that "moral support" was all the Russians could expect in East Asia, the atmosphere in Moscow chilled noticeably. When negotiations on debts and credits began in March, 1934, the Russians were firm and unyielding. Roosevelt's agreement with Litvinov had left important issues unresolved—notably whether a loan or a credit was to be extended to finance Soviet purchases inside the United States, how much of the Kerensky government's debt the Soviets would pay, and whether this debt would be paid with interest. The Russians clearly were interested in securing American economic assistance, but not to the point of yielding the right to control Soviet purchases in the United States or of accepting the American position on the Kerensky debt, something that would have to be done, under the Johnson Act of 1934, if a loan were to be extended. Stalin might have compromised in return for an open American stand against Japan, but public opinion made this course unfeasible for the Roosevelt administration, while a gradual improvement in Soviet-Japanese relations made it seem, after a time, less vital to the Russians.[14]

Bullitt at first attributed the breakdown in negotiations to "misunderstandings," but by the spring of 1934 he was reporting that "the honeymoon atmosphere has evaporated completely." The Russians were convinced that the Japanese were not going to attack; moreover they expected pressure from export-hungry businessmen to make Washington compromise on the debt negotiations. "I do not take the matter so tragically," Litvinov told an infuriated Bullitt: "No nation today pays its debts." The Soviet foreign minister and the American ambassador were soon reduced to hurling insults at one another, and the Russians withdrew their offer of land for a new Monticello in Moscow. Bullitt's efforts to improve the situation by organizing polo matches and baseball games with Soviet officials had little effect. "The nub of the matter is this," he re-

---

[13] Bullitt to Roosevelt, January 1, 1934, in Bullitt, ed., *For the President*, pp. 72–73.

[14] Maddux, *Years of Estrangement*, pp. 27–43; Bishop, *The Roosevelt-Litvinov Negotiations*, pp. 152–178.

ported to the State Department: "If the Soviet Government should again become convinced that an attack by Japan was likely or imminent we should probably find Litvinov willing to reach an agreement on the basis of our proposals. So long as the Soviet Union feels completely secure I believe that no agreement acceptable to us will be acceptable to the authorities in Moscow."[15]

The final disillusionment, for Bullitt, came over the question of the Comintern's relationship with the Communist Party of the United States. Litvinov had indicated orally that he did not regard his agreement with Roosevelt as applying to Comintern activities, and it seems doubtful that administration officials really expected a cessation of communist activities in the United States. Roosevelt was under considerable domestic pressure to secure strict compliance with the agreement, however, and when plans for a seventh Comintern Congress became known in Moscow in the summer of 1935, Bullitt, with the State Department's approval, made it clear that Washington would regard participation by American communists as a violation of the Roosevelt-Litvinov pledge. Litvinov's only response was to feign ignorance of the forthcoming meeting.

The Comintern Congress did meet, American communists did participate, and Soviet newspapers published their attacks on the United States. Bullitt viewed these developments as "a flagrant violation of Litvinov's pledge to the President" and recommended, in retaliation, restrictions on Soviet visas and consular privileges. Roosevelt rejected these reprisals but did authorize a stiff note, released simultaneously to the press, threatening "most serious consequences" if the USSR failed to prevent further acts in violation of Litvinov's promise. The Russians responded predictably by disavowing responsibility for the Comintern and charging interference in Soviet internal affairs by anti-Bolshevik Russian émigrés in the United States. Soviet Ambassador Alexander Troyanovsky concluded the exchange somewhat less predictably with the Biblical interroga-

---

[15] Bullitt to Hull, March 28, May 21, June 16, 1934, *FR: Soviet Union*, pp. 74, 100, 109–111; Bullitt to Roosevelt, April 13 and August 5, 1934, in Bullitt, ed., *For the President*, pp. 83, 93.

tory: "Why beholdest thou the mote which is in thy brother's eye, but perceivest not the beam that is in thine own eye?"[16]

"It is perfectly clear, Bullitt wrote in July, 1935, "that to speak of 'normal relations' between the Soviet Union and any other country is to speak of something which does not and cannot exist." Litvinov, for once, agreed. He admitted to the American ambassador some months later that "there was no such thing as friendship or 'really friendly' relations between nations." The truth was that the United States wanted "to remain aloof from all active interest in international affairs." For this reason, he implied, friendly relations with the United States were not of great importance to the Soviet Union.[17]

Both sides had expected too much from recognition. The Russians anticipated that establishing formal relations with the United States would help counterbalance the growing power of Germany and Japan. Convinced that the United States had been "compelled," for similar reasons, to deal with the Russians, Kremlin officials failed to understand why American diplomats attached greater importance to strict implementation of the Roosevelt-Litvinov agreements than to common action against the aggressors. Only gradually did they come to realize that the Roosevelt administration's preoccupation with unpaid debts and Comintern activities had been sincere; that, because of the depth of American isolationism, whatever prospects of cooperation against aggression Roosevelt had held out lay more in the realm of rhetoric than reality.[18]

For the Americans, recognition had been expected to achieve what nonrecognition had not: a fundamental change in the external behavior of the Soviet Union which would make it an acceptable member of the international community. The new policy turned out to be no more successful than its predecessor, for the simple reason that neither the existence nor absence of relations with the United States provided sufficient incentive to

---

[16] *FR: Soviet Union*, pp. 221–223, 244–245. See also Bishop, *The Roosevelt-Litvinov Agreements*, pp. 31, 44–53; and Bennett, *Franklin D. Roosevelt and the Search for Security*, pp. 61–68.

[17] Bullitt to R. Walton Moore, July 15, 1935, and to Hull, November 9, 1935, *FR: Soviet Union*, pp. 134, 265.

[18] On this point, see Keith David Eagles, "Ambassador Joseph E. Davies and American-Soviet Relations, 1937–1941" (Ph. D. Dissertation, University of Minnesota, 1966), pp. 49–50.

Stalin to change the internal structure of his regime, upon which foreign policy ultimately depended. The Americans' preconditions for recognition meant little, partly because they were so vaguely worded as to be susceptible of varying interpretations, partly because, once recognition had been granted, there was no sure way to compel compliance.[19] Both sides, in sum, exaggerated the effects establishing formal diplomatic relations would have on the other; the failure of the Roosevelt-Litvinov agreements must be seen, in the end, as a triumph of internal over external considerations in foreign policy.

## III

The disillusionment that followed the breakdown of negotiations on the debt question coincided with the beginning of the massive purges that were to mark the consolidation of Stalin's dictatorship. It was a period when surface appearances corresponded only sporadically with what was in fact taking place: it is symptomatic that the new Soviet constitution of 1936, guaranteeing free elections and the rights of Soviet citizens, went into effect four months after the first great purge trial and one month before the second. This disparity between appearance and reality made it unusually difficult for American observers to come to grips with the phenomenon of Stalinism.

There was by this time a core of professionally trained Russian experts on the staff of the American embassy in Moscow, among them George F. Kennan and Charles E. Bohlen, both of whom would later play a significant role in shaping United States policy toward the Soviet Union. Another influential career diplomat, Loy W. Henderson, though not specifically a Russian specialist, served in Moscow from 1934 to 1938. These officials had, in turn, been much influenced by the long-time chief of the State Department's Division of East European Affairs, Robert F. Kelley. The purport of their voluminous reports back to Washington during this period was that there existed little reliable basis for cooperation with the Soviet Union, even against potential adversaries. As Kennan later put it, "Never— neither then nor at any later date—did I consider the Soviet

---

[19] Bishop, *The Roosevelt-Litvinov Agreements*, p. 15.

Union a fit ally or associate, actual or potential, for this country."[20]

The Soviet specialists based this view in part on ideological considerations. "I am convinced," Henderson wrote in 1936, "that the establishment of a Union of World Soviet Socialist Republics is still the ultimate objective of Soviet foreign policy." Henderson conceded that the prospect of world revolution was not as bright, in the eyes of Russian leaders, as it once had been. He even raised the possibility that "Soviet leaders might eventually become so engrossed in the accomplishment of their more immediate objectives that they will lose sight of it altogether." But, for the moment, the Soviet Union was clearly seeking to control revolutionary movements throughout the world, both to promote its own foreign policy interests and also out of "fear that if it loses all guidance over those forces they are likely to develop into implacable foes of the Soviet Union and the Soviet system." Such considerations could not be ignored in assessing bases for cooperation between Washington and Moscow.[21]

Henderson and his colleagues did not go so far as to share the view Bullitt had come to by this time—that relations with the Soviet Union were merely "a subordinate part of the problem presented by communism as a militant faith designed to produce world revolution and the 'liquidation, ' (that is to say, murder) of all non-believers."[22] The Soviet specialists always tended to see ideology more as the instrument rather than the determinant of Stalin's policy. Still, international communism was a matter of sufficient concern to cause embassy experts to discount Moscow's sincerity in seeking a united front against the aggressors. Henderson, for example, interpreted Russian aid to the Spanish Republicans as a demonstration of sympathy for the world revolutionary movement, while Kennan regarded

---

[20] George F. Kennan, *Memoirs: 1925–1950* (Boston: 1967), p. 57. See also Thomas R. Maddux, "American Diplomats and the Soviet Experiment: The View from the Moscow Embassy, 1934–1939," *South Atlantic Quarterly*, LXXIV(Autumn, 1975), 470–471; Franz Knipping, *Die Amerikanische Russlandpolitik in der Zeit des Hitler-Stalin-Pakts, 1939–1941* (Tübingen: 1974), pp. 25–26.

[21] Henderson to Hull, November 16, 1936, *FR: Soviet Union*, pp. 310–311, 313. See also Baer, ed., *Henderson Memoirs*, pp. 463–470.

[22] Bullitt to Hull, April 20, 1936, *FR: Soviet Union*, p. 292.

Chinese Communist efforts to form an anti-Japanese coalition with Chiang Kai-shek as an attempt by Moscow, using Trojan horse tactics, to take over China.[23] In neither case were these assessments necessarily in error as far as Moscow's ultimate objectives were concerned. But they did downplay more than appears warranted in retrospect the Kremlin's interest in resisting Germany and Japan.

Another problem that served to inhibit Soviet-American cooperation, in the view of the Russian specialists, was the Stalin regime's increasing suspicion of foreigners. Xenophobia was, of course, nothing new in Russia—Bullitt in 1936 submitted a long report on the subject taken entirely from the dispatches of Neill Brown, the American minister in St. Petersburg in the early 1850s. But the scope and intensity of Stalin's antiforeign campaign soon surpassed anything achieved by Nicholas I. It took the form of restrictions on travel, intimidation of Soviet citizens to discourage contacts with outsiders, discriminatory currency exchange rates, repeated attempts to penetrate embassy security, and even, in 1937, an accusation that an American cotton expert had tried to import the boll weevil into Soviet Turkestan. "One is inclined to wonder," Henderson observed, "whether, in view of the manner in which the Soviet Government is inculcating hatred for, and suspicion of, all foreigners,... that Government seriously desires genuinely friendly relations between the Soviet Union and any other country."[24]

The brutal purges of the 1936–1938 period only confirmed this view. Although skeptical of official charges that there had been a conspiracy directed against Stalin's regime, the embassy staff despaired of proving their falsity. "The Russian mind," Kennan noted, "sometimes carries both truth and falsehood to such infinite extremes that they eventually meet in space, like parallel lines, and it is no longer possible to distinguish between them." They were unanimous, however, in their belief that these internal upheavals had so weakened the Soviet government and military that it would be difficult, in the immedi-

---

[23] Henderson to Hull, October 17, 1936, FR: 1936, II, 540; Dorothy Borg, *The United States and the Far Eastern Crisis of 1933–1938* (Cambridge, Massachusetts: 1964), pp. 232–234.
[24] Henderson to Hull, August 20, 1937, FR: *Soviet Union*, p. 390. See also Bullitt to Hull, March 4, 1936, ibid., pp. 289–291.

ate future, for Moscow to play a major role in world affairs. And despite their training, which encouraged a dispassionate and reasoned approach to events, the embassy staff could not help reacting with horror and repugnance at the events they were witnessing. "I felt that the top of my head was coming off," Bohlen recalled, after sitting through the sentencing of eighteen leading Bolsheviks "to be shot." "So prolonged and incessant were the hammer-blow impressions," Kennan later wrote, "each more outrageous and heartrending than the other —that the effect was never to leave me. Its imprint on my political judgment was one that would place me at odds with official thinking in Washington for at least a decade thereafter."[25]

There was another interpretation of events in the Soviet Union, however, and this was provided by Bullitt's successor, Joseph E. Davies, a wealthy lawyer with no diplomatic experience whom Roosevelt named ambassador to the Soviet Union in November 1936. Davies went to Russia at a time when relations were so bad that they could hardly do anything but improve. Instructed by the President to evaluate elements of strength in the Soviet system, Davies saw what he wanted to see, and his impressions, often very different from those of his staff, formed the basis of his reports back to Washington. Certain that the combination of capitalism and nationalism constituted the strongest possible base of national power, Davies persuaded himself that both were developing inside the Soviet Union. Revolutionary internationalism, he argued, was a thing of the past:

To maintain its existence, this Government has to apply capitalistic principles. Otherwise it will fail and be overthrown. ... I expect to see this Government, while professing devotion to Communism, move constantly more to the Right, in practice, just as it has for the past eight years.

Fabian socialism, Davies thought, might be the end product of Stalin's gradual evolution away from communism.[26]

---

[25] Kennan memorandum, February 13, 1937, *FR: Soviet Union*, p. 369; Charles E. Bohlen, *Witness to History, 1929–1969* (New York: 1973), p. 51; Kennan, *Memoirs; 1925–1950*, p. 70.

[26] Davies to Hull, June 6, 1938, *FR: Soviet Union*, p. 557. See also Eagles, "Davies," pp. 208–212; and Maddux, *Years of Estrangement*, pp. 57–59.

Like his staff, Davies found the purges "horrifying." Stalin's tyranny continued indefinitely, he argued, would provoke the Russian people into destroying their own government. But, unlike his subordinates, Davies saw legitimate reasons for the terror. Foreign plots against the government had been real, in his view; the trials and the terror that surrounded them had been an unpleasant necessity. ("Great revolutions cannot be projected by spraying perfume," he quoted Soviet officials as arguing). Stalin and his associates were wrapping themselves "in the mantle of angels to serve the devil. They are undoubtedly a strong, able group of ruthless idealists. But tyranny is tyranny." Despite this ambivalence, Davies did not see the purges as significantly weakening the Soviet Union, because of its almost unlimited supplies of manpower and massive industrial base. Nor did these events preclude cooperation against the aggressors: the purges had, after all, been directed against German and Japanese influences. An isolated Soviet Union might threaten world economic and political security, but "friendly relations in the future may be of great general value."[27]

Both Davies and his staff agreed that, despite all difficulties, diplomatic relations with the Soviet Union should be maintained. Whatever happened to Stalin's regime, the USSR was too important to ignore; bad relations were better than no relations at all. But the ambassador and the career diplomats disagreed sharply over the question of whether two governments with such diametrically opposed political systems could find any basis for joint action in the pursuit of common interests. The question has bedeviled Soviet-American relations ever since. The negative answer of Kennan, Bohlen, and Henderson would, in time, gain its hearing, but for the moment it was Davies' affirmative reply that found a response where it counted—in the White House.

---

[27] Davies to Hull, April 1 and June 6, 1938, *FR: Soviet Union*, pp. 546, 549, 557–559. See also Eagles, "Davies," pp. 216–225, 250–251; Richard H. Ullman, "The Davies Mission and United States-Soviet Relations, 1937–1941," *World Politics*, IX(January, 1957), 220–239; and James S. Herndon and Joseph O. Baylen, "Col. Philip R. Faymonville and the Red Army, 1934–43," *Slavic Review*, XXXIV(September, 1975), 493–499.

IV

Roosevelt had, of course, regretted the failure of his agreement with Litvinov, but he never let his disappointment carry him to the point of accepting Bullitt's view that Soviet communism posed a greater danger to the world than German fascism. Whatever its methods, the president took the view that the ultimate intentions of communism were meritorious—the improvement of the human condition. And he had never given up his original hope of working with the Russians to increase the strain under which Germany and Japan operated.[28] Accordingly, Roosevelt found Davies' assessment of the Russian situation more credible than that of the State Department. (It seems doubtful that the president ever saw the reports of the Moscow embassy staff, but he was familiar with the position of top State Department officials, which paralleled theirs.) And, following his triumphant reelection in 1936, he took steps to try to rebuild the briefly cordial Soviet-American relationship.

Davies' appointment in November, 1936, had been one of those steps. The president instructed his new ambassador not to raise the old issue of debts but to concentrate on learning as much as possible about the Soviet Union's economic and military potential, with a view toward determining which side Moscow would likely support in the event of a European war. Davies resolved, presumably with the president's approval, to approach his mission "free from prejudice and with an open mind." In what was probably not an unrelated move, Roosevelt authorized, or at least did not oppose, a reorganization of the State Department in the spring of 1937 which eliminated Robert Kelley's Division of East European Affairs, a major center of skepticism regarding the possibility of cooperation with the Russians.[29]

Later that year, concerned about the resumption of Sino-Japanese hostilities, Roosevelt began toying with ideas for organizing resistance to Japan. These included a refusal to invoke

---

[28] Knipping, *Die Amerikanische Russlandpolitik*, pp. 5–6; Sumner Welles, *Where Are We Heading?* (New York: 1946), pp. 37–38; William L. Langer and S. Everett Gleason, *The Challenge to Isolation: The World Crisis of 1937–1940 and American Foreign Policy* (New York: 1952), pp. 126–127.

[29] Joseph E. Davies, *Mission to Moscow* (New York: 1941), pp. xii–xiv, xvii, 6. See also Kennan, *Memoirs: 1925–1950*, pp. 83–85; Bohlen, *Witness to History*, pp. 39–41; and Maddux, *Years of Estrangement*, pp. 88–90.

provisions of the Neutrality Act, on the grounds that an arms embargo would only hurt China, and the October 5 "quarantine speech," in which he called for joint action against the aggressors. They also involved highly tentative discussions with the State Department on the feasibility of United States collaboration with the British, the French, and the Russians to preserve peace in East Asia. Precisely what Roosevelt had in mind is not clear, but State's reaction, despite the abolition of Kelley's division, was not favorable. Secretary Hull and his advisers distrusted Soviet intentions in China, suspected Moscow of seeking a Japanese-American war, and, in the light of the purges, doubted the effectiveness of the Red Army in any East Asian conflict. Roosevelt did not object when the department sought unsuccessfully to block Soviet participation at the Brussels Conference on East Asia in November, or when United States representatives at that conference rebuffed inquiries from Litvinov about prospects for common action against Japan.[30]

The bombing of the American gunboat *Panay* in December, however, pushed Roosevelt again toward the idea of an anti-Japanese coalition. The president secretly proposed to the British consideration of a naval blockade against Japan, and dispatched Captain Royal E. Ingersoll, director of the Navy's War Plans Division, to London to discuss the matter. He also instructed Ambassador Davies, in January, 1938, to suggest to the Russians an exchange of military information regarding Pacific problems in general, and Japan in particular. Significantly, Roosevelt instructed Davies to keep this initiative secret from both the State Department and the Moscow embassy staff. Litvinov responded lukewarmly to Davies's proposal, complaining that without a definite pact there seemed to be little purpose to the plan, but in June, Stalin himself endorsed it. By this time, though, the Ingersoll mission had become public and Roosevelt, fearing further revelations, refused to pursue the initiative.[31]

The president had, however, given the Russians reason to hope that military cooperation might be possible in another

---

[30] Maddux, *Years of Estrangement*, pp. 91–96; Eagles, "Davies," pp. 178–192.

[31] Davies to Hull, January 17, 1939, *FR: Soviet Union*, pp. 596–597. See also Maddux, *Years of Estrangement*, pp. 96–97; Langer and Gleason, *The Challenge to Isolation*, p. 127; and John McVickar Haight, "Franklin D. Roosevelt and a Naval Quarantine of Japan," *Pacific Historical Review*, XL(May, 1971), 203–226.

area. In November, 1936, the Soviet government began a campaign, which it was to pursue with remarkable patience and tenacity over the next three years, to have private American firms construct warships for the Soviet navy. Stalin was seeking, at this time, to build a substantial balanced fleet, but the USSR lacked the facilities for constructing large vessels, and, for political reasons, the use of German, Japanese, British, or French firms was impractical. The proposal required Washington's approval, since it involved the release of confidential specifications, but the State Department and the White House quickly made it clear that they had no objections. Even Robert Kelley approved, on the grounds that if the Soviet Union evolved eventually "into a purely national Government, the strengthening of the naval forces of the Soviet Union would not run counter to the national interests of the United States."[32]

However, the Navy Department, and, in particular, Admiral William D. Leahy, Chief of Naval Operations, had deep reservations about the propriety both of building foreign warships in the United States and of aiding a communist country. Navy officials privately let it be known that American firms cooperating with the Russians might not, in the future, receive Navy contracts, and this threat was enough to halt all action on the proposal. The Russians made repeated efforts to revive it, even promising to station the vessels in question at Vladivostok, where they could be used against the Japanese, but without success. Roosevelt complained in May, 1939, of the Navy's tendency to consider "as a military secret every possible item of naval equipment" and reiterated that he "wanted this deal...to go through." But by this time, domestic shipbuilding capacity was almost wholly committed to American naval rearmament, and this situation, together with the rapid deterioration in Soviet-American relations that followed the Nazi-Soviet Pact in August, prevented further action.[33]

---

[32] Kelley memorandum of March 24, 1937, FR: Soviet Union, p. 466.

[33] The Soviet effort to have warships built in the United States is fully documented in FR: Soviet Union, pp. 457–490, 670–707, 869–903. See also Robert Ward Herrick, *Soviet Naval Strategy: Fifty Years of Theory and Practice* (Annapolis: 1968), pp. 36–38; and Thomas R. Maddux, "United States-Soviet Naval Relations in the 1930's: The Soviet Union's Efforts to Purchase Naval Vessels," *Naval War College Review*, XXIX(Fall, 1976), 28–37.

Given presently available evidence, it is difficult to know how seriously the Russians regarded prospects for American participation in an anti-Japanese coalition. Certainly the petty harassment of American diplomats in the Soviet Union continued throughout this period, and the Russians were never willing to make significant compromises on debts. Stalin does appear to have attached great importance to his plan for the construction of warships by American firms—otherwise, it is difficult to account for the persistence with which he pursued that objective, in the face of continual discouragement. Nor does it seem likely that Soviet officials had abandoned the hopes they had held in 1933 for diplomatic cooperation in East Asia, though what form they expected it to take remains unclear.[34]

In fact, however, the possibility of joint Soviet-American action of any kind was remote. Fears of "entanglements" were still strong enough to inhibit positive moves by the Roosevelt administration to resist the aggressors. And even if these sentiments had not been a problem, there still would have been significant constraints on the Soviet-American relationship. For one thing, although Roosevelt worried about the rise of Germany and Japan, he did not become clear in his own mind until after Munich as to whether accommodation or resistance was the best way to handle these countries.[35] Nor was he willing to devote the kind of sustained attention to foreign affairs that would have allowed him to override objections to Soviet-American cooperation within the State and Navy Departments. And even if all these impediments had been removed, there still would have been the problem of internal differences between the two countries—differences that had never been more obvious than they were in the late 1930s.

The reality of the situation was simply that Stalin, in his desperate effort to secure his regime at all costs against internal challenge, had made the Soviet Union in the eyes of the exter-

---

[34] For the general Soviet attitude on collective security during this period, see Jonathan Haslam, *The Soviet Union and the Struggle for Collective Security in Europe, 1933–39* (New York: 1984); and Jiri Hochman, *The Soviet Union and the Failure of Collective Security, 1934–1938* (Ithaca: 1984).

[35] See, on this point, Dallek, *Franklin D. Roosevelt and American Foreign Policy*, pp. 161–166.

nal world an unacceptable partner in the task of keeping peace. Englishmen, Frenchmen, Poles, and Czechs were no more willing to join in Litvinov's anti-fascist crusade than were Americans, whose interests were far less directly engaged. The Munich agreement of September, 1938, represented the triumph of a widely shared view that communism was at least as dangerous as fascism, if not more so. It was a view that was to persist until Hitler's violation of that agreement six months later made his ultimate intentions clear. But by that time the Soviet Union had decided that, in the absence of cooperation from the West, the best chance of preventing war lay in collaboration with Hitler, not resistance to him.

## V

Despite its revolutionary implications for Russian foreign policy, the Nazi-Soviet Pact of August, 1939, came as no surprise in Washington. Davies had expressed fears of a German-Russian rapprochement if the West made no effort to join with the USSR in resisting the aggressors, and rumors of such a reconciliation periodically reached the Moscow embassy staff. During the summer of 1939, leaks from a German diplomat in that city gave United States officials the opportunity to monitor the secret Ribbentrop-Molotov negotiations on almost a day-by-day basis.[36] Still, the pact, when it came, was a bitter disappointment to those who had hoped for some improvement in Soviet-American relations. For those who had thought such improvement unlikely, it was a striking confirmation of their belief that the Russians could not be trusted.

Stalin's actions during the next six months only reinforced that judgment. The Nazi-Soviet Pact made it possible for Hitler, on September 1, to invade Poland, an action which, in turn, provoked British and French declarations of war. On September 17, in accordance with secret provisions of that pact, the Red Army entered Poland from the East, seizing almost half the country. By the end of October, the Russians had demanded

---

[36] Bohlen, *Witness to History*, pp. 67–87. See also *FR: Soviet Union*, pp. 373, 555, 584, 750; *FR: 1939*, I, 312–337; Davies, *Mission to Moscow*, pp. 450, 453–454; and Johnnie von Herwarth with S. Frederick Starr, *Against Two Evils: Memoirs of a Diplomat-Soldier during the Third Reich* (London: 1981), pp. 145–167.

and obtained base rights in the Baltic states of Latvia, Lithuania, and Estonia. Finland's refusal to grant similar rights and boundary concessions brought about a Soviet invasion of that country on November 30, but unexpected resistance delayed the Red Army's victory until the following March. By the summer of 1940, Stalin had extracted territorial concessions from the Rumanians as well and had incorporated the Baltic states into the Soviet Union. These boundary changes regained for the Russians most of the territory lost during the Revolution and Civil War, but the fact that they had been achieved by intimidation and force made Moscow's actions seem, in the eyes of Western observers, little different from those of the Germans or the Japanese.

Nonetheless, the Roosevelt administration chose quite deliberately to make a fundamental distinction between the behavior of the Soviet Union and that of Germany and Japan. Tentatively at first, but by the summer of 1940 with increasing purposefulness, official Washington moved toward a strategy of seeking to undermine the Hitler-Stalin alliance while at the same time working to prevent a similar relationship from developing between Moscow and Tokyo.[37]

There had been intimations from the first that the Nazi-Soviet association could not last. "It reverses the processes of men's minds in a way which I do not believe can be permanent," Assistant Secretary of State Adolf Berle noted in September 1939; "winning or losing, that combination must eventually break up." The problem, though, was to determine how long such a development might take. Reports from the Moscow embassy stressed Russian-German cooperation, giving little reason to hope for an early break. State Department officials worried that the Hitler-Stalin split might come only after the Germans had defeated the Western democracies, and that the eventual outcome would be the Soviet domination of Europe. To some, including Assistant Secretary of State Breckinridge Long and Joseph P. Kennedy, United States ambassador to Great Britain, such thoughts suggested the wisdom of encouraging the British and French to make peace with Hitler.

---

[37] Knipping, *Die Amerikanische Russlandpolitik*, pp. 34–35; Maddux, *Years of Estrangement*, pp. 107–113.

"It would be a shame," Long noted, "[to] continue a war which would mean the victory of Communism in Europe and confront us with our eventual enemy—Russia."[38]

For Roosevelt, however, the ultimate enemy had always been Germany. Accordingly, he categorically refused to promote negotiations with Hitler to keep Stalin out of Europe, and set about doing what was possible, within the framework of existing neutrality legislation, to aid the Western democracies. At the same time, he avoided actions that might unnecessarily antagonize the Russians. Despite its use of military force against Poland, Roosevelt chose not to regard the Soviet Union as a belligerent and so avoided invoking the arms embargo which had, since September, been in effect against Germany and its opponents. Nor did the administration make an issue over Soviet demands on the Baltic states, which, for the moment, remained nominally independent. In East Asia, Roosevelt encouraged the Chinese to maintain good relations with Moscow, with a view, as he put it, "to keep[ing] Russia and Japan apart."[39]

But the Soviet invasion of Finland on November 30, 1939, greatly complicated Roosevelt's strategy. Coming at a time when the war between Germany and the Allies had lapsed into inactivity, the assault received full media coverage in the United States. Finland quickly become an object of sympathy, because not only had the Russians launched an unprovoked attack against a small democracy with close ethnic ties to the United States; they had also managed to invade the only European country that had maintained regular payments on its World War I debts. The Russians further compounded their problems by failing to defeat the Finns quickly, thereby earning for themselves the reputation not only of predators but of inefficient ones at that.

---

[38] Berle Diary, September 3, 1939, quoted in Langer and Gleason, *The Challenge to Isolation*, p. 203; Long Diary, October 11, 1939, Fred L. Israel, ed., *The War Diary of Breckinridge Long* (Lincoln: 1966), p. 27. See also Kennedy to Hull, September 11 and 25, 1939, *FR: 1939*, I, 423–424, 454.

[39] Maddux, *Years of Estrangement*, p. 111. See also Langer and Gleason, *The Challenge to Isolation*, pp. 245, 320–321; John Morton Blum, *From the Morgenthau Diaries: Years of Urgency, 1938–1941* (Boston: 1965), p. 124; Robert A. Divine, *Roosevelt and World War II* (Baltimore: 1969), p. 78.

Roosevelt made no attempt to conceal his disgust. "The whole of the United States is not only horrified but thoroughly angry," he wrote, on November 30. "People are asking why one should have anything to do with the present Soviet leaders because their idea of civilization and human happiness is so totally different from ours." Congress had repealed the arms embargo by this time, but after Soviet planes bombed Finnish cities, the president did invoke a "moral embargo," discouraging American firms from shipping aircraft and related equipment to the USSR. On December 22, he instructed the State Department to let the Russians know that their attitude showed "such a complete disregard for the ordinary politeness and amenities between civilized governments that the President honestly wonders whether the Soviet Government considers it worthwhile to continue diplomatic relations." And on February 10, 1940, he publicly characterized the USSR as a "dictatorship as absolute as any other dictatorship in the world."[40]

Nonetheless, the president held fast against pressure, which quickly became considerable, to break relations with the Soviet Union or to place the Russians in the same category with Nazi Germany. Despite a strong personal inclination to help the Finns, Roosevelt yielded to Hull's objections against sending surplus military equipment and agreed to refer consideration of a loan to Congress, which failed to act until it was too late. The administration's restraint in this matter may have been motivated as much by fear of isolationist criticism as by the hope of playing the Russians off against the Germans, but the latter consideration was present as well and was not inconsistent with the first.[41] Settlement of the Russo-Finnish War in March, 1940, together with the German invasion of Denmark and Norway in April and the attack on France and the Low Countries in May, reinforced Roosevelt's belief that the Germans were more dangerous than the Russians. Following France's unexpectedly quick defeat in June, the State Department, with

---

[40] Roosevelt to Joseph Grew, November 30, 1939, in Elliott Roosevelt, ed., *F. D. R.: His Personal Letters, 1928–1945* (New York: 1950), II, 961; Roosevelt to Hull and Welles, December 22, 1939, *FR: Soviet Union*, p. 869; Samuel I. Rosenman, ed., *The Public Papers and Addresses of Franklin D. Roosevelt* (New York: 1938–1950), IX, 93.

[41] Maddux, *Years of Estrangement*, pp. 121–122.

the president's approval, began a concerted effort to try to improve United States relations with the Soviet Union.

This initiative took the form of a long series of negotiations, beginning in late July, 1940, between Under Secretary of State Sumner Welles and Constantine Oumansky, the Soviet ambassador to the United States. The atmosphere under which these talks were conducted was hardly promising. The Russians had just completed their absorption of the Baltic states into the Soviet Union, and the administration had responded by freezing assets of those countries in the United States and by continuing to recognize them as independent states. The moral embargo on aircraft equipment remained in effect, and with American rearmament getting under way, the Russians experienced increasing difficulties in obtaining export licenses for other strategic materials which they wanted to purchase. Soviet Foreign Minister Molotov was not exaggerating the situation when he commented in a speech on August 1: "I will not dwell on our relations with the United States of America, if only for the reason that there is nothing good that can be said about them."[42]

But both Moscow and Washington had by this time developed enough common concerns to keep the negotiations going. The United States had committed itself to providing all aid to Britain short of war; uncertainty on Germany's part about Russian intentions would obviously ease Britain's task. Uncertainty might also be useful in dealing with Japan, which was attempting to settle its differences with the Soviet Union to facilitate expansion into Southeast Asia. For the Russians, Hitler's rapid victories upset expectations that the Germans would be tied down in Western Europe for some time to come, while growing German activity in the Balkans and Finland hinted at the direction in which Hitler might move next. The Tripartite Pact, signed late in September, 1940, further surprised the Russians, raising the possibility of a Berlin-Rome-Tokyo axis directed against Moscow.[43] Stalin was by no means ready to break his ties with Hitler at this stage, but this series of events did make clear the advantages of projecting a bit of unpre-

---

[42] Molotov speech of August 1, 1940, Degras, ed., *Soviet Documents*, III, 468. For the Welles-Oumansky talks, see Maddux, *Years of Estrangement*, pp. 128–146.

[43] Ulam, *Expansion and Coexistence*, pp. 296–303.

dictability himself. For this purpose, the Welles-Oumansky negotiations were useful.

These talks did not go smoothly. Oumansky's abrasive personality alone was enough to try the patience of any diplomat, and he remained unrepentant in his insistence that the United States recognize Soviet territorial conquests and sell the Russians whatever was necessary for their defense efforts. Still, the discussions did provide Washington with assurances that the Russians had no immediate plans to align themselves with the Japanese; on its part, the Roosevelt administration agreed early in 1941 to end the moral embargo. Few concrete results grew out of these exchanges, but the psychological atmosphere had definitely improved. Even Molotov admitted that the United States had demonstrated "in a very small way" a desire to improve relations with the Soviet Union.[44]

The Welles-Oumansky negotiations were not popular with Soviet specialists in the Department of State or in the Moscow embassy. The tendency in those quarters had been to stress Russo-German solidarity and to warn strongly against making unilateral concessions which Moscow would only interpret as a sign of weakness. The Russians feared a German attack, Ambassador Laurence A. Steinhardt argued in a letter from Moscow in October, 1940, but they would never risk such an attack merely to improve relations with the United States or Great Britain. Similarly, in East Asia, the true Soviet interest was to get the United States embroiled in a war with Japan from which only the Russians would benefit. "If I am correct in this interpretation," Steinhardt noted, ". . . the best policy to pursue is one of aloofness, indicating strength, rather than an approach which can have no prospect of success."[45]

But the Russians were not to enjoy the luxury of deciding whether to remain aligned with Germany. Hitler had been planning an invasion of the Soviet Union since the summer of 1940, and by January, 1941, the American embassy in Berlin, with the help of a disaffected official in the German foreign ministry, had obtained hard evidence to this effect. Steinhardt opposed telling the Russians, on the grounds that the informa-

---

[44] *FR: 1940*, III, 440.
[45] Steinhardt to Henderson, October 20, 1940, ibid., p. 407.

tion would encourage them to settle their differences with Japan and try to appease Hitler, but Welles, presumably with Roosevelt's approval, went ahead. On March 1, 1941, he gave Oumansky the news. "Oumansky turned very white," Welles recalled, and then briefly expressed thanks. Further exchanges with Welles provided additional information, which the Russians were able to confirm from the British and from their own intelligence service.[46] As a result, by the spring of 1941, Stalin had clear indications of what to expect.

Meanwhile, the Roosevelt administration was working to ensure that the United States could assist the Russians if it chose to when the German invasion came. In January, 1941, the president had submitted the Lend-Lease Act to Congress. The bill's primary purpose was to facilitate aid to Great Britain, but Roosevelt carefully insisted on having language inserted authorizing assistance to *any* country whose defense he deemed vital to that of the United States. Congressional critics pointed out that such wording would make it possible to aid even the Soviet Union, however remote that prospect might seem, but Roosevelt, in possession by now of secret information suggesting that the prospect was not remote at all, refused to accept amendments specifically excluding the USSR. The bill passed on this basis, and Roosevelt signed it on March 11, slightly more than a week after Welles had informed Oumansky of the impending German attack.[47]

If the Russians were grateful for the information the Americans had provided them or for Roosevelt's cautious handling of the Lend-Lease bill, they did painfully little to show it. Instead, as Steinhardt had predicted, Stalin moved to appease Berlin and repair his relations with Tokyo. The Soviet dictator made no protest early in April when Hitler invaded Yugoslavia one day after the Russians had signed a treaty of friendship

---

[46] *FR: 1941*, I, 712–714; Summer Welles, *The Time for Decision* (New York: 1944), pp. 170–171; William L. Langer and S. Everett Gleason, *The Undeclared War: 1940–1941* (New York: 1953), pp. 336–345; James E. McSherry, *Stalin, Hitler, and Europe* (Cleveland: 1970), II, 202–203, 218–220; Waldo Heinrichs, *Threshold of War: Franklin D. Roosevelt and American Entry into World War II* (New York: 1988), pp. 54–56.

[47] Raymond H. Dawson, *The Decision to Aid Russia, 1941: Foreign Policy and Domestic Politics* (Chapel Hill: 1959), pp. 22–41.

with that country. Later that month, the Soviet Union negotiated a treaty with Japan pledging both countries to remain neutral if the other became involved in war with a third power.
"Now that the Soviet Union and Japan have arranged their
affairs," Stalin told the departing Japanese foreign minister,
"Japan will straighten out the East, and the Soviet Union and
Germany will take care of Europe and later on between them
they will take care of the Americans." In May, the Russians
withdrew recognition from the Norwegian, Belgian, and
Yugoslav governments-in-exile, all of them victims of German
aggression. Soviet economic deliveries to Germany were actually increased in the weeks before the German attack, and on
June 14, a week before the invasion, TASS branded as an "obvious absurdity" rumors of an impending Russo-German war.[48]

The Roosevelt administration's policy of seeking to undermine the Hitler-Stalin alliance by improving relations with
Moscow had not been easy to maintain, given the contempt the
Russians showed for world opinion during their period of alignment with Germany, given the intensely hostile American public reaction to their behavior. Nor can it be said that the policy
was successful—Stalin, after all, clung to his pact with Hitler
until after German troops had begun marching into the Soviet
Union. But the fact that the effort was made did ease problems
of Soviet-American cooperation after June 22, 1941. It also provides interesting evidence that American policymakers, are,
from time to time, capable of balancing interests against principles with some degree of sophistication and realism.

---

[48] McSherry, *Stalin, Hitler, and Europe*, II, 209–221; Ulam, *Expansion and Coexistence*, pp. 307–311. A recent Soviet account acknowledges that: "Some information about nazi Germany's preparations for an attack on the USSR was received by the Soviet government also from foreign sources, but it had to reckon
with the fact that any information coming from the US and British governments
was from countries that were pursuing imperialist aims and had repeatedly
demonstrated their hostility towards the USSR." [Pavel Sevostyanov, *Before the
Nazi Invasion: Soviet Diplomacy in September 1939–June 1941*, translated by David
Skvirsky (Moscow: 1984), p. 292.]

CHAPTER VI

# The Grand Alliance: 1941–1945

A FUNDAMENTAL PRINCIPLE IN THE CONDUCT OF INTERNA-
TIONAL RELATIONS, it has been argued, is that great nations
should not unnecessarily increase the number of adversaries
with which they have to deal.[1] Like most principles of strategy
and diplomacy, this one appears self-evident when stated.
Practical implementation, however, has been surprisingly infre-
quent. A rare demonstration of the principle correctly applied
can be found in Roosevelt's policy of trying to maintain some
semblance of friendly relations with the Soviet Union during
the difficult period from September 1939 through June 1941. For
an egregious example of a failure to apply the principle, one
need only turn to Hitler's diplomacy between June and
December of 1941, a period which saw him perform the remarkable feat, within six months, of declaring war on *both* the Soviet
Union and the United States. The result was to make possible
the association of the United States, Great Britain, and the Soviet Union in what Winston Churchill called a "Grand Alliance"
against their common German foe.

I

There is great irony in the fact that Stalin, who habitually
trusted no one, was virtually the last person in a position of
high responsibility to become convinced of Hitler's intention to
attack the Soviet Union. Soviet intelligence had picked up nu-
merous indications that an invasion was imminent, and both
the Americans and the British had warned the Russians as well.

---

[1] See Frederick H. Hartmann, *The Relations of Nations*, Fourth Edition (New
York: 1973), pp. x, 82–83.

But intelligence is no better than the preconceptions national leaders bring to its evaluation. Wanting to believe that his policy of buying time for Russia had not failed, Stalin refused until the very night of the attack to allow defensive preparations, with the result that the Soviet Union suffered such severe early losses in men, equipment, and territory as to make problematic its continuation in the war.[2]

Few in Washington failed to recognize the earthshaking implications of the Russo-German conflict, but there was from the start disagreement as to what to do about it. Obviously, it could only benefit the Anglo-American cause to have Britain's chief enemy tied down in the East. But if, as seemed likely, the Russians collapsed as Hitler's previous victims had done, then the British would have enjoyed at best a temporary respite. Any aid sent to Russia would only detract from Britain's ability to repel the renewed German offensive which would soon be hurled against it. If, on the other hand, there could be assurance that the Russians would fight, then it would clearly be advantageous to send them all possible aid. But a victory achieved in collaboration with the Soviet Union would raise serious questions about the peace settlement, since congruence between Stalin's war aims and those of his Western allies could not be assumed. Roosevelt's military and diplomatic advisers, accordingly, recommended caution in responding to this new development.[3]

From London, however, there came another view, powerfully and eloquently expressed. "I have only one purpose, the destruction of Hitler, and my life is much simplified thereby," Winston Churchill proclaimed. "If Hitler invaded Hell, I would make at least a favorable reference to the Devil in the House of Commons." Churchill had already sounded out Roosevelt on the idea of publicly welcoming Stalin as an ally if the Germans

---

[2] See, on the early course of the Russo-German war, Albert Seaton, *The Russo-German War, 1941–45* (London: 1971), pp. 70–152; Adam B. Ulam, *Stalin: The Man and His Era* (New York: 1973), pp. 536–539; Alexander Werth, *Russia at War, 1941–45* (New York: 1964), pp. 131–260; John Erickson, *The Road to Stalingrad* (New York: 1975), pp. 50–222.

[3] Langer and Gleason, *The Undeclared War*, pp. 537–541; Dawson, *The Decision to Aid Russia*, pp. 112–118; Maddux, *Years of Estrangement*, pp. 149–151; Heinrichs, *Threshold of War*, pp. 100–107.

attacked. The President had raised no objections; hence, on the evening of June 22, the British prime minister announced in a radio address that "any man or state who fights on against Nazidom will have our aid. Any man or state who marches with Hitler is our foe.... It follows, therefore, that we shall give whatever help we can to Russia and the Russian people."[4]

Roosevelt wholeheartedly agreed. To a greater extent than has been appreciated, his approach to strategy and diplomacy during the early years of World War II rested on a coherent set of assumptions, chief among which was the conviction that the security of the Western Hemisphere required Britain's survival as an independent state. It followed from this premise that, to the extent that other nations could be enlisted in the anti-German cause, Britain's plight would be eased thereby. Germany's invasion of the Soviet Union, he recognized, might provide such an opportunity. If it proved to be more than a di-version, he wrote on June 26, "it will mean the liberation of Europe from Nazi domination—and at the same time I do not think we need worry about any possibility of Russian domin-ation."[5]

This last observation reflected Roosevelt's long-standing be-lief that although the Soviet Union was a dictatorship, officially committed to a repellent ideology, it was by no means as dan-gerous to American interests as was Hitler's Germany. "Russia is defending its own soil," he argued. "At the present time Russia is defending its own soil," he argued. "At the present time Russia is in no sense the aggressor nation—Germany is." It was true, the president noted, that the Russians had, in the past, used propaganda to try to spread their influence beyond their borders. But the Germans used force as well, a major dif-ference. "The survival of Russia is less dangerous to religion, to the church as such, and to humanity in general than would be the survival of the German form of dictatorship," he wrote to Pope Pius XII on September 3. "I can't take communism nor can

---

[4] Winston S. Churchill, *The Grand Alliance* (Boston: 1950), pp. 369–372. See also Martin Gilbert, *Winston S. Churchill: Finest Hour, 1939–1941* (Boston: 1983), pp. 1117–1121.

[5] Roosevelt to William D. Leahy, June 26, 1941, in Roosevelt, ed., *F. D. R., His Personal Letters*, II, 1177.

you," he explained to former Ambassador Joseph Davies, "but to cross this bridge I would hold hands with the Devil."[6]

Roosevelt had the authority, under the Lend-Lease Act, to make American aid available to the Soviet Union, but Congress retained control of appropriations and could, if it disagreed with the president's decision, cut off funds. This possibility could not easily be dismissed, given public attitudes toward the Soviet Union in the summer of 1941. Russian actions in Poland, Finland, and the Baltic states during the previous two years had provoked bitterness which even the German attack could not be expected to dispel overnight. Isolationists found in the Soviet Union's association with Great Britain all the more reason why the United States should have nothing to do with the war. Even interventionists had difficulty in rationalizing cooperation with a power so recently Germany's ally. Public opinion polls reflected ambivalence: while an overwhelming majority of the public wanted the Russians to defeat the Germans, only a minority expected them to, or thought that the United States should assist them.[7]

The president thus had to move warily. He authorized an interim program of aid to Russia, but carefully refrained from financing it under Lend-Lease. Instead he worked behind the scenes to float trial balloons, disarm opponents, and allow pro-Soviet sentiment gradually to build. He encouraged former Ambassador Davies to speak in favor of all-out aid to the USSR and to publish a sanitized version of his largely pro-Russian 1937–1938 dispatches from Moscow. In hopes of defusing opposition from religious organizations, Roosevelt cajoled the Kremlin into issuing a largely meaningless affirmation of the right of religious freedom in the Soviet Union, and worked simultaneously through the Vatican to discourage criticism of Russia by American Catholics. When critics in Congress attempted in October to exclude the USSR from future Lend-Lease aid, the

---

[6] Roosevelt to Myron C. Taylor, September 1, 1941, Franklin D. Roosevelt Papers, PSF: Italy, Franklin D. Roosevelt Library, Hyde Park, New York; Roosevelt to Pius XII, September 3, 1941, in Roosevelt, ed., *F. D. R., His Personal Letters*, II, 1205; Eagles, "Davies," p. 328.

[7] Dawson, *The Decision to Aid Russia*, pp. 99–101, 218–230; George C. Herring, Jr., *Aid to Russia, 1941–1946: Strategy, Diplomacy, the Origins of the Cold War* (New York: 1973), pp. 6–7.

president lobbied quietly but successfully to defeat their amendment while refraining from public opposition.[8]

Roosevelt had, by this time, received a series of increasingly optimistic reports regarding the Russians' capacity to resist, notably from Harry Hopkins, who had gone to Moscow in late July, and from W. Averell Harriman, who visited the Soviet capital in September with Lord Beaverbrook, British minister of supply. American and British military leaders, who had at first resented the diversion of vital supplies to the USSR, had come now to see the strategic value of this course of action: "The maintenance of an active front in Russia," the American Joint Board noted in September, "offers by far the best opportunity for a successful land offensive against Germany." Public opinion polls detected decreasing opposition to helping the Russians, along with a growing conviction that a Soviet victory would be in American interests. Accordingly, President Roosevelt encountered little opposition when, on November 7, 1941, he made Lend-Lease available to the Kremlin, on the grounds that the defense of the Soviet Union was vital to the security of the United States.[9]

Events had, in the course of two years, transformed the Russians from aggressors to allies, a process greatly facilitated by Roosevelt's concentration on congruities of interests between the United States and the Soviet Union, not differences of principle. There remained only Washington's formal affiliation with what was already in fact a tripartite coalition against Germany. This came about in an unexpected way on December 7, 1941, when the Japanese, taking advantage of a major American failure of intelligence, attacked Pearl Harbor. Hitler's declaration of war followed within three days. Three weeks later, on January 1, 1942, representatives of the United States, Great Britain, and the Soviet Union signed in Washington a

---

[8] Dawson, *The Decision to Aid Russia*, pp. 230–238, 274–282; Langer and Gleason, *The Undeclared War*, pp. 793–798, 816–818; Herring, *Aid to Russia*, pp. 18–24. See also Elizabeth Kimball MacLean, "Joseph E. Davies and Soviet-American Relations, 1941–43," *Diplomatic History*, IV (Winter, 1980), 73–94.

[9] Joint Board estimate of September 11, 1941, quoted in Langer and Gleason, *The Undeclared War*, p. 792. See also Dawson, *The Decision to Aid Russia*, pp. 282–289; and W. Averell Harriman and Elie Abel, *Special Envoy to Churchill and Stalin, 1941–1946* (New York: 1975), pp. 82–105.

"Declaration of the United Nations," committing each signatory to fight until victory had been achieved.[10] Hitler's inadvertent creation, the Grand Alliance, was now complete.

## II

Churchill claims to have worried that, in view of all that had transpired between 1939 and 1941, the Russians might be shy about requesting help from the West in their fight against Hitler. Such proved not to be the case. As early as July 1941, Stalin asked the British, who were in no position to comply, to invade northern France. Later that month, he told Harry Hopkins that he would welcome American troops, under American command, anywhere on the Russian front. In September, he argued that Churchill could "without risk" send "twenty-five or thirty" British divisions to Archangel or the Caucasus—this at a time when London was straining shipping capabilities to the limit just to put two additional divisions into the Middle East. "By her passive attitude Britain is helping the Nazis," Stalin complained to the Soviet ambassador in London: "Do the British understand this? I think they do. What is it then that they want? It seems they want us to be weakened."[11]

This was an unjust accusation, but it did reflect the frustrations the Russians felt over a fundamental strategic fact of life in World War II: neither Great Britain nor the United States had come under direct ground attack. Both enjoyed, as a result, a certain flexibility in deciding how and when to strike back at the enemy. For the Russians, there could be no such choice: reeling from invasion on a broad front, their only option, short of capitulation, was all-out resistance. Obtaining relief from this pressure, whether through the dispatch of American a[nd] British troops to the Soviet Union or the creation of a sec[ond]

[10] Rosenman, ed., *Roosevelt Public Papers*, XI, 3–5.

[11] Churchill, *The Grand Alliance*, pp. 380, 384, 462–465; Hopkins to [Roosevelt,] July 31, 1941, FR: 1941, I, 814; Stalin to Maisky, August 30, 1941, M[inisterstvo] innostrannykh del SSSR, *Sovetsko-angliiskie otnosheniia vo v[remia Velikoi otechestvennoi voiny, 1941–1945* (Moscow: 1983), I, 109. See also [Steven Merritt] Miner, *Between Churchill and Stalin: The Soviet Union, Great Brita[in, and the Origins] of the Grand Alliance* (Chapel Hill, North Carolina: 1988), pp. [For a] recent Soviet account that reflects Stalin's attitude, Viln[?] *Great Victory: Soviet Diplomacy, 1914–1945* (Moscow: 198[?])

.ont against the Germans in Europe, accordingly became Stalin's chief diplomatic priority.

Roosevelt was not, at first, averse to creating an early second front. His military advisers, trained in the tradition of striking the enemy in the most direct manner and concerned about the strategic implications of a Soviet defeat, pushed strongly for an attack across the English Channel as soon as possible. Roosevelt, too, favored such an operation, partly out of a desire to stave off growing pressures inside the United States for an all-out offensive against Japan, partly out of fear that delay in confronting the Germans might lead Stalin to seek a separate peace, partly as an inducement to the Soviet leader to postpone discussion of postwar territorial claims in Europe, which Roosevelt feared might disrupt the common war effort. (That Stalin would not have been thinking about postwar territorial claims had he not expected to win does not seem to have occurred to the president, whose ability to see the interconnection of military and diplomatic problems was sometimes limited.) Accordingly, in June 1942, Roosevelt publicly promised Soviet Foreign Minister Molotov that a second front would be established somewhere in Europe before the end of the year.[12]

In the end, however, Roosevelt had to break this promise. The slow pace of American mobilization and training ensured that any 1942 attack would be primarily a British operation, and Churchill, haunted by memories of World War I trench warfare, was not inclined to launch costly attacks to relieve an ally whose concern over Britain's plight between 1939 and 1941 had been minimal. And even if the British had been willing, it would not have been possible in 1942 to accumulate sufficient transports to launch an invasion of Europe with any prospect of success. As a result, Roosevelt and Churchill agreed on a substitute plan involving joint Anglo-American landings in Vichy-occupied North Africa in November 1942. This operation met Roosevelt's desire to get American troops into action against the Germans before the end of the year, but it did little to take pressure off the Red Army. Delays in clearing the Germans out of

lease of June 11, 1942, FR: 1942, III, 594. See also Robert Beitzell, ance: America, Britain and Russia, 1941–1943 (New York: 1972), pp. ard W. Steele, The First Offensive: 1942 (Bloomington: 1973), pp.

"Declaration of the United Nations," committing each signatory to fight until victory had been achieved.[10] Hitler's inadvertent creation, the Grand Alliance, was now complete.

## II

Churchill claims to have worried that, in view of all that had transpired between 1939 and 1941, the Russians might be shy about requesting help from the West in their fight against Hitler. Such proved not to be the case. As early as July 1941, Stalin asked the British, who were in no position to comply, to invade northern France. Later that month, he told Harry Hopkins that he would welcome American troops, under American command, anywhere on the Russian front. In September, he argued that Churchill could "without risk" send "twenty-five or thirty" British divisions to Archangel or the Caucasus—this at a time when London was straining shipping capabilities to the limit just to put two additional divisions into the Middle East. "By her passive attitude Britain is helping the Nazis," Stalin complained to the Soviet ambassador in London: "Do the British understand this? I think they do. What is it then that they want? It seems they want us to be weakened."[11]

This was an unjust accusation, but it did reflect the frustrations the Russians felt over a fundamental strategic fact of life in World War II: neither Great Britain nor the United States had come under direct ground attack. Both enjoyed, as a result, a certain flexibility in deciding how and when to strike back at the enemy. For the Russians, there could be no such choice: reeling from invasion on a broad front, their only option, short of capitulation, was all-out resistance. Obtaining relief from this pressure, whether through the dispatch of American and British troops to the Soviet Union or the creation of a second

[10] Rosenman, ed., *Roosevelt Public Papers*, XI, 3–5.

[11] Churchill, *The Grand Alliance*, pp. 380, 384, 462–465; Hopkins to Roosevelt, July 31, 1941, *FR: 1941*, I, 814; Stalin to Maisky, August 30, 1941, Ministerstvo innostrannykh del SSSR, *Sovetsko-angliiskie otnosheniia vo vremia velikoi otechestvennoi voiny, 1941–1945* (Moscow: 1983), I, 109. See also Stev~
Miner, *Between Churchill and Stalin: The Soviet Union, Great Brita~
of the Grand Alliance* (Chapel Hill, North Carolina: 1988
recent Soviet account that reflects Stalin's atti~
*Great Victory: Soviet Diplomacy, 1914–1945* (Mosc

front against the Germans in Europe, accordingly became Stalin's chief diplomatic priority.

Roosevelt was not, at first, averse to creating an early second front. His military advisers, trained in the tradition of striking the enemy in the most direct manner and concerned about the strategic implications of a Soviet defeat, pushed strongly for an attack across the English Channel as soon as possible. Roosevelt, too, favored such an operation, partly out of a desire to stave off growing pressures inside the United States for an all-out offensive against Japan, partly out of fear that delay in confronting the Germans might lead Stalin to seek a separate peace, partly as an inducement to the Soviet leader to postpone discussion of postwar territorial claims in Europe, which Roosevelt feared might disrupt the common war effort. (That Stalin would not have been thinking about postwar territorial claims had he not expected to win does not seem to have occurred to the president, whose ability to see the interconnection of military and diplomatic problems was sometimes limited.) Accordingly, in June 1942, Roosevelt publicly promised Soviet Foreign Minister Molotov that a second front would be established somewhere in Europe before the end of the year.[12]

In the end, however, Roosevelt had to break this promise. The slow pace of American mobilization and training ensured that any 1942 attack would be primarily a British operation, and Churchill, haunted by memories of World War I trench warfare, was not inclined to launch costly attacks to relieve an ally whose concern over Britain's plight between 1939 and 1941 had been minimal. And even if the British had been willing, it would not have been possible in 1942 to accumulate sufficient transports to launch an invasion of Europe with any prospect of success. As a result, Roosevelt and Churchill agreed on a substitute plan involving joint Anglo-American landings in Vichy-occupied North Africa in November 1942. This operation met Roosevelt's desire to get American troops into action against the Germans before the end of the year, but it did little to take pressure off the Red Army. Delays in clearing the Germans out of

---

ss release of June 11, 1942, *FR: 1942*, III, 594. See also Robert Beitzell,
*Alliance: America, Britain and Russia, 1941–1943* (New York: 1972), pp.
ichard W. Steele, *The First Offensive: 1942* (Bloomington: 1973), pp.

"Declaration of the United Nations," committing each signatory to fight until victory had been achieved.[10] Hitler's inadvertent creation, the Grand Alliance, was now complete.

## II

Churchill claims to have worried that, in view of all that had transpired between 1939 and 1941, the Russians might be shy about requesting help from the West in their fight against Hitler. Such proved not to be the case. As early as July 1941, Stalin asked the British, who were in no position to comply, to invade northern France. Later that month, he told Harry Hopkins that he would welcome American troops, under American command, anywhere on the Russian front. In September, he argued that Churchill could "without risk" send "twenty-five or thirty" British divisions to Archangel or the Caucasus—this at a time when London was straining shipping capabilities to the limit just to put two additional divisions into the Middle East. "By her passive attitude Britain is helping the Nazis," Stalin complained to the Soviet ambassador in London: "Do the British understand this? I think they do. What is it then that they want? It seems they want us to be weakened."[11]

This was an unjust accusation, but it did reflect the frustrations the Russians felt over a fundamental strategic fact of life in World War II: neither Great Britain nor the United States had come under direct ground attack. Both enjoyed, as a result, a certain flexibility in deciding how and when to strike back at the enemy. For the Russians, there could be no such choice: reeling from invasion on a broad front, their only option, short of capitulation, was all-out resistance. Obtaining relief from this pressure, whether through the dispatch of American and British troops to the Soviet Union or the creation of a second

---

[10] Rosenman, ed., *Roosevelt Public Papers*, XI, 3–5.

[11] Churchill, *The Grand Alliance*, pp. 380, 384, 462–465; Hopkins to Roosevelt, July 31, 1941, *FR: 1941*, I, 814; Stalin to Maisky, August 30, 1941, Ministerstvo innostrannykh del SSSR, *Sovetsko-angliiskie otnosheniia vo vremia velikoi otechestvennoi voiny, 1941–1945* (Moscow: 1983), I, 109. See also Ste... Miner, *Between Churchill and Stalin: The Soviet Union, Great Brit...* *of the Grand Alliance* (Chapel Hill, North Carolina: 198... recent Soviet account that reflects Stalin's att... *Great Victory: Soviet Diplomacy, 1914–1945* (Mos...

front against the Germans in Europe, accordingly became Stalin's chief diplomatic priority.

Roosevelt was not, at first, averse to creating an early second front. His military advisers, trained in the tradition of striking the enemy in the most direct manner and concerned about the strategic implications of a Soviet defeat, pushed strongly for an attack across the English Channel as soon as possible. Roosevelt, too, favored such an operation, partly out of a desire to stave off growing pressures inside the United States for an all-out offensive against Japan, partly out of fear that delay in confronting the Germans might lead Stalin to seek a separate peace, partly as an inducement to the Soviet leader to postpone discussion of postwar territorial claims in Europe, which Roosevelt feared might disrupt the common war effort. (That Stalin would not have been thinking about postwar territorial claims had he not expected to win does not seem to have occurred to the president, whose ability to see the interconnection of military and diplomatic problems was sometimes limited.) Accordingly, in June 1942, Roosevelt publicly promised Soviet Foreign Minister Molotov that a second front would be established somewhere in Europe before the end of the year.[12]

In the end, however, Roosevelt had to break this promise. The slow pace of American mobilization and training ensured that any 1942 attack would be primarily a British operation, and Churchill, haunted by memories of World War I trench warfare, was not inclined to launch costly attacks to relieve an ally whose concern over Britain's plight between 1939 and 1941 had been minimal. And even if the British had been willing, it would not have been possible in 1942 to accumulate sufficient transports to launch an invasion of Europe with any prospect of success. As a result, Roosevelt and Churchill agreed on a substitute plan involving joint Anglo-American landings in Vichy-occupied North Africa in November 1942. This operation met Roosevelt's desire to get American troops into action against the Germans before the end of the year, but it did little to take pressure off the Red Army. Delays in clearing the Germans out of

ss release of June 11, 1942, *FR: 1942*, III, 594. See also Robert Beitzell,
Alliance: America, Britain and Russia, 1941–1943 (New York: 1972), pp.
ichard W. Steele, *The First Offensive: 1942* (Bloomington: 1973), pp.

Africa in turn made it impossible to launch a cross-Channel attack in 1943—the invasion of Italy, and that state's forced withdrawal from the Axis coalition, was, for the Russians, small comfort. The true second front would not come until June 1944, a year and a half later than Roosevelt had promised.[13]

The Russians believed at the time, and have charged since, that the delay in constituting the second front was deliberate. Roosevelt and Churchill, the argument runs, resolved to let the Soviet Union bear the brunt of the fighting, leaving the British and Americans to step in at the last moment to shape the peace settlement.[14] There can be no doubt that it was the Russians who, as Churchill put it, "tore the guts" out of the German army. Total German losses, including killed, wounded, and missing, came to over six million on the eastern front, as compared to just over one million in Western Europe and the Mediterranean. Throughout most of the war the Red Army was confronting, on the eastern front, more than 200 enemy divisions. Prior to the Normandy landings in June 1944, the British and Americans rarely faced more than 10 German divisions at any one time. One Soviet account has noted pointedly but accurately that for every American killed in the war against the Axis, fifty Russians died.[15]

It is frequently forgotten, though, that the British and the Americans had their own second front problem in East Asia where the Soviet Union had refrained from declaring war on the Japanese. Roosevelt and Churchill appreciated the Russians' unwillingness to take on an additional enemy at a time when the German army was just outside Moscow. At no point did they ask Stalin to enter the Pacific war until after Germany's defeat. But requirements of the war against Japan did

---

[13] Ibid., pp. 143–182; Beitzell, *The Uneasy Alliance*, pp. 42–107, 303–365. See also Mark A. Stoler, *The Politics of the Second Front: American Military Planning in Diplomacy and Coalition Warfare, 1941–1943* (Westport, Connecticut: 1977).

[14] See, for example, "Diplomatic History of the Opening of the Second Front," p. 76; B. Ponomaryov, A. Gromyko, and V. Khvostov, eds., *History of Soviet Foreign Policy, 1917–1945* (Moscow: 1969), p. 428; also Hugh Phillips, "Mission to America: Maksim M. Litvinov in the United States, 1941–43," *Diplomatic History*, XII (Summer, 1988), 272–273.

[15] N. N. IAkovlev, "SSSR-SShA: Motivy sotrudnichestva i konflikta (1941–1945)," *SShA: Ekonomika, Politika, Ideologiia*, 1970, #5, p. 21. See also Seaton, *The Russo-German War*, p. 586; and Beitzell, *The Uneasy Alliance*, p. 369.

significantly restrict the United States' ability to amass the troops and equipment—particularly landing craft—necessary to launch an early cross-Channel attack in Europe.[16] The delayed second front was, thus, part of the price the Russians paid for neutrality in the Pacific.

It is also not often taken into account what impact the recruitment of additional manpower would have had on American war production, much of which went to Great Britain and the Soviet Union in the form of Lend-Lease. Some $43.6 billion, or 14% of total American defense expenditures in World War II, was allocated for Lend-Lease; of this, approximately $11 billion, or 3.5% of total expenditures, went to the Soviet Union. As it was, the United States mobilized almost as high a percentage of its population as did the USSR (12% versus 13%); its factories produced 35% of all the combat munitions used against Germany and its allies and 85% of those used against the Japanese. The United States might have been able to collect enough men in Britain in 1943 to launch a second front, but only by taking pressure off Japan (thereby increasing the Soviet Union's security problems in Northeast Asia) and cutting back on the industrial production which played such a vital role in shaping the outcome of the war.[17]

Anglo-American reluctance to incur casualties also worked to delay the second front. Churchill's preoccupation with this matter has been well documented; less well known is the extent to which Roosevelt shared this concern.[18] The Russians, denied the luxury of deciding how to use their manpower, naturally resented this situation. But the fact that the British and Americans refused to launch suicide attacks to take pressure off the Red Army does not necessarily imply a determination on their part to deny Stalin the legitimate fruits of victory. Had such been

---

[16] Kent Roberts Greenfield, *American Strategy in World War II: A Reconsideration* (Baltimore: 1963), pp. 30–41.

[17] Richard M. Leighton, "The American Arsenal Policy in World War II: A Retrospective View," in Daniel R. Beaver, ed., *Some Pathways in Twentieth Century History* (Detroit: 1969), pp. 221–252. See also Robert Huhn Jones, *The Roads to Russia: United States Lend-Lease to the Soviet Union* (Norman, Oklahoma: 1969), pp. 238–239; and Leon Martel, *Lend-Lease, Loans, and the Coming of the Cold War: A Study of the Implementation of Foreign Policy* (Boulder, Colorado: 1979), pp. 35–50.

[18] Harriman and Abel, *Special Envoy to Churchill and Stalin*, p. 74.

their intent, the best strategy would have been to invade Europe at once regardless of casualties, so as to keep the Russians out of as much of it as possible. Rather, Anglo-American strategy reflected the rational balancing of objectives and resources which any wise statesman will engage in, *if he has the choice*. Stalin, in part as a result of his own bungling diplomacy between 1939 and 1941, was simply unfortunate enough not to have had that choice.

## III

Anglo-American military strategy was not without its price, though. The caution Roosevelt and Churchill demonstrated in planning military operations gave the Russians a credible basis for claiming that, having borne a disproportionate share of the costs of fighting the war, they should in turn enjoy disproportionate influence in determining the postwar settlement.[19] There is, to be sure, nothing automatic about the proposition that investments in blood necessarily produce equivalent dividends in political influence; if anything, the World War I experience had demonstrated precisely the opposite. Stalin's great fear was that Roosevelt and Churchill might try to repeat Wilson's performance in that earlier conflict—let the major belligerents bleed each other white, then demand, at a decisive moment, the right to shape the peace settlement. But for a variety of reasons, London and Washington failed to take advantage of their strategic flexibility to secure for themselves a decisive role at the peace table. Much to his surprise, Stalin found himself being petitioned to grant concessions to the West, rather than the other way around.[20]

Stalin probably had no precise blueprint for the kind of settlement he wanted, but he did have a set of operating assumptions that had consistently governed his foreign policy. These included the convictions: (1) that the outside world would, for the foreseeable future, remain hostile to the Soviet Union; (2)

---

[19] Frederick C. Barghoorn, *The Soviet Image of the United States* (New York: 1950), p. 51.

[20] Ulam, *Stalin*, pp. 564–565. See also Vojtech Mastny, *Russia's Road to the Cold War: Diplomacy, Warfare and the Politics of Communism, 1941–1945* (New York: 1979), pp. 110–112, 122.

that, despite this circumstance, the security of the USSR should not be risked to promote world revolution; (3) that such security could best be obtained (a) by taking advantage of conflicts between potential adversaries to keep them divided, and (b) by dominating spheres of influence along Russia's periphery, in order to place as much controlled territory between the Soviet Union and its enemies as possible.[21] These principles had governed Stalin's diplomacy during his abortive period of collaboration with Hitler; given the opportunity, he could be expected to apply them as well in his dealings with his Western allies.

The Soviet leader had sought as early as December 1941 to have the British confirm the territorial gains Russia had made from the Nazi-Soviet Pact—eastern Poland, the Baltic states, and parts of Finland and Rumania. "All we ask for," he told Anthony Eden, "is to restore our country to its former frontiers." Stalin advanced these claims cautiously, however, and when the Americans objected, refrained from insisting upon their inclusion in a bilateral pact the Soviet Union signed with Great Britain in May, 1942. This apparent deference to American sensibilities may have grown out of Stalin's concern not to let anything interfere with creation of an early second front, but new evidence from Soviet sources now suggests an alternative explanation: Litvinov reported having received assurances from Roosevelt several months earlier that although public opinion was not yet prepared, he himself "[did] not foresee any difficulties regarding our border desires after the war."[22] By 1943, however, Soviet military fortunes had decidedly improved, even without a cross-Channel attack. Gradually Stalin let it be known that he would require, not just a return to his 1939–1941 frontiers, but the installation as well of govern-

---

[21] This analysis follows Ulam, *Expansion and Coexistence*, pp. 345–348, 360–361; but see also William Taubman, *Stalin's American Policy: From Entente to Detente to Cold War* (New York: 1982), pp. 74–75.

[22] Litvinov to Narkomindel, March 12, 1942, Ministerstvo innostrannykh del SSSR, *Sovetsko-amerikanskie otnosheniia vo vremia velikoi otechestvennoi voiny, 1941–1945* (Moscow: 1984), I, 155. See also Sipols, *The Road to Great Victory*, pp. 73–74. For evaluations of this evidence, see Phillips, "Mission to America," pp. 268–270; and Miner, *Between Churchill and Stalin*, p. 218n. The Stalin quotation is from *The Reckoning: The Memoirs of Anthony Eden, Earl of Avon* (Boston: 1965), p. 335.

ments "friendly" to the Soviet Union throughout Eastern Europe and the Balkans. The result promised to be an intrusion of Russian power into Europe unprecedented since the days of Alexander I.

Such a development would pose great problems for Britain and the United States, whose policies, both in World Wars I and II, had been based on the proposition that a balance of power on the European continent was crucial to their security. Complicating the issue was the fact that Roosevelt had chosen to justify American entry into the war, not solely in terms of the considerations of power politics that weighed most heavily in his own mind, but in idealistic terms as well. Thus the president, with Churchill, had pledged himself in the Atlantic Charter to oppose "territorial changes that do not accord with the freely expressed wishes of the peoples concerned," and to seek to have "sovereign rights and self government restored to those who have been forcibly deprived of them."[23] Whether on grounds of *realpolitik* or Wilsonian ideals, therefore, the massive expansion of Soviet power in Europe was not a prospect Anglo-American leaders could view with equanimity.

Options for avoiding this prospect, however, were decidedly limited. One would have been to negotiate a separate peace with Germany before the Soviet Union had moved into a position of dominance. Certainly Stalin feared this possibility—his suspicious mind could never completely free itself from the fear that his capitalist allies might make common cause with his capitalist foes.[24] In fact, though, such an arrangement was never seriously considered. Roosevelt and Churchill stuck strictly to the view that Hitler was more dangerous than Stalin, and even if they had not, public opinion in neither Britain nor the United States would have tolerated dealings with the Germans. The furor set off by General Dwight Eisenhower's relatively innocent discussions with Admiral Darlan of Vichy France in November 1942, gives some clue to what the reaction would have been had

---

[23] *FR: 1941*, I, 368. For a discussion of Roosevelt's war aims, see John Lewis Gaddis, *The United States and the Origins of the Cold War, 1941–1947* (New York: 1972), pp. 1–31.

[24] Ulam *Expansion and Coexistence*, p. 348.

Roosevelt and Churchill tried to deal with the Germans at Soviet expense.[25]

Furthermore, there was always the danger that the Russians might play the same game. Not having public opinion to worry about, Stalin could have carried off such an arrangement far more easily than could his Western colleagues, as indeed his 1939 actions had demonstrated. In an effort to guard against this possibility and to reassure public opinion, Roosevelt and Churchill proclaimed the doctrine of unconditional surrender at Casablanca in January 1943. Despite this, the evidence indicates that Stalin did authorize tentative contacts with the Germans the following summer, a low point in Russian relations with the West because of the delay in creating the second front. It was his own increasingly frequent military successes, not his allies' assurances, that kept him from pursuing these initiatives.[26]

Another way of avoiding the expansion of Soviet power into central Europe would have been to organize military operations in such a way as to interpose British and American forces between the Russians and the Germans. An Anglo-American invasion of the Balkans was the most frequently mentioned possibility, but one which carried with it overwhelming difficulties. Logistical and topographical obstacles were so great there could be no assurance of reaching Germany ahead of the Russians. And, although Stalin from time to time suggested such a plan,[27] it seems unlikely that he would have welcomed large-scale Western military operations in the Balkans, an area he regarded as within his postwar sphere of influence. Such an operation also would have encountered stiff opposition from the American military, already impatient with Churchill's "indirect" strategy of attrition, suspicious of him (unjustly, as it turned out) for seeking to substitute in place of the cross-Channel attack operations that would promote British political objectives in the eastern Mediterranean.[28]

---

[25] Ibid., p. 349; Arthur Layton Funk, *The Politics of TORCH* (Lawrence, Kansas: 1974), pp. 249–255.

[26] Vojtech Mastny, "Stalin and the Prospects of a Separate Peace in World War II," *American Historical Review,* LXXVII(December, 1972), 1365–1388.

[27] Harriman and Abel, *Special Envoy,* p. 379.

[28] See, on this point, Richard M. Leighton, "OVERLORD Revisited: An Interpretation of American Strategy in the European War, 1942–1944," *American Historical Review,* LXVIII(July, 1963), 919–937.

Still another way of attempting to ensure Russian postwar cooperation might have been to impose political conditions on the Lend-Lease aid which the United States was sending, in increasing quantities, to the USSR. By the spring of 1943, several of Roosevelt's top advisers were recommending such a course of action.[29] But there were problems with this strategy too. Although aid to Russia did speed military operations against the Germans, the tide of battle on the eastern front had largely been reversed before aid had begun to arrive in quantity. The Russians at no point were so dependent on Lend-Lease that they would have been willing to compromise, in any significant way, their postwar plans.[30] Then, too, even if promises had been made, there was no way of ensuring that the Russians would keep them, as American officials had learned to their dismay during the years following the Roosevelt-Litvinov agreements of 1933.

Other problems as well inhibited direct opposition to Stalin's program. Washington officials attached great importance to securing Soviet participation in the war against Japan, which projections indicated would last at least a year and a half after Germany's defeat and would cost at least as many casualties.[31] Similarly, Moscow's cooperation was deemed essential in the organization of the United Nations, which many Americans expected to be the major instrument for maintaining world order after the war. It is significant that when Ambassador Harriman proposed raising the question of Poland at the Moscow Foreign Ministers' Conference in October 1943, Secretary of State Cordell Hull rejected the idea: "I don't want to deal with these piddling little things," he complained. "We must deal with the main issues."[32] As it turned out, the USSR probably would have entered both the Pacific war and the United Nations without inducements from the United States, simply because Stalin considered both moves advantageous to the Soviet Union's

---

[29] Herring, *Aid to Russia*, pp. 80–109.

[30] Ulam, *Expansion and Coexistence*, pp. 330; Herring, *Aid to Russia*, pp. 139–140.

[31] See Ernest R. May, "The United States, the Soviet Union, and the Far Eastern War, 1941–1945," *Pacific Historical Review*, XXIV (May, 1955), 153–174; and Louis Morton, "Soviet Intervention in the War with Japan," *Foreign Affairs*, XL(July, 1962), 653–662.

[32] Harriman and Abel, *Special Envoy*, p. 236.

position as a great power. The Kremlin autocrat was shrewd enough to appear reluctant, though, thereby further limiting his allies' ability to contest his postwar claims.

This complex of considerations convinced Roosevelt that there was no feasible way to employ Anglo-American strategic flexibility to block Soviet expansion. Instead, he concluded that the only way to achieve both military victory and a favorable postwar settlement would be to try to integrate Stalin's war aims with those of his Western allies. This would not be, Roosevelt thought, an impossible task. Proceeding on the assumption that insecurity, not ideology, drove Stalin's expansionism, the president reasoned that if the Soviet dictator's fears could be relieved, his motives for seeking to project influence beyond his borders would disappear and a settlement agreeable to all might be reached. Roosevelt sought to accomplish this end: (1) by ensuring the total destruction of German and Japanese power; (2) by meeting, where possible, Stalin's legitimate security needs in Europe and East Asia and (3) by seeking to build an atmosphere of mutual trust between the Soviet leader and his Western allies which would assure him that he had nothing to fear.

Unconditional surrender had been part of that strategy; so too had been the president's insistence, over the objections of the State Department, on the postwar partition of Germany. On Eastern Europe, Roosevelt had at first opposed Stalin's proposed boundary changes, on grounds that they would have violated the spirit of the Atlantic Charter. But he soon came to the conclusion that the West lacked the means of denying Stalin the gains he wanted, and that his own efforts should be directed toward arranging the best possible compromise. Accordingly, he worked to restore relations between Moscow and the staunchly anti-Soviet Polish government-in-exile, located in London. He also hoped to convince Stalin to hold plebiscites in the Baltic states in order to make their incorporation into the USSR palatable to American and world opinion.[33] But

---

[33] This analysis of Roosevelt's views follows Gaddis, *The United States and the Origins of the Cold War,* pp. 6–7, 64–65, 100–101, 136–137. See also Phillips, "Mission to America," pp. 268–269. For more on Roosevelt's thinking, see John Lewis Gaddis, *Strategies of Containment: A Critical Appraisal of Postwar American National Security Policy* (New York: 1982), pp. 1–13.

Roosevelt's chief priority was to arrange a personal meeting with the Soviet dictator, in the expectation that the feeling of trust that had come to characterize the Roosevelt-Churchill relationship could be expanded to include Stalin as well. After several delays, occasioned by the president's unsuccessful attempts to exclude Churchill and by Stalin's reluctance to leave Moscow, the Big Three finally agreed to meet in Teheran at the end of November 1943.

The conference was, to all appearances, a great success. Roosevelt and Churchill made the final commitment to Stalin to launch a second front in the spring of 1944, and the Soviet leader promised in turn to enter the war against Japan three months after Germany's surrender. The president also indicated to Stalin that he would not oppose territorial changes in Eastern Europe, although the Russians must not expect public acknowledgment until after the 1944 election. Roosevelt appealed to Stalin to handle Eastern European issues in such a way as not to offend world opinion and urged upon him, without success, the idea of a plebiscite for the Baltic states. Stalin enthusiastically seconded Roosevelt's advocacy of harsh treatment for Germany, though no final agreements were reached on specifics.[34] Most important, the conference took place in the atmosphere of hearty good-fellowship that Roosevelt considered essential if his goal of integrating Stalin's war aims with those of the Western allies was to be achieved.

## IV

It seems likely that the Big Three left Teheran with differing ideas of what had been accomplished. To Stalin, the fact that his Anglo-American colleagues had not objected to the Eastern European boundary changes he wanted probably suggested that they viewed the Atlantic Charter as window dressing;

---

[34] The record of the Teheran Conference can be traced in *Foreign Relations: The Conference at Cairo and Tehran, 1943* (Washington: 1961), but see also Keith Eubank, *Summit at Teheran: The Untold Story* (New York: 1985); and Keith Sainsbury, *The Turning Point: Roosevelt, Stalin, Churchill, and Chiang Kai-Shek, 1943: The Moscow, Cairo, and Teheran Conferences* (New York: 1985). For a Soviet account, see Valentin Berezhkov, *History in the Making: Memoirs of World War II Diplomacy* (Moscow: 1983), pp. 238–304.

Roosevelt and Churchill, he believed, had tacitly recognized the Soviet Union's right to have subservient governments along its borders. After all, the British prime minister himself had proclaimed that in the postwar world the big powers must be satisfied, like rich, happy men.[35] Roosevelt, on the other hand, believed that by demonstrating that he had found Stalin's requests reasonable, he had thereby won the Soviet leader's trust. Stalin, he thought, would not presume upon this relationship to press extreme demands. Provided the Poles could be made to see the futility of their anti-Russian position, there was no reason why free elections could not be held throughout Eastern Europe which would, in turn, produce governments friendly to the Soviet Union.[36]

That there was a considerable gap between these perceptions quickly became apparent, most obviously with regard to Poland. While Roosevelt and Churchill had reluctantly accepted Stalin's position on boundaries, they were not prepared to see the independence of what remained of that country compromised. Britain had gone to war in 1939 on Poland's behalf, and, in the United States, a large and vociferous Polish-American community ensured that any East European settlement would be strictly tested against the principles of the Atlantic Charter. Stalin, however, took advantage of the Red Army's entry onto Polish soil to establish the nucleus of a new government, subservient to the Soviet Union, independent of the Polish government-in-exile in London, unrecognized by either the British or the Americans. George Kennan noted the significance of these developments in his diary on August 1: "The jealous and intolerant eye of the Kremlin can distinguish, in the end, only vassals and enemies; and the neighbors of Russia, if they do not wish to be the one, must reconcile themselves to being the other."[37]

---

[35] FR: *Tehran*, p. 568. See also Ulam, *Expansion and Coexistence*, p. 360; and Vojtech Mastny, "Soviet War Aims at the Moscow and Teheran Conferences of 1943," *Journal of Modern History*, XLVII(September, 1973), 503.

[36] Gaddis, *The United States and the Origins of the Cold War*, pp. 139–145; Dallek, *Franklin D. Roosevelt and American Foreign Policy*, pp. 438–441.

[37] Kennan, *Memoirs: 1925–1950*, p. 209. For background on wartime Polish-American relations, see Richard C. Lukas, *The Strange Allies: The United States and Poland, 1941–1945* (Knoxville: 1978).

The same day Kennan wrote those lines, the Polish underground organization in Warsaw, knowing that the Red Army was approaching the city and encouraged by Soviet broadcasts to take action, launched an uprising against the Germans. To the horror of Western observers, Stalin refused to order an advance to help the Poles, or to allow British and American planes to land at Soviet airfields after dropping supplies. It is to this day unclear whether Stalin's behavior was based solely on military considerations or was a calculated move to decimate the pro-Western Polish underground.[38] The latter was clearly the effect, however, and from this point many of Roosevelt's advisers came strongly to doubt Soviet willingness to allow anything but satellite governments in Eastern Europe. Kennan himself thought that the time had come to cut off all aid to the Soviet Union until Moscow became more cooperative. Ambassador Harriman was not willing to go that far, but he did warn Washington that "unless we take issue with the present policy there is every indication the Soviet Union will become a world bully wherever their interests are involved."[39]

By this time, problems had developed in other areas as well. Citing the Anglo-American occupation of Italy as a precedent, Stalin refused to allow his allies anything more than a token role in the occupation of Rumania, Bulgaria, and Hungary, into which the Red Army also marched in 1944. Attempts to arrange the exchange of military information for the coming joint effort against Japan produced little fruit, while the Russians insisted on terminating a plan for the shuttle-bombing of Germany, using Ukrainian air bases, after only a few missions. The Russians had, by the fall, expressed reservations about voting procedures in the United Nations; they also persistently refused, despite repeated requests, to distinguish between Lend-Lease aid intended for military purposes and that to be used for post war reconstruction. Wartime collaboration brought no change in the policies of harassment to which Westerners in Moscow had

---

[38] Werth, *Russia at War*, pp. 869–883; Ulam, *Expansion and Coexistence*, pp. 361–363; Seaton, *The Russo-German War*, pp. 453–456. As Vojtech Mastny points out, these two considerations need not have been inconsistent. [*Russia's Road to the Cold War*, pp. 183–186, 194–195.]

[39] Kennan, *Memoirs: 1925–1950*, p. 211; Harriman and Abel, *Special Envoy*, p. 344; Bohlen, *Witness to History*, p. 161.

*European Territorial Changes, 1939–1947.*

long been subject. And, finally, Roosevelt and his principal military advisers had evidence, by this time, of a sustained effort by Soviet intelligence to penetrate the security of the top-secret Anglo-American project to develop the atomic bomb.[40]

Roosevelt refused, however, to interpret these events as evidence that his policy of winning Stalin's trust had failed. Himself a realist when it come to international affairs, the president saw little surprising or reprehensible in the Soviet leader's desire to have friendly governments in Eastern Europe. He still nursed the hope that, with Germany's defeat and demilitarization, Stalin's demands would become less severe—such sentiments may well have influenced his brief support for the punitive Morgenthau Plan in the fall of 1944.[41] At the same time, though, as a realist in domestic politics, Roosevelt could not allow Stalin a completely free hand. Eastern Europe had the potential of becoming a major campaign issue in the 1944 election; it might also generate sufficient opposition within the Senate to block American participation in the United Nations.[42] Accordingly, the president tried throughout 1944 to keep the issue as quiet as possible, in the hope of achieving some kind of compromise between the legitimate security interests of the USSR and the principles of the Atlantic Charter.

Roosevelt was not wholly without resources in seeking such a compromise. The president rejected his advisers' recommendation that he impose political conditions on future Lend-Lease aid, but he did make clear his intention not to grant postwar credits to the Russians "until we get what we want." In a reversal from his previous support for the Morgenthau Plan,

---

[40] Gaddis, *The United States and the Origins of the Cold War*, pp. 80–91; Herring, *Aid to Russia*, pp. 126–138; Harriman and Abel, *Special Envoy*, pp. 295–300. For Balkan and East European issues, see also Thomas T. Hammond, ed., *Witnesses to the Origins of the Cold War* (Seattle: 1982); and Michael M. Boll, *Cold War in the Balkans: American Foreign Policy and the Emergence of Communist Bulgaria, 1943–1947* (Lexington: 1984). On Soviet atomic espionage, see Ronald Radosh and Joyce Milton, *The Rosenberg File: A Search for the Truth* (New York: 1983); and Robert Chadwell Williams, *Klaus Fuchs, Atom Spy* (Cambridge, Massachusetts: 1987).

[41] See, on this point, Robert Murphy, *Diplomat among Warriors* (Garden City, New York: 1964), p. 227; also Warren F. Kimball, *Swords or Ploughshares? The Morgenthau Plan for Defeated Nazi Germany* (Philadelphia: 1976).

[42] Gaddis, *The United States and the Origins of the Cold War*, pp. 139–157.

Roosevelt had also come, by the end of 1944, to accept the State Department's argument that United States and Great Britain should retain as much control as possible over the flow of reparations from Germany to the Soviet Union. He had further decided, by this time, not to inform the Russians of the atomic bomb project, even though he knew they were aware, through espionage, of the program's existence.[43] Although the president's motives in making these decisions are not entirely clear, there is reason to believe that he may have anticipated the possibility, at some point in the future, of trading reconstruction aid and information about the bomb for political concessions. His chief resource in winning Stalin's cooperation, however, remained his own belief in his ability to "get through" to the Soviet leader in face-to-face negotiations. To this end, he attached great importance to arranging another meeting of the Big Three, which took place at Yalta, in the Crimea, in February 1945.

Like Teheran, Yalta produced surface conviviality and surface agreements. The Big Three agreed that the Lublin Polish government, which Stalin had recognized the month before, would "be reorganized on a broader democratic basis with the inclusion of democratic leaders from Poland itself and from Poles abroad." Elections for a permanent government, Stalin promised, would be held soon, possibly within a month. Roosevelt, Churchill, and Stalin also signed a "Declaration on Liberated Europe,"calling for the creation of governments in Eastern Europe "broadly representative of all democratic elements in the population and pledged to the earliest possible establishment through free elections of governments responsible to the will of the people." No final agreements were reached on Germany, other than to accept, "as a basis for negotiations," a Soviet request for reparations in the amount of $10 billion. In East Asia, Roosevelt and Churchill promised Stalin, in return for his agreement to enter the war against Japan after Germany's

---

[43] Herring, *Aid to Russia*, pp. 169–170; Gaddis, *The United States and the Origins of the Cold War*, pp. 86–88, 126–127; Barton J. Bernstein, "The Quest for Security: American Foreign Policy and International Control of Atomic Energy, 1942–1946," *Journal of American History*, LX(March, 1974), 1003–1010; Martin J. Sherwin, *A World Destroyed: The Atomic Bomb and the Grand Alliance* (New York: 1975), pp. 108–135.

defeat, the Kurile Islands, lower Sakhalin, leases at Port Arthur (Lushun) and Dairen (Dalian), control of the Chinese Eastern and South Manchurian railroads, and recognition of the independence from China of Outer Mongolia.[44]

Contrary to charges made in later years, Roosevelt gave up nothing at Yalta not already under Stalin's actual or potential control. His chief concern was cosmetic: to put the best possible face on a bad situation in order to make palatable to the American people the postwar expansion of Soviet influence. Otherwise, he feared, the gap between the ideals for which the war had been fought and its very realistic outcome would be so great as to render peacetime Soviet-American cooperation impossible. The president relied heavily on Stalin's cooperation in this process: the Soviet leader, he hoped, would be discreet in projecting power beyond his borders, operating behind the facade of democratic procedures wherever possible. Perhaps, in time, Soviet insecurity might decline to the point that illusion might approach reality. Yalta, Roosevelt told the Congress in his final appearance before that body, was not a perfect peace. "But it can be a peace—and it will be a peace—based on the sound and just principles of the Atlantic Charter."[45]

Stalin would not cooperate, however, in conveying even the appearance of action consistent with Western ideals. Within two weeks of signing the Declaration on Liberated Europe, he violated it by forcing a subservient government on Rumania. Tedious negotiations to broaden the Soviet-sponsored government of Poland got nowhere. In March, reports began reaching Washington that the Russians were mistreating American prisoners-of-war liberated from the Germans; that same month, Moscow announced that Foreign Minister Molotov would be too busy to attend the San Francisco Conference on the organization of the United Nations. "Our gallant allies," Ambassador Harriman's daughter noted in a letter from Moscow, "are being most bastard-like." Worst of all, Stalin chose to interpret an abortive Anglo-American effort to arrange the surrender of

---

[44] The fullest record of the Yalta Conference is *Foreign Relations: The Conferences at Malta and Yalta, 1945* (Washington: 1955). See also Diane Shaver Clemens, *Yalta* (New York: 1970); and Russell D. Buhite, *Decisions at Yalta: An Appraisal of Summit Diplomacy* (Wilmington, Delaware: 1986).

[45] Rosenman, ed., *Roosevelt Public Papers*, XIII, 579.

German forces in Italy as a plot, coordinated with Berlin, to keep the Red Army out of Central Europe. "I cannot avoid a feeling of bitter resentment," Roosevelt fumed, "toward your informers, whoever they are, for such vile misrepresentations of my actions and those of my trusted subordinates."[46]

There are indications that Roosevelt was reassessing his policy toward the Soviet Union at the time of his death. "Averell [Harriman] is right," he told a friend on March 23. "We can't do business with Stalin. He has broken every one of the promises he made at Yalta." Roosevelt remained firm in his refusal to consider a postwar loan until Russian intentions had become clearer, nor did he object when Congress that month prohibited the use of Lend-Lease for reconstruction purposes. Nor did the president alter his policy of withholding information about the atomic bomb. "We must not permit anybody to entertain a false impression that we are afraid," he wrote to Churchill on April 6. "Our armies will in very few days be in a position that will permit us to become 'tougher' than has heretofore appeared advantageous to the war effort."[47]

None of this means that Roosevelt had abandoned his hope of cooperating with the Russians to build a new postwar order. "I would minimize the general Soviet problem as much as possible," he observed in his last cable to Churchill, "because these problems, in one form or another, seem to arise every day and most of them straighten out."[48] It does seem likely, however, that events since Yalta had convinced Roosevelt of the futility of trying to win Stalin's trust and of the need to place dealings with the Russians henceforth on the strict *quid-pro-quo* basis that Harriman and the other Soviet specialists had been recommending for more than a year.

Critics would charge, in retrospect, that Roosevelt had been naive to the point of irresponsibility by persisting in the belief that he could win Stalin's trust through personal cordiality, political appeasement, and unconditional aid. In fact, his ap-

---

[46] Roosevelt to Stalin, April 4, 1945, *FR: 1945*, III, 746. See also Harriman and Abel, *Special Envoy*, pp. 419–428; and Bradley F. Smith and Elena Agarossi, *Operation Sunrise: The Secret Surrender* (New York: 1979).

[47] Harriman and Abel, *Special Envoy*, p. 444; Herring, *Aid to Russia*, pp. 174–178; Sherwin, *A World Destroyed*, pp. 136–139; Warren F. Kimball, ed., *Churchill and Roosevelt: The Complete Correspondence* (Princeton: 1984), III, 617.

[48] Ibid., p. 630.

proach was more realistic than that. A policy that withheld the second front for two years, tied reconstruction aid to political concessions, and rejected the sharing of atomic bomb information can hardly be regarded as one of timid acquiescence. When Roosevelt did make concessions, it was generally in areas where Anglo-American power could not feasibly be brought to bear to deny the Russians what they wanted. The president saw more clearly than most observers that insecurity, not world revolutionary ambitions, drove Soviet expansionism; he was also correct in his perception that only Stalin was in a position to modify the tradition of institutionalized suspicion that separated Russia from the West.

Roosevelt's mistakes, it would appear, were three: (1) He underestimated the depth of Stalin's paranoia—not until after Yalta did he see that the Soviet dictator's distrust of his allies had been just as great as his fear of the Germans. (2) He overestimated the intensity of American isolationism, thus discounting the United States' capacity to project political influence in the postwar world—it is significant that he told Stalin at Yalta that public opinion would not tolerate the retention of American troops overseas for more than two years after the war.[49] (3) He failed, whether because of want of insight or energy, to use his own considerable persuasive powers to prepare the American people for the kind of realistic postwar settlement his own instincts told him would be inevitable. It was Roosevelt's fate to live just long enough to see that these mistakes had been made; devising strategies to correct them would be up to his diligent but ill-informed and inexperienced successor.

## V

Harry S. Truman knew very little of the deterioration that had taken place in Soviet-American relations when he came into office because Roosevelt had not kept him informed. He quickly sought recommendations from the late president's advisers, most of whom had long favored a firmer policy than Roosevelt had been prepared to implement. Unsure of himself, yet eager to appear decisive, Truman quickly accepted their advice to "get tough," a course of action consistent with his own favorite

---

[49] FR: Yalta, p. 617.

method of handling crises. He was not afraid of the Russians, the new president told Harriman; after all, "the Soviet Union needed us more than we needed them." He would not expect to get 100% of what the United States wanted, but "we should be able to get 85 percent." He was going ahead with plans for the San Francisco conference, and if the Russians disapproved, "they could go to hell."[50]

The president's first opportunity to demonstrate his toughness came on April 23, 1945, when Soviet Foreign Minister Molotov stopped off in Washington on his way to San Francisco (Stalin had reversed his earlier decision and ordered Molotov to attend, as a mark of respect for Roosevelt's memory.) The Soviet diplomat's reception at the White House was not warm, however: Truman lectured him in the manner of a World War I artillery captain shaping unruly troops into line. An agreement had been made at Yalta, the president stated, and all that remained was for Stalin to carry it out. When Molotov tried to explain that the Soviet government was carrying out what it considered to be the correct interpretation of the Yalta agreements, Truman cut him off. The United States wanted cooperation with Russia, he snapped, but not as a one-way proposition. The usually imperturbable Molotov emerged from this experience badly shaken. "I gave it to him straight," Truman later bragged, "one-two to the jaw."[51]

Some historians have seen this as the moment at which the Cold War began.[52] Certainly the new president's truculence upset the Russians, who had grown used to the smooth and slippery platitudes of his predecessor. In fact, however, Truman had no intention of reversing Roosevelt's Russian policy; he had reason to believe he was continuing it. Roosevelt himself had come to see the need for a tougher approach by the time of his death, and the new president's advisers were almost unanimous in urging a firm stand. In his eagerness to appear decisive Truman

---

[50] *FR: 1945*, V, 232–233, 253.

[51] Joseph E. Davies Diary, April 30, 1945, Joseph E. Davies Papers, Library of Congress. See also *FR: 1945*, V, 256–258; and Harry S. Truman, *Year of Decisions* (Garden City, New York: 1955), pp. 79–82.

[52] See, for example, Clemens, *Yalta*, pp. 268–274; D. F. Fleming, *The Cold War and Its Origins, 1917–1960* (Garden City, New York: 1961), I, 265–269; Gar Alperovitz, *Atomic Diplomacy: Hiroshima and Potsdam* (New York: 1965), pp. 12–13; Alexander Werth, *Russia: The Postwar Years* (New York: 1971), pp. 56–61, 117–118.

probably overreacted, as he himself later realized,[53] but he did so in an effort to solidify his own authority, not to wreck chances for postwar accommodation with the USSR.

During this period, Truman made other decisions that had the effect of avoiding, rather than encouraging, conflict with the Soviet Union. He agreed to support Roosevelt's Yalta pledge that the Russians could have three seats in the United Nations General Assembly, even though he himself disapproved of this arrangement. He turned down Winston Churchill's proposal that Allied troops in Central Europe remain in the advanced positions they had attained by V-E Day, not withdrawing into previously agreed-upon occupation zones until the Russians had become more cooperative. He made no change in the agreement Roosevelt had concluded with Stalin at Yalta whereby the Russians would receive political concessions in return for entering the war against Japan.[54]

By mid-May 1945, Truman had nonetheless begun to fear that the Russians had misunderstood his intentions. The fate of Poland remained unsolved. The San Francisco Conference seemed to be turning into a forum for the airing of differences instead of their resolution. Shortly after V-E Day, overzealous subordinates ordered ships transporting Lend-Lease supplies to Russia to return to port if the material they carried was not intended for use against Japan. Truman, who had intended a more gradual curtailment of Lend-Lease, immediately countermanded this order, but not before the Russians had complained bitterly. The incident convinced the president of the extreme anti-Soviet hostility that existed among some Washington officials and of the need to make a new effort to settle differences with Moscow.[55]

Truman entrusted this delicate responsibility to Roosevelt's favorite unofficial emissary, Harry Hopkins, who went to Moscow in late May. "I told Harry he could use diplomatic language or he could use a baseball bat if he thought that was the proper approach," Truman wrote.[56] Hopkins' sympathetic atti-

---

[53] Jonathan Daniels, *Man of Independence* (Philadelphia: 1950), pp. 269–270.

[54] Gaddis, *The United States and the Origins of the Cold War*, pp. 206–215; Lisle A. Rose, *Dubious Victory: The United States and the End of World War II* (Kent, Ohio: 1973), pp. 126–170.

[55] Herring, *Aid to Russia*, pp. 180–211; Margaret Truman, *Henry S. Truman* (New York: 1972), p. 255.

[56] Ibid., p. 252.

tude toward the Russians was no secret, though; Truman knew very well that his approach would be conciliatory. The Hopkins-Stalin conversations did much to clear the air. They produced a compromise on Poland which preserved Soviet influence there but allowed the West to save face; Stalin reiterated his promise to enter the war against Japan and help resolve a stalemate at San Francisco by accepting the American formula on voting in the United Nations Security Council; and finally, the Russian leader agreed to meet Truman and Churchill in July at Potsdam, just outside Berlin.[57]

Potsdam was the longest of the wartime summits—two and a half weeks—but it produced the fewest agreements. With Poland's difficulties resolved, however unsatisfactorily from the viewpoint of London and Washington, the German question moved to center stage. The need for joint occupation and demilitarization provoked no disagreement, but there were serious differences over the question of German reparations. The Russians, eager to use German resources for reconstruction, sought the right to extract up to $10 billion in reparations from the country as a whole, regardless of the effect such removals would produce on the German economy. Truman and Churchill strongly opposed this course of action, recalling the impact arbitrary reparations demands had had on Germany in the 1920s, reluctant to have to employ British and American resources to prevent economic collapse there. In the end, the Big Three reached a complicated accord giving each occupying power the authority to take what it wanted from its own zone and promising the Russians such additional deliveries from the industrialized Western zones as were not vital to the German economy. This arrangement placed London and Washington in a position to control the flow of reparations to Russia, but only at the expense of undermining prospects for central administration of the defeated state.[58]

---

[57] For the Hopkins-Stalin negotiations, see Robert E. Sherwood, *Roosevelt and Hopkins: An Intimate History* (New York: 1948), pp. 887–912; also Dwight William Tuttle, *Harry L. Hopkins and Anglo-American-Soviet Relations, 1941–1945* (New York: 1983), pp. 268–306. For a Soviet account, see Berezhkov, *History in the Making,* pp. 436–443.

[58] Bruce Kuklick, *American Policy and the Division of Germany* (Ithaca: 1972), pp. 114–172; John H. Backer, *The Decision to Divide Germany: American Foreign Policy in Transition* (Durham: 1978), pp. 88–101.

On other issues, little was accomplished. The Big Three agreed to set up a Council of Foreign Ministers to begin work on peace treaties with former Axis satellites. Attempts to secure stronger Soviet compliance with the Yalta Declaration on Liberated Europe failed, though, as the Russians insisted on equating the situation in Eastern Europe with that in Italy and Greece. Stalin did renew his promise to enter the war against Japan and obligingly provided the Americans with news of peace feelers from Tokyo. Other matters, including the disposition of Italian colonies, revision of the Montreux Convention governing access to the Turkish Straits, troop withdrawals from Iran, and an American proposal for the internationalization of strategic waterways, had to be referred to the foreign ministers for further consideration.[59]

One week after the Potsdam Conference ended, on August 6, 1945, the United States dropped the first atomic bomb on Hiroshima. Two days later, on August 8, the Soviet Union declared war against Japan, three months to the day after Germany's defeat, as had been promised. The second bomb followed on August 9, and on August 14 the Japanese government announced its acceptance of Allied surrender terms. Stalin, as startled as anyone by this swift series of events, nonetheless seized the occasion to request participation by Soviet troops in the occupation of Japan. Truman in an equally peremptory manner rejected this claim. "I...had not anticipated that such would be your reply," Stalin complained. But Truman's position on Japan, together with another decision, made at the same time, to have American troops occupy southern Korea, simply reflected Washington's acceptance of a proposition Stalin himself had asserted repeatedly in Europe: that "this war is not as in the past; whoever occupies territory also imposes his own social system as far as his army can reach. It cannot be otherwise."[60]

---

[59] For the Potsdam Conference, see *Foreign Relations: The Conference of Berlin (The Potsdam Conference), 1945* (Washington: 1960); also Rose, *Dubious Victory,* pp. 270–304; Herbert Feis, *Between War and Peace: The Potsdam Conference* (Princeton: 1960), pp. 155–324, and Charles L. Mee, Jr., *Meeting at Potsdam* (New York: 1975).

[60] Milovan Djilas, *Conversations with Stalin* (New York: 1962), p. 114. See also Truman, *Year of Decisions,* pp. 440–443; Herbert Feis, *Contest Over Japan* (New York: 1967); and Marc S. Gallicchio, *The Cold War Begins in Asia: American East Asian Policy and the Fall of the Japanese Empire* (New York: 1988).

The atomic bomb's effect on the Soviet-American relationship has been the subject of intense speculation and debate.
There is no doubt that the bomb's political implications had
concerned American officials since the early days of its development: both the Roosevelt and Truman administrations expected
the new weapon to strengthen considerably the American bargaining position in future negotiations with the Soviet Union.[61]
But this fact does not justify charges that Truman's motives in using the bomb were as much to intimidate the Russians as to defeat
the Japanese.[62] Despite the fact that American cryptographers had
long since cracked the Tokyo government's codes, no conclusive
evidence existed indicating an immediate willingness on Japan's
part to surrender. An invasion of Kyushu, with anticipated heavy
casualties, appeared to be the only alternative to use of the bomb.
Given conditions of almost total war, given the expenditure of
time and resources that had gone into its production, given the
prospect of saving thousands of American lives, the decision to
use the bomb took on a logic of its own, never entirely separated
from considerations of postwar international politics but never
dominated by them either.[63]

To the extent that these considerations did play a role, it was
with the expectation that a combat demonstration of the new
weapon's effectiveness would facilitate, not impair, chances for

---

[61] Sherwin, *A World Destroyed*, pp. 165–219. See also Bernstein, "The Quest
for Security," pp. 1003–1015; Barton J. Bernstein, "Roosevelt, Truman, and the
Atomic Bomb, 1941–1945: A Reinterpretation," *Political Science Quarterly*,
XC(Spring, 1975), 23–69; and Robert S. Messer, *The End of an Alliance: James F.
Byrnes, Roosevelt, Truman, and the Origins of the Cold War* (Chapel Hill: 1982), pp.
71–92.

[62] See, for example, Alperovitz, *Atomic Diplomacy*, *passim*.

[63] Rose, *Dubious Victory*, pp. 305–355; Sherwin, *A World Destroyed*, pp. 198–
200; Walter Smith Schoenberger, *Decision of Destiny* (Athens, Ohio: 1969),
pp. 285–307. Recent research has called into question Truman's retrospective
claim [*Year of Decisions*, p. 417] that intelligence estimates predicted the loss of
500,000 American lives if the Japanese home islands had to be invaded without
using the atomic bomb. [See Rufus E. Miles, Jr., "Hiroshima: The Strange Myth
of Half a Million American Lives Saved," *International Security*, X(Fall, 1985),
121–140; also Barton J. Bernstein, "A Postwar Myth: 500,000 U.S. Lives Saved,"
*Bulletin of the Atomic Scientists*, XLII (June–July, 1986), 38–40.] But in the context
of total war, Truman and his advisers would have found it difficult to justify *any*
substantial number of additional American casualties once the bomb had become available.

an amicable resolution of differences with the Soviet Union. The simple fact that the United States possessed the bomb would make possible a firmer American negotiating position, something Truman, and his advisers increasingly regarded as necessary if talks with the Russians were to succeed. The bomb would also give the United States a bargaining chip, in the sense that information regarding its production—or a commitment to seek its control by an international agency—might be exchanged for Soviet political concessions. Finally, much in the minds at least of several of the scientists involved in the bomb project was the conviction that only a graphic illustration of what the new weapon could do would shock the world into taking those measures necessary to prevent its future use. As one of them noted, "Without a military demonstration it may be impossible to impress the world with the need for national sacrifices to gain lasting security."[64]

These hopes never materialized; plans for the international control of atomic energy foundered on the mutual distrust with which Russians and Americans had come, by the end of the war, to regard each other. In time, however, once both sides had perfected nuclear weapons and the means of delivering them, mutual deterrence would come to discourage the use of such devices as efficiently as proposed schemes for their international control might have done. It may be in this respect that the decision to end World War II with atomic weapons has had its most beneficial, if wholly unforeseen, effect: without the awesome demonstrations Hiroshima and Nagasaki provided of the consequences of failure, it is difficult to imagine how the "balance of terror" could have been maintained with the success that it has during the past four and a half decades.

The Grand Alliance represented a triumph of interests over ideologies in a moment of shared peril; without its potent combination of Russian manpower and Western technology, it is difficult to see how Hitler's defeat, not to mention that of the

---

[64] Arthur H. Compton to Henry L. Stimson, June 12, 1945, quoted in Bernstein, "Roosevelt, Truman, and the Atomic Bomb," p. 60n. See also Sherwin, *A World Destroyed*, pp. 200, 212, 218; Gaddis, *The United States and the Origins of the Cold War*, p. 267; and Richard Rhodes, *The Making of the Atomic Bomb* (New York: 1986), pp. 308, 324–325, 508–509.

Japanese, could have been accomplished in less than four years. At no point during that conflict, though, were politics adjourned, whether in Washington, London, or Moscow: military strategy on each side reflected visions of a postwar settlement not always congruent with what the other side had in mind. As a result, seeds of future conflicts began to grow, even as fruits of victory were being harvested. In whatever particular Hell he inhabited, the Austrian corporal must have enjoyed a fleeting moment of consolation, for the coalition he had inadvertently forged had now, through the act of destroying him, begun to destroy itself.

CHAPTER VII

# The Origins of the Cold War: 1945–1953

IT IS, OF COURSE, A TRUISM THAT COALITIONS TEND NOT TO SURVIVE THEIR ENEMIES' DEFEAT. Certainly during World War II most observers of the international scene had expected differences eventually to arise among the victors. The hope had been, though, that a sufficiently strong framework of common interests—whether the United Nations or some mutually acceptable agreement on spheres of influence—would develop that could keep these differences within reasonable limits. This did not happen. Although both sides sought security, although neither side wanted a new war, disagreements over how to achieve those goals proved too great to overcome. With a rapidity that dismayed policymakers in both Washington and Moscow, allies shortly before united against the Axis found themselves in a confrontation with each other that would determine the shape of the postwar era. Russian-American relations, once a problem of rarely more than peripheral concern for the two countries involved, now became an object of rapt attention and anxiety for the entire world.

I

It is no simple matter to explain how national leaders in the United States and the Soviet Union came to hold such dissimilar concepts of postwar security. There did exist, in the history of the two countries' encounters with one another, an ample basis for mutual distrust. But there were also strong motives for cooperation, not the least of which was that, had they been able to act in concert, Russians and Americans might have achieved something close to absolute security in an insecure world. Their failure to do so may be attributed, ultimately, to irreconcilable differences in four critical areas: perceptions of history, ideology, technology, and personality.

Clearly the divergent historical experiences of the two countries conditioned their respective views of how best to attain security.[1] The Russians tended to think of security in terms of space—not a surprising attitude, considering the frequency with which their country had been invaded, or the way in which they had used distance to defeat their adversaries. That such a concept might be outmoded in an age of atomic weapons and long-range bombers appears not to have occurred to Stalin; Hitler's defeat brought no alteration in his determination to control as much territory along the periphery of the Soviet Union as possible. "He regarded as sure only whatever he held in his fist," the Yugoslav Communist Milovan Djilas has written. "Everything beyond the control of his police was a potential enemy."[2]

Americans, on the other hand, tended to see security in institutional terms: conditioned by their own atypical historical experience, they assumed that if representative governments could be established as widely as possible, together with a collective security organization capable of resolving differences between them, peace would be assured. That such governments might not always harbor peaceful intentions toward their neighbors, that the United Nations, in the absence of great power agreement, might lack the means of settling disputes, occurred to only a few informed observers. The general public, upon whose support foreign policy ultimately depended, tended to accept Cordell Hull's vision of a postwar world in which "there will no longer be need for spheres of influence, for alliances, for balance of power, or any of the special arrangements through which, in the unhappy past, the nations sought to safeguard their security or to promote their interests."[3]

---

[1] See, on this point, Louis J. Halle, *The Cold War as History* (New York: 1967), pp. 10–29.

[2] Djilas, *Conversations with Stalin*, p. 82. See also Taubman, *Stalin's America Policy*, p. 74.

[3] *Congressional Record*, November 18, 1943, p. 9679. See also Michael Donelan, *The Ideas of American Foreign Policy* (London: 1963), p. 36; and John Lewis Gaddis, *The Long Peace: Inquiries into the History of the Cold War* (New York: 1987), pp. 51–52.

There was, of course, room for compromising these conflicting viewpoints. Neither the United States nor its British ally had been prepared wholly to abandon spheres of influence as a means of achieving their own postwar security; both accepted the premise that the USSR was entitled to have friendly countries along its borders. The great difficulty was that, unlike the expansion of American and British influence into Western Europe and the Mediterranean, the Soviet Union's gains took place without the approval of most of the governments and most' of the people in the areas involved. The Anglo-Americans simply did not find it necessary, in the same measure as did the Russians, to ensure their own security by depriving people within their sphere of influence of the right to self-determination.[4] Given Western convictions that only the diffusion of democratic institutions could guarantee peace, given Hitler's all-too-vivid precedent, Moscow's imposition of influence in Eastern Europe seemed ominous, whatever its motives. Stalin found himself able to implement his vision of security only by appearing to violate that of the West. The result was to create for the Soviet Union new sources of hostility and, ultimately, insecurity in the world.

Ideological differences constituted a second source of antagonism. Stalin had deliberately downplayed the Soviet commitment to communism during the war, even to the point of abolishing the Comintern in 1943. Some Americans concluded that the Russians had abandoned that ideology altogether, if on no other grounds than that a nation that fought Germans so effectively could not be all bad.[5] The European communist movement remained very much the instrument of Soviet policy, however, and the Russians used it to facilitate their projection of influence into Eastern Europe. This development raised fears in the West that Soviet collaboration against the Axis had been nothing but a marriage of convenience and that, victory having been achieved, the Kremlin was now embarking upon a renewed crusade for world revolution.

This was, it now appears, a mistaken view. Stalin had always placed the security of the Soviet state above the interests of in-

---

[4] See, on this point, Geir Lundestad, "Empire by Invitation? The United States and Western Europe, 1945–1952," *Journal of Peace Research*, XXIII(1986), 263–276.

[5] Gaddis, *The United States and the Origins of the Cold War*, pp. 32–42.

ternational communism; it had been the former, not the latter, that had motivated his expansion into Eastern Europe. Far from encouraging communists outside the Soviet Union to seize power, Stalin initially advised restraint, especially in his dealings with such movements in France, Italy, Greece, and China.[6] But the Soviet leader's caution was not all that clear in the West. Faced with the sudden intrusion of Russian power into Europe, faced with a revival of anticapitalist rhetoric among communists throughout the world,[7] faced with painful evidence from the recent past of what happened when dictators' rhetoric was not taken seriously, observers in both Western Europe and the United States jumped to the conclusion that Stalin, like Hitler, had insatiable ambitions, and would not stop until contained.[8]

Technological differences created a third source of tension. The United States alone emerged from World War II with an industrial plant superior to what it had possessed before that conflict started; the Soviet Union, in turn, had come out of the war with its land ravaged, much of its industry destroyed, and some twenty million of its citizens dead. The resulting disparity of power caused some Americans to exaggerate their ability to influence events in the rest of the world; it simultaneously produced in the Russians deep feelings of inferiority and vulnerability.[9]

This problem manifested itself most obviously with regard to reconstruction. Stalin had hoped to repair war damage with the help of Lend-Lease and a postwar loan from the United States; his conviction that Americans would soon be facing a postwar

---

[6] On this point, see Djilas, *Conversations with Stalin*, pp. 27, 74, 132, 182; Mastny, *Russia's Road to the Cold War*, pp. 67–68, 85–97, 114, 231; William O. McCagg, Jr., *Stalin Embattled, 1943–1948* (Detroit: 1978), pp. 31–71. But, as William Taubman points out, Stalin's attempts to restrain communists outside the Soviet Union did not mean that he had abandoned efforts to project influence there. [*Stalin's American Policy*, pp. 75–82].

[7] John C. Campbell, *The United States in World Affairs, 1947–48* New York: 1948), pp. 4—7.

[8] See Gaddis, *The Long Peace*, pp. 34–40.

[9] Thomas G. Paterson, *Soviet-American Confrontation: Postwar Reconstruction and the Origins of the Cold War* (Baltimore: 1973), pp. 8–14. See also Paul Kennedy, *The Rise and Fall of the Great Powers: Economic Change and Military Conflict from 1500 to 2000* (New York: 1987), pp. 362–363.

depression led him to believe—drawing on clear Leninist principles—that Washington would have no choice but to provide such aid as a means of generating foreign markets for surplus products. His surprise was great when the United States passed up the economic benefits it would have derived from granting a loan in favor of the political concessions it hoped to obtain by withholding it. Nor would Washington allow the use of Lend-Lease for reconstruction; to compound the offense, the Truman administration also cut off, in 1946, the flow of reparations from the American zone in Germany. Whether more generous policies on these matters would have produced better relations with the Soviet Union is impossible to prove—certainly the Russians were never in such need of aid as to be willing to make major political concessions in order to get it. There is no doubt, though, that they bitterly resented their exclusion from these "fruits" of Western technology.[10]

Another "fruit" of Western technology that impressed the Russians was, of course, the atomic bomb. Although Soviet leaders carefully avoided signs of concern about this new weapon, they did secretly accelerate their own bomb development project while simultaneously calling for the abolition of all such weapons of mass destruction.[11] After much debate within the government, the United States, in the summer of 1946, proposed the Baruch Plan, which would have transferred control of all fissionable materials to the United Nations. In fact, however, neither the Russians nor the Americans had sufficient faith in the world organization to entrust their security completely to it. Washington at no point was willing to surrender its bombs until the control system had gone into effect, while Moscow was unwilling to accept the inspection provisions which would allow the plan to operate. Both sides had concluded by 1947 that they

---

[10] Paterson, *Soviet-American Confrontation*, pp. 54–56, 260–264. See also Susan J. Linz, "Foreign Aid and Soviet Postwar Recovery," *Journal of Economic History*, XLV(December, 1985), 947–954.

[11] David Holloway, *The Soviet Union and the Arms Race* (New Haven: 1983), pp. 19–20; McGeorge Bundy, *Danger and Survival: Choices about the Bomb in the First Fifty Years* (New York: 1988), pp. 176–184. See also Nikita S. Khrushchev, *Khrushchev Remembers: The Last Testament*, translated and edited by Strobe Talbott (Boston: 1974), pp. 58–59.

would find greater security in an arms race than in an unproven system of international control.[12]

Finally, accidents of personality made it more difficult than it might otherwise have been to achieve a mutually agreeable settlement. The Russians perceived in the transition from Roosevelt to Truman an abrupt shift from an attitude of cooperation to one of confrontation. "The policy pursued by the US ruling circles after the death of Franklin D. Roosevelt," the official history of Soviet foreign policy asserts, "amounted to renunciation of dependable and mutually beneficial cooperation with the Soviet Union, a cooperation that was so effective...in the period of joint struggle against the nazi aggressors."[13] In fact, though, Roosevelt's policy had been firmer than Stalin realized; Truman's was not as uncompromising as his rhetoric suggested. What was different was style: where Roosevelt had sought to woo the Soviet leader by meeting his demands wherever possible, the new chief executive, like a good poker player, tried to deal from positions of rhetorical, if not actual, strength. His tough talk was designed to facilitate, not impede, negotiations—any appearance of weakness, he thought, would only encourage the Russians to ask for more.[14]

What Truman failed to take into account was the possibility that Stalin might also be bluffing. Given the history of Western intervention to crush Bolshevism, given the Soviet Union's ruined economy and weakened population, and given the atomic bomb's unexpected confirmation of American technological superiority, it seems likely that the aging Soviet dictator was as frightened of the West as the West was of him. Truman's tough

---

[12] See, on this point, PPS/7, "General United States Policy with Respect to International Control of Atomic Energy," August 21, 1947, *FR: 1947*, I, 607; also Larry G. Gerber, "The Baruch Plan and the Origins of the Cold War," *Diplomatic History*, VI(Winter, 1982), 69–95.

[13] A. A. Gromyko and B. N. Ponomarev, eds., *Soviet Foreign Policy: 1917–1980*, translated by David Skvirsky (Moscow: 1981), II, 27. See also Nikita S. Khrushchev, *Khrushchev Remembers*, translated and edited by Strobe Talbott (Boston: 1970), p. 232.

[14] Truman also drew on his domestic political background in attempting to deal with Stalin, who he thought resembled the late Kansas City political boss, Tom Pendergast. See Deborah Welch Larson, *Origins of Containment: A Psychological Explanation* (Princeton: 1985), p. 178.

rhetoric, together with Hiroshima's example, may well have reinforced Stalin's conviction that if *he* showed any signs of weakness, all would be lost. Both leaders had learned too well the lesson of the 1930s: that appeasement never pays. Prospects for an amicable resolution of differences suffered accordingly.

There was nothing in this set of circumstances that made the Cold War inevitable—few things ever are inevitable in history. But a situation such as existed in Europe in 1945, with two great powers separated only by a power vacuum, seemed almost predestined to produce hostility, whether either side willed it or not. As a result, the United States, the Soviet Union, and much of the rest of the world as well would have to suffer through that prolonged period of insecurity that observers at the time, and historians since, have called the "Cold War."

## II

The evolution of United States policy toward the Soviet Union between 1945 and 1947 can be seen as a three-stage process of relating national interests to national capabilities. From V-J Day through early 1946, there existed genuine confusion in Washington as to both Soviet intentions and appropriate methods for dealing with them. Coordination between power and policy was, as a result, minimal. By the spring of 1946, a consensus had developed favoring resistance to further Soviet expansion, but little had been done to determine what resources would be necessary to accomplish that goal or to differentiate between areas of primary and secondary concern. It was not until 1947 that there began to emerge an approach to the Soviet Union that bore some reasonable relationship to American capabilities for projecting influence in the world.

There appeared to be no lack of power available to the United States for the purpose of ordering the postwar environment as it saw fit, but the task of transforming technological superiority into political influence proved frustratingly difficult. Secretary of State James F. Byrnes had hoped to trade reconstruction assistance and a commitment to the international control of atomic energy for Soviet concessions on such outstanding issues as implementation of the Yalta Declaration on Liberated Europe, peace treaties with former German satellites, and, ultimately, a final resolution of the German question itself. But the Russians maintained a posture of ostentatious unconcern about the atomic bomb, nor would they yield on significant issues to obtain reconstruction assistance. Congressional skepticism about Moscow's intentions ensured that any loan would carry a political price far beyond what the Russians would willingly pay, while public opinion pushed Truman into a decision to seek United Nations control of atomic energy before Byrnes had made any attempt to extract Soviet concessions in return. Economic and technological superiority thus won the United States surprisingly few practical benefits in its early postwar dealings with the USSR.[15]

In Washington, moreover, there still existed a substantial number of officials who viewed Soviet hostility as the product of misunderstandings and who expected that, with restraint on both sides, a mutually satisfactory resolution of differences might still occur. It is significant that as late as November, 1945, a State Department representative could rebuke the Joint Chiefs of Staff for confidentially suggesting that the wartime alliance might not survive victory. "We must always bear in mind," a Department memorandum noted the following month, "that because of the differences between the economic and political systems [of the United States and the Soviet Union], the conduct of our relations requires more patience and diligence than with other countries." Despite his tough rhetoric, President Truman shared this view. Disagreements with the Russians were to be expected once the common bond of military necessity had been removed, he told his advisers; in time, they would disappear because "Stalin was a fine man who wanted to do the right thing."[16]

But events made this position increasingly difficult to sustain. The Russians remained adamant in their determination to exclude Western influence from Eastern Europe and the Balkans, while a continued Soviet presence in Iran and

---

[15] Gaddis, *The United States and the Origins of the Cold War*, pp. 244–276; Messer, *The End of an Alliance, 1945–1948*, pp. 1–131.

[16] *FR: 1946*, I, 1126–1127; Thomas M. Campbell and George C. Herring, eds., *The Diaries of Edward R. Stettinius, Jr., 1943–1946* (New York: 1975), p. 437; John Morton Blum, ed., *The Price of Vision: The Diary of Henry A. Wallace, 1942–1946* (Boston: 1973), p. 490.

Manchuria raised fears that Moscow might try to impose control over those territories as well. Russian interest in the eastern Mediterranean seemed to be growing, with demands for trusteeships over former Italian colonies, boundary rectifications at Turkey's expense, and a revision of the Montreux Convention governing passage through the Dardanelles. And in February, 1946, news of Soviet atomic espionage became public for the first time with the revelation that the Canadian government had arrested a group of Russian agents for trying to steal information about the bomb. That same month, Stalin in his first major postwar foreign policy speech stressed the incompatibility between communism and capitalism, implying that future wars were inevitable until the world economic system was restructured along Soviet lines.[17]

It was at this point that there arrived at the State Department a dispatch from George F. Kennan, now *chargé d'affaires* at the American embassy in Moscow, which did much to clarify official thinking regarding Soviet behavior. Russian hostility toward the West, Kennan argued, stemmed chiefly from the internal necessities of the Stalinist regime: the Soviet dictator required a hostile outside world in order to justify his own autocratic rule. Marxism provided Soviet leaders with

justification for their instinctive fear of the outside world, for the dictatorship without which they did not know how to rule, for cruelties they did not dare not to inflict, for sacrifices they felt bound to demand.... Today they cannot dispense with it. It is the fig leaf of their moral and intellectual respectability.

It followed that Stalin was, by nature, incapable of being reassured. "Nothing short of complete disarmament, delivery of our air and naval forces to Russia and resigning of the powers of government to American Communists would even dent this problem," Kennan noted in a subsequent dispatch, "and even then Moscow would smell a trap and would continue to harbor the most baleful misgivings." The solution, Kennan suggested, was to strengthen Western institutions in order to render them

---

[17] *Vital Speeches*, XII (March 1, 1946) 300–304. See also Gaddis, *The United States and the Origins of the Cold War*, pp. 299–302; and, for the significance of Stalin's speech, McCagg, *Stalin Embattled*, pp. 217–237; Taubman, *Stalin's American Policy*, pp. 133–135.

invulnerable to the Soviet challenge while simultaneously awaiting the eventual mellowing of the Soviet regime.[18]

There was little in Kennan's analysis that he and other career Soviet experts had not been saying for some time. What was new was Washington's receptivity to the message, a condition brought about both by frustration over Soviet behavior and by growing public and Congressional resistance to further concessions. In contrast to its earlier optimism about relations with Moscow, the State Department now endorsed Kennan's analysis as "the most probable explanation of present Soviet policies and attitudes." The United States, it concluded, should demonstrate to the Kremlin, "in the first instance by diplomatic means and in the last analysis by military force if necessary that the present course of its foreign policy can only lead to disaster for the Soviet Union."[19]

The spring and summer of 1946 did see a noticeable toughening of United States policy toward the Soviet Union. In early March, Truman lent public sanction to Winston Churchill's strongly anti-Soviet "iron curtain" speech by appearing on the platform with him at Fulton, Missouri. That same month, Secretary of State Byrnes insisted on placing the issue of Iran before the United Nations, even after the Russians had agreed to withdraw their troops from that country. The termination of German reparations shipments came in May; three months later, Byrnes publicly committed the United States to support German rehabilitation, with or without the Russians. In July, Truman endorsed the continued presence of American troops in southern Korea on the grounds that that country constituted "an ideological battleground upon which our whole success in Asia may depend." Soviet pressure on Turkey for bases produced a decision in August to maintain an American naval force indefinitely in the eastern Mediterranean. In September, White House aide Clark Clifford submitted a report to the president, prepared after consultation with top military and diplomatic advisers, arguing that "this government should be prepared ... to

---

[18] Kennan to Byrnes, February 22 and March 20, 1946, *FR: 1946*, VI, 696–709, 721–723. See also Kennan, *Memoirs: 1925–1950*, pp. 292–295.

[19] H. Freeman Matthews to the State-War-Navy Coordinating Committee, April 1, 1946, *FR: 1946*, I, 1167–1169.

resist vigorously and successfully any efforts of the U.S.S.R. to expand into areas vital to American security."[20]

But these policies were decided upon without precise assessments as to whether the means existed to carry them out. The atomic bomb was of little use for such purposes, given the strong inhibitions American officials felt about brandishing their new weapon in peacetime and given the limited number of bombs and properly equipped bombers available, if war came.[21] Nor could the administration hold out the prospect of economic aid as a means of inducing more cooperative Soviet behavior, in the face of continued Congressional reluctance to appropriate funds for such purposes.[22] Such conventional military power as the United States possessed was rapidly melting away under the pressures of demobilization, and although most Americans supported firmer policies toward the Soviet Union, the election of an economy-minded, Republican-controlled Congress in November suggested that few were prepared to assume the burdens, in the form of high taxes and military manpower levels, such policies would require.

Shortly thereafter a severe economic crisis, the product of remaining wartime dislocations and an unusually harsh winter, hit Western Europe. This development caused the British to announce their intention, in February, 1947, of terminating economic and military aid to Greece and Turkey, countries that had, up to that point, been regarded as within London's sphere of responsibility. It also raised the longer-range but even more frightening prospect that economic conditions in Western

---

[20] Truman to Edwin Pauley, July 16, 1946, ibid., VII, 713; Clifford report, "American Relations with the Soviet Union," September 24, 1946, in Thomas H. Etzold and John Lewis Gaddis, eds. *Containment: Documents on American Policy and Strategy, 1945–1950* (New York: 1978), p. 66. See also Fraser J. Harbutt, *The Iron Curtain: Churchill, America, and the Origins of the Cold War* (New York: 1986), pp. 151–208; Bruce R. Kuniholm, *The Origins of the Cold War in the Near East: Great Power Conflict and Diplomacy in Iran, Turkey, and Greece* (Princeton: 1980), pp. 303–382; and Charles M. Dobbs, *The Unwanted Symbol: American Foreign Policy, the Cold War, and Korea, 1945–1950* (Kent, Ohio: 1981), pp. 56–83.

[21] We now know that there were 9 atomic bombs in the American arsenal in mid-1946; the number had risen only to 13 by mid-1947. [See David Alan Rosenberg, "U. S. Nuclear Stockpile, 1945 to 1950," *Bulletin of the Atomic Scientists*, XXXVIII(May, 1982), 25–30; also Harry R. Borowski, *A Hollow Threat: Strategic Air Power and Containment Before Korea* (Westport, Connecticut: 1982)].

[22] Paterson, *Soviet-American Confrontation*, pp. 51–54.

Europe generally might deteriorate to the point that communist parties there could seize power through coups or even free elections. Suddenly the whole European balance of power, which the United States had gone to war to restore, seemed once again in peril.[23]

This situation, which appeared so to threaten European stability, was one the Russians had done little if anything to instigate; it was rather the product primarily of internal conditions within the countries involved. But there was little doubt of Moscow's ability to exploit the European economic crisis if nothing was done to alleviate it. And action was taken, with such energy and dispatch that the fifteen weeks between late February and early June, 1947, have come to be regarded as a great moment in the history of American diplomacy, a rare instance in which "the government of the United States operat[ed] at its very finest, efficiently and effectively."[24]

Such plaudits may be too generous. Certainly the language Truman used to justify aid to Greece and Turkey ("at the present moment in world history nearly every nation must choose between alternative ways of life. . . . I believe that it must be the policy of the United States to support free peoples who are resisting attempted subjugation by armed minorities or by outside pressures")[25] represented a projection of rhetoric far beyond either the administration's intentions or capabilities.[26] Whatever its usefulness in prying funds out of a parsimonious Congress, the sweeping language of the "Truman Doctrine" would cause problems later on as the president and his foreign policy advisers sought to clarify distinctions between vital and peripheral interests in the world. That such distinctions were important became apparent with the announcement in June, 1947, of the Marshall Plan, an ambitious initiative that reflected,

---

[23] For the origins of this crisis, see Terry H. Anderson, *The United States, Great Britain, and the Cold War, 1944–1947* Columbia, Missouri: 1981), pp. 144–175; and Robert M. Hathaway, *Ambiguous Partnership: Britain and America, 1944–1947* (New York: 1981), pp. 295–299.

[24] Joseph M. Jones, *The Fifteen Weeks (February 21–June 5, 1947)* (New York: 1955), p. vii.

[25] *Public Papers of the Presidents: Harry S. Truman, 1947* (Washington: 1963), pp. 178–179.

[26] See, on this point, John Lewis Gaddis, "Was the Truman Doctrine a Real Turning Point?" *Foreign Affairs*, LII(January, 1974), 390–393.

far more than did the Truman Doctrine, the careful calibration of ends to means characteristic of the administration's policy during this period.

The European Recovery Program, to use its official title, proposed spending some $17 billion for economic assistance to the non-communist nations of Europe over the next four years.[27] (Aid was offered to the Soviet Union and its East European satellites as well, but with the expectation, which proved to be correct, that Moscow would turn it down.) It was a plan directed, not against Soviet military attack, a contingency United States officials considered remote, but against the economic malaise that had sapped self-confidence among European allies, rendering them vulnerable to internal communist takeovers. It involved no direct military commitments; rather, its architects assumed, much as had advocates of the "arsenal of democracy" concept before World War II, that the United States could most efficiently help restore the balance of power in Europe by contributing its technology and raw materials, but not its manpower. It represented a deliberate decision to focus American energies on the recovery of Europe at the expense of commitments elsewhere: it is significant that the spring of 1947 also saw the Truman administration move toward liquidating its remaining responsibilities in China and Korea.[28] What took place in Washington during the famous "fifteen weeks," then, was not so much a proliferation of commitments as a reordering of priorities, executed with a sharp awareness of what the United States would have to accept in the world and what, given limited resources, it could realistically expect to change.

Unfortunately, rhetoric again obscured the point, this time by way of a mysterious article, entitled "The Sources of Soviet Conduct," which appeared in the July, 1947, issue of *Foreign Affairs*. Attributed only to a "Mr. X," it advanced the notion that

the main element of any United States policy toward the Soviet Union must be that of a long-term, patient but firm and vigilant contain-

---

[27] The definitive study is now Michael J. Hogan, *The Marshall Plan: America, Britain, and the Reconstruction of Western Europe, 1947–1952* (Cambridge: 1987); but see also Robert J. Pollard, *Economic Security and the Origins of the Cold War, 1945–1950* (New York: 1985).

[28] See William Whitney Stueck, Jr., *The Road to Confrontation: American Policy toward China and Korea, 1947–1950* (Chapel Hill: 1981), pp. 31–110.

ment of Russian expansive tendencies....Soviet pressure against the free institutions of the Western world is something that can be contained by the adroit and vigilant application of counter-force at a series of constantly shifting geographical and political points, corresponding to the shifts and maneuvers of Soviet policy.[29]

Then, as now, nothing remained secret for very long, and word soon leaked out that "Mr. X" had been none other than Kennan, who had recently become head of the State Department's new Policy Planning Staff. This information gave the "X" article something of the character of an official document, and it quickly came to be seen as the definitive expression of administration policy toward the Soviet Union.

In fact, Kennan had not intended his article as a comprehensive prescription for future action; it was, rather, an elaboration of the analysis of Soviet behavior he had submitted in his February, 1946, telegram to the State Department. Such policy recommendations as Kennan did include reflected only in the most approximate and incomplete way the range of his thinking on Soviet-American relations. The article implied an automatic commitment to resist Russian expansionism wherever it occurred; there was in it little sense of the administration's preoccupation with limited means and of the consequent need to distinguish between primary and secondary interests. Nor did the piece make it clear that economic rather than military methods were to be employed as the chief instrument of containment.[30] The safest generalization that can be made about the "X" article is that, like the Truman Doctrine, it was an outstanding demonstration of the obfuscatory potential of imprecise prose. It was not an accurate description of the policies the United States was, at that moment, in the process of implementing.

Kennan provided a much clearer explanation of what he meant by "containment" in a secret review of the world situation prepared for Secretary of State George C. Marshall in November, 1947. Soviet efforts to fill power vacuums left by

---

[29] "X," "The Sources of Soviet Conduct," *Foreign Affairs*, XXV(July, 1947), 575–576.

[30] For Kennan's own critique of the "X" article, and an account of the circumstances surrounding its publication, see his *Memoirs: 1925–1950*, pp. 354–367. See also Gaddis, *Strategies of Containment*, pp. 25–53.

German and Japanese defeats had largely been halted, Kennan argued, but this accomplishment had dangerously strained American resources: "The program of aid to Europe which we are now proposing to undertake will probably be the last major effort of this nature which our people could, or should, make....It is clearly unwise for us to continue the attempt to carry alone, or largely singlehanded, the opposition to Soviet expansion." Further dispersal of resources could be avoided only by identifying clearly those parts of the world upon whose defense American security depended. Aside from the Western Hemisphere, Kennan's list included only non-communist Europe, the Middle East, and Japan. In China there was little the West could do, although there were as well "definite limitations on both the military and economic capabilities of the Russians in that area." Since Korea was "not of decisive strategic importance to us, our main task is to extricate ourselves without too great a loss of prestige." All in all, Kennan concluded, "our best answer is to strengthen in every way local forces of resistance, and persuade others to bear a greater part of the burden of opposing communism."[31]

"Containment," then, involved no indiscriminate projection of commitments around the world: it was, instead, a policy precise in its identification of American interests, specific in its assessment of threats to those interests, frugal in its calculation of means required to ward off those threats, vague only in its public presentation. But this very vagueness would, in time, corrupt the concept, for where gaps between policy and rhetoric exist, it is often easier to bring the former into line with the latter than the other way around. The eventual consequence would be the promulgation of policies under the rubric of "containment" far removed from what that doctrine had been originally intended to mean.

### III

Despite its limited character, the vigor of the American response to Soviet postwar probes apparently caught Stalin by surprise. His response was to try to strengthen further the security of his own regime, first by increasing safeguards against

---

[31] PPS/13, "Resume of World Situation," November 6, 1947, *FR: 1947*, I, 770–777.

Western influences inside the Soviet Union; second, by tightening control over Russia's East European satellites; and finally by working to ensure central direction of the international communist movement. By a perverse kind of logic, each of these moves backfired, as did a much earlier Soviet initiative whose existence only came to light at this point—the establishment, in the United States during the 1930s, of a major espionage network directed from Moscow. The result, in each of these cases, was to produce consequences that only made it more difficult for Stalin to obtain the kind of security he sought.

Soviet leaders had always faced a dilemma regarding contacts with the West. Such associations might carry substantial benefits—certainly this had been true of collaboration with Great Britain and the United States during World War II. But there were also costs, not the least of which was the possibility that prolonged exposure to Western ideas and institutions might erode the still vulnerable base of the Soviet regime. It is an indication of the seriousness with which Stalin viewed this problem that he shipped hundreds of thousands of returning prisoners-of-war off to labor camps in 1945, much to the horror of Americans who had forcibly repatriated many of them at the Russians' request.[32] By 1947, Moscow's campaign against Western influences had extended to literature, music, history, economics, and even genetics. As a result, Soviet prestige suffered throughout the world; the effect of these policies on science, and, in turn, on the advancement of Russian military capabilities, can only be guessed at.[33]

Even more striking in its impact on the West, though, was Stalin's harsh effort to consolidate his control over Eastern

---

[32] The classic account is Alexander Solzhenitsyn, *The Gulag Archipelago* (New York: 1973), especially pp. 237–276; but see also Russell D. Buhite, "Soviet-American Relations and the Repatriation of Prisoners of War, 1945," *Historian*, XXXV(May, 1973), 394–397; and Mark Elliott, "The United States and Forced Repatriation of Soviet Citizens, 1944–47," *Political Science Quarterly*, LXXXVIII (June, 1973), 253–275. The British also deferred to Soviet wishes in this matter. [See Nikolai Tolstoy, *Victims of Yalta* (London: 1979)].

[33] Barghoorn, *The Soviet Image of the United States*, pp. 102–124; Ulam, *Stalin*, pp. 643–652; McCagg, *Stalin Embattled*, pp. 243–254; and, for an account that places the defeat of "moderate" elements somewhat later than suggested here, Werner G. Hahn, *Postwar Soviet Politics: The Fall of Zhdanov and the Defeat of Moderation, 1946–53* (Ithaca: 1982).

Europe. Subservience to Moscow, not ideological uniformity, had been the chief Soviet priority in that area until 1947, but in June of that year the Russians imposed a communist-dominated government in Hungary, a country in which relatively free elections had been held in the fall of 1945. "I think it's an outrage," President Truman told a press conference on June 5. "The Hungarian situation is a terrible one." In February, 1948, the Communist Party of Czechoslovakia overthrew the duly-constituted government of that country—an event that produced the death, by either murder or suicide, of the popular Czech foreign minister, Jan Masaryk. It would be difficult to exaggerate the impact of this development in the West, where guilty consciences still existed over what had been done to the Czechs at Munich ten years before. One immediate effect was to ensure Congressional passage of the Marshall Plan; another was to provoke Britain, France, and the Benelux countries into forming the Western Union, the first step toward a joint defensive alliance among the non-communist nations of Europe. There also followed the stimulation of something approaching a war scare in the United States, an administration request for Universal Military Training and the reinstitution of the draft, and a public condemnation by Truman of the Soviet Union as the "one nation [that] has not only refused to cooperate in the establishment of a just and honorable peace, but—even worse—has actively sought to prevent it."[34]

Meanwhile, attempts to resolve the question of divided Germany had produced no results, despite protracted and tedious negotiations. In February, 1948, the three Western occupying powers, plus the Benelux countries, met in London and decided to move toward formation of an independent West German state. Stalin's response, after initial hesitation, was to impose a blockade on land access to Berlin, which the World War II settlement had left a hundred miles inside the Soviet zone. The Berlin crisis brought the United States and the Soviet

---

[34] Truman press conference, June 5, 1947, *Truman Public Papers, 1947*, p. 265; Truman address to Congress, March 17, 1948, *Public Papers of the Presidents: Harry S. Truman, 1948* (Washington: 1964), p. 183. For the impact of the Czech crisis, see Herbert Feis, *From Trust to Terror: The Onset of the Cold War, 1945–1950* (New York: 1970), pp. 291–305; and Daniel Yergin, *Shattered Peace: The Origins of the Cold War and the National Security State* (Boston: 1977), pp. 343–358.

*Divided Germany and Austria.*

Union as close to war as they would come during the early postwar years. Truman was determined that Western forces would stay in the beleaguered city, however untenable their military position there, and to reinforce this policy he ostentatiously transferred to British bases three squadrons of B-29 bombers. No atomic bombs accompanied these planes, nor were they even equipped to carry them.[35] But this visible reminder of American nuclear superiority may well have deterred the Russians from interfering with air access to Berlin, and through this means the United States and its allies were able to keep their sectors of the city supplied for almost a year. Stalin finally agreed to lift the blockade in May, 1949, but not before repeating the dubious distinction he had achieved in the Russo-Finnish War a decade earlier: of appearing to be brutal and incompetent at the same time.

The Berlin blockade had two important consequences, both of which were detrimental from the Soviet point of view. It provided the impetus necessary to transform the Western Union into the North Atlantic Treaty Organization, a defensive alliance linking the United States, Canada, and ten Western European nations, established in April, 1949.[36] Simultaneously, the blockade lessened prospects for a settlement of the German problem in collaboration with the Russians;[37] the result was to accelerate implementation of the London program, a goal accomplished with the formation, in September, 1949, of the Federal Republic of Germany.

---

[35] Borowski, *A Hollow Threat*, pp. 125–128. See also Gregg Herken, *The Winning Weapon: The Atomic Bomb in the Cold War, 1945–1950* (New York: 1980), pp. 257–260; and, on the Berlin blockade crisis in general, Avi Shlaim, *The United States and the Berlin Blockade, 1948–1949: A Study in Crisis Decision-Making* (Berkeley: 1983). For Soviet behavior prior to and during the crisis, see Hannes Adomeit, *Soviet Risk-Taking and Crisis Behavior: A Theoretical and Empirical Analysis* (London: 1982), pp. 67–182.

[36] For the origins of NATO, see Timothy P. Ireland, *Creating the Entangling Alliance: The Origins of the North Atlantic Treaty Organization* (Westport, Connecticut: 1981); Lawrence S. Kaplan, *The United States and NATO: The Formative Years* (Lexington: 1984); and, for the strong British role in these developments, Martin H. Folly, "Breaking the Vicious Circle: Britain, the United States, and the Genesis of the North Atlantic Treaty," *Diplomatic History*, XII(Winter, 1988), 59–77.

[37] For evidence that such an option was still under consideration in Washington, see Gaddis, *Strategies of Containment*, pp. 74–76.

Stalin's efforts to tighten control over communists outside the Soviet Union also produced unintended consequences. In apparent reaction to the Marshall Plan, he authorized in September, 1947, the revival of a central directorate for the international communist movement, this time to be known as the Cominform. It is unlikely that Stalin had anything more in mind than to make international communism a more reliable instrument of Soviet foreign policy, but the effect in the West was to confirm lurking suspicions that his objective had always been world revolution. As Elbridge Durbrow, the American *chargé d'affaires* in Moscow, put it, the move was "patently a declaration of political and economic war against the U.S. and everything the U.S. stands for in world affairs."[38]

Establishment of the Cominform substantially weakened the position of communist parties in Western Europe, whose success, up to that point, had been based largely on their ability to convince followers of their nationalist rather than internationalist credentials. Even worse, from the Soviet point of view, the effort to enforce ideological uniformity provoked an open split with Tito's Yugoslavia, heretofore the Kremlin's most reliable satellite. In Washington, the State Department's Policy Planning Staff immediately saw the importance of this development:

For the first time in history we may now have within the international community a communist state....independent of Moscow....A new factor of fundamental and profound significance has been introduced into the world communist movement by the demonstration that the Kremlin can be successfully defied by one of its own minions.[39]

Winning support from within the government and from Congress for a policy of actually aiding a communist regime took

---

[38] Durbrow to Marshall, October 6, 1947, *FR: 1947*, IV, 596. For Stalin's motives in creating the Cominform, see Taubman, *Stalin's American Policy*, pp. 176–178; and McCagg, *Stalin Embattled*, pp. 261–284.

[39] PPS/35, "The Attitude of This Government Toward Events in Yugoslavia," June 30, 1948, *FR: 1948*, IV, 1079–1080. For background on U.S. policy toward Yugoslavia, see Charles G. Stefan, "The Emergence of the Soviet-Yugoslav Break: A Personal View from the Belgrade Embassy," *Diplomatic History*, VI(Fall, 1982), 387–404; and Robert M. Blum, "Surprised by Tito: The Anatomy of an Intelligence Failure," ibid., XII(Winter, 1988), 39–57.

time, but by 1949 the United States was supporting Tito's position in the United Nations and providing economic assistance. After the outbreak of the Korean War, military aid would follow as well. Stalin's effort to impose monolithic unity had the ironic effect of producing the first visible crack in the monolith—an error of which the United States was quick to take advantage.[40]

Yet another of Stalin's errors—this one made years earlier—came to light only at this point. There had long been rumors, and even some fragmentary evidence, of a Soviet espionage network operating within the United States, but Washington officials had not taken this information seriously nor had it been thoroughly investigated prior to the end of World War II. That situation changed, though, with the defection of Soviet code-clerk Igor Gouzenko in Ottawa shortly after V-J Day, together with the almost simultaneous confession of Elizabeth Bentley, an American who claimed to have been running spies for the Soviet KGB since 1940. These revelations suggested not only that Russians had been trying to steal atomic bomb secrets, but that an entire network of Soviet agents had been created during the 1930s for the purpose of infiltrating government agencies and conveying sensitive information to Moscow. The Truman administration responded by quietly removing suspected individuals from official positions and strengthening its security checks, but by 1948 the Congress had launched a series of sensational public hearings into the matter during which several highly-placed former officials—notably Harry Dexter White of the Treasury Department and Alger Hiss of the State Department—were accused of having committed espionage. White died before formal charges could be brought, but Hiss was convicted early in 1950 of having lied about his earlier communist connections; there quickly followed the arrests of British scientist Klaus Fuchs, who confessed to having transmitted atomic bomb information to the Russians while working on the wartime Manhattan Project, and of Julius and Ethel Rosenberg, who were eventually executed for the same crime in 1953.[41]

---

[40] Lorraine M. Lees, "The American Decision to Aid Tito, 1948–1949," ibid., II(Fall, 1978), 407–422; Henry W. Brands, Jr., "Redefining the Cold War: American Policy toward Yugoslavia, 1948–60," ibid., XI(Winter, 1987), 41–53.

[41] The best sources on these still-controversial issues are Allen Weinstein, *Perjury: The Hiss-Chambers Case* (New York: 1978); Ronald Radosh and Joyce

Because of the highly-charged political atmosphere in which these events took place—and because that atmosphere had largely made possible the opportunistic anti-communism of Senator Joseph McCarthy—there persisted for years afterward the belief that these charges of espionage had been exaggerated: that even if Fuchs had been guilty, Hiss and the Rosenbergs had been the victims of a second American "Red Scare," hardly less virulent in its indiscriminate accusations than its predecessor of 1919–1920.[42] Recent evidence suggests, however, that espionage did in fact take place, and on a significant scale: access to FBI documents has confirmed the case against Hiss, and it has now been acknowledged—as it could not have been at the time—that the government's case against Fuchs, the Rosenbergs, and a number of other alleged spies was based on intercepted and laboriously deciphered communications from the Soviet KGB itself.[43] It has also become clear that the Russians managed even more successfully to infiltrate the British government, to the point in 1944 of placing their own agent, Kim Philby, in charge of *counterespionage* activities within the British Secret Service.[44]

It might be argued that there was nothing unusual in all of this: espionage, after all, has a long and colorful history in relations between great powers. But there is, as yet, no evidence that the Americans or the British attempted to spy on the Russians in any substantial way during World War II; despite their success in breaking German and Japanese codes, they ap-

Milton, *The Rosenberg File: A Search for the Truth* (New York: 1983); Robert J. Lamphere and Tom Shachtman, *The FBI-KGB War: A Special Agent's Story* (New York: 1986); and Robert Chadwell Williams, *Klaus Fuchs, Atom Spy* (Cambridge, Massachusetts: 1987).

[42] See, for example, John Chabot Smith, *Alger Hiss: The True Story* (New York: 1976); and Walter and Miriam Schneir, *Invitation to an Inquest* (New York: 1965). On McCarthy, see Thomas C. Reeves, *The Life and Times of Joe McCarthy: A Biography* (New York: 1982); and David M. Oshinsky, *A Conspiracy So Immense: The World of Joe McCarthy* (New York: 1983).

[43] Weinstein, *Perjury*, p. 565; Radosh and Milton, *The Rosenberg File*, pp. 7–8; Lamphere and Shachtman, *The FBI-KGB War*, pp. 78–98.

[44] See Anthony Boyle, *The Fourth Man: The Definitive Account of Kim Philby, Guy Burgess, and Donald MacLean and Who Recruited Them to Spy for Russia* (New York: 1979); Anthony Glees, *The Secrets of the Service: A Story of Soviet Subversion of Western Intelligence* (New York: 1987).

pear to have refrained from attempting a similar coup against the Russians, for fear of compromising the wartime alliance.[45] The fact that Stalin felt no comparable inhibitions is revealing, both about his own mentality and about his expectations for cooperation after the war. It also causes one to wonder what the Russians gained from their elaborate espionage activities in Britain and the United States, as balanced against what they lost. For although Fuchs's treason may have accelerated the Soviet atomic bomb project by about a year, and although the Russians—through Philby and his associates—may well have picked up sensitive inside information about the size of the American atomic stockpile, the cost to the Russians of their indulgence in espionage, once it became known in the West, was considerable. If Stalin ever hoped to win the trust of Western statesmen—and there is some reason to think he did[46]—then this evidence of his own failure to reciprocate a wartime trust extended to him could only have defeated that purpose.

Through his own policies, therefore, Stalin brought about many of the things he most feared: an American commitment to defend Western Europe; a revived West German state, closely tied to his adversaries; the beginnings of fragmentation within the international communist movement; and a conviction on the part of Western leaders that, because the Soviet Union could not be trusted, negotiations with it on the resolution of outstanding differences could only be approached with the greatest caution and from positions of strength, if they were to take place at all. It was a sobering demonstration of the consequences that can follow from a chronic inability to anticipate the impact of one's own actions; it also provides evidence for the view that one of the West's major—if unappreciated—assets during the early Cold War was the persistent ineptitude of the Soviet dictator himself.[47]

---

[45] Ibid., pp. 246–252; Anthony Cave Brown, *The Last Hero: Wild Bill Donovan* (New York: 1982), pp. 417–419.

[46] See Taubman, *Stalin's American Policy*, pp. 8–9.

[47] See Vojtech Mastny, "Stalin and the Militarization of the Cold War," *International Security*, IX(Winter, 1984–1985), 109–129; also Townsend Hoopes, *The Devil and John Foster Dulles* (Boston: 1973), p. 285.

IV

By 1949, containment had largely achieved its primary objective—restoration of a balance of power in Europe. A sense of self-confidence had begun to reappear, and simultaneously fears of further Soviet expansion, whether by military attack or internal subversion, had begun to subside. In tacit acknowledgment that its previous policies had failed, the Soviet Union in the spring of that year launched a massive "peace campaign," the precursor, as it turned out, of the shift from the doctrine of "inevitable conflict" between communism and capitalism to that of "peaceful coexistence."[48] But success in international relations is an elusive, sometimes undetectable quality, and the Truman administration in 1949 felt anything but buoyant. Perversely, containment's very achievements raised problems of such magnitude as to prevent Washington from taking advantage of them.

Kennan himself had never believed that the United States should remain content simply with limiting Soviet expansion in Europe and East Asia. His concept of containment, as worked out in the Policy Planning Staff during 1947 and 1948, had two additional goals, to be sought once the original objective of geographically restricting Soviet power had been achieved: (1) to bring about a split between the Soviet Union and its chief instrument for projecting power beyond its borders, the international communist movement; and (2) through a combination of pressures and inducements, to alter Moscow's view of the outside world as hostile, and thus to make possible a negotiated mutual withdrawal of Soviet and American forces from the advanced positions they had occupied since the end of World War II.[49]

The idea of exploiting differences between the Soviet Union and international communism had been based on the assumption that the Russians would not indefinitely be able to control that movement, partly because of their own inability to tolerate diversity, and partly because the very act of coming to power in other countries would tend to make communist leaders less dependent on Moscow. Kennan and his associates on the Policy

---

[48] Marshall D. Shulman, *Stalin's Foreign Policy Reappraised* (Cambridge, Massachusetts: 1963), pp. 81–103.

[49] See Gaddis, *Strategies of Containment,* pp. 36–51.

Planning Staff saw Soviet expansionism as a new form of imperialism, subject to all the frailties, vulnerabilities, and self-destructive tendencies of that earlier phenomenon. In time, they thought, two opposing blocs might develop in the communist world—one dominated by the Soviet Union, the other made up of communists defiant of Moscow's leadership. As a report to the National Security Council observed in 1949, "a situation of this description might eventually provide us with an opportunity to operate on the basis of a balance in the communist world and to foster the tendencies toward accommodation with the West implicit in such a state of affairs."[50]

Efforts were undertaken, between 1947 and 1949, to implement this strategy. The offer of Marshall Plan aid to the Soviet Union and Eastern Europe in 1947 had been made in the hope that a Russian rejection would reveal the nakedness of Moscow's control and place strains on its relations with its satellites.[51] The Truman administration moved swiftly to exploit Tito's split with Moscow the following year, and Kennan's Policy Planning Staff saw that event as a precedent for what might happen elsewhere: "The possibility of defection from Moscow, which has heretofore been unthinkable for foreign communist leaders, will from now on be present in one form or another in the mind of every one of them."[52] We now know, as well, that at Kennan's suggestion the National Security Council in June, 1948, authorized creation of a covert action capability for the newly-organized Central Intelligence Agency: resulting activities included secret assistance to left-wing but non-communist political parties and labor unions in Western Europe, the creation of ostensibly private (but also quietly-subsidized) organizations to assist Soviet and East European emigres, the establishment of Radio Free Europe, which broadcast anti-Soviet

---

[50] NSC 58/2, "United States Policy Toward the Soviet Satellite States in Eastern Europe," December 8, 1949, *FR: 1949*, V, 51. See also NSC 20/1, "U.S. Objectives with Respect to Russia," August 18, 1948, in Etzold and Gaddis, eds., *Containment*, pp. 182–187.

[51] Ibid., pp. 182–183. See also Kennan, *Memoirs: 1925–1950*, p. 342.

[52] PPS/35, June 30, 1948, *FR: 1948*, IV, 1030. See also Lees, "The American Decision to Aid Tito," pp. 407–422; Brands, "Redefining the Cold War: American Policy toward Yugoslavia," pp. 41–47; and, on the general strategy of seeking to separate international communists from Moscow's control, Gaddis, *The Long Peace*, pp. 147–164.

propaganda into the satellite countries, and ultimately—although with growing reservations on Kennan's part—a series of mostly unsuccessful efforts actually to conduct clandestine operations in Eastern Europe and the Balkans aimed at further eroding Moscow's control there.[53]

Unfortunately, though, the administration made few attempts to explain the distinction between Soviet expansionism and international communism to the American people. In part, this failure reflected the belief of many in Washington that only the prospect of an undifferentiated global threat could shake Americans out of the isolationist tendencies that remained latent among them. "The only way we can sell the public on our new policy," one official had written at the time of the Truman Doctrine speech, "is by emphasizing the necessity of holding the line: communism vs. democracy should be the major theme."[54] In part, lack of clarity on this issue reflected genuine confusion on the part of many in Washington as to whether ideology motivated, or was the instrument of, Kremlin policy: Kennan's analyses themselves had not been entirely clear on that point.[55] In part, it reflected also domestic political expediency: in a period characterized by an unrelenting, sometimes hysterical, search for subversive elements at home, it was no easy task to justify making distinctions between varieties of communism overseas.

The result was to institutionalize, in much of American thinking about the communist world, what one political scientist has called "casual ascription"—the tendency to picture "all Communist moves, with whatever party or state they originate, as manifestations of...Soviet strategy."[56] This phenomenon

---

[53] See NSC 10/2, "National Security Council Directive on Office of Special Projects," June 18, 1948, in Etzold and Gaddis, eds., *Containment*, pp. 125–128; also Gaddis, *The Long Peace*, pp. 159–160; George F. Kennan, *Memoirs: 1950–1963* (Boston: 1972), pp. 202–203; John Ranelagh, *The Agency: The Rise and Decline of the CIA* (New York: 1986), pp. 133–138; and, for an elaborate operation against the communist government of Albania that Kim Philby almost certainly compromised, Nicholas Bethell, *Betrayed* (New York: 1984).

[54] Quoted in Jones, *The Fifteen Weeks*, p. 151.

[55] See Charles Gati, "What Containment Meant," *Foreign Policy*, #7 (Summer, 1972), p. 25.

[56] William Welch, *American Images of Soviet Foreign Policy* (New Haven: 1970), p. 83.

had its most obvious effect on United States policy in East Asia where, by the end of 1949, efforts to leave the way open for possible dealings with Mao Zedong's new communist government in China had generated strong opposition in Congress; after the outbreak of the Korean war, such approaches would become almost impossible.[57] "Casual ascription" produced perceptions of unity among adversaries where it either did not exist or would not last; the result was an unnecessary proliferation of enemies in the world, an outcome very different from what the original concept of containment had intended.

Kennan had also stressed the importance of eventually negotiating a settlement of differences with Moscow in both Europe and East Asia. Neither the Russians nor the Americans could indefinitely man World War II truce lines, he believed; the emergence of independent centers of power, particularly in Germany and Japan, would best serve United States long-term interests. Achieving such an objective peacefully would require the voluntary contraction of Soviet power; this, in turn, would necessitate an American willingness to talk with the Russians and, ultimately, to arrange for mutual troop withdrawals.[58]

American officials at this time, however, tended to view such negotiations as involving unacceptable risks. Hence, when on Kennan's recommendation word was discreetly passed to Moscow in April, 1948, that the United States stood prepared "for full discussion and composing of our difficulties," the Russians were able to torpedo the initiative simply by making public the fact that it had taken place.[59] Six months later, during the final days of the 1948 presidential campaign, Secretary of State Marshall vetoed a hastily contrived scheme put together by Truman's political advisers to send Chief Justice Fred Vinson

---

[57] Gaddis, *The Long Peace*, pp. 164–173. See also Nancy Bernkopf Tucker, *Patterns in the Dust: Chinese-American Relations and the Recognition Controversy, 1949–1950* (New York: 1983).

[58] PPS/23, February 24, 1948, *FR: 1948*, I, 522; PPS/37, "Policy Questions Concerning a Possible German Settlement" August 12, 1948, ibid., II, 1287–1297. See also Kennan, *Memoirs: 1925–1950*, p. 365; and Gaddis, *Strategies of Containment*, pp. 38–42.

[59] Kennan, *Memoirs: 1925–1950*, pp. 346–347. See also J. Samuel Walker, "No More Cold War: American Foreign Policy and the 1948 Soviet Peace Offensive," *Diplomatic History*, V(Winter, 1981), 75–91.

to Moscow for talks with the Russians.[60] Behind both of these responses was the fear that anything approaching substantive discussions would undermine the morale of American allies, convey to Moscow an impression of weakness, and raise in the minds of the general public images of another "Yalta," a symbol of appeasement now almost as potent as "Munich."[61]

As a result, no real effort was made to determine what possibilities existed for a joint reduction of forces of the kind Kennan had recommended. Instead, the energies of American diplomats went into building up such bastions as NATO, an independent West Germany, and, by 1951, a postoccupation Japan closely linked to the United States by security treaty. Kennan had definite reservations about the wisdom of these moves: "There is no logical stopping point in the development of a system of anti-Russian alliances," he wrote late in 1948, "until that system has circled the globe and has embraced all of the non-communist countries of Europe, Asia, and Africa."[62] But in the absence of any concrete assurances that negotiations would bear fruit, in the presence of the understandable tendency within the administration to prefer safety over risk and to defer to the wishes of frightened allies,[63] Kennan's recommendations no longer carried the weight they once had.

The announcement, in September, 1949, that the Russians had exploded their first atomic bomb further set back prospects for negotiations by producing in the West fears of military inferiority. The United States and its allies had never equaled the Russians in conventional manpower, but Washington's monopoly over the atomic bomb, it had been thought, would deter Moscow from taking advantage of its numerical superiority. News of the Soviet atomic test led to arguments that the American deterrent would have to be bolstered if it was to remain effective; these considerations produced a presidential decision, early in 1950, to authorize construction of a hydrogen

---

[60] Robert A. Divine, *Foreign Policy and U.S. Presidential Elections: 1940–1948* (New York: 1974), pp. 254–260.

[61] See Athan G. Theoharis, *The Yalta Myths: An Issue in U.S. Politics, 1945–1955* (Columbia, Missouri: 1970), especially pp. 39–69.

[62] PPS/43, "Considerations Affecting the Conclusion of a North Atlantic Security Pact," November 24, 1948, *FR: 1948*, III, 286.

[63] See, on this point, Gaddis, *The Long Peace*, pp. 61–71.

bomb.[64] They also contributed to a growing conviction in Western capitals that, because the Russians would soon have their own nuclear deterrent, Washington and its NATO allies would have to try to counterbalance, for the first time, Soviet conventional force levels in Europe.[65] Restoration of confidence—the original goal of containment—would in time require not only economic aid but also military assistance, the long-term stationing of United States forces in Europe, and eventually the rearmament of West Germany.

"The issues that face us are momentous, involving the fulfillment or destruction not only of this Republic but of civilization itself." So ran the introduction to NSC-68, a comprehensive review of American policy toward the Soviet Union conducted by the National Security Council early in 1950 and largely drafted by Paul H. Nitze, Kennan's successor as Policy Planning Staff director. There was much in this important document that paralleled Kennan's thinking: it associated American interests in the world with diversity, not uniformity; it viewed Soviet expansionism as stemming more from internal insecurities than from ideological compulsions; it recommended dealing with that threat "by developing the moral and material strength of the free world [so] that the Soviet regime will become convinced of the falsity of its assumptions and that the preconditions for workable agreements can be created."[66]

But Kennan had based his prescriptions for action on the assumption that, although the Russians were fully capable of

---

[64] David Alan Rosenberg, "American Atomic Strategy and the Hydrogen Bomb Decision," *Journal of American History*, LXVI(June, 1979), 62–87. There is now evidence that the Russians had begun work on their own hydrogen bomb prior to the American decision to do so. See Holloway, *The Soviet Union and the Arms Race*, pp. 24–26; and Bundy, *Danger and Survival*, pp. 197–198.

[65] Kaplan, *The United States and NATO*, p. 154; Gaddis, *Strategies of Containment*, p. 82. Western estimates of Soviet conventional force strength were almost certainly exaggerated. See Matthew A. Evangelista, "Stalin's Postwar Army Reappraised," *International Security*, VII(Winter, 1982–1983), 110–138.

[66] NSC-68, "United States Objectives and Programs for National Security," April 14, 1950, *FR, 1950*, I, 238, 242. See also Gaddis, *Strategies of Containment*, pp. 90–109; and Paul Y. Hammond, "NSC-68: Prologue to Rearmament," in Warner R. Schilling, Paul Y. Hammond, and Glenn H. Snyder, *Strategy, Politics, and Defense Budgets* (New York: 1962), pp. 267–378. For Nitze's role, see Steven L. Rearden, *The Evolution of American Strategic Doctrine: Paul H. Nitze and the Soviet Challenge* (Boulder, Colorado: 1984), pp. 19–26.

starting a war, they would not in fact do so, except by miscalculation. Such judgments, based on what he admitted was "the unfirm substance of the imponderables,"[67] were not enough to satisfy those in Washington responsible for national security policy, especially after the Soviet Union's demonstration of an atomic capability. These analysts, among them Nitze and Secretary of State Dean Acheson, argued that the only safe way to proceed was to base United States planning, not on what the Russians were likely to do, but on what they *could* do—on Soviet capabilities rather than Soviet intentions. Viewed in this light, the drafters of NSC-68 calculated that the Russians had the *immediate* capability

a. To overrun Western Europe, with the possible exception of the Iberian and Scandinavian Peninsulas; to drive toward the oil-bearing areas of the Near and Middle East; and to consolidate Communist gains in the Far East;

b. To launch air attacks against the British Isles and air and sea attacks against the lines of communications of the Western Powers in the Atlantic and the Pacific;

c. To attack selected targets with atomic weapons, now including the likelihood of such attacks against targets in Alaska, Canada, and the United States.[68]

"No need to ask *why* [the adversary] should be moved to take certain hostile actions, or whether he would be likely to take them," Kennan noted years afterward, in describing the kind of thinking that went into NSC-68; "that he has the capability of taking them suffices."[69]

Measured against that standard, NSC-68 found the military position of the United States dangerously inadequate, leaving Washington officials in many situations with "no better choice than to capitulate or precipitate a global war." The solution, the document argued, was "a build-up of military strength by the

---

[67] Kennan diary note, July 12, 1950, quoted in Kennan, *Memoirs: 1925–1950*, p. 499.

[68] NSC-68, April 14, 1950, *FR: 1950*, I, 249.

[69] George F. Kennan, "The United States and the Soviet Union, 1917–1976," *Foreign Affairs*, LIV(July, 1976), 682. See also Bundy, *Danger and Survival*, p. 347, on the very different effects produced by assessing Soviet intentions on the basis of practical experience, on the one hand, and from the standpoint of quantitative systems analysis, on the other.

United States and its allies to the point at which the combined strength will be superior... to the forces that can be brought to bear by the Soviet Union and its satellites." Such a program would require a significant increase in expenditures: "Budgetary considerations will need to be subordinated to the stark fact that our very independence as a nation may be at stake." It would mean postponing negotiations with the Russians until the buildup had been completed: "The present world situation is one which militates against successful negotiations with the Kremlin—for the terms of agreement... would reflect present realities and would therefore be unacceptable, if not disastrous." It would require recognition "by this Government, the American people, and all free peoples, that the cold war is in fact a real war in which the survival of the free world is at stake."[70]

"Containment" had thus evolved, in the course of three years, from the assumption that international stability required only the limited application of economic power in a few key areas to the conviction that such equilibrium depended upon willingness to wield military force wherever Western interests were threatened. "The assault on free institutions is world-wide now," NSC-68 had argued. "In the... present polarization of power a defeat of free institutions anywhere is a defeat everywhere."[71] It was a proposition to be tested sooner than anyone had expected—in the mountains and rice paddies of Korea.

## V

There is, to this day, no entirely adequate explanation of why North Korean forces crossed the 38th parallel on June 25, 1950. Circumstantial evidence suggests that Stalin, acting under the impression that the United States had come to regard East Asian mainland positions as less than vital to its security, had given general authorization for an invasion sometime that summer, perhaps to be coordinated with a Chinese Communist attack on Taiwan. The North Korean leader, Kim Il-sung, however, had always seen the postwar division of his country as the product of civil rather than international rivalry, and in the

---

[70] NSC-68, April 14, 1950, *FR: 1950*, I, 264, 283, 285, 291–292.
[71] Ibid., p. 240.

*The Korean War, 1950–1953.*

hope of catching his South Korean adversaries off guard, apparently decided to attack several weeks early. The Russians, as surprised as anyone by this turn of events, were unable to veto United Nations participation in the defense of South Korea, having walked out of the Security Council to protest its failure to seat the newly-organized People's Republic of China. Whatever the facts surrounding its origins, Stalin probably did not regard his Korean gambit as a departure from his usual policy of avoiding direct confrontations with the West. It seems, rather, to have been intended as a "probe by proxy," designed perhaps to recoup lost prestige resulting from the Berlin blockade's failure; perhaps to strengthen the Soviet position against Mao Zedong, of whom Stalin was already suspicious; perhaps also to compound the security problems of Japan, a country in which American troops seemed likely to remain stationed for the indefinite future.[72]

To the Russians' astonishment, Truman quickly ordered United States troops to defend South Korea. The reasons for this decision are not hard to grasp, even in the light of the administration's relative inaction in China between 1947 and 1949 and Secretary of State Acheson's explicit exclusion of Korea from the American "defensive perimeter" some months earlier.[73] The attack across the 38th parallel was far more blatant than anything that had happened in China; it resembled nothing so much as the Japanese invasion of Manchuria in 1931, an

---

[72] This account of what is still a very murky episode follows Robert R. Simmons, *The Strained Alliance: Peking, Pyongyang, Moscow and the Politics of the Korean Civil War* (New York: 1975), pp. 102–136. See also Burton I. Kaufman, *The Korean War: Challenges in Crisis, Credibility, and Command* (New York: 1986), pp. 32–33; William Stueck, "The Korean War as International History," *Diplomatic History*, X(Fall, 1986), 292–294; and, for the United States attitude toward its East Asian "defensive perimeter," Gaddis, *The Long Peace*, pp. 72–103. Soviet historians have so far provided almost no information about the conflict's origins, but see *Khrushchev Remembers*, pp. 400–402; and Roy A. Medvedev, *Let History Judge: The Origins and Consequences of Stalinism*, translated by Colleen Taylor (New York: 1972), p. 479. For some very fragmentary Chinese perspectives, see Warren I. Cohen, "Conversations with Chinese Friends: Zhou Enlai's Associates Reflect on Chinese-American Relations in the 1940s and in the Korean War," *Diplomatic History*, XI(Summer, 1987), 288–289.

[73] Acheson National Press Club speech, January 12, 1950, *Department of State Bulletin*, XXIII(January 23, 1950), 111–118. See also Gaddis Smith, *Dean Acheson* (New York: 1972), pp. 175–176.

uncomfortable precedent with obvious implications. It also represented a direct challenge to the authority of the United Nations, a consideration whose importance to Truman would be difficult to overstate. NSC-68 had only recently sensitized administration officials to the dangers of "piecemeal aggression"—to the prospect of "gradual withdrawal under the direct or indirect pressure of the Soviet Union, until we discover one day that we have sacrificed positions of vital interest."[74] Finally, Korea was one of the few places in the world where the United States could respond quickly, thanks to the presence in and around Japan of the Eighth Army and the Seventh Fleet. As General J. Lawton Collins later noted, "Nowhere else abroad did we have such forces of all arms immediately available for employment."[75]

"The attack on Korea makes it plain beyond all doubt," Truman told the nation on June 27, "that communism has passed beyond the use of subversion to conquer independent nations and will now use armed invasion and war."[76] This widely shared but inaccurate impression, foreshadowed in NSC-68, led to three important developments: It brought about the approval and implementation of that document, with the result that the fiscal 1951 defense budget shot up from an original request for $13.5 billion to a final authorization of $48.2 billion.[77] It transformed NATO from a traditional mutual defense alliance into an integrated military structure, involving the appointment of an American supreme commander and the stationing of United States troops in Europe.[78] Finally, by speeding decisions to rearm West Germany and to sign, with or without Soviet participation, a peace treaty with Japan, it accelerated the process by which former enemies became future allies. Stalin's Korean adventure thus demonstrated once again his uncanny ability, through his own actions, to rally his adversaries against himself.

---

[74] NSC-68, April 14, 1950, *FR: 1950*, I, 264, 278.

[75] J. Lawton Collins, *War in Peacetime: The History and Lessons of Korea* (Boston: 1969), p. 4.

[76] *Public Papers of the Presidents: Harry S. Truman, 1950* (Washington: 1965), p. 492.

[77] Hammond, "NSC-68: Prologue to Rearmament," p. 351. See also NSC-68/2, "United States Objectives and Programs for National Security," September 30, 1950, *FR: 1950*, I, 400.

[78] Kaplan, *The United States and NATO*, pp. 145–175.

That the Truman administration was capable of similar accomplishments becomes clear when one considers the consequences of its decisions, made within hours of the North Korean attack, to neutralize the Taiwan Strait and to step up aid to French forces in Indochina. These two actions had been directed more against the Russians than the Chinese Communists: concern over Taiwan reflected fears of what might happen if Mao should grant the Russians air and naval bases there, while support for counterinsurgency efforts in Indochina had been decided upon, even before the Korean War broke out, as a means of facilitating a more substantial French contribution to NATO.[79] The new Beijing government could regard neither move with equanimity, however; its resulting suspicion of Washington's motives goes far toward explaining Mao's decision to intervene in the Korean War following General Douglas MacArthur's crossing of the 38th parallel in the fall of 1950. Hopes for driving a wedge between Moscow and Beijing never totally disappeared in Washington—as late as May, 1951, a National Security Council paper could still list this as a major objective of United States East Asian policy.[80] But most officials, and probably most Americans, would have agreed with President Truman when he told British Prime Minister Clement Attlee in December, 1950, that the Chinese "are satellites of Russia and will be satellites as long as the present Peiping regime is in power. . . . The Russians cannot dominate them forever, but that is a long-range view and does not help us just now."[81]

There is, thus, both irony and justification in the argument that the United States, far from exploiting latent Sino-Soviet antagonism, may inadvertently have moderated it.[82] Admittedly, it was difficult for Washington officials at that time to know the exact nature of the Moscow-Beijing relationship: outward appearances, at least, did project an impression of unity. But the original strategy of containment had based itself on the assumption that, in the end, national differences would prove more de-

---

[79] See Gaddis, *The Long Peace,* pp. 80–94.

[80] NSC-48/5, "United States Objectives, Policies and Courses of Action in Asia," May 17, 1951, *FR: 1951,* VI, 35. See also Gaddis, *The Long Peace,* pp. 170–171.

[81] Minutes, Truman-Attlee meeting of December 4, 1950, *FR: 1950,* VII, 1368–1369.

[82] See, on this point, Franz Schurmann, *The Logic of World Power* (New York: 1974), pp. 242–243.

cisive than ideological similarities in shaping relations between Russia and China. It was an acute and farsighted judgment, amply borne out by subsequent events.

That it did not become the basis for American policy during the Korean War may be attributed to the triumph of short-term military considerations over long-term political ones, to the administration's conviction that generalization in the public identification of threats more often produced popular and Congressional support than did precision, and to the peculiar American tendency, destined to manifest itself time and time again in the future, to rely excessively on ideology as an instrument with which to predict the behavior of adversaries. As a consequence, the United States fell into the paradoxical error of treating international communism as a monolith at almost exactly the moment that it had ceased to be one.

By May of 1951, Stalin apparently was ready to accept what had become a military stalemate in Korea. Informal soundings produced indications that the Russians would be willing to arrange armistice negotiations with the North Koreans and the Chinese Communists,[83] and in July of that year these talks got underway. They would take no less than two years to complete, during which time the fighting in Korea continued unabated.[84] It did so, however, with some assurance on the part of the major powers involved that the conflict would be kept limited—that the small war many had thought might be the prelude to World War III would not, in fact, become so.

Nonetheless, the Korean War had exposed a fundamental contradiction in the original concept of containment. That strategy had sought to achieve its objective by means ultimately psychological in nature: the restoration of self-confidence in areas threatened by Soviet expansionism. Kennan had also stressed the need, though, to distinguish carefully between vital and peripheral interests: only in this way, it was thought, could limited resources be applied with maximum effectiveness. What Korea showed was that interests once considered peripheral could become vital if attacked, that victories for communism in peripheral areas could undermine self-confidence in

---

[83] Kennan, *Memoirs: 1950–1963*, pp. 35–38.
[84] See Kaufman, *The Korean War*, pp. 183–357; also Rosemary Foot, *The Wrong War: American Policy and the Dimensions of the Korean Conflict, 1950–1953* (Ithaca: 1985), pp. 131–231.

vital ones, unless resisted. The need to choose between the competing claims of credibility and economy, to avoid the twin dangers of inaction on the one hand and dispersal of resources on the other, would constitute a central dilemma for American policymakers for years to come.

## VI

On December 21, 1951, President Truman announced the nomination of George F. Kennan to be the next United States ambassador to the Soviet Union. Kennan's appointment sailed through the Senate with no difficulty—he was, after all, the country's most prominent Soviet expert, a man whose experience with the USSR stretched back beyond the establishment of diplomatic relations in 1933, a man who, more than anyone else, had shaped the strategy of containment. It was, Kennan recalled in his *Memoirs*, "a task for which my whole career had prepared me, if it had prepared me for anything at all."[85]

Unfortunately for Kennan, though, Soviet-American tensions had moved beyond the point at which diplomacy could play any meaningful role. Kennan found himself wholly without instructions from either the White House or the State Department; upon inquiry, he discovered that the administration's priorities lay more in the direction of solidifying alignments against the Russians than in negotiating differences with them. "So far as I could see, we were expecting to be able to gain our objectives...without making any concessions whatsoever to the views and interests of our adversaries." It was a position justifiable, Kennan thought, only "if we were really all-powerful, and could hope to get away with it. I very much doubted that this was the case."[86]

Upon proceeding to Moscow, Kennan found the atmosphere there even more stifling than on previous tours of duty. Plainclothes police guards followed Kennan everywhere, discouraging contacts with Soviet citizens. The ambassador's residence had come to resemble a prison, with floodlit walls and fences on all sides, patrolled by armed guards. The rooms, as always, were bugged; the servants even more surly and unfriendly than before.

---

[85] Kennan, *Memoirs: 1950–1963*, pp. 106.
[86] Ibid., pp. 107–110.

Looking out the window, I could see the Soviet citizens piously crossing the street to avoid walking in the dangerous proximity of our
fence. I could hear, night after night, the testing of jet engines somewhere off across the Moscow River. Sometimes I would wander
around the building without turning the lights on, go down into the
great, dimly lit white ballroom and play the grand piano, or, having no
one with whom to speak Russian, establish myself in one of the gilded
chairs of the several living rooms and read Russian aloud to myself just
to indulge my love of the language.... So I wandered in my gilded
prison, comforting myself with the reflection that if this venerable
building, with its unhappy history, had a ghost, the ghost was un-
questionably I.

Diplomatic contacts with Soviet officials were confined to unavoidable formalities; the new ambassador was not invited, and
never tried, to see Stalin. Soviet propaganda was full of charges
about American preparations for future war; charges that
Kennan, out of sympathy with much of the administration's
policy, could not wholly dismiss. "I began to ask myself
whether...we had not contributed, and were not continuing to
contribute—by the overmilitarization of our policies and statements—to a belief in Moscow that it was war we were after."[87]

While passing through Berlin in September, 1952, Kennan,
in answer to a press conference question, compared the conditions of diplomats in Moscow to those he had encountered
while interned in Germany during the first months of World
War II. Bristling at this implied analogy with Hitler's regime,
the Soviet government declared Kennan *persona non grata* and
refused to allow him to reenter the country. It was, Kennan acknowledged in retrospect, "an extremely foolish thing for me to
have said."[88] Yet his statement was neither untrue nor unprecedented: his frustrations had been felt by American diplomats in
Russia for more than a century. The problem was not so much
Kennan's qualifications as a diplomat (although he would later
judge himself severely on that score) as it was the general invulnerability of Soviet-American hostility to the usages of traditional
diplomacy. As such, Kennan's abortive ambassadorship may
stand as a fitting symbol of what the Cold War had become.

---

[87] Ibid., pp. 112–134.
[88] Ibid., p. 159.

# CHAPTER VIII

# From Confrontation To Confrontation: 1953–1962

UNTIL THE ADMINISTRATION OF DWIGHT D. EISENHOWER CAME INTO OFFICE, most Washington officials—Kennan among them—had regarded the Cold War as a transitory phenomenon. Either a real war would end it or, more likely, the Russians would come to see that they could not achieve their objectives by means short of war, and would shift toward policies of accommodation with the West. If anyone had been rash enough to predict, early in 1953, that the American troops then still fighting in Korea and on guard in Western Europe would be present in both locations three and a half decades later, the idea would have been dismissed as implausible, even preposterous. The possibility that the Soviet Union and the United States might maintain so intense a rivalry for so long without war but also without surrender was something few Americans had begun to grasp. It was Eisenhower who, out of concern over the twin dangers of nuclear war and economic exhaustion, began to acclimate the United States to that prospect. And it would be under his successor, John F. Kennedy, that the task of evading annihilation and capitulation would meet its severest test.

I

Diplomacy and politics are never completely separate from one another, of course, but the quadrennial process of running for president in the United States does seem to generate, with particular regularity, public commitments on foreign policy that tend to restrict candidates' options once in office.[1] The cam-

---

[1] See, on this point, Robert A. Divine, *Foreign Policy and U.S. Presidential Elections: 1952–1960* (New York: 1974), p. ix.

paign of 1952 was no exception. Eisenhower, faced not so much with the problem of winning the election as of securing the Republican Party's nomination, felt obliged to assure his conservative rivals that he would abandon the Truman administration's strategy of simply "containing" the Soviet Union. That approach, critics argued, had risked dispersing scarce resources by relying too heavily on American manpower and not enough on American technology, had acquiesced too willingly in the "enslavement" of millions behind the "Iron Curtain," had concentrated too heavily on resisting Soviet expansionism in Europe while neglecting it in Asia, and had been administered, at least in part, by individuals sympathetic, possibly even subservient, to the interests of Moscow.[2] Not all opponents of containment endorsed all of these charges; not all of the charges themselves were consistent. But they did all arise in one form or another during the 1952 campaign, and the new administration accordingly found it difficult to ignore them.

Fears that containment would lead to a dispersal of resources were nothing new. Kennan's original strategy had assumed only limited means and had insisted, as a consequence, upon a rigid differentiation between vital and peripheral interests. But Korea had demonstrated how a country of apparently peripheral importance could become vital once attacked. The Truman administration's response had been to improvise the concept of limited war—conventional military operations tightly controlled both in geographical scope and in levels of violence. But it had given little thought, by the time it left office, to how such operations could be sustained over protracted periods of time, given their costs, given growing public impatience, and given the need simultaneously to protect other more critical areas.

Eisenhower's answer was what came to be known as the "New Look," a strategy first proposed by John Foster Dulles during the 1952 campaign. Containment, Dulles argued, had left decisions as to the time, place, and method of aggression up to the enemy; the United States had been saddled, as a result, with the impossible task of organizing resistance on all fronts. What was needed instead was a determination on the part of

---

[2] Norman A. Graebner, *The New Isolationism* (New York: 1956), pp. 18–30; James T. Patterson, *Mr. Republican: A Biography of Robert A. Taft* (Boston: 1972), pp. 476–496. See also Gaddis, *Strategies of Containment*, pp. 117–125.

the West "to retaliate, instantly, by means and at places of our own choosing." If the United States and its allies could select their own weapons and the most favorable circumstances in which to employ them, the result, Dulles insisted, would be "maximum protection at bearable cost."[3]

There was both more, and less, to this "New Look" than met the eye. It departed from Truman's strategy by placing "solvency" on a par with "security" as an irreducible national interest. Since nuclear weapons cost less than large conventional forces, this appeared to imply a greater willingness than in the past actually to use them. But what critics quickly dubbed the doctrine of "massive retaliation" did not mean automatic escalation to nuclear war in every crisis; rather, the idea was to create uncertainty in the minds of potential adversaries in the hope of deterring them from committing aggression in the first place.[4] Nor did the strategy exclude employing alternative means—including local forces of resistance, covert action, and even psychological warfare—where appropriate.[5] Nor was the "New Look" as dramatic a departure as it seemed from the previous administration's strategic concept: seared by the experience of Korea, Truman and his advisers had already decided not to allow "privileged sanctuaries" should war break out again in Asia, and to rely chiefly on air and naval power, if not nuclear weapons, to accomplish American objectives there.[6] What was new about the "New Look" was its public announcement—a maneuver Dulles, now Secretary of State, performed in a more bellicose manner than was necessary—together with its emphasis on nuclear deterrence, the rigidity with which it

---

[3] Speech to the Council on Foreign Relations, January 12, 1954, *Department of State Bulletin*, XXX(January 25, 1954), 107–110. See also John Foster Dulles, "A Policy of Boldness," *Life*, XXXII(May 19, 1952), 146–160.

[4] Glenn H. Snyder, "The 'New Look' of 1953," in Schilling, Hammond, and Snyder, *Strategy, Politics and Defense Budgets*, pp. 463–470; Gaddis, *Strategies of Containment*, pp. 147–152.

[5] Ibid., pp. 152–159. See also Seyom Brown, *The Faces of Power: Constancy and Change in United States Foreign Policy from Truman to Reagan* (New York: 1983), pp. 74–75.

[6] NSC-118/2, "United States Objectives and Courses of Action in Korea," *FR: 1951*, VII, 1385–1386; NSC-124/2, "United States Objectives and Courses of Action with Respect to Southeast Asia," *FR: 1952–1954*, XII, 131–132. See also Foot, *The Wrong War*, pp. 143–156; and Kaufman, *The Korea War* pp. 225–226.

tied defense policy to budgetary considerations, and, most important, its attempt to achieve security through blurring, rather than clarifying, distinctions between primary and secondary interests.

"Liberation" was not a new concept either. As early as December, 1949, President Truman had approved a National Security Council paper calling for efforts "to foster a heretical drifting-away process on the part of the [East European] satellite states." That document had stressed the need to avoid provoking Soviet retaliation, however, and had cautioned against taking actions beyond United States capabilities to support.[7] Privately, Dulles had no quarrel with this approach; his view, like Kennan's, was that the West could do little other than to wait for fissures within the Soviet Union's sphere of influence to manifest themselves.[8] But Dulles went out of his way in public to call for the "liberation" of Eastern Europe, and to contrast this active approach with the Truman administration's "purely defensive" policy. The Republican platform of 1952 went even further, condemning "the negative, futile and immoral policy of 'containment' which abandons countless human beings to... despotism and Godless terrorism," and calling for the repudiation of "all commitments contained in secret understandings such as those of Yalta which aid Communist enslavements."[9]

Events soon made it clear, however, that "liberation" had been aimed more at freeing the government in Washington from the Democrats' control than at contesting Soviet influence in Eastern Europe. Moscow's authority in that part of the world did come under challenge in June, 1953, when riots broke out in East Germany, but the Eisenhower administration had no plans for exploiting such a situation and was reduced to the role of a passive spectator as the Russians crushed the revolt. Nor did Eisenhower honor campaign pledges to repudiate the Yalta

---

[7] NSC-58/2, "United States Policy toward the Soviet Satellite States in Eastern Europe," December 8, 1949, *FR: 1949*, V, 51. See also Gaddis, *The Long Peace*, pp. 158–161.

[8] Hoopes, *Dulles*, pp. 127–133: Michael A. Guhin, *John Foster Dulles: A Statesman and His Times* (New York: 1972), pp. 170–180.

[9] Arthur M. Schlesinger, Jr., ed., *History of American Presidential Elections, 1789–1968* (New York: 1971), IV, 3284.

agreements, fearing that any such unilateral disavowal might call into question United States rights in the occupied cities of Berlin and Vienna.[10] Even more than had been the case on matters of strategic doctrine, then, the new administration's policies regarding Eastern Europe constituted a tacit endorsement, rather than a rejection, of the principles of containment.

Another charge made against Truman's foreign policy had been that it concentrated too heavily on Europe, neglecting events in Asia. It is true that the original containment strategy had seen Europe as the most vital area of concern for the United States, but Japan had also rated high on Washington's list of priorities, and the Korean War had focused attention on much of the rest of Asia as well. By the time Truman left office, the United States had security treaties with Japan, the Philippines, Australia, and New Zealand, and had begun providing military and economic aid to the French in Indochina. The major difference between the Truman and Eisenhower administrations as far as East Asia was concerned was the latter's willingness to associate itself openly with Chinese Nationalist aspirations to reconquer the mainland, a move that Truman and Acheson had carefully avoided. Here, once again, domestic politics came into play: by promising early in 1953 to "unleash" Chiang Kai-shek, Eisenhower and Dulles sought to placate the right wing of the Republican Party, which had been vociferous in its support of the Nationalists since China's "fall" to communism in 1949. The price of "releashing" Chiang during the delicate Quemoy-Matsu crisis a year and a half later was an explicit American commitment to defend Taiwan if attacked.[11]

Finally, containment had become a target for attacks by Senator Joseph R. McCarthy and his followers, on the grounds that officials disloyal to the United States had formulated and implemented it. Again, this was not a new charge: the Truman administration since 1947 had maintained its own domestic loyalty program designed to screen out security risks, at times on a less

---

[10] Dwight D. Eisenhower, *The White House Years: Mandate for Change, 1953–1956* (Garden City, New York: 1963), p. 221.

[11] Foster Rhea Dulles, *American Foreign Policy toward Communist China, 1949–1969* (New York: 1972), p. 150–160; J. H. Kalicki, *The Pattern of Sino-American Crises: Political-Military Interactions in the 1950s* (London: 1975), pp. 120–155.

than discriminating basis.[12] The program had not prevented Republicans from making "communism in government" a major campaign issue in 1952, however, and as a consequence Senator McCarthy gained an indirect veto over almost all State Department appointments during the first year of the Eisenhower administration. This situation produced the resignation, either forcibly or voluntarily, of a number of career Foreign Service officers associated with the doctrine of containment, including Kennan himself; it also led to a major Senate fight over the nomination of his successor as ambassador to the Soviet Union, the equally highly-qualified Charles E. Bohlen, largely on the grounds that he had been Roosevelt's interpreter at Yalta.[13] We now know that Eisenhower, appalled by what was happening, worked craftily behind the scenes to discredit McCarthy;[14] as a result, the senator's anti-communist crusade soon fizzled, but not before it had made the nation look ridiculous abroad and constrained debate over foreign policy at home.

Aware of containment's unpopularity, President Eisenhower in the summer of 1953 ordered a top-secret study, known as Project Solarium, to investigate alternatives to it. Separate teams carefully examined the advantages and disadvantages of continuing the Truman administration's approach, of drawing clear lines beyond which Russian expansionism would be resisted, and of seeking to roll back existing areas of Soviet influence. Despite having just been forced out the State Department, Kennan was asked to chair the first team and, upon completion of the exercise, Eisenhower appeared to endorse his group's recommendations. In fact the president would incorporate aspects of all three approaches into his strategy and would add firm ideas of his own, notably the need to devise a strategy that

---

[12] Alan D. Harper, *The Politics of Loyalty: The White House and the Communist Issue, 1946–1952* (Westport, Connecticut: 1969), pp. 1969), 232–254; Richard M. Fried, *Men against McCarthy* (New York: 1976), pp. 23–29.

[13] Kennan, *Memoirs: 1950–1963.* pp. 168–189; E. J. Kahn Jr., *The China Hands: America's Foreign Service Officers and What Befell Them* (New York: 1975), pp. 246–263; Bohlen, *Witness to History*, pp. 309–336; T. Michael Ruddy, *The Cautious Diplomat: Charles E. Bohlen and the Soviet Union, 1929–1969* (Kent, Ohio: 1986), pp. 109–124. For McCarthy's relations with the State Department, see Oshinsky, *A Conspiracy So Immense*, pp. 260–264.

[14] See Fred I. Greenstein, *The Hidden Hand Presidency: Eisenhower as Leader* (New York: 1982), pp. 155–227.

the nation could sustain without bankrupting itself.[15] But by lending his prestige to Kennan's position, Eisenhower quietly signalled his intention to abandon the Republican platform rather than containment: the new administration's strategy would be formulated within the framework of its predecessor's.

The critical difference between the Truman and Eisenhower approaches to containment had to do with means, not ends. Convinced, along with the authors of NSC-68, that the nation could afford to spend whatever was necessary to be secure, the Truman administration had stressed the need to minimize risks by undertaking to resist aggression wherever and whenever it took place, without escalation or capitulation, whatever the expense. Eisenhower, convinced that the nation could not sustain high military expenditures over extended periods of time, sought to minimize costs by undertaking to resist aggression not necessarily where adversaries acted, but rather at times, in places, and in ways the nation could afford. Truman's "risk-minimizing" approach to containment expended resources to avoid escalation; Eisenhower's "cost-minimizing" approach tolerated escalation to avoid bankruptcy.[16] Both, though, were variations on the theme of containment, whose continuation as the dominant concept for policy toward the Soviet Union now seemed assured.

## II

"The Government of the United States tenders its official condolences to the Government of the U.S.S.R. on the death of Generalissimo Joseph Stalin, Prime Minister of the Soviet Union." Such, in its entirety, was the Eisenhower administration's public response to the passing of the Soviet autocrat on March 5, 1953. The White House had, the day before, taken the occasion to express sympathy for the Russian people "regardless of the identity of government personalities"; Secretary of State Dulles, who looked forward to the possibility now of

---

[15] Kennan, *Memoirs: 1950–1963*, pp. 181–182; Gaddis, *Strategies of Containment*, pp. 145–146. For documentation on the "Solarium" study, see *FR: 1952–1954*, II, 360–366, 387–442.

[16] See John Lewis Gaddis, "Containment and the Logic of Strategy," *National Interest*, #10(Winter, 1987/8), 27–38.

exploiting "confusion and rivalries" within the Kremlin, warned American embassies overseas to avoid any comments that might "exceed [the] bounds [of] good taste, thereby confirming [the] Soviet propaganda image of Americans as crude barbarians."[17] These initiatives having been taken, the new administration then turned its attention to the problems of dealing with the Soviet Union in a post-Stalin era.

Changes in Moscow's policy were not long in coming. The new collective leadership there seemed to welcome, rather than discourage, friendly ties with the West; it also partially dismantled Stalin's secret police apparatus, emphasized the production of consumer goods, relaxed controls over Eastern Europe, and advanced cautious but increasingly frequent denunciations of the "cult of personality." It renewed, as well, an intriguing offer Stalin himself had made in 1952: to consider the establishment of a reunified, partially rearmed, but neutral German state.[18] The problem, for Washington officials, was to determine whether the congenial appearance Malenkov, Khrushchev, and their associates presented to the world did in fact reflect a new concept of international relations, or was merely another in a long series of tactical modifications designed to further the ultimate aim of Soviet expansionism.

Dulles acknowledged the possibility that Soviet ideology might change in the face of evolving circumstances, but he also believed deeply that Western unity depended upon the existence of a credible threat.[19] For this reason, he viewed the new Kremlin regime with extreme wariness, fearing that any lessening of Cold War tensions might induce dangerous complacency

---

[17] *Public Papers of the Presidents: Dwight D. Eisenhower, 1953* (Washington: 1963) pp. 75, 91. See also Dulles to certain diplomatic posts, March 5, 1953, *FR: 1952–1954*, II, 1681.

[18] Ronald Bitzer, "Soviet Policy on German Reunification in 1952," *World Politics*, CXXXII(1969), 245–255; Ann L. Phillips, *Soviet Policy toward East Germany Reconsidered* (Westport, Connecticut: 1986), pp. 119–126. For a recent German account, see Rolf Steininger, *Eine vertane Chance: Die Stalin-Note vom 10, Marz 1952 und die Wiedervereinigung* (Bonn: 1985).

[19] Guhin, *Dulles*, pp. 136–138, 143–149. See also John Foster Dulles, *War, Peace and Change* (New York: 1939), p. 90; and John Lewis Gaddis "The Unexpected John Foster Dulles: Nuclear Weapons, Communism, and the Russians," in Richard Immerman, ed., *John Foster Dulles and the Diplomacy of the Cold War* (Princeton: 1989), forthcoming.

inside the United States and among its allies. Domestic political considerations reinforced this conviction: the new secretary of state was a strong partisan, given to framing foreign policy as much in terms of what looked good at home as to what effect it would produce on the international scene.[20] Having campaigned on a platform of vigorous resistance to an implacable foe, he found himself unprepared when confronted instead by an apparently reasonable and humane rival, eager for negotiations. In this sense, as one biographer has put it, Stalin did Dulles a profound disservice by dying too soon.[21]

Eisenhower, on the other hand, inclined toward measured optimism. Stalin's death might well clear the way for fundamental changes in the Soviets' view of the world, he thought: "Consequently, a major preoccupation of my mind throughout most of 1953 was the development of approaches to the Soviet leaders that might be at least a start toward the birth of mutual trust."[22] The president's most notable effort in this regard was a speech made over Dulles's objections in April, 1953, in which he drew a clear distinction between Stalin and the new Soviet leadership; he also offered, if the Russians would make concrete gestures toward resolving outstanding differences, to begin negotiations looking toward a mutual reduction of armaments.[23] Eisenhower held out no great hope that the Russians would respond favorably to this initiative, but he did attach a higher priority than did Dulles to clearing the way for negotiations should negotiable issues prove to exist.

Conciliatory signs of the kind Eisenhower had requested were not long in coming. In an unusual step, *Pravda* reprinted the full text of the president's address; shortly thereafter, Soviet officials began seeking informal social contacts with American diplomats in Moscow for the first time in years.[24] More importantly, the Russians in the spring of 1953 began applying pressure on the Chinese Communists and the North Koreans to end

---

[20] Hoopes, *Dulles*, pp. 124–125; Herbert S. Parmet, "Power and Reality: John Foster Dulles and Political Diplomacy," in Theodore A. Wilson and Frank Merli, ed., *Makers of American Diplomacy* (New York: 1974), pp. 596–601.

[21] Hoopes, *Dulles*, p. 171.

[22] Eisenhower, *Mandate for Change*, p. 144. See also Stephen E. Ambrose, *Eisenhower: The President* (New York: 1984), pp. 91–94.

[23] Speech of April 16, 1953, *Eisenhower Public Papers, 1953*, pp. 179–188.

[24] Bohlen, *Witness to History*, pp. 348–352, 359–362.

the fighting in Korea. It was not clear at the time, nor is it completely clear today, whether the July, 1953, armistice agreement resulted primarily from internal developments in China, Soviet influence, or veiled threats by Eisenhower and Dulles to use nuclear weapons in Korea if the fighting did not stop.[25] But, whatever brought it about, the Russians had not been unhelpful in arranging the cease-fire, and this was an encouraging sign.

Pressures, especially from the British, had begun to build as early as the summer of 1953 for a summit conference with Stalin's successors, but Dulles had strongly discouraged this course of action. Negotiations, he feared, might suggest to the Russians lack of resolve on the part of the West. They might also weaken NATO, an organization whose internal cohesion seemed to require the existence of a strong external threat, particularly if French opposition to the integration of West German forces into a European defense structure was to be overcome. Finally, negotiations might cause difficulties at home, where repeated Republican invocations of "Yalta" as a symbol of appeasement made it no easy task, even for an administration as popular as Eisenhower's, to agree to the first top-level contacts with Kremlin officials since the end of World War II.[26]

By early 1955, though, even Dulles was finding it difficult to hold out. The Soviet leadership, now increasingly dominated by the irrepressible Khrushchev, agreed in May to sign a long-delayed peace treaty with Austria, thus bringing to an end the four-power occupation of that country.[27] That same month the Russians offered, for the first time, to consider disarmament plans involving limited on-site inspection within the USSR. McCarthyism in the United States had lost much of its potency by then; in Europe the French had agreed, if not to the integra-

---

[25] Foot, *The Wrong War*, pp. 205–231; Kaufman, *The Korean War*, pp. 306–321; Bundy, *Danger and Survival*, pp. 238–243. Surviving Chinese officials deny that American threats to use nuclear weapons played a role in Beijing's acceptance of an armistice, but there is, as yet, no documentary evidence to confirm this. See Cohen, "Conversations with Chinese Friends," pp. 288–289.

[26] M. Steven Fish, "After Stalin's Death: The Anglo-American Debate over a New Cold War," *Diplomatic History*, X(Fall, 1986), 333–356. See also Theoharis, *The Yalta Myths*, pp. 130–194.

[27] See Audrey Keith Cronin, *Great Power Politics and the Struggle over Austria, 1945–1955* (Ithaca: 1986), pp. 143–159.

tion of West German forces into an all-European army, at least to the Bonn government's membership in NATO. With public opinion in both the United States and Western Europe coming to favor summit talks, Eisenhower overrode Dulles's objections and agreed to meet with the leaders of Great Britain, France, and the Soviet Union at Geneva in July, 1955.

Substantive progress at Geneva was minimal. The Russians backed away from discussions of German reunification because, as Khrushchev candidly admitted, the East Germans had not yet had time "to be educated to the great advantage of Communism."[28] Eisenhower rejected Russian disarmament proposals as inadequate, suggesting instead the mutual aerial surveillance of all Soviet and American military installations. This "open skies" plan won the Americans propaganda points but had little chance of acceptance, given the disproportionate benefits it would have provided the United States, an open society with few secrets to hide, as compared to the Soviet Union.[29]

Atmospherics are sometimes more important than accomplishments, though, and the sight of capitalist and communist leaders amiably agreeing to disagree had a curiously reassuring effect on world opinion, leading to newspaper headlines about something called "the spirit of Geneva." If such a spirit existed, it lay in the personal relationships formed during the five days of the conference. Khrushchev found Eisenhower to be "a good man," if very much under Dulles's influence. Eisenhower jokingly assured the Russians of his relief at finding them not to be fourteen feet high, with horns and a tail.[30] The conference thus established an unspoken assumption that would underlie much subsequent summit diplomacy: that nations whose leaders had dealt with each other face to face would find it difficult to be enemies. It was a simplistic view of international relations, but to the extent that direct acquaintance could free Soviet and American leaders from the tendency to explain each other's be-

---

[28] Eisenhower, *Mandate for Change*, p. 523.

[29] See W. W. Rostow, *Open Skies: Eisenhower's Proposal of July 21, 1955* (Austin: 1982).

[30] *Khrushchev Remembers*, p. 434; Peter Lyon, *Eisenhower: Portrait of the Hero* (Boston: 1974), p. 660. See also Eisenhower, *Mandate for Change*, p. 527; and Ambrose, *Eisenhower: The President*, pp. 261–267.

havior in narrow ideological terms, perhaps not an entirely inaccurate one.

The Twentieth Party Congress, which met in Moscow in February, 1956, provided striking confirmation of the changes that had taken place in the Soviet Union since Stalin's death. In a long, rambling, emotional secret speech—which the Central Intelligence Agency subsequently obtained and released to the world[31]—Khrushchev condemned the dead dictator and most of his works, thereby acknowledging fallibility, an unexpected trait in a system based on the "scientific" application of theory to human events. The concept of "peaceful coexistence," employed on and off in the past for tactical purposes, now became a fixed principle of Soviet foreign policy; simultaneously the new leadership officially repudiated the Stalinist doctrine of inevitable conflict between states of differing social systems.[32] From the perspective of more than three decades, it seems clear that these developments marked a turning point of fundamental importance in the history of Soviet foreign policy—an adaptation of ideology to fit reality much along the lines of what Kennan had predicted some years earlier.[33] But there ensued no immediate improvement in relations with the West, a fact for which both sides must bear some responsibility.

Despite the fact that he took quite seriously growing indications of change within the Soviet Union, Dulles continued to resist negotiations even after the summit. His attitude reflected a continuing distrust of the Russians' long-term intentions, doubt that they would keep whatever agreements were made, and concern that such negotiations might disrupt the still-delicate NATO alliance. Eisenhower took a less pessimistic view, but in the end deferred to Dulles's judgment.[34] It may very well be that there was little to negotiate about: distrust on both sides was high and would remain so for years to come. Still, the So-

---

[31] Ranelagh, *The Agency*, pp. 285–288.

[32] Wolfgang Leonhard, *The Three Faces of Marxism* (New York: 1974), pp. 144–154. For a well-informed Soviet account, see Roy Medvedev, *Khrushchev*, translated by Brian Pearce (Garden City, New York: 1983), pp. 83–103.

[33] See William Zimmerman, *Soviet Perspectives on International Relations, 1956–1967* (Princeton: 1969), pp. 4–6.

[34] Gaddis, *Strategies of Containment*, pp. 189–193. Dulles's assessment of internal changes in the Soviet Union is discussed in Gaddis, "The Unexpected John Foster Dulles," forthcoming.

*United States and USSR Overseas Commitments.*

viet leadership did undergo a period of uncertainty following Stalin's death which the West might have exploited to its advantage, particularly on the issues of disarmament and German reunification, had it been more confident of its own strength and more willing to employ the normal processes of diplomacy.[35] After 1955, such a course of action would become more difficult. The integration of West Germany into NATO, together with the creation, in the East, of the Warsaw Treaty Organization, institutionalized the division of Europe into two hostile camps; if there had ever been any realistic prospect of reunifying Germany, it ceased to exist after this point.[36]

But it was not just Western rigidity that undermined the "spirit of Geneva." De-Stalinization, which should have improved relations with the West, had just the opposite effect in the fall of 1956 when revolts broke out in Poland and Hungary; the Russians' brutal suppression of the Hungarian uprising would embitter East Europeans—and many in the West as well—for years to come. With all its talk of "liberation" and despite indications that the Central Intelligence Agency had even been covertly training anti-Soviet paramilitary groups for possible use in Eastern Europe, the Eisenhower administration was as unprepared for this crisis as it had been for the East German riots three years earlier; it could only respond with a combination of public denunciation, frustration over its own impotence, and in some circles guilt over having at least indirectly encouraged the East Europeans to test the limits of Soviet control.[37]

The dismantling of Stalin's dictatorship, therefore, did little to lower Cold War tensions; indeed it may even have increased them as an insecure Khrushchev attempted the difficult task of implementing reform without undermining authority. Spheres of influence were becoming more sharply defined and hence less susceptible to adjustment; meanwhile new developments in the technology of warfare—the proliferation of nuclear weap-

---

[35] Bohlen, *Witness to History*, p. 371; Adam B. Ulam, *The Rivals: America and Russia since World War II* (New York: 1971), pp. 230–232.

[36] A. W. DePorte, *Europe between the Superpowers: The Enduring Balance* (New Haven: 1979), pp. 142–165.

[37] Ranelagh, *The Agency*, pp. 287, 305–307. See also David C. Martin, *Wilderness of Mirrors* (New York: 1980), p. 90; and Stephen E. Ambrose and Richard H. Immerman, *Ike's Spies: Eisenhower and the Espionage Establishment* (New York: 1981), pp. 237–240.

ons together with the development of long-range rockets to carry them—were creating a new sense of vulnerability in both Washington and Moscow. The Cold War had taken on a dynamic of its own, with indications of restraint on one side producing, not a corresponding response, but a hardening of position on the part of the other.

## III

It is, by now, commonplace to note that the geographical scope of Soviet-American competition expanded, during the 1950s, from Europe and Northeast Asia into East and Southeast Asia, the Middle East, and Latin America. Nor are the reasons for this development hard to grasp: they are connected, most obviously, with the acceleration of decolonization brought about by World War II, together with the efforts of Stalin's successors to profit from the antagonism toward the West that process generated. Less clear is why the United States responded in the way that it did: why it so consistently exaggerated the strength of communism in the "Third World" and, correspondingly, neglected what would prove to be the more durable ideology there—nationalism.

The Eisenhower administration sought to contain Soviet expansionism in those parts of the world in three ways: by employing covert operations to overthrow governments suspected of promoting, either consciously or unconsciously, the interests of international communism; by working to stimulate and support nationalism where it could be expected to assume a reliably anti-communist orientation; and, finally, by attempting to build safeguards against both external attack and internal subversion through a network of multilateral defense pacts modeled on NATO.

The United States is on record as having attempted, through the Central Intelligence Agency, at least four major covert operations against foreign governments during the Eisenhower administration: the successful overthrow of Prime Minister Mohammed Mossadeqh in Iran in August, 1953; the equally efficient dispatch of President Jacobo Arbenz Guzman's left-wing regime in Guatemala in June, 1954; an unsuccessful effort to undermine the position of Indonesian President Sukarno in 1958; and the abortive attempt to organize a rebellion against Fidel

Castro's government in Cuba, planned during the final months of Eisenhower's term, but actually implemented in April, 1961, three months after President Kennedy took office.[38] What these four targets of American intervention had in common was not communism—none of the four openly adhered to the doctrines of Marxism-Leninism—but rather anti-Americanism; that such sentiments might not automatically mean subservience to the Soviet Union does not appear to have impressed administration officials. Nor, in planning these operations, did they weigh fully the long-term costs of covert action, successful or not, in provoking suspicion of American motives both at home and abroad.

Covert action was not the administration's preferred method of operation, however; instead it sought, where possible, to encourage governments that would be both nationalist *and* anti-communist. In many parts of the world this was not an unrealistic objective: the examples of South Korea, the Philippines, Pakistan, Iran (after Mossadeqh's overthrow), Saudi Arabia, and much of Latin America come to mind. But there were regions where nationalism was indissolubly linked to communism, despite the best efforts of the United States to drive them apart. One was Vietnam, where by 1954 France's long effort to suppress Ho Chi Minh's communist insurgency had come close to collapse. Although Ho had, in recent years, received considerable amounts of military and economic assistance from Moscow and Beijing, there was little doubt in Washington about the genuinely national base of his movement.[39] The Eisenhower administration found it impossible to align the United States with nationalism in this case, though, for the simple reason that in Vietnam it proceeded under the rubric of "communism." Instead, following the partition of that territory

---

[38] For details, see Ranelagh, *The Agency*, pp. 260–269, 332–335, 353–376; also Kuross A. Samii, *Involvement by Invitation: American Strategies of Containment in Iran* (University Park, Pennsylvania: 1987), pp. 95–145; Richard H. Immerman, *The CIA in Guatemala: The Foreign Policy of Intervention* (Austin: 1982); and Peter Wyden, *The Bay of Pigs: The Untold Story* (New York: 1979).

[39] See Eisenhower, *Mandate for Change*, p. 372. For background, see Ronald H. Spector, *Advice and Support: The Early Years of the United States Army in Vietnam* (New York: 1985), pp. 3–218; also Andrew J. Rotter, *The Path to Vietnam: Origins of the American Commitment to Southeast Asia* (Ithaca: 1987); and Melanie Billings-Yun, *Decision against War: Eisenhower and Dien Bien Phu, 1954* (New York: 1988).

at the 1954 Geneva Conference, Washington embarked on a long and costly effort to develop an anti-communist variety of nationalism through support of the Ngo Dinh Diem regime in Saigon, a course of action destined ultimately to involve the United States in its most protracted and least successful war.[40]

In other parts of the world, regimes that were both national-ist and anti-communist existed, but the administration did not always recognize or support them. The most conspicuous ex-ample was Egypt, where the United States initially endorsed the strongly nationalist government of Gamal Abdel Nasser but backed off when, in 1955, Nasser made it clear that he intended to maintain close ties with the Soviet Union and the People's Republic of China as well. Suspecting, incorrectly in this case, that association with communists meant control by them (and motivated as well by Congressional skepticism and a desire to expose as a bluff Soviet offers of aid), Dulles in the summer of 1956 withdrew an earlier offer to fund construction of Nasser's pet project, the Aswan Dam. This action led in turn to Egyptian seizure of the Suez Canal, an abortive Anglo-French-Israeli mil-itary operation to take it back, and the odd sight of the United States and the Soviet Union cooperating in the United Nations to restore order in that part of the world.[41]

By all logic, the United States should have emerged from the Suez crisis with an enhanced reputation in the Middle East for having resisted the last major effort by colonial powers to im-pose their will there. That it did not may be attributed, in large part, to the workings of a third administration approach to the problem of communism and nationalism: the extension of mul-tilateral, bilateral, and at times unilateral security guarantees to those areas of the Third World seen as vulnerable to Soviet or Chinese influence.

It had been the Eisenhower administration's role in organiz-ing the 1955 Baghdad Pact (made up of Great Britain, Turkey,

---

[40] Spector, *Advice and Support*, pp. 219–373. The search for an anti-communism version of nationalism in Vietnam and the Phillipines is percep-tively analyzed in D. Michael Shafer, *Deadly Paradigms: The Failure of U.S. Counterinsurgency Policy* (Princeton: 1988).

[41] The most comprehensive account is Donald Neff, *Warriors at Suez: Eisenhower Takes America into the Middle East* (New York: 1981); but see also Robert Rhodes James, *Anthony Eden: A Biography* (New York: 1986), pp. 441–598.

Iraq, Iran, and Pakistan) that had provoked Nasser into improving his relations with Moscow and Beijing in the first place. Now, early in 1957, Dulles asked Congress to approve the "Eisenhower Doctrine," a declaration of intent by the United States to defend the entire Middle East against "overt armed aggression from any nation controlled by International Communism."[42] Dulles had expected this statement to deter Soviet efforts to exploit Western weakness in the region after Suez; paradoxically it had the effect of raising doubts, both in Congress and in the country at large, about the administration's ability to gauge threats precisely or to formulate appropriate responses. Reaction in the Middle East was largely negative, a trend intensified the following year when the United States, acting under terms of the doctrine, landed troops in Lebanon to protect that country's government against a coup that turned out to have been instigated more by forces of Arab nationalism (and Nasserism) than by the machinations of the Kremlin.[43]

The Eisenhower Doctrine was but the final link in a chain of security commitments the administration had assumed since taking office—the Southeast Asian Treaty of 1954, the Taiwan Defense Treaty of 1954, and the Baghdad Pact (with which the United States was closely associated, even though it did not formally join). By 1958, Washington had taken on explicit obligations to defend some forty-five countries against attack, and, by implication, several more. Critics accused Eisenhower and Dulles of "pactomania," an unfair charge since all but four of these commitments had been made by the Truman administration.[44] But this system of alliances was consistent with the president's strategy of seeking maximum deterrence at minimum cost: the administration sought to convey the impression that, although it could never defend all allies all at once, it could shield enough to render aggression unprofitable. If aggressive ambitions did exist in Moscow or Beijing—there is no way to be certain of this until Soviet and Chinese archives become available—the use of deterrent alliances may well have discouraged

---

[42] *Department of State Bulletin*, XXXV(January 21, 1957), 86.

[43] Steghen J. Genco, "The Eisenhower Doctrine: Deterrence in the Middle East, 1957–1958," in Alexander L. George and Richard Smoke, *Deterrence in American Foreign Policy: Theory and Practice* (New York: 1974), pp. 355–358.

[44] See Gaddis, *Strategies of Containment*, p. 152n.

them. What it could not deter, though, was the process of revolutionary change. The administration persistently ascribed such developments to its adversaries, thus exaggerating their unity and capabilities while simultaneously offending the sense of nationalism that probably afforded Third World nations their best long-term protection against hegemonial aspirations from the outside.

In retrospect, though, the most significant developments in the evolving relationship between communism and nationalism during this period were taking place, not in the "nonaligned" world at all, but in the increasingly uneasy partnership between the two giants of the communist world, the Soviet Union and the People's Republic of China. Here the Eisenhower administration was more prescient than its Third World policies might have suggested. Historians have long assumed that Dulles's staunch support for Chiang Kai-shek during the offshore island crises of 1954–1955 and 1958 reflected his fear of monolithic communism and his deference to the pro-Nationalist China lobby in the United States. But new evidence suggests an alternative explanation: that the administration's tough stand had as its goal not so much placation of the China lobby as fragmentation of the Sino-Soviet alliance, paradoxically by forcing the two communist giants into a position of dependence on each other.

Dulles had seen no possibility of splitting the Chinese Communists from the Russians by attempting to win their favor, as Acheson had hoped to do prior to the Korean War: after two and a half years of fighting, bitterness on both sides was too great to permit that. But, as the secretary of state pointed out late in 1953, making friends with Beijing was not the only way to promote Sino-Soviet differences: indeed, a policy of uncompromising toughness toward China, in addition to paying domestic political dividends, might drive the Chinese into a position of *greater* dependence on the Russians, forcing them to demand economic and military assistance that Moscow would be unable to provide. The hard-pressed Chinese would then break with the Russians out of frustration.[45]

---

[45] See, especially, Dulles's briefing for Eisenhower, Churchill, and Bidault at the Bermuda Conference, December 7, 1953, *FR: 1952–1954*, V, 1808–1818; also Gaddis, *The Long Peace*, pp. 174–187; and David Allan Mayers, *Cracking the Monolith: U.S. Policy against the Sino-Soviet Alliance, 1949–1955* (Baton Rouge: 1986).

We do not know, to this day, the full story of how the Sino-Soviet alliance did in fact collapse during the late 1950s. But enough evidence has accumulated to suggest that the Russians saw the Chinese as running unnecessary risks in challenging Washington's hard line on Quemoy and Matsu: former Soviet Foreign Minister Andrei Gromyko has even revealed a Mao Zedong plan, put forward in August, 1958, to lure American ground forces onto the Chinese mainland and then have the Russians attack them with nuclear weapons. Gromyko immediately rejected the scheme, and shortly thereafter, to the disgust of the Chinese, the Russians withdrew an earlier offer to provide them with their own atomic bomb.[46] The Dulles strategy of seeking to drive the Soviet Union and Communist China apart by forcing them together may not have directly caused these disputes, but it was an uncannily accurate anticipation of how they appear to have come about.[47]

But the Dulles of 1958 was not the Richard Nixon of 1971: beyond an agreement to hold informal talks with Chinese representatives, the administration made no effort to exploit growing Sino-Soviet differences by improving relations with Beijing. Dulles refused to consider diplomatic recognition or China's admission to the United Nations; he also opposed cultural exchanges, the reciprocal visits of newsmen, and, in one case, the acquisition of a Chinese panda for an American zoo.[48] Domestic politics had something to do with this: Dulles knew very well that communism was no longer monolithic, but he also knew that Mao's intervention in Korea had given his regime, in the eyes of many Americans, a reputation for evil surpassing even that of the Soviet Union. The resulting anti-Chinese atmosphere provided little incentive for those within the government who perceived the depth of Sino-Soviet antagonism—as Dulles clearly did—to push for better relations with Beijing.

There was, throughout the Eisenhower administration's attempts to wrestle with problems of communism and national-

---

[46] A. A. Gromyko, *Pamiatnoe* (Moscow: 1988), II, 132–134. See also the *New York Times*, February 22, 1988.

[47] See, for example, Donald S. Zagoria, *The Sino-Soviet Conflict, 1956–1961* (Princeton: 1962), pp. 152–221; and John Gittings, *Survey of the Sino-Soviet Dispute, 1963–1967* (London: 1968), pp. 20–26, 89–109.

[48] Hoopes, *Dulles*, pp. 415–423.

ism in the Third World, a curious pessimism regarding the ability of the first ideology to sustain itself against the second. This lack of faith in the "staying power" of nationalism caused the administration to feel that it had to extend security guarantees to vulnerable states. The same phenomenon made Eisenhower and Dulles less sensitive than they might have been to the backlash such efforts would produce in the "nonaligned" world, where perfervid American attempts to recruit allies appeared at least as intrusive and destabilizing as anything the Russians were doing. It also caused Washington to lose sight of the distinction between revolutions its adversaries had instigated and those upon which they were merely trying to capitalize. Finally, it may have delayed by some years exploitation of the Sino-Soviet split, the most important alteration in the global balance of power since the end of World War II, and one Dulles at least had been wise enough to foresee.

The early strategists of containment had taken the view that in any competition between communism and nationalism, the latter would, in the end, prevail; that this had already happened inside the USSR, where communism had become the instrument of Soviet national interests; and that by discreetly encouraging nationalism elsewhere in the world, the Kremlin's ability to project influence beyond its borders might be significantly reduced. The Eisenhower administration was not completely unsympathetic to this approach: it continued to support communist Yugoslavia on the basis of its demonstrated independence from Moscow, and one of Dulles's chief concerns in the Middle East was to disassociate United States policies from the activities of former colonial regimes there.[49] But the domestic political costs of dealing with governments which, though nationalist, were also communist, neutralist, or in some other way not inclined to follow Washington's wishes, proved in many cases to be greater than the administration was willing to pay. As a result, containment, a strategy originally designed to work with the forces of nationalism to restrain Soviet expansion, now took on the appearance of a crusade against nationalism itself, an approach very different from what its original architects had intended.

---

[49] Guhin, *Dulles*, pp. 266, 288.

## IV

If the 1950s witnessed an expansion of the Cold War into geographical areas previously untouched by it, these years also saw an unprecedented intrusion of that conflict into the realm of technology. Up to that point, the chief impact of technology on the Cold War had been to confirm the superior power of the United States over the Soviet Union. Lend-Lease, the atomic bomb, the European Recovery Program, and the development of a strategic bombing force capable of reaching the USSR—all had been, in one way or another, the products of sophisticated American technology, much resented by the Russians but also, one suspects, much envied. This situation changed dramatically when, on October 4, 1957, the Soviet Union successfully launched Sputnik, the first artificial earth satellite. Russian scientists seemed to have made a major breakthrough, carrying with it the potential for a major shift in the strategic balance of power.

Obtuse though he was in many ways, Stalin must be given credit for having had a clear vision of the course developments in strategic weapons technology were going to take during the 1950s. Thanks to programs he initiated, the Soviet Union was able to test a primitive thermonuclear device as early as August, 1953; the first such American test had taken place only the previous November. The Russians had an operational hydrogen bomb ready by November, 1955; this achievement, when coupled with the Soviet Air Force's developing long-range bomber capability, led President Eisenhower to conclude by early 1956 that the United States had lost its historic invulnerability to attack. Despite the fact the Strategic Air Command's overwhelming retaliatory strength could devastate the Soviet Union several times over, there would be no way to prevent some Russian weapons from getting through. The result, Eisenhower noted, would be "literally a matter of digging ourselves out of ashes, [and] starting again."[50]

---

[50] Eisenhower diary, January 23, 1956, Robert H. Ferrell, ed., *The Eisenhower Diaries* (New York: 1981), p. 312. See also Herbert F. York, *The Advisors: Oppenheimer, Teller, and the Superbomb* (San Francisco: 1976), p. 94–96; David Alan Rosenberg, "The Origins of Overkill: Nuclear Weapons and American Strategy, 1945–1960," *International Security* VII(Spring, 1983), 39–40; and, on Soviet nuclear weapons development, Holloway, *The Soviet Union and the Arms Race*, pp. 23–27.

But Stalin had also decided, at some point after World War II, to seek an even more lethal technological advantage over the West: instead of attempting to match the rapidly-growing American strategic bombing force, the USSR would concentrate its scarce resources on developing long-range missiles capable of carrying nuclear weapons.[51] Stalin's successors, kept in the dark about much of this, found a missile development program well underway at the time of the dictator's death. The new leadership had a great deal to learn: "We were like peasants in a marketplace," Khrushchev recalled, describing the occasion on which members of the Politburo viewed a long-range missile for the first time. "We walked around and around the rocket, touching it, tapping it to see if it was sturdy enough—we did everything but lick it to see how it tasted."[52] Whatever their lack of sophistication, however, Khrushchev and his associates were not slow to take advantage of the technological lead their unlamented predecessor had given them.

"It always sounded good to say in public speeches that we could hit a fly at any distance with our missiles," Khrushchev subsequently admitted,[53] but in fact problems of guidance and cost prevented the Soviet Union, at any point during his leadership, from deploying a sufficient number of launchers to obtain an assured first-strike capability against the United States. Instead the Russians accepted strategic inferiority while simultaneously working to convince the West that *it* was operating from a position of weakness. This massive bluff—resembling as nothing else the old Chinese tactic of building paper forts, then painting bellicose dragons on them to ward off aggressors—depended for its success upon Moscow's ability to conceal from outsiders the nature and extent of Soviet military deployments, and on the Kremlin's confidence that the United States would never take advantage of its actual strategic superiority to attack the USSR.

The first requirement could, for the moment, be taken for granted: despite frequent penetrations of Soviet air space by American reconnaissance aircraft and even, during the early

---

[51] Walter A. McDougall, *The Heavens and the Earth: A Political History of the Space Age* (New York: 1985), pp. 41–55.

[52] *Khrushchev Remembers: The Last Testament*, p. 46.

[53] Ibid., p. 47.

1950s, an extensive effort to photograph Russian military installations from unmanned balloons,[54] Western observers were reduced to gleaning most of their knowledge of the Kremlin's military capabilities from weapons displays in May Day parades,
occasional closely guarded trips around the country, and the
scraps of information that appeared in the official press. The
limitations of this process became evident following Moscow
Aviation Day ceremonies in July, 1955, when the Russians managed to set off a major "bomber gap" scare in the West, and a
substantial acceleration in the production of American B-52s,
through the simple expedient of flying a single squadron of
their own "Bison" bombers over the reviewing stand several
times.[55]

Soviet leaders could not be entirely certain of Washington's
peaceful intentions: there is evidence that the Eisenhower administration's talk of "massive retaliation" frightened them, setting off debates within the Kremlin on how best to deter the
United States. The 1955 Geneva summit appears to have lessened fears of an American attack, however, while the West's
failure to support the uprising in Hungary the following year
may well have confirmed impressions that the Eisenhower-
Dulles version of containment would differ little in practice
from what had gone before.[56] It is significant that Khrushchev's
first public threat to rain rockets on European capitals, delivered in reaction to the Anglo-French-Israeli invasion of Egypt,
occurred just as Soviet troops were reimposing control over
their unfortunate East European satellite.

The summer of 1957 saw two important developments that
facilitated exploitation of a "strategic deception" strategy. One
was the elimination, in June, of Khrushchev's remaining rivals
for power in the Kremlin, an event that left him, for the time

---

[54] See Jeffrey Richelson, *American Espionage and the Soviet Target* (New York:
1987), pp. 100–140.
[55] Allen Dulles, *The Craft of Intelligence* (New York: 1963), p. 149: Arnold L.
Horelick and Myron Rush, *Strategic Power and Soviet Foreign Policy* (Chicago:
1966), pp. 27–28.
[56] Ibid., pp. 18–29, 211–212. See also Thomas W. Wolfe, *Soviet Power and
Europe, 1945–1970* (Baltimore: 1970), pp. 133–135; and, for evidence that the idea
of "preventive war" was discussed within the Eisenhower administration, Marc
Trachtenberg, "A 'Wasting Asset': American Strategy and the Shifting Nuclear
Balance, 1949–1954," *International Security*, XIII(Winter, 1988/89), 5–49.

being, in full control of Soviet foreign policy. The other was the first successful test, in August, of an intercontinental ballistic missile. Claims regarding this test were greeted with incredulity in the outside world, until in October the Russians demonstrated their capability for all to see by launching Sputnik. This development provoked alarm, even panic, in the West, with a previously-appointed presidential commission headed by Ford Foundation chairman H. Rowan Gaither, Jr., now calling for the expenditure of an additional $44 billion over the next five years to improve American missile strength and civil defense facilities; Khrushchev himself responded with a gradually escalating series of carefully worded claims designed to imply, if not overtly assert, Soviet strategic superiority over the United States.[57]

Khrushchev did not at first tie his assertions regarding ICBM development to specific political issues, but in November, 1958, he abruptly threatened to turn over control of Berlin access routes to the East Germans if the Western powers did not agree to terminate their occupation rights in West Berlin within six months. Shortly thereafter, Soviet Foreign Minister Gromyko warned that should fighting break out over Berlin, "modern military technology" would make it certain that the flames of war "would inevitably spread to the continent of America."[58] Khrushchev's decision to instigate a new Berlin crisis almost certainly reflected fears that the West Germans might gain access, through NATO, to tactical nuclear weapons and intermediate-range ballistic missiles—such devices were already being deployed in Western Europe, ironically in response to fears the Russians themselves had provoked, first of a conventional force attack there, and subsequently of a "missile gap." Then, too, West Berlin's continued existence as a bastion of capitalism deep within communist East Germany remained a perpetual irritant; Khrushchev may also have hoped to impress the Chinese, who now doubted Soviet resolve as a result of Moscow's caution during the second Quemoy-Matsu crisis earlier that

---

[57] Horelick and Rush, *Strategic Power and Soviet Foreign Policy*, pp. 42–49. See also McDougall, *The Heavens and the Earth*, pp. 237–249; and, for the Gaither Committee report, Gaddis, *Strategies of Containment*, pp. 184–186.

[58] Quoted in Horelick and Rush, *Strategic Power and Soviet Foreign Policy*. pp. 119–120.

year.[59] But whatever his objectives, the Kremlin leader clearly expected Soviet achievements in missile and space technology to help him attain them.

Significantly, Khrushchev coupled his demands on Berlin with a series of conciliatory gestures aimed apparently at recreating the "spirit of Geneva." These included an invitation for Eisenhower to visit the Soviet Union, trips by subordinates Anastas Mikoyan and Frol Kozlov to the United States, a return trip by Vice President Richard Nixon to Moscow (the occasion of a spirited debate between Nixon and Khrushchev, held in the unlikely setting of a model kitchen in an American exhibition then visiting the Soviet capital), and finally, an agreement to hold a foreign ministers' meeting on the subject of Berlin. Eisenhower, who following Dulles's death in May, 1959, had decided to play a more active personal role in the conduct of Soviet-American relations, responded by inviting Khrushchev to visit the United States if the foreign ministers' meeting in Geneva produced progress on Berlin. It did not, but through a misunderstanding the president's precondition was not made clear to the Russians, and Khrushchev, to Eisenhower's chagrin, decided to come anyway.[60]

The Soviet leader attached great importance to this visit: "we had finally forced the United States to recognize the necessity of establishing closer contacts with us." To all appearances, he enjoyed himself hugely, bantering with reporters, sipping champagne with leading capitalists in Averell Harriman's apartment, debating methods of corn production with Iowa farmers, allowing himself to be scandalized by a cancan dance on a Hollywood sound stage, and working himself up into a considerable tantrum over not being allowed, for security reasons, to visit Disneyland. Talks between Eisenhower and Khrushchev at the president's Maryland mountain retreat led inevitably to press speculation about the "spirit of Camp David" (it is a sign of

[59] Ulam, *The Rivals*, pp. 287–295; Jack M. Schick, *The Berlin Crisis, 1958–1962* (Philadelphia: 1971), p. 233. See also note 46, above.

[60] Dwight D. Eisenhower, *The White House Years: Waging Peace, 1956–1961* (Garden City, New York: 1965), pp. 405–408. See also Ambrose, *Eisenhower: The President*, pp. 532–537; and, on the Nixon-Khrushchev "kitchen" debate, Stephen E. Ambrose, *Nixon: The Education of a Politician, 1913–1962* (New York: 1987), pp. 523–525.

how spotty the Russians's information about the United States was at this time that Khrushchev and his entourage had some difficulty in determining what Camp David was, and in reassuring themselves that their invitation to this out-of-the-way place had not been meant as an insult).[61] But beyond Eisenhower's acknowledgment that the Berlin situation was "abnormal" and Khrushchev's agreement not to press for a settlement until after a four-power summit the following spring, practical results of the Khrushchev visit appeared minimal.

Meanwhile, alarm over Soviet missile developments had begun to subside. The United States had, by the end of 1959, convincingly demonstrated its own satellite and ICBM capability. Even more important, secret means of detection had begun to reveal that Soviet missile deployments had come nowhere close to what American estimates had projected. High-altitude U-2 reconnaissance aircraft, developed by the Central Intelligence Agency, had been overflying the Soviet Union since 1956. The information they provided could not be conclusive because of the limited frequency and coverage of the flights,[62] but it was enough, when combined with Eisenhower's own deeply-felt concern about excessive military spending, to cause him to resist calls like those of the Gaither Committee for massive increases in the defense budget following Sputnik.[63]

The U-2 also became the occasion of a major crisis, though, when in May, 1960, one crashed, or was shot down, near Sverdlovsk in central Russia two weeks before the Paris summit. Khrushchev gave Eisenhower the opportunity to disavow responsibility for the overflight, but the president, in an unprecedented public acknowledgment of a covert operation, refused to do so, announcing that he had indeed authorized the mission and that others like it had been going on for almost four years. This left Khrushchev little choice: "[Eisenhower]

---

[61] See Khrushchev's lengthy and revealing account of this trip in *Khrushchev Remembers: The Last Testament*, pp. 368–416.

[62] For the development and use of the U-2, see Michael R. Beschloss, *Mayday: Eisenhower, Khrushchev and the U-2 Affair* (New York: 1986), pp. 73–242.

[63] Bundy, *Danger and Survival*, pp. 334–350. See also Richard A. Aliano, *American Defense Policy from Eisenhower to Kennedy* (Athens, Ohio: 1975), pp. 6–8, 47–60.

had, so to speak, offered us his back end, and we obliged by kicking it as hard as we could."[64] The Soviet leader traveled to Paris but, once there, broke up the summit meeting (and cancelled an invitation for the president to visit the Soviet Union) in an outburst of offended rhetoric: "We shall not tolerate insults, we have our pride and our dignity. We represent a mighty socialist state."[65]

Whether the Paris summit would have produced progress on Berlin is difficult to say. Khrushchev clearly had staked his personal reputation on talks with Eisenhower; indeed, the Chinese would later claim that he repudiated his commitment to share nuclear weapons with them as a means of facilitating the discussions at Camp David.[66] Certainly he gave the president every chance to sweep the U-2 incident under the rug. On the other hand, Khrushchev was already under considerable pressure from both within his own government and from the Chinese for yielding too much.[67] The U-2 episode gave him a convenient excuse for avoiding negotiations—an excuse all the more important since, presumably, recovered photographs from the downed plane had given the Russians some indication of how good American intelligence on Soviet missile deployments had been. What is clear is that Eisenhower made his decision to accept public responsibility for the overflight, and thus risk the summit, more for reasons of personal honesty and a desire to avoid the appearance of not controlling his own administration[68] than from any sensitivity to Khrushchev's internal problems or the way in which these might affect future Soviet-American relations.

The United States had to give up U-2 overflights, but this meant only a brief gap in the flow of intelligence before a new and even better source became available—satellite reconnaissance. This new instrument, which Eisenhower had ordered

---

[64] *Khrushchev Remembers: The Last Testament,* pp. 448.

[65] Khrushchev press conference, May 18, 1960, *Documents on International Affairs, 1960* (London: 1961), p. 34. See also Beschloss, *Mayday,* pp. 243–304.

[66] Schurmann, *The Logic of World Power,* pp. 302–303, 308–309.

[67] Ulam, *The Rivals,* pp. 310–312; Michel Tatu, *Power in the Kremlin: From Khrushchev to Kosygin* (New York: 1969), pp. 41–122.

[68] Eisenhower, *Waging Peace,* pp. 553–553. See also, for an overall assessment, Beschloss, *Mayday,* pp. 355–382.

developed as an eventual successor to the U-2, quickly confirmed what had been suspected for some time: that the Soviet
missile buildup had been more rhetorical than real and that the
Russians had deployed only a fraction of the ICBMs they could
have built had they chosen to do so.[69] That they did not can be
seen both as evidence of efficient budgetary management—it
made sense to delay deployment of clumsy, first-generation
rockets until more reliable versions had come along—and as an
attempt by Khrushchev to implement his own "new look" strategy of maximum deterrence at minimum cost. The practice of
"strategic deception" can also be taken, though, as reflecting a
high degree of confidence on the Russians' part regarding
Washington's peaceful intentions: the Kremlin leadership decided that it could live comfortably with strategic inferiority because the United States was unlikely to put its strategic superiority to actual use.[70]

"Of course, we tried to derive maximum political advantage
from the fact that we were the first to launch our rockets into
space," Khrushchev later recalled. "We wanted to exert pressure on American militarists—and also influence the minds of
more reasonable politicians—so that the United States would
start treating us better. However, ... we had no intention of
starting a war."[71] Not surprisingly, this approach backfired.
The problem with any such effort to translate apparent technological superiority into political benefits is that the very act of
demonstrating that superiority is likely to impress potential adversaries more with the need to catch up than with the desirability of resolving differences. Certainly the United States had
found this to be the case in its own sporadic attempts to exploit
a technological edge over the Soviet Union after World War II.
Khrushchev's "strategic deception" ploy represented a more
ambitious and blatant effort to obtain such political gains, on
the basis of a technological advantage considerably less impres-

---

[69] McDougall, *The Heavens and the Earth*, pp. 112–124. See also Paul B. Stares,
*The Militarization of Space: U.S. Policy, 1945–1984* (Ithaca: 1985), pp. 22–58; and
William E. Burrows, *Deep Black: Space Espionage and National Security* (New York:
1986) pp. 55–112.

[70] Horelick and Rush, *Strategic Power and Soviet Foreign Policy*, pp. 105–107.

[71] *Khrushchev Remembers: The Last Testament*, p. 53.

sive than what the United States had enjoyed a decade earlier. Such minimal dividends as his strategems did produce were largely the result, not of the skill or dexterity with which they were executed, but of the Eisenhower administration's reluctance to divulge the means by which it had discovered the fraudulent ground upon which they rested.

V

There is little reason to question Khrushchev's assertion that he did not want a war. Indeed, it now appears that a principal objective of Soviet foreign policy during the decade in which he controlled it was to *improve* relations with the West—a goal Khrushchev came to regard, in the end, as more important than maintaining the solidarity of the international communist movement. Nor is there much doubt as to what motivated this policy: the Soviet leader apparently meant it when he repeatedly warned his Chinese Communist critics that there could be no winners in a nuclear exchange.[72] Yet Khrushchev's methods for seeking a relaxation of tension were distinctly odd. One historian has compared them to those of a man

who seeks to have a friendly chat with a man next door, ... [but] instead of knocking politely on the door of the apartment, climbs on the window ledge outside, makes ferocious faces through his neighbor's window or loudly bangs at the door, threatening to break it open. In the interval, he explains that all he wants is friendship and neighborly comity.[73]

This strategy of seeking detente through intimidation reached its climax between 1960 and 1962.

It was a period that saw Khrushchev publicly threaten, in the wake of the abortive Paris summit, to "take the American imperialists by the scruff of the neck [and] give them a good shaking."[74] It witnessed the Soviet leader making a spectacle of himself at the United Nations in September, 1960, jeering speakers, pounding the desk with his fists and, in several in-

---

[72] Zagoria, *The Sino-Soviet Conflict*, pp. 156, 280–284, 290–294.
[73] Ulam, *The Rivals*, pp. 285–286.
[74] Khrushchev press conference, May 18, 1960, *Documents on International Affairs, 1960*, p. 36.

stances, his shoe. ("Some people did not seem to understand this unparliamentary method," he admitted afterwards.)[75] In January, 1961, Khrushchev made it clear that the Soviet Union's desire to avoid nuclear war in no way precluded support for "wars of national liberation." Eight months later, he shocked the world by ordering construction of a fortified wall separating East and West Berlin; there quickly followed a unilateral resumption of nuclear weapons tests in the atmosphere—there had been a moratorium on such tests since 1958—and a new barrage of threats based on Soviet space achievements:

The Soviet Union has worked out designs for creating a series of super-powerful nuclear bombs equivalent to 20, 30, 50 and 100 million tons of T.N.T., and many powerful rockets . . . [which] can lift and deliver such nuclear bombs to any point on the globe . . . It would be unjustifiable thoughtlessness not to draw the appropriate conclusions.[76]

Finally, sometime in the spring or summer of 1962, Khrushchev made the risky decision to place medium- and intermediate-range ballistic missiles in Cuba, a maneuver that would bring the world closer to nuclear war than ever before, or since. These were policies more bellicose and provocative than anything Stalin had ever attempted. And yet they paralleled persistent efforts on Khrushchev's part to move toward detente with the West.

The Soviet leader had hoped that the coming to power of a new administration in Washington would produce such a result. Khrushchev had quietly rooted for John F. Kennedy in his close 1960 contest with "that son-of-a-bitch Richard Nixon";[77] fortunately for the Democrats, however, he showed uncharacteristic discretion and kept his sympathies to himself. Immediately after Kennedy's inauguration and as a sign of goodwill, Khrushchev ordered the release of two American airmen shot down on a reconnaissance mission over the Barents Sea several

---

[75] *Khrushchev Remembers: The Last Testament*, p. 473.

[76] Soviet government statement of August 30, 1961, *Documents on International Affairs, 1961* (London: 1965), p. 463. For Khrushchev's January 6, 1961, speech on wars of national liberation, see ibid., pp. 259–273. The Berlin Wall and the nuclear test moratorium are covered in Norman Gelb. *The Berlin Wall: Kennedy, Khrushchev, and a Showdown in the Heart of Europe* (New York: 1986); and Robert A. Divine, *Blowing on the Wind: The Nuclear Test Ban Debate, 1954–1960* (New York: 1978), especially pp. 225–240.

[77] *Khrushchev Remembers*, p. 507.

months earlier;[78] he also let it be known that he would welcome an opportunity to meet with the new president. Kennedy quickly agreed, and a summit conference was scheduled for Vienna in early June, 1961.[79] It was not, from Washington's point of view, the most auspicious moment: the month of April had brought embarrassing humiliations, with the failure of the Central Intelligence Agency's Bay of Pigs operation against Castro in Cuba and with a new Soviet space feat, the first manned orbital flight around the earth. Kennedy attempted to recoup what prestige he could by committing the United States to placing a man on the moon by the end of the decade; this lofty (and expensive) objective set, the new president set off for Europe and his encounter with the unpredictable Soviet premier.

If there was a "spirit of Vienna," it was one very different from the temporarily optimistic moods generated by the earlier Geneva and Camp David summits. The responsibility, it would appear, lay on both sides. Khrushchev once again brought up the subject of Berlin, threatening to sign a peace treaty with the East Germans cutting off Western access rights by the end of the year. Kennedy responded by insisting that the West would keep its commitments. The American president in turn berated the Soviet leader for his "wars of national liberation" strategy; Khrushchev struck back with a denunciation of American attempts to freeze the status quo in the Third World. Arguments on both sides reflected a reversion to ideological stereotypes: Kennedy appeared to be assuming Moscow's responsibility for revolutionary movements everywhere, while Khrushchev charged that "monopolists" who could not afford to disarm ran the United States. The Vienna summit produced one unexpected agreement to work for the neutralization of Laos, but in general the effect was to increase rather than lower the level of tension. As Kennedy put it in a report to the American people: "We have wholly different views of right and wrong, of what is

---

[78] Beschloss, *Mayday*, pp. 321–322, 341–344.

[79] Theodore C. Sorensen, *Kennedy* (New York: 1965), pp. 541–543; Arthur M. Schlesinger, Jr., *A Thousand Days: John F. Kennedy in the White House* (New York: 1965), pp. 278–286.

an internal affair and what is aggression, . . . of where the world is and where it is going."[80]

Two months later, following an announcement by Khrushchev of a large increase in the Soviet defense budget, Kennedy ordered a tripling of draft calls, asked Congress for authority to call up the reserves, and endorsed implementation of a new and elaborate civil defense program.[81] If these moves were intended to impress Khrushchev, they apparently succeeded. It seems likely that his decision in August to erect the Berlin Wall, although it appeared at the time as a new provocation, was in fact an effort to defuse the crisis: it is significant (and typical) that Khrushchev coupled his announcement in October of a fifty-megaton nuclear test with yet another postponement of the deadline for a Berlin settlement.[82] Khrushchev also picked this moment to initiate a personal exchange of correspondence with Kennedy outside normal diplomatic channels, a means of communication that was to prove of great value during the events that followed.[83]

Since shortly after taking office, Kennedy and his top advisers had known from reconnaissance satellite photographs that the so-called "missile gap," which had figured prominently in the 1960 campaign, was nonexistent.[84] They chose not to make this information public, however, until late October of 1961, when Deputy Secretary of Defense Roswell Gilpatric, in a carefully worded public address, announced that "[the] Iron Curtain is not so impenetrable as to force us to accept at face value the Kremlin's boasts. . . . We have a second-strike capability which is at least as extensive as what the Soviets can deliver by

---

[80] Kennedy television address of June 6, 1961, *Public Papers of the Presidents: John F. Kennedy, 1961* (Washington: 1962), p. 443. See also Sorensen, *Kennedy,* pp. 543–550; and Schlesinger, *A Thousand Days,* pp. 333–348.

[81] Kennedy television address of July 25, 1961, *Kennedy Public Papers, 1961,* pp. 533–535.

[82] Khrushchev speech of October 17, 1961, *Documents on International Affairs, 1961,* pp. 224–225.

[83] Sorensen, *Kennedy,* pp. 552–555.

[84] Lawrence Freedman, *U.S. Intelligence and the Soviet Strategic Threat,* Second Edition (Princeton: 1986), pp. 72–77; John Prados, *The Soviet Estimate: U.S. Intelligence Analysis and Russian Military Strength* (New York: 1982), pp. 110–122. For newly-available satellite reconnaissance capabilities, see Burrows, *Deep Black,* pp. 82–112.

striking first."[85] The administration's motives in making this
and similar statements at that time were mixed: there were domestic political advantages to dispelling once and for all the
myth of the "missile gap"; there may also have been the expectation that such action would increase the credibility of the
American deterrent. Certainly the Gilpatric speech was a useful
reassurance to nervous allies.[86] Whatever its purposes, though,
its effect was to challenge, openly and authoritatively, the inflated strategic claims upon which Khrushchev's policies of the
past four years had been based.

Those policies had involved accepting a position of actual
strategic inferiority as long as a facade of superiority could be
maintained, if not with those Washington officials privy to U-2
and satellite intelligence, at least with the informed public in
the West, the Soviet Union, and, significantly, China. The
Gilpatric speech ripped away that facade, leaving Moscow in an
embarrassingly exposed strategic position, a condition made all
the more alarming by the Kennedy administration's careful refusal to rule out, as a response to conventional military aggression, the possibility of initiating a nuclear exchange.[87] It was
this uncomfortable situation that appears to have driven
Khrushchev to take the risk of sending missiles to Cuba.

Such Soviet accounts as exist of the "Caribbean crisis" stress
the defensive purposes of the missile deployment: it was intended, they argue, to protect Castro's regime from another
American invasion.[88] Khrushchev has added that a secondary
objective was to "equalize" the balance of power: "The
Americans had surrounded our country with military bases and

---

[85] *New York Times*, October 22, 1961.

[86] See, on the Gilpatric speech, Horelick and Rush, *Strategic Power and Soviet Foreign Policy*, pp. 83–84; Bundy, *Danger and Survival*, pp. 382, 419; and Gerald M. Steinberg, *Satellite Reconnaissance: The Role of Informal Bargaining* (New York: 1983), pp. 49–51.

[87] See, on this point, Jerome H. Kahan, *Security in the Nuclear Age: Developing U.S. Strategic Arms Policy* (New York: 1975), pp. 90–92; and Marc Trachtenberg, "The Influence of Nuclear Weapons in the Cuban Missile Crisis," *International Security*, X(Summer, 1985), 159–160.

[88] A. A. Gromyko, "Karibskii krizis," *Voprosy istorii*, 1971, #7, pp. 135–144, #8, pp. 121–129, and *Through Russian Eyes: President Kennedy's 1036 Days* (Washington: 1973), pp. 169–171; also Gromyko and Ponomarev, eds., *Soviet Foreign Policy: 1917–1980*, II, 336–338.

threatened us with nuclear weapons, and now they would learn just what it feels like to have enemy missiles pointed at you."[89] Both objectives may well have been present, but the weight of the evidence suggests that the latter in fact dominated. Missiles with ranges of from 1100 to 2200 nautical miles were hardly appropriate weapons for use against another Bay of Pigs style landing; moreover the risks Khrushchev took in sending such weapons outside the Soviet Union for the first time—accompanied, the Russians have now acknowledged, by 20 nuclear warheads—seem far out of proportion to the gains envisaged had the defense of Cuba been his sole objective.[90]

A more satisfactory explanation is to view Khrushchev's action as a "post-strategic deception" maneuver, necessitated by the Kennedy administration's exposure of the "missile gap" as a myth. Although the Russians, despite Khrushchev's claims, had never produced enough ICBMs to obtain an assured first-strike capability against the United States, there was nothing fraudulent or illusory about their buildup of medium- and intermediate-range missiles targeted against Europe. Here the Russians had gone all out, producing some 700 such weapons by the end of 1962 as against approximately 20 ICBMs capable of reaching the United States.[91] Whatever early lead Moscow might have had in ICBM development had long since been eclipsed by the assembly line production in the United States of Atlas, Titan, and Minuteman rockets (almost 300 by the time of the missile crisis) and of the submarine-launched Polaris (144 missiles by late 1962), all of which could reach targets inside the Soviet Union.[92] Cuba offered Khrushchev a quick means of re-

---

[89] *Khrushchev Remembers*, p. 547. See also Medvedev, *Khrushchev*, p. 186.

[90] Graham T. Allison, *Essence of Decision: Explaining the Cuban Missile Crisis* (Boston: 1971), p. 49; Horelick and Rush, *Strategic Power and Soviet Foreign Policy*, pp. 127–128. For the Soviet acknowledgement on nuclear warheads, see the *New York Times*, January 29, 1989.

[91] Horelick and Rush, *Strategic Power and Soviet Foreign Policy*, pp. 49, 94; Wolfe, *Soviet Power and Europe*, pp. 41–42, 98, 154, 183–184; Holloway, *The Soviet Union and the Arms Race*, p. 43. The estimate of 20 Soviet ICBMs is from Soviet sources quoted in the *New York Times*, January 29, 1989.

[92] Horelick and Rush, *Strategic Power and Soviet Foreign Policy*, pp. 35–36, 83; Wolfe, *Soviet Power and Europe*, pp. 182–183; Freedman, *U.S. Intelligence and the Soviet Strategic Threat*, p. 101; Robin Edmonds, *Soviet Foreign Policy, 1962–1973: The Paradox of Super Power* (London: 1975), p. 27.

dressing the unfavorable balance to which the Kennedy administration had now called attention: it provided an unsinkable
platform from which to aim MRBMs and IRBMs, which the
Russians possessed in abundance, at American targets. The effect, had it succeeded, would have been to more than double
overnight the Soviet Union's offensive missile capability against
the United States.[93]

Khrushchev was probably telling the truth when he asserted,
both at the time and subsequently, that he never intended to
use the missiles he dispatched to Cuba in an offensive
capacity.[94] What he presumably did hope to do was to reveal
the missiles' presence in a dramatic fashion and then demand,
as the price for removing them, concessions from the West, almost certainly on Berlin, possibly also on nuclear-free zones in
Central Europe and East Asia.[95] Such a maneuver would have
been consistent with his repeated attempts, since the mid-1950s,
to bludgeon the West into a settlement of Cold War issues. But it
was a risky gamble in every sense: Khrushchev had to depend
upon the Americans not learning of the missile deployment until
it was fully in place, and then upon their willingness to bargain
over its removal. Neither assumption turned out to be valid.

The actions the Kennedy administration took upon discover-
ing the Soviet missiles in Cuba—a "quarantine" of the island,
together with what was virtually a public ultimatum to remove
the weapons—have never been free from retrospective criticism. The president has been charged with having exaggerated
the strategic significance of the Soviet deployment; critics are
fond of quoting Secretary of Defense Robert S. McNamara's observation, made at the time, that "it makes no great difference
whether you are killed by a missile fired from the Soviet Union
or from Cuba." It has also been argued that Kennedy made no

---

[93] Soviet officials have now unofficially conceded this point. See Raymond
L. Garthoff, "Cuban Missile Crisis: The Soviet Story," *Foreign Policy*, #72(Fall,
1988), pp. 65–66.

[94] Khrushchev to Kennedy, October 26, 1962, *Department of State Bulletin*,
LXIX(November 19, 1973), 640; *Khrushchev Remembers*, p. 549.

[95] Dean Rusk and George Ball comments, October 16, 1962, ExComm meeting, "White House Tapes and Minutes," pp. 177–178, 190. See also Tatu, *Power
in the Kremlin*, pp. 231–233; Ulam, *The Rivals*, p. 329.

effort to resolve the crisis through diplomatic means but instead welcomed a public confrontation with the Russians; the implication is that he had forthcoming Congressional elections much in mind. Finally, it has been asserted that the episode was not the finely orchestrated exercise in crisis management it is often pictured as having been; that what brought about its favorable resolution was not skill but simply, in Dean Acheson's words, "plain dumb luck."[96]

None of these arguments is wholly fallacious, but they do share a certain narrowness of perspective for which allowances should be made. A doubling of the number of launchers capable of reaching the United States was no insignificant event, even if it did leave unchanged the overall strategic balance. Shorter distances to targets meant improved accuracy and reduced warning time; moreover United States detection systems had not been designed to pick up missiles coming from the south.[97] It is true that the Russians would have had difficulty in coordinating simultaneous launches from the Soviet Union and Cuba, but Khrushchev could be sure that no such action was contemplated—Kennedy could not. No doubt the administration did want to avoid another humiliation like the Bay of Pigs, but this desire reflected more than mere partisan concerns. Appearances are by no means insignificant components of international power; as Kennedy himself noted, the possibility that Khrushchev's maneuver would have altered only the *appearance* of power relationships gave no guarantee that very real, and undesirable, consequences might not flow from it.[98]

Diplomacy might have accomplished the same end that was in fact achieved, but there could be no assurance of that: McNamara thought it "likely to lead to no satisfactory result,

[96] Robert A. Divine, ed., *The Cuban Missile Crisis*, Second Edition (New York: 1988), *passim*. See also Richard J. Walton, *Cold War and Counterrevolution: The Foreign Policy of John F. Kennedy* (New York: 1972), pp. 103–142; and Louise FitzSimons, *The Kennedy Doctrine* (New York: 1972), pp. 126–172.

[97] Allison, *Essence of Decision*, p. 54; Horelick and Rush, *Strategic Power and Soviet Foreign Policy*, pp. 137–138.

[98] Sorensen, *Kennedy*, p. 678; Bundy, *Danger and Survival*, p. 412. See also the ExComm discussion of October 16, 1962, "Documentation: White House Tapes and Minutes of the Cuban Missile Crisis," *International Security*, X(Summer, 1985), pp. 184–186.

and it almost stops subsequent military action."[99] The advantage of a public challenge to the Russians was that it made Kennedy's determination all the more credible by greatly increasing the price he would have to pay to back down. It also precluded any attempt by Khrushchev to reveal the missiles' presence himself, in an effort to reap at least some of the dividends he had hoped for. It is true that Kennedy risked nuclear war by openly demanding that Khrushchev yield,[100] but given the Soviet Union's inferiority, in this instance both in strategic and conventional capabilities, he would appear to have had better rational grounds on which to anticipate achieving his objectives peacefully than his Soviet counterpart did when he made his high-risk decision to install missiles in Cuba in the first place.

The crisis reached its climax with an unsubtle hint, delivered through the president's brother, Robert Kennedy, that the United States would remove the missiles from Cuba forcefully if the Russians did not immediately agree to withdraw them.[101] Khrushchev at first agreed to do so, in a long, emotional message on October 26, in return for a public pledge from Kennedy to attempt no further invasions of Cuba. But before the president could respond a second and more formal message arrived from Moscow demanding as well the removal of American intermediate-range missiles from Turkey, installed there by the

---

[99] McNamara comments, October 16, 1962, ExComm meeting, ibid., p. 182. See also Bundy, *Danger and Survival*, pp. 408–410.

[100] Two recent revelations, one from Soviet, the other from American sources, suggest how easily things could have gotten out of hand. First, although American intelligence had estimated that there were between 8,000 and 10,000 Soviet military personnel in Cuba in October, 1962, Soviet sources now suggest the actual figure was 42,000. [Garthoff, "Cuban Missile Crisis: The Soviet Story," p. 67.] This suggests that, despite American conventional and strategic superiority, Khrushchev might have found it difficult to take no retaliatory action if a Soviet force of that size was being overrun. Second, Oleg Penkovsky, a high-ranking official in Soviet Military Intelligence who was also an American and British spy, was arrested in Moscow on October 22, at the height of the missile crisis. There are indications that, before being taken into custody, Penkovsky managed to send a coded telephone signal to his American and British handlers to the effect that war was imminent. After some agonizing, they suppressed it, without passing it on to the top level of the CIA, or to the White House. [Raymond Garthoff, *Reflections on the Cuban Missile Crisis* (Washington: 1987), pp. 39–41.]

[101] Robert F. Kennedy, *Thirteen Days: A Memoir of the Cuban Missile Crisis* (New York: 1969), pp. 108–109. See also, for the Soviet side of this episode, Garthoff, "Cuban Missile Crisis: The Soviet Story," p. 75.

Eisenhower administration in 1959 to balance the alleged "missile gap." Kennedy, we now know, was prepared to make this concession despite the political loss of face it would have entailed: if it should become known that the United States could have avoided invading Cuba by trading missiles in Turkey, the president worried, then "I don't see how we'll have a very good war."[102]

As it turned out, though, no such American compromise was necessary. One of the president's advisers—it is not clear who—at this critical point recalled the plot of an Anthony Trollope novel—it is not clear which—in which an ambitious heroine had interpreted an ambiguous gesture as a proposal of marriage. It was decided, on this basis, simply to accept the first Khrushchev communication and ignore the second; Khrushchev agreed to go along.[103] The "Trollope ploy" worked, thereby averting a Soviet-American confrontation that might have led to World War III as well as demonstrating the unarguable benefits, to policymakers, of a broad liberal education.

Kennedy's no-invasion pledge allowed both sides to emerge from the crisis claiming victory, but there was little doubt as to who the real winners and losers were."I won't deny," Khrushchev later admitted, "that we were obliged to make some big concessions in the interests of peace."[104] The United States had its way in the Cuban Missile Crisis because Kennedy was able to convince Khrushchev that American strategic power might actually be put to military use against the Soviet Union. It had been the Soviet leader's skepticism on that point that had allowed him to tolerate actual strategic inferiority for the previous five years while simultaneously claiming superiority. The tone of Khrushchev's October 26 message—which he appears to have dic-

---

[102] Kennedy comment, October 27, 1962, ExComm meeting, McGeorge Bundy, transcriber, and James G. Blight, editor, "The Eleventh Hour of the Cuban Missile Crisis: October 27, 1962: Transcripts of the Meetings of the ExComm," *International Security*, XII(Winter, 1987/88), 83. See also David A. Welch and James G. Blight, "The Eleventh Hour of the Cuban Missile Crisis: An Introduction to the ExComm Transcripts," ibid., pp. 15–16; Bundy, *Danger and Survival*, pp. 427–436; and James G. Blight, Joseph S. Nye, Jr., and David A. Welch, "The Cuban Missile Crisis Revisited," *Foreign Affairs*, LXVI(Fall, 1987), 178–179.

[103] Welch and Blight, "Introduction to the ExComm Transcripts," pp. 11, 19.

[104] *Khrushchev Remembers*, p. 553.

tated himself and dispatched without revision[105]—reflects the degree to which his self-confidence had been shaken:

> ...[W]e are normal people.... Consequently, how can we permit the incorrect actions which you ascribe to us? Only lunatics or suicides, who themselves want to perish and to destroy the whole world before they die, could do this. We, however, want to live and do not at all want to destroy your country.[106]

Several weeks later, in a long and self-serving explanation of his actions to the Supreme Soviet, Khrushchev reflected ruefully that while "imperialism today is no longer what it used to be," those who had described it as a "paper tiger" (meaning, of course, the Chinese) should know that "this 'paper tiger' has atomic teeth. It can use them and it must not be treated lightly."[107]

The Cuban missile crisis has been seen as a fundamental turning point in the history of the Cold War.[108] This may be to exaggerate its significance: that conflict was, after all, a multifarious phenomenon, aspects of which had disappeared long before 1962, while others would persist long afterward. What the missile crisis did do was to force Khrushchev to abandon once and for all his disruptive strategy of seeking detente through intimidation: the Soviet leader appears to have been genuinely shocked by the proximity with which the world approached a nuclear holocaust. Paradoxically, however, the crisis also demonstrated, more clearly than any other single event since World War II, the beneficent effect of nuclear weapons in managing international crises. The level of tension in this crisis was sufficiently great that if both sides had not possessed such weapons, war almost certainly would have started. That it did not can be attributed, not so much to skilled diplomacy on each side, as to a sober realization on the part of both of what a failure of diplomacy would mean.

---

[105] Medvedev, *Khrushchev*, p. 190. Soviet officials now suggest that Khrushchev's October 26 message was dispatched in haste because Soviet intelligence had obtained information suggesting that an American invasion of Cuba was imminent. See Garthoff, "Cuban Missile Crisis: The Soviet Story," p. 74.

[106] *Department of State Bulletin*, LXIX(November 19, 1963), 641.

[107] Speech of December 12, 1962, *Documents on International Affairs, 1962* (London: 1971), p. 257.

[108] Halle, *The Cold War as History*, pp. 408–411.

CHAPTER IX

# From Confrontation to Negotiation: 1962–1976

RELATIONS BETWEEN WASHINGTON AND MOSCOW, it some-times appears, are conducted in a kind of acronymic short-hand—ICBM, SLBM, ABM, MIRV, MARV, MBFR, CSCE, MFN, even MAD—all have specific meanings, if not to laymen, at least to those responsible for monitoring developments in the frequently arcane fields these abbreviations represent. There is yet another acronym, though, that might usefully be employed more often than it is: this is GRIT, or "graduated reciprocation in tension reduction." Proposed by psychologist Charles E. Osgood in 1962, GRIT assumed that the process that had pro-duced the Cold War—graduated, reciprocal increases in tension —could be reversed: that a "spiral of terror" could become a "spiral of trust."[1] It would be foolish to claim that in the years that followed the Cuban Missile Crisis trust became the basis of relations between the superpowers. Still, the relative impor-tance of terror in that relationship did decline, in a manner roughly in accordance with Osgood's prescription. Both Russians and Americans sought to avoid future confrontations on the scale of what had happened in 1962; as a result, there gradually emerged more congruities of interest than either side thought existed. This did not mean an end to the Cold War, as events of the late 1970s and early 1980s would make clear. But it did mean that the Soviet-American relationship had begun slowly to shift to a less perilous level.

---

[1] Charles E. Osgood, *An Alternative to War or Surrender* (Urbana: 1962), pp. 86–87.

I

The Cuban Missile Crisis did not, as is sometimes asserted, frighten Soviet and American leaders into embracing a policy of detente. Whatever their motives, both sides had for some time sought a relaxation of Cold War tensions, although by different methods. What the missile crisis did was to bring these methods into closer correspondence with one another. By far the greater movement took place on the Soviet side as Khrushchev now abandoned his obviously counterproductive strategy of seeking to bully the West into an easing of antagonisms. On the American side the change was less dramatic: the Kennedy administration made no significant alteration in its earlier policy of seeking agreement on such negotiable issues as existed while at the same time taking care not to convey to the Russians an appearance of weakness. Kennedy could pursue this approach with greater assurance of domestic support than in the past, however, thanks to the enhanced respectability the events of October, 1962, had brought to the cause of detente.

Statements of Soviet leaders during the months following the missile crisis reflected what one observer at the time described as a "decidedly chastened spirit."[2] "It wasn't in the interests of socialism to allow the crisis over Cuba to develop into a thermonuclear war," Khrushchev told the Supreme Soviet with unconscious irony in December, 1962: "Why should we invite ourselves to go to the Devil?...Nobody has yet returned from there to tell us that it is better there than it is on earth." Foreign Minister Gromyko blandly observed that if only the Americans had asked, he would gladly have told them of the Soviet missiles in Cuba. Less disingenuously, he congratulated Kennedy and his advisers for having "acted with circumspection, since it is dark, indeed, in this abyss and the bottom is not to be seen." Significantly, Gromyko also resurrected Lenin's 1921 call for friendly relations with the United States, observing that there were "sober voices" within that country "calling for...a policy which takes the interests of the Soviet Union and other socialist countries into consideration."[3]

---

[2]Richard P. Stebbins, *The United States in World Affairs. 1963* (New York: 1964), p. 10.

[3]*Documents on International Affairs, 1962*, pp. 260, 277–281.

The confrontation over Cuba had a sobering effect in the United States as well, although not in such an obvious way. With the conspicuous exception of the Bay of Pigs incident, each of the major foreign policy crises the Kennedy administration had faced since 1961 had been provoked by Khrushchev in pursuit of his "detente through intimidation" strategy. Renunciation of that approach would, in and of itself, have produced a considerable improvement in Soviet-American relations. Kennedy sought to hasten the process, though, with a carefully worded expression of willingness to move beyond ideological rigidities. "No government or social system is so evil that its people must be considered as lacking in virtue," he told an audience at American University in June, 1963. "No nation in the history of battle ever suffered more than the Soviet Union suffered in the course of the Second World War." Kennedy then went on to assess realistically the prospects for detente:

Both the United States and its allies, and the Soviet Union and its allies, have a mutually deep interest in a just and genuine peace and in halting the arms race. Agreements to this end are in the interests of the Soviet Union as well as ours, and even the most hostile nations can be relied upon to accept and keep those treaty obligations, and only those treaty obligations, which are in their own interest.

"Our most basic common link," he concluded, "is that we all inhabit this planet. We all breathe the same air. We all cherish our children's future. And we are all mortal."[4]

It was a speech that could not have been given a year earlier without provoking outcries of "appeasement" and "softness toward communism," not just from Republicans but from members of the president's own party as well. As it was, criticism of the address was curiously muted, suggesting that the trauma of the missile crisis had at least expanded the range of politically feasible discourse within the United States on the subject of detente.[5] Khrushchev's reaction too was moderately favorable, and there developed as a result a propitious atmosphere for talks that were about to begin in Moscow looking toward the long-awaited conclusion of a limited nuclear test ban treaty.

---

[4]*Public Papers of the Presidents: John F. Kennedy, 1963* (Washington: 1964), pp. 461–462.
[5]Sorensen, *Kennedy*, p. 733.

The "Treaty Banning Nuclear Weapons Tests in the Atmosphere, in Outer Space and Under Water," signed by representatives of the United States, the Soviet Union, and Great Britain on August 5, 1963, left open the possibility of underground weapons tests, and so represented a retreat from earlier attempts to achieve a comprehensive test ban treaty. Still, the agreement marked an important milestone for several reasons. It was the first formal undertaking between major Cold War antagonists to place some restraints, however limited, on the nuclear arms race. It avoided the problems of on-site inspection, upon which previous arms control discussions with the Russians had come to grief, by addressing itself only to those forms of testing capable of being monitored from outside the Soviet Union. It also constituted, for Khrushchev, a public endorsement of detente with the West at the expense of whatever appearance still remained of Sino-Soviet solidarity: his final attempt to resolve differences with the Chinese, vociferous critics of the treaty, had ended in failure five days before that document was initialed.[6] Finally, the steadily mounting enthusiasm with which the treaty was received in the United States, and the corresponding decline of opposition to it in the Senate, which gave its approval in September, suggested that suspicion of the Soviet Union was not so deep as to preclude taking some minimal risks to reduce the danger of war.[7]

The test ban treaty was only one of several public accords reached with the Russians during the sudden flowering of mutual amiability that took place in 1963. An agreement establishing a Moscow-Washington "hot line" had been concluded in June—the purpose of this direct communications link was to avoid delays of the kind that had held up exchanges between Kennedy and Khrushchev during the tense days of the missile crisis.[8] In October, the United States and the Soviet Union agreed to endorse a United Nations resolution calling for a ban

---

[6]Gittings, *Survey of the Sino-Soviet Dispute*, pp. 184–192.

[7]Stebbins, *The United States in World Affairs, 1963*, pp. 26–29. See also Sorensen, *Kennedy*, pp. 739–740; and, on the negotiation of the treaty, Glenn T. Seaborg with Benjamin S. Loeb, *Kennedy, Khrushchev, and the Test Ban* (Berkeley: 1981).

[8]For speculations about the reasons for those delays, see Bundy, *Danger and Survival*, pp. 443–444.

on the placement (as opposed to the testing, covered in the test ban treaty) of nuclear weapons in outer space. Prospects for economic contacts brightened noticeably that same month when Kennedy approved the sale of some $250 million worth of surplus American wheat to the Soviet Union to help meet one of that country's chronic agricultural shortfalls. In none of these understandings did either side compromise anything approaching a vital national interest. But, as Kennedy noted in one of his last foreign policy addresses, delivered on October 19, the fact that even "a few limited, enforceable agreements" could be reached was "of mutual benefit to both sides and to the world."[9]

Kennedy could not publicly speak of two other highly significant areas of Soviet-American cooperation that were proceeding behind the scenes. One had to do with reconnaissance satellites: Moscow's initial response to early American launches had been to regard these devices as instruments of espionage, different from the U-2 overflights they had replaced only in the higher altitude at which they functioned. Protests were lodged in the United Nations, and there was reason to expect that as soon as the Soviet Union developed the capability to intercept such satellites and destroy them, it would do so. But, by the summer of 1963, the Russians had had their own reconnaissance satellites in orbit for over a year and presumably knew something of the intelligence they could produce: at that point they abruptly shifted their position, withdrew their protests, and settled into a pattern of tacit cooperation with the United States in tolerating this polite form of spying. The result was to give each side an unprecedented capacity to monitor what the other was doing: that capacity was at least as important to the future of arms control as the just-concluded and far more visible Limited Test Ban Treaty.[10]

An even more secret area of tacit Soviet-American cooperation had to do with what both sides were coming to see as the emerging Chinese threat. Embittered by Khrushchev's withdrawal of economic and military assistance during the late 1950s and by his more recent efforts to improve relations with the

---

[9]*Kennedy Public Papers, 1963*, p. 796.

[10]Gaddis, *The Long Peace*, pp. 199–206. See also Steinberg, *Satellite Reconnaissance*, pp. 103–127.

West, the People's Republic of China no longer bothered to conceal its differences with the Russians: indeed, by 1963, Moscow and Beijing were exchanging unrestrained public insults. More ominous, though, were indications that the Chinese were about to test their own atomic bomb; what they might do with such a weapon was not something either Soviet or American leaders could comfortably think about. There developed, as a consequence, a series of top-secret exchanges with the Russians about cooperative action to preclude Chinese nuclear weapons development, up to and apparently including the possibility of a joint Soviet-American nuclear strike against Beijing's test facility in the Gobi desert.[11] Although no action was ever taken against the Chinese, who did in fact explode an atomic bomb in October, 1964, the fact that strategic planners in Moscow and Washington could even contemplate such a course of action so soon after having contemplated the use of nuclear weapons against each other suggests how far Soviet-American relations had come since the dramatic events of October, 1962.

John F. Kennedy's assassination in Dallas in November, 1963, occasioned a degree of sorrow in Moscow comparable only to that generated by Roosevelt's death eighteen years earlier. Khrushchev personally paid his respects at the American embassy; some years later he recorded this tribute in his oral reminiscences:

Kennedy was...someone we could trust. When he gave us public assurances that the US would not organize an invasion of Cuba,...we trusted him. We accepted the concession he was making and made a concession of our own by withdrawing our nuclear weapons from Cuba....Despite the irreconcilability of our class antagonisms.... Kennedy and I found common ground and a common language when it came to preventing a military conflict....He showed great flexibility and, together, we avoided disaster.[12]

Khrushchev, too, came to be regarded, during his last year in power, with a surprising degree of indulgence in the United States. When false rumors of his death swept Western capitals in April, 1964, the *Washington Post* noted: "We felt a leap at the

---

[11]Gordon H. Chang, "JFK, China, and the Bomb," *Journal of American History*, LXXIV(March, 1988), 1287–1310.
[12]*Khrushchev Remembers: The Last Testament*, pp. 513–514.

heart and a great concern that a man vital to the balance of the world had been lost."[13] The Soviet leader's abrupt deposition six months later brought more apprehension than rejoicing; it also elicited from Lyndon B. Johnson an assessment curiously parallel to Khrushchev's eulogy for Kennedy:

There were times when he was guilty of dangerous adventure. It required great American firmness and good sense—first in Berlin and later in the Cuban missile crisis—to turn back his threats and actions without war. Yet he learned from his mistakes, and he was not blind to realities. In the last 2 years, his Government has shown itself aware of the need for sanity in the nuclear age.[14]

Speculation as to the relative importance of men and circumstances in history tends to slide easily into the realm of the unverifiable. Still, it does not seem wholly irresponsible to suggest that the cause of peace was well served by the presence, during and immediately after a period of unprecedented tension, of leaders on both sides capable of perceiving shared interests through the distractions created by ideological differences, unwieldy bureaucracies, dissimilar backgrounds, and the allurements of pride and prestige. Such had not always been the case in the history of Russian-American relations, nor would it invariably be so in the future. Whatever their shortcomings as custodians of national power—and these are not difficult to point out—the unlikely "partnership" of Kennedy and Khrushchev must be given credit for having reversed, in however limited a fashion, the lockstep process of escalation and counterescalation that had characterized the first two decades of the postwar era.

## II

Kennedy had felt obliged to caution shortly before his death, however, that "a pause in the cold war is not a lasting peace, and a *detente* does not equal disarmament."[15] This is a useful

---

[13]Quoted in Abraham Brumberg, "The Fall of Khrushchev—Causes and Repercussions," in John W. Strong, ed., *The Soviet Union under Brezhnev and Kosygin* (New York: 1971), p. 2.

[14]Radio-television address, October 18, 1964, *Public Papers of the Presidents: Lyndon B. Johnson, 1963–1964* (Washington: 1965), p. 1377.

[15]Speech of October 19, 1963, *Kennedy Public Papers, 1963*, p. 795.

qualification to keep in mind in assessing the post-missile crisis "thaw" in Soviet-American relations, for although elements of change had clearly manifested themselves in the foreign policies of Washington and Moscow, there were also elements of continuity with what had gone before that placed definite limitations on how far the process of reconciliation could proceed.

One of these was the strategic arms race. It is becoming clear in retrospect that among the Kennedy administration's most significant steps, in terms of its long-term consequences, was its decision to press on with the production of ICBMs and SLBMs after it had become clear that there was no missile gap. Eisenhower's final defense budget would have given the United States, by the mid-1960s, 19 missile-firing Polaris submarines and 450 silo-launched Minuteman missiles. Kennedy expanded this program, first to 29 submarines and 800 Minutemen, then, *after* public exposure of the "missile gap" myth late in 1961, to 41 submarines and 1000 Minutemen. This buildup reflected no quest for a first-strike capability against the USSR— American experts had, by 1963, ruled out any possibility of destroying all Soviet strategic weapons in a single attack. Rather, it was the product of interservice compromises within the Pentagon and a reluctance on the part of the administration to admit having overestimated the Soviet missile threat.[16] The effect, however, was to give the United States, by the time of Khrushchev's downfall, a considerable advantage over the Soviet Union in numbers of strategic weapons. As late as April, 1965, Secretary of Defense McNamara could claim for the United States a superiority of three or four to one and could announce that the Russians had "lost the quantitative race."[17]

In its misreading of the future, this remark compares favorably with Neville Chamberlain's famous April, 1940, comment

---

[16]Kahan, *Security in the Nuclear Age*, pp. 84–94; Harland B. Moulton, *From Superiority to Parity: The United States and the Strategic Arms Race, 1961–1971* (Westport, Connecticut: 1973), p. 79. See also Charles R. Morris, *Iron Destinies, Lost Opportunities: The Arms Race between the U.S.A. and the U.S.S.R., 1945–1987* (New York: 1988), pp. 183–192.

[17]"Interview with Robert S. McNamara, Defense Secretary: Is Russia Slowing Down the Arms Race?" *U.S. News and World Report*, LVIII(April 12, 1965), 52.

that Hitler had "missed the bus," for the year 1965 saw the Soviet Union begin a massive deployment of SS-9 and SS-11 ICBMs, together with improved missile-firing submarines, that would within five years bring it to the point of numerical parity with the United States.[18] To say that the Kennedy administration's missile buildup provoked this response would be to oversimplify—the strategic arms race has never been a straightforward cycle of action on one side and reaction on the other.[19] Still, it is clear that the new Soviet leadership of Leonid Brezhnev and Alexei Kosygin was not prepared to tolerate, as had Khrushchev, the prospect of indefinite strategic inferiority. This position involved no repudiation of Khrushchev's hopes for relaxing tensions with the West, but it did delay that process, since it proceeded from the assumption that the Soviet Union should not negotiate on arms control until rough strategic equivalency had been achieved. To the extent that Kennedy's program increased the number of weapons the Russians would have to build before reaching that point, it can be said to have contributed, as McNamara later admitted,[20] to some retardation in the progress of detente.

Another set of circumstances that threatened detente was, of course, the growing American involvement in Indochina. Historians still puzzle over what motivated the Kennedy and Johnson administrations to send United States forces to Vietnam; certainly the Russians must have marveled at the logic by which Washington could tolerate an avowed Soviet satellite ninety miles off Florida while expending vast sums of money and blood halfway around the world to suppress an indigenous guerrilla movement whose deference to either Moscow or Beijing was, at best, limited. Despite continued references, as if by reflex, to the "Sino-Soviet bloc," American officials had long since moved beyond regarding all communist movements everywhere as agents of the Kremlin. As Secretary of State Dean Rusk put it in February, 1964: "The Communist world is no longer a single flock of sheep following blindly behind one

---

[18]Holloway, *The Soviet Union and the Arms Race*, pp. 43–44.

[19]See Albert Wohlstetter, "Is There a Strategic Arms Race?" *Foreign Policy*, #15 (Summer, 1974), pp. 3–20, and #16(Fall, 1974), pp. 48–81.

[20]Robert S. McNamara, *The Essence of Security* (New York: 1968), pp. 57–59.

leader."[21] Still, administration spokesmen sought repeatedly to justify the war as one more stage in the long process of containment that had begun twenty years before. "The American people...have learned the great lesson of this generation," President Johnson told the Congress in May, 1965:

Wherever we have stood firm aggression has been halted, peace restored, and liberty maintained. This was true in Iran, in Greece and Turkey, and in Korea. It was true in the Formosa Strait and in Lebanon. It was true at the Cuban missile crisis. It will be true again in Southeast Asia.[22]

What had happened was that the process of containment had come to be regarded as of greater importance than precision as to who, or what, was being contained. As Johnson argued:

The aim in Vietnam is not simply the conquest of the South, tragic as that would be. It is to show that American commitment is worthless. Once that is done, the gates are down and the road is open to expansion and endless conquest.[23]

From a policy initially designed to rally forces of nationalism, even where communist, against the expanding power of the Soviet Union, containment had evolved into a program of resistance to communism, even where nationalist, for the purpose of preserving American credibility in the world. It is significant that George Kennan, more than anyone else the architect of the original concept of containment, now publicly condemned this application of it, noting that "there is more respect to be won in the opinion of this world by a resolute and courageous liquidation of unsound positions than by the most stubborn pursuit of extravagant and unpromising objectives."[24] Ironically, the Johnson administration now came to place a considerable reli-

---

[21]Speech of February 25, 1964, in Jules Davids, ed., *Documents on American Foreign Relations, 1964* (New York: 1965), p. 146. See also Gaddis, *Strategies of Containment*, pp. 208–213; and Lyndon Baines Johnson, *The Vantage Point: Perspectives on the Presidency, 1963–1969* (New York: 1971), p. 470.

[22]Message to Congress, May 4, 1965, *Public Papers of the Presidents: Lyndon B. Johnson, 1965* (Washington: 1966), p. 487.

[23]Ibid., p. 486.

[24]Senate Committee on Foreign Relations, Hearings, *Supplemental Foreign Assistance Fiscal Year 1966—Vietnam* (Washington: 1966), pp. 335–336. See also David Mayers, *George Kennan and the Dilemmas of American Foreign Policy* (New York: 1988), pp. 275–292.

ance, for its extrication from the Vietnam morass, upon the original target of containment, the Soviet Union itself.

Johnson saw no reason why the Kremlin should not help arrange a Vietnam settlement: "We seek in southeast Asia an order and security that we think would contribute to the peace of the whole world," he announced in August, 1966, "and in that, we think, the Soviet Union has a very large stake."[25] Not surprisingly, the Russians took a somewhat different view. Where Khrushchev had regarded the Indochina conflict with relative detachment, Brezhnev and Kosygin initiated a program of aid to North Vietnam which, although in no way comparable to American expenditures ($1.6 billion versus $99.2 billion for 1965–1971, by one estimate),[26] nonetheless did play a significant role in sustaining Hanoi's war effort. Nor did the Russians exert themselves unduly to speed an end to the fighting, although they did at several points serve as an intermediary between the Americans and the North Vietnamese. Clearly Washington's preoccupation with Southeast Asia served Soviet interests by distracting the attention of policymakers, dispersing men and resources in an area of peripheral importance, and isolating the United States from a considerable body of world opinion. As long as the struggle showed signs of escalating beyond the region involved, the Russians were not at all averse to seeing it continue.[27]

Still, Johnson was probably correct when he argued, in retrospect, that his Vietnam policy did not significantly impede the progress of detente.[28] The Russians have never been hesitant to sacrifice interests of allies when in conflict with their own: even the systematic American bombardment of a "fraternal" socialist country, initiated with particularly graceless timing during Kosygin's February, 1965, visit to Hanoi, was not enough to cause the Kremlin to give up its policy of avoiding

---

[25]Speech of August 26, 1966, *Johnson Public Papers, 1966*, p. 902.

[26]International Institute for Strategic Studies, *Strategic Survey, 1972* (London: 1973), pp. 49–50.

[27]Edmonds, *Soviet Foreign Policy*, pp. 45–46; W. W. Kulski, *The Soviet Union in World Affairs: A Documented Analysis, 1964–1972* (Syracuse: 1973); George C. Herring, *America's Longest War: The United States and Vietnam, 1950–1975*, Second Edition (New York: 1986), pp. 168–169.

[28]Johnson, *The Vantage Point*, pp. 475–476. See also W. W. Rostow, *The Diffusion of Power: An Essay in Recent History* (New York: 1972), pp. 376–377.

direct confrontations with the United States. Certainly the war did not, as many had feared, drive the Russians and Chinese back together: arguments over who was doing more to help Ho Chi Minh provoked such bitterness that, by 1967, Moscow and Beijing were accusing each other of collusion with the Americans in Southeast Asia.[29] Furthermore, the war had the unanticipated effect of facilitating the Soviet drive for strategic parity: the Johnson administration decided not to try to stay ahead of the Russians in the quantitative ICBM race, as much because of budgetary pressures growing out of Vietnam as from informed judgments that the point of diminishing returns had been reached in long-range missile strength.[30]

The new American attitude toward the arms race became clear early in 1967 in response to indications that the Russians were constructing anti-ballistic missile emplacements around Moscow. While ostensibly defensive, the Soviet ABM deployment had definite offensive implications, for in the new and strange logic of strategic weapons competition, anything that might prevent one side's missiles from reaching their targets could be seen as tempting the other side into trying a first strike. Instead of seeking a comparable deployment of this expensive and unstable weapons system, Johnson proposed negotiations with the Russians to limit ICBMs, ABMs, and to conclude work on a treaty banning the further proliferation of nuclear weapons, on which exchanges had already taken place. Encouraged by the restraint the Russians had shown during the June, 1967, Arab-Israeli War (during which the "hot line" had been used for the first time to defuse a crisis), Johnson agreed to meet with Kosygin while the Soviet premier was in New York for an emergency United Nations session on the Middle East. The ensuing three-day summit, held on a college campus in Glassboro, New Jersey, at the end of June, produced generally friendly discussions but no agreement on negotiations to limit the strategic arms race. Yielding to growing domestic pressure, the administration later that year decided to go ahead

---

[29]Edmonds, *Soviet Foreign Policy*, pp. 47–48; Gittings, *Survey of the Sino-Soviet Dispute*, pp. 259–260.

[30]Moulton, *From Superiority to Parity*, pp. 283–287. See also Strobe Talbott, *The Master of the Game: Paul Nitze and the Nuclear Peace* (New York: 1988), pp. 99–101.

with construction of a "thin" ABM system, officially described as directed against the Chinese.[31]

By the summer of 1968, however, the situation had changed in several respects. In quantitative terms, the Russians were approaching their goal of strategic parity. Johnson had limited the bombing of North Vietnam and had announced his forthcoming retirement from the presidency. Discussions on the Non-Proliferation Treaty had borne fruit, and as that document was signed, on July 1, the Russians announced their willingness to begin talks "in the nearest future" on the limitation of offensive and defensive weapons systems. On August 19, they proposed starting the negotiations in Moscow in October and extended an invitation for Johnson to visit the Soviet capital on that occasion. The next day though, Soviet ambassador Anatolii Dobryin had to inform Johnson that

in connection with the further aggravation of the situation... created by a conspiracy of the external and internal forces of aggression against the existing social order in Czechoslovakia..., the Government of the Czechoslovak Socialist Republic [has] approached the allied states, the Soviet Union among them, with the request of rendering assistance, including the assistance by military forces.

Much as Johnson had often done with regard to Vietnam, Dobryin added his government's hope that "current events should not harm Soviet-American relations," but in fact the invasion of Czechoslovakia forced the administration to shelve, for the remainder of its term, plans for arms control talks with the Russians.[32]

The Czech crisis was at once the product of detente and an indication of its limitations. Both major European alliances—NATO and the Warsaw Pact—depended for their cohesion in large part on shared perceptions of external threat. As Soviet-American tensions began to decline after 1962, friction developed within each system. In the West, it manifested itself in the failure of the cumbersome Multilateral Nuclear Force concept

---

[31]Morris, *Iron Destinies, Lost Opportunities*, pp. 246–254; Kahan, *Security in the Nuclear Age*, pp. 121–123. See also Johnson, *The Vantage Point*, pp. 297–301, 481–485; and Ernest J. Yanarella, *The Missile Defense Controversy: Strategy, Technology, and Politics, 1955–1972* (Lexington: 1977), pp. 105–142.

[32]Johnson, *The Vantage Point*, pp. 487–491.

for sharing control of nuclear weapons and in General Charles DeGaulle's 1966 decision to withdraw French forces from military participation in NATO. The Eastern European scene was also one of disarray, with the Rumanians in particular approaching the Chinese in their ostentatious demonstrations of independence from Moscow. Not surprisingly both sides sought to profit from these trends. Johnson as early as 1964 had initiated a campaign to "build bridges" to Eastern Europe, a project endorsed with even greater enthusiasm by West Germany following the coming to power there of the Kiesinger-Brandt coalition in late 1966. The Russians responded by accelerating their own efforts to supplant NATO with an all-European security system, an idea they had first broached more than a decade earlier. Neither Washington nor Moscow could avoid noting, however, that the price of progress in either of these enterprises would likely be some attrition in the solidity of their own alliances.[33]

What the invasion of Czechoslovakia showed was that the West could more easily afford this price than could the Soviet Union. The Russians had made no effort to oppose the coming to power of Alexander Dubcek in early 1968, but as the new government in Prague began to move toward an abandonment of censorship, secret police rule, and restrictions on political activity by non-communists, Moscow became alarmed. One can discount the official explanation the Russians gave for their decision to send Soviet and satellite forces into Czechoslovakia on the night of August 20–21: there is no evidence of NATO or West Germany collusion with the Dubcek regime; indeed the United States and its allies had gone out of their way to avoid any appearance of provocation during that spring and summer. What the Russians feared was rather the impact of "reform communism" on their long-range military position in Eastern Europe and, ultimately, on the security of the Soviet regime itself.[34] Because it served, to a greater extent than did NATO,

---

[33]Wolfe, *Soviet Power and Europe*, pp. 312–313, 348–385. See also Lawrence S. Kaplan, *NATO and the United States: The Enduring Alliance* (Boston: 1988), pp. 89–101; and Lincoln Gordon, "Interests and Policies in Eastern Europe: The View from Washington," in Gordon, ed., *Eroding Empire: Western Relations with Eastern Europe* (Washington: 1987), pp. 73–74.

[34]Wolfe, *Soviet Power and Europe*, pp. 359–392.

the interests of a single dominant state, the Warsaw Pact simply could not accommodate the diversities of viewpoint, and hence of political systems, that characterized its Western counterpart.

Both Vietnam and Czechoslovakia represented efforts by the superpowers to secure what each had perceived to be an eroding power base; paradoxically, the effect of the actions each took was to accelerate that process of erosion. Far from enhancing the credibility of American commitments, the war in Vietnam raised widespread doubts about Washington's ability to wield power in a manner consistent with its own self-interest, world opinion, and sheer common sense. The war weakened NATO, fueled inflation, shattered a domestic consensus on foreign policy dating back to the 1940s, accelerated the Soviet achievement of strategic parity, and, ultimately forced Johnson from the presidency. The Soviet invasion of Czechoslovakia, far from eliminating the threat of "reform communism," actually strengthened that trend within Western European communist parties, especially after the Russians sought clumsily to legitimize their action through the "Brezhnev Doctrine," an assertion of Moscow's right to intervene in the affairs of any "socialist" country to suppress "counterrevolution." It also did much to repair the damage Vietnam had inflicted on NATO, weakened the military potential of Warsaw Pact forces, and tarnished overnight the image of moderation the new Soviet leadership had been trying to project since Krushchev's downfall.[35]

Significantly, however, neither Vietnam nor Czechoslovakia did lasting damage to the cause of detente. Both superpowers managed in time to swallow these respective insults in the interest of pursuing agreement on matters of mutual concern, notably arms control, trade, and the "management" of conflict among third parties. Arguing from effect to intent, some critics, including the Chinese, even asserted that a tacit understanding had been reached between Washington and Moscow to perpetuate the status quo.[36] That puts the matter too strongly, but what one can accurately say is that by 1969 both the United States and the Soviet Union had demonstrated a greater incli-

---

[35]See, on the impact of Czechoslovakia, ibid., pp. 383–385, 393–426.
[36]Lester A. Sobel, ed., *Kissinger and Detente* (New York: 1975), pp. 67–70.

nation than had previously been present to frame their relationship, not in terms of instruments of diplomacy—alliances, weapons buildups, rhetorical posturing, quests for credibility—but in terms of its chief end: the resolution of outstanding differences. It was on this basis that the achievements of the next four years would rest.

### III

Historians have come to regard 1969 as a major turning point in the evolution of the Cold War, for it was in that year that the internal situation in each of the major countries involved simultaneously came to favor detente. The year saw the Soviet Union achieve its long-sought goal of numerical parity with the United States in ICBMs; at the same time, however, Moscow's hopes for economic parity receded with the realization that capitalist assistance would be necessary to solve Russia's industrial and agricultural problems. In China, the calculated irrationality known as the "Great Cultural Revolution" was coming to an end, at least insofar as it had been directed against American influences; meanwhile fighting had broken out between Chinese and Soviet forces along the Ussuri River. In the United States, the slow process of disengagement from Vietnam had begun; there had also come to power in Washington an administration that could hardly be accused of "softness" toward communism and that therefore, in the odd logic of American politics, enjoyed greater latitude in negotiating with its ideological adversaries than had been available to its predecessors. This unusual juxtaposition of circumstances produced no overnight disappearance of Soviet-American tensions, but it did make possible, over the next three years, their considerable reduction.

"After a period of confrontation, we are entering an era of negotiation."[37] It was an unexpected tone for Richard M. Nixon to take in his inaugural address, given his long record of hostility toward the communist world. One advantage of protracted ideological rigidity, though, is that by abandoning it one

---

[37] *Public Papers of the Presidents: Richard M. Nixon, 1969* (Washington: 1970), p. 3.

can enhance one's reputation for statesmanship; if this process alienates old supporters, then the influx of new-found and pleasantly surprised allies can more than compensate for them. Another useful trait in a statesman is not to bear grudges: this characteristic (not often applied by Nixon in other situations, one must add) enabled the new president to obtain the services of Henry A. Kissinger as his assistant for national security affairs, despite the fact that the Harvard professor had only months before proclaimed the Republican nominee unfit to occupy the White House.[38] Students of diplomacy, politics, and human behavior will be arguing for years over the precise nature of this remarkable partnership; what is clear now is that Nixon and Kissinger grasped the significance of the moment at which they had come to power and were determined to use it to try to bring about an end to the Cold War.

Their approach, as both men later described it, was to take advantage of uncertainties created by the Soviet achievement of strategic parity, economic difficulties within the USSR, and the fragmentation of the international communist movement to reinforce attitudes on the part of Kremlin leaders conducive to detente. As Nixon put it in 1972:

There were ambiguous tendencies in Soviet policy; the same factors that might lead the USSR toward greater hostility also suggested the opportunity for a relaxation of tension. The task of American policy was to recognize the persistence of this ambiguity and to take action to strengthen the more positive tendencies.

Kissinger described the same strategy in a slightly different manner two years later: "When Soviet policy moved toward conciliation we sought to turn what may have started as a tactical maneuver into a durable pattern of conduct."[39] It is important to emphasize that neither Nixon or Kissinger contemplated any immediate abandonment of containment: their intent rather was to explore possibilities for altering the Soviet approach to

---

[38]Marvin Kalb and Bernard Kalb, *Kissinger* (Boston: 1974), pp. 15–19; Henry Brandon, *The Retreat of American Power* (Garden City, New York: 1973), pp. 24–25. See also Henry A. Kissinger, *White House Years* (Boston: 1979), p. 7.

[39] Richard M. Nixon, *U.S. Foreign Policy for the 1970's: The Emerging Structure of Peace: Report to the Congress, February 9, 1972* (Washington: 1972), p. 18; Kissinger statement before the Senate Foreign Relations Committee, September 19, 1974, *Department of State Bulletin*, LXXI(October 14, 1974), 508.

international order for a post–Cold War era; if it succeeded, then containment would have achieved its purpose.[40]

Because there exists no generally agreed-upon standard of strength in this field, it is difficult to say precisely when Soviet strategic power began to approach that of the United States. In numbers of land-based ICBMs the Russians passed the Americans sometime in 1969: by the end of that year they had approximately 1,200 such weapons, as compared to 1,054 for the United States, a figure that had not changed since 1967. The Russians had also deployed by that time an ABM system of questionable reliability. The United States retained almost a three-to-one advantage in SLBMs, though (656 versus 230), and an even larger lead in long-range bombers (540 versus 150). The Americans also led the Russians in missile accuracy and in numbers of warheads, an index of increasing significance with the Johnson administration's decision to proceed with the development of MIRV (multiple independently-targetable re-entry vehicle) technology.[41]

In the end, however, numbers and characteristics of weapons are not as significant as the attitudes of political leaders who control their use. In this respect, the turning point in the arms race may well have come with Nixon's first press conference as president, on January 27, 1969. In it, he explicitly renounced the goal of strategic "superiority," which he had strongly advocated during the campaign, in favor of "sufficiency," a concept Kissinger had supported.[42] Nixon thereby served notice that he would not reverse the Johnson administration's tacit acceptance of Soviet numerical parity in ICBMs. The new chief executive had come to his decision for many of the same reasons his predecessor had: studies had shown that further increases in missile strength would provide little additional protection against a Soviet attack; such an effort would cost too much at a time when pressures were intensifying for

---

[40]Gaddis, *Strategies of Containment*, p. 289; Raymond L. Garthoff, *Detente and Confrontation: American-Soviet Relations from Nixon to Reagan* (Washington: 1985), p. 29.

[41] Institute for Strategic Studies, *Strategic Survey, 1969* (London: 1970), p. 27; Yanarella, *The Missile Defense Controversy*, pp. 58–59, 165–166.

[42]*Nixon Public Papers, 1969*, p. 19. See also Kissinger, *White House Years*, pp. 202–203.

cuts in the defense budget; and, finally, the Russians appeared capable of matching any new escalation of the arms race weapon for weapon.[43]

Transforming a necessity into a virtue is easier, however, if one can avoid the appearance of having been pushed, and this Nixon and Kissinger skillfully did. The president coupled his blessing of "sufficiency" with the announcement that he would not proceed immediately into talks on the limitation of strategic weapons, stalled the previous year by the Soviet invasion of Czechoslovakia but now eagerly advocated by both the Russians and by former officials of the Johnson administration. He also announced, shortly thereafter, decisions to go ahead with construction of an American ABM system and to deploy MIRVs. The ABM program was almost certainly intended as a bargaining chip in future SALT negotiations: the costly system was untestable short of nuclear war and so provided little assurance of protection. The MIRVs were far more reliable; moreover, Kissinger doubted whether they would ever be included in a SALT agreement, since verification would require on-site inspection, something the Russians had always resisted. Only after carefully establishing what arms control measures they could accept without violating the standard of "sufficiency" did Nixon and Kissinger, in October, 1969, agree to begin SALT talks with the Russians the following month.[44]

Several things are noteworthy about Kissinger's approach to SALT. He appears to have viewed the early discussions as an opportunity to "educate" the Soviet negotiators, who at times demonstrated a surprising unfamiliarity with their own strategic weapons systems and the intricacies of arms control issues generally. He did all he could to avoid bureaucratic delays—especially useful in this regard were what he called "building blocks," a series of proposals, all cleared in advance, which the American delegation could put before the Russians in various combinations without consulting Washington on each change of position. During the latter stages of the talks Kissinger relied heavily on "back channel" contacts with Moscow, carried on independently of and at times without the knowledge of the

---

[43] Gaddis. *Strategies of Containment*, pp. 279–280.
[44] Kissinger, *White House Years*, pp. 131–138, 147–149. See also Kahan, *Security in the Nuclear Age*, pp. 144–145, 172–177.

SALT negotiators for the purpose of clarifying positions. And, most important, Kissinger sought to circumvent the touchy issue of on-site inspection by focusing the talks on those weapons systems capable of being monitored by "national technical means"—a euphemism for satellite reconnaissance.[45]

It would be difficult to say who came out on top in the strategic arms limitation agreements Nixon and Brezhnev signed in Moscow in May, 1972. On the one hand, the Russians, by agreeing to a mutual limitation of ABM deployments to two sites (one defending an ICBM emplacement, the other the national capital), in effect endorsed the long-standing American argument that stability in the nuclear arms race could best be attained by foregoing attempts to defend population centers. Approval of this "mutual assured destruction" concept (MAD) represented a significant change of attitude on the part of the security-conscious Soviet state. On the other hand, the imposition of a freeze on existing numbers of land-based and submarine-launched ballistic missiles constituted not just an acknowledgment of Soviet parity—it actually left the United States with a substantial numerical inferiority in ICBMs (1,618 versus 1,054) and a smaller one in SLBMs (740 versus 656).[46]

Whether the Russians and the Americans would have done without SALT what they promised not to do under it is open to question. The costly and unreliable characteristics of ABMs might have kept the Russians from deploying them on a larger scale in any event; similarly the United States, convinced of the greater accuracy of its missiles—and well on the way to installing multiple warheads on them—might never have matched

---

[45]Kissinger, White House Years, pp. 534–551, 805–823. See also John Newhouse, Cold Dawn: The Story of SALT (New York: 1973), pp. 166–249; and Gerard Smith, Doubletalk: The Story of SALT I (New York: 1980), pp. 222–246.

[46]U.S. Arms Control and Disarmament Agency, Arms Control and Disarmament Agreements: Texts and Histories of Negotiations (Washington: 1982), pp. 132–157. Under the terms of the SALT I Interim Agreement, the Soviet Union could complete those ICBM launchers still under construction over and above the 1,618 figure: the United States had no ICBMs under construction at this time. Both sides were also allowed to expand their SLBM launchers to a limit of 950 for the Russians and 710 for the Americans, but only as replacements for older ICBM or SLBM launchers, which would then have to be destroyed. By mutual consent, the SALT I treaty was amended in 1974 to allow each side only one, rather than two, ABM emplacements.

Soviet increases in ICBMs and SLBMs. Certainly the SALT accords did little to forestall such qualitative improvements: satellite reconnaissance was of only limited use in determining a missile's range and accuracy, or the number of warheads it carried. Nor did the negotiations produce restrictions on unmanned bombers or cruise missiles, weapons systems with considerable actual and potential strategic implications. None of this is to say, however, that the agreements were without value.

The SALT I agreements should be assessed, not in terms of whether they hastened or retarded the Soviet Union's emergence as the strategic equal of the United States, but in terms of the political context they created within which to deal with that probably unavoidable development. Predictions of what would happen when the Russians reached strategic parity had tended to range between two very different alternatives: either Moscow would use its new-found strength to intimidate the West, as Khrushchev had tried to do a decade earlier, or the achievement of parity would give Kremlin leaders the self-confidence necessary to engage, for the first time, in meaningful negotiations to resolve outstanding issues.[47] It was the policy of the Nixon administration, through SALT, to encourage the latter over the former alternative.

The United States could have responded to the Soviet achievement of parity by embarking on a new arms buildup of its own, but such a decision would have required a major escalation of the Cold War in return for only transitory benefits. It could, alternatively, have lapsed into some combination of isolationism and appeasement, but the disadvantages here, too, were obvious. A third option, the one actually followed, was to explore with the Soviet Union opportunities for declaring "off limits" certain areas of strategic weapons competition, to the extent that this could be done without adversely affecting the military balance. There is no reason to believe that the agreements reached at Moscow threatened that equilibrium; in fact, they probably reinforced it by removing the possibility of a race to develop ABMs and by limiting the further deployment of Soviet ICBMs and SLBMs. SALT may well have represented, then, the

---

[47] Wolfe. *Soviet Power and Europe,* pp. 510–515; Horelick and Rush, *Strategic Power and Soviet Foreign Policy,* pp. 176–195.

best of the available possibilities for coming to grips with the undeniable reality of Soviet strategic parity.[48]

But if detente was the product of Soviet self-confidence growing out of the attainment of strategic parity, it also developed in large part from anxieties generated by chronic economic difficulties. Such problems were, of course, nothing new—dislocations stemming from the effort to make economics fit ideology had long been a prominent feature of life in the USSR. What was new was the leadership's awareness that the economic gap between Russia and the West was growing, particularly in the areas of advanced technological and managerial skills, at a time when it confronted the twin necessities of maintaining Soviet military strength while satisfying growing internal demands for consumer goods. Prospects for resolving this dilemma through autarkic means appeared increasingly unpromising; it began to look as though the Soviet Union would not be able to compete with the West without help from the West, in the form of trade, investment, and—most important—technology transfers.[49]

As had been the case half a century earlier when the new Soviet state had sought to industrialize by importing foreign technology, Kremlin leaders counted on capitalist entrepreneurial instincts to override whatever political or strategic objections might exist to such exchanges. "The facts of contemporary reality," Soviet Foreign Trade Minister Nikolai Patolichev wrote in 1970, "confirm anew Lenin's thesis to the effect that objective economic interest is stronger than the policies of those imperialist powers who seek to hold back the development of business cooperation with the Socialist world."[50] On a superficial level, one could find some basis for Patolichev's assessment: after all, the Nixon administration's sudden relaxation of restrictions on truck and machine tool exports to the Soviet Union in

---

[48]See Gaddis, *Strategies of Containment*, pp. 324–329, for an elaboration of this argument.

[49]Edmonds, *Soviet Foreign Policy*, pp. 84–86; Garthoff, *Detente and Confrontation*, pp. 87–89; Herbert S. Dinerstein, "The Soviet Outlook: America, Europe, and China," in Robert F. Osgood, ed., *Retreat from Empire: The First Nixon Administration* (Baltimore: 1973), pp. 113–117.

[50]Quoted in Seyom Brown, *New Forces in World Politics* (Washington: 1974), p. 69.

1971 did coincide with the most severe balance of payments crisis since World War II.[51]

But the Soviet leadership's interest in expanding trade with the West stemmed as much from considerations of security as from economics: riots over food prices in Poland the previous December had forced the resignation of Party Secretary Wladyslaw Gomulka and had very nearly provoked Soviet military intervention. This sobering demonstration of how internal discontent could shake the authority of the state was not lost on either Moscow or Washington: it was no accident that, three months later, the Twenty-Fourth Congress of the Soviet Communist Party endorsed a Five-Year Plan which, for the first time, emphasized raising consumer living standards over the needs of heavy industry. Nor was it fortuitous that, soon thereafter, the Nixon administration informed the Russians that it might be willing to loosen export restrictions in return for cooperation on outstanding political and military issues.[52]

Although the overall volume of trade remained relatively small, considerable progress had been made by the end of 1972 in expanding Soviet-American economic ties. The Russians agreed to remedy an old grievance by making at least a token payment ($722 million over the next three decades) on their long-overdue World War II Lend-Lease debt; in return the Nixon administration promised to seek Export-Import Bank credits to finance Soviet purchases in the United States and the restoration by Congress of "most-favored nation" tariff status to imports from the USSR, which had been withdrawn in 1951. Soviet buyers quietly placed orders for an astonishing 25% of the 1972 United States wheat crop—some 440 million bushels—to meet an unexpected shortfall in their own harvest. Several major American corporations, among them Pepsi-Cola and the Chase Manhattan Bank, made arrangements to open offices or manufacture their products in the Soviet Union; by mid-1973, even the First National City Bank, a prominent fixture of economic life in prerevolutionary Russia, had reopened its Moscow

---

[51]Philip J. Funigiello, *American-Soviet Trade in the Cold War* (Chapel Hill: 1988), p. 181; Alfred E. Eckes, Jr., *A Search for Solvency: Bretton Woods and the International Monetary System, 1941–1971* (Austin: 1975), pp. 259–266.

[52]Edmonds, *Soviet Foreign Policy*, pp. 89, 99–100; Kalb and Kalb, *Kissinger*, p. 213; Funigiello, *American-Soviet Trade in the Cold War*, pp. 181–182.

branch after an absence of fifty-one years. And in what may have been the most grandiose project of all, the Soviet government had opened negotiations with the El Paso Natural Gas Company and the Occidental Petroleum Company (the latter headed by Armand Hammer, one of the few successful foreign concessionaires in Russia during the 1920s) for a $10 billion, seven-year plan to build pipelines and tankers with which to transport Siberian natural gas to Japan and the United States.[53]

The Nixon administration encouraged these trends on the assumption that a proliferation of economic relationships would render the Soviet Union dependent on American trade and technology, thereby lessening the danger of war. "Our purpose," Secretary of Commerce Peter G. Peterson explained in August, 1971,

is...to build in both countries a vested economic interest in the maintenance of an harmonious and enduring relationship. A nation's security is affected not only by its adversary's military capabilities but by the price which attends the use of those capabilities. If we can create a situation in which the use of military force would jeopardize a mutually profitable relationship, I think it can be argued that our security will have been enhanced.

Two years later, Kissinger, by that time secretary of state, described the same approach even more succinctly: "Over time, trade and investment may leaven the autarkic tendencies of the Soviet system, invite gradual association of the Soviet economy with the world economy, and foster a degree of interdependence that adds an element of stability to the political equation."[54]

Fissures within the international communist movement also provided the Nixon administration with opportunities to encourage movement toward detente. There had been earlier efforts to exploit such fragmentation—Washington had long dealt with Yugoslavia almost as an ally, the Johnson administration had made similar overtures toward Eastern Europe—and throughout the Cold War American officials had known that

---

[53]Ibid., pp. 54, 182–184; Brown, *New Forces in World Politics*, pp. 72–73; Sobel, ed., *Kissinger and Detente*, pp. 67–70.

[54]Peter G. Peterson, *U.S.–Soviet Commercial Relations in a New Era* (Washington: 1972), pp. 3–4; Kissinger statement of September 19, 1974, *Department of State Bulletin*, LXXI (October 14, 1974), 512.

the Sino-Soviet "alliance" only imperfectly concealed substantial Sino-Soviet differences. There had been no sustained effort to improve relations with the People's Republic of China, though, in part because of that state's unremitting hostility toward the United States and in part because both Kennedy and Johnson feared raising ghosts from the "who lost China" debates of the early 1950s. There is obvious irony in the fact that the president who made the breakthrough to Beijing had himself led the attack on the Democrats' China policy two decades earlier. But Nixon's views on the subject had never been as dogmatic as his public rhetoric suggested: he had noted the importance of Sino-Soviet differences as early as 1954, and by 1967 he was arguing publicly against any policy that would seek to keep China indefinitely isolated.[55]

Nixon entered the White House at a delicate moment in the history of Sino-Soviet relations: worried by the border clashes that had taken place along the Ussuri River—and perhaps recalling similar feelers in 1963 from the Kennedy administration[56]—Soviet diplomats during the summer of 1969 began sounding out American officials on what Washington's response would be to a preemptive strike by the USSR on Chinese nuclear installations. In the course of the subsequent SALT talks, the Russians formally proposed what would have been in effect a Soviet-American alliance designed to discourage "provocative" actions by China.[57]

Far from encouraging such cooperation with Moscow against Beijing, Nixon instead initiated a series of gestures aimed at bringing about a Sino-American reconciliation: these concluded with the surprise announcement in July, 1971, that Kissinger had secretly traveled to the Chinese capital to meet with Zhou Enlai, and that the President himself would soon follow. Both Nixon and Kissinger were careful to deny that their China "opening" was directed against the Russians, but there is little doubt that such considerations were present. "The worst thing that could happen for us," Nixon had told his staff in August,

[55]Gaddis, The Long Peace, pp. 181–182; Richard M. Nixon, "Asia After Vietnam," Foreign Affairs, XLVI (October, 1967), 121–123.

[56]See above, p. 258.

[57]Kissinger, White House Years, pp. 183, 548, 554; Garthoff, Detente and Confrontation, pp. 175–176, 207–210.

1969, "would be for the Soviet Union to gobble up Red China.... We're not doing this because we love the Chinese. We just have to see to it that the U.S. plays both sides." In addition to maintaining the global balance of power, such tactics might induce Soviet cooperation on other issues. "They haven't helped on Vietnam, on the Mideast, on the arms talks," Nixon added. "We've got to give them a reason to help us."[58]

The president's strategy of "linkage"—as this approach came to be known—never produced the results he expected from it, partly because he publicized it too widely and partly because he exaggerated Moscow's ability to shape events in the Middle East and Southeast Asia.[59] But there are convincing indications that the China initiative did cause the Russians to speed up efforts to reach agreements on SALT;[60] certainly it was responsible for the invitation, issued in October, 1971, for Nixon to visit Moscow the following spring after his return from Beijing. Brezhnev, in a speech delivered in March, 1972, described the Sino-American rapprochement as a "natural" development, although he could not help wondering whether Nixon's talks with the Chinese had not gone "beyond the framework of bilateral relations between the USA and China. How else is one to understand, for instance, the statement made during the banquet in Shanghai that 'today our two peoples hold the future of the world in their hands'?"[61] It was the tone of a man resigned to relinquishing at last the luxury of having adversaries who despised each other more than they despised him.

"Linkage" did work in other ways, though. Attempts to solve the perennial German question had received a major boost in September, 1969, with the victory of the Social Democrats in West Germany and the emergence, as chancellor, of Willy Brandt. Three separate series of negotiations with the Russians soon got underway, with progress on each linked to

---

[58]Quoted in William Safire, *Before the Fall: An Inside View of the Pre-Watergate White House* (New York: 1975), p. 370. See also Kissinger, *White House Years*, pp. 182, 684–763.

[59]On the limitations of "linkage," see Gaddis, *Strategies of Containment*, pp. 311–313; also Kalb and Kalb, *Kissinger*, pp. 102–106.

[60]Kissinger, *White House Years*, pp. 837–840; Newhouse, *Cold Dawn*, pp. 234–236. But see also Smith, *Doubletalk*, p. 339.

[61]Leonid Brezhnev, *On the Policy of the Soviet Union and the International Situation* (Garden City, New York: 1973), p. 178.

developments in the others: (1) discussions between West Germany, Poland, and the Soviet Union confirming existing boundaries in Eastern Europe, including the controversial Oder-Neisse frontier—Brandt signed treaties to this effect with the Russians in August, 1970, and with the Poles the following December; (2) negotiations among the four powers occupying Berlin aimed at normalizing the position of that divided city— the resulting agreement, recognizing Western access rights there, was signed in September, 1971; and (3) contacts between representatives of NATO and the Warsaw Pact looking toward eventual talks on mutual and balanced force reductions (MBFR) and the Russians' long-sought Conference on Security and Co-operation in Europe (CSCE).

What emerged from these overlapping and interlocking negotiations was the outline of a European settlement based on tacit West German abandonment of reunification, Soviet recognition of the Western position in Berlin, a continued American military presence on the Continent, and a greater reliance than in the past on diplomacy as a means of resolving differences.[62] These agreements by no means removed Europe from the arena of Cold War rivalries, but they did represent an acknowledgment by the major powers of the status quo there. And since postwar Soviet policy in Europe can be explained as much by fear of the Germans as of anyone else, this achievement of at least partial stabilization was no insignificant accomplishment.[63]

"Linkage" also appeared to be an effective tool for "crisis management." Intelligence reports in September, 1970, indicated that the Russians might be building a nuclear submarine base in Cuba. Whatever its purpose, construction at the offending site soon stopped after Kissinger warned that such activity could impair prospects for detente. Another dangerous situa-

---

[62]Garthoff, *Detente and Confrontation*, pp. 108–126; Karl E. Birnbaum, *East and West Germany: A Modus Vivendi* (Lexington, Massachusetts: 1973), pp. 91–96; Jonathan Dean, "Berlin in a Divided Germany: An Evolving International Regime," in Alexander L. George, Philip J. Farley, and Alexander Dallin, eds., *U.S.–Soviet Security Cooperation: Achievements, Failures, Lessons* (New York: 1988), pp. 83–105.

[63]See, on the stability of the postwar European system, A. W. DePorte, *Europe between the Super-powers: The Enduring Balance* (New Haven: 1979).

tion developed that same month in the Middle East, when Syrian tanks crossed into Jordan to aid Palestinian commandos in their struggle with King Hussein. "You and your client started it," Kissinger is said to have told a Soviet diplomat, "and you have to end it." Whether on Moscow's orders or not, the Syrians did turn back, but not before Kissinger had arranged for joint Israeli-Jordanian-American operations against both Syrian and Russian forces, if necessary. Fifteen months later, in December, 1971, war broke out between India and Pakistan over the secession from the latter of Bangladesh (formerly East Pakistan). Concerned over rumors that the Indians, with Soviet encouragement, might dismember West Pakistan as well, Kissinger threatened to cancel the forthcoming Moscow summit unless the Russians induced New Delhi to show restraint.[64]

To what extent these crises actually reflected hostile intent on the part of the Soviet Union—or, alternatively, overreaction by the United States—is still not wholly clear. Certainly Washington appears to have exaggerated Soviet responsibility for the India-Pakistan confrontation (although this may have been done deliberately to impress the pro-Pakistani Chinese).[65] What these incidents do illustrate is the administration's conviction that the Russians needed detente badly enough to pay a substantial price for it: that they would pass up opportunities to exploit specific crises at the expense of the West in order to make progress toward a general relaxation of tensions. Moscow's response to the events of early May, 1972, suggests that these were not entirely invalid assumptions.

On May 8, Nixon, acting in response to a large-scale North Vietnamese offensive against South Vietnam, ordered the mining of Haiphong and several other ports, together with an intensification of air strikes against Hanoi's overland supply lines. Closing North Vietnamese harbors had long been talked about in Washington, but the option had been rejected in the past for fear of provoking Chinese or even Soviet intervention.[66] Nixon

---

[64]Kissinger, *White House Years*, pp. 594–652, 842–918. See also Kalb and Kalb, *Kissinger*, pp. 196–215, 257–263; and Garthoff, *Detente and Confrontation*, pp. 76–82, 262–288.

[65]Ibid., pp. 263–266.

[66]See Johnson, *The Vantage Point*, p. 369.

now chose to act only two weeks before a long-planned meeting with Kremlin leaders in Moscow, at which final discussions were to take place on the normalization of economic relations and on the laboriously negotiated treaties limiting the deployment of offensive and defensive strategic weapons systems. For a moment, it appeared as though prospects for detente had been ruined. "What would happen," *Pravda* complained, "if the several states, whose legitimate interests...are threatened by the unilateral action of the USA, were to respond in the same manner?"[67] Certainly Nixon and Kissinger were prepared for the possibility that the Russians might cancel the summit: "The summit isn't worth a damn if the price for it is losing in Vietnam," the president told his advisers: "My instinct tells me that the country can take losing the summit, but it can't take losing the war."[68]

And yet, when Soviet Foreign Trade Minister Patolichev visited the White House three days after Nixon's announcement, he responded to newsmen's questions about the summit with bland reassurances: "We never had any doubts about it. I don't know why you asked this question. Have you any doubts?"[69] That the decision to escalate in Vietnam did not produce the same effect that the U-2 incident had on the 1960 Paris summit, or the invasion of Czechoslovakia on Johnson's projected 1968 trip to Moscow, suggests that the Russians had developed an even greater stake in the improvement of Soviet-American relations than existed in Washington. Or so it was made to appear. The borderline between illusion and reality, like that between luck and skill, is an exceedingly fine one in diplomacy: clearly all of those qualities were present in the series of maneuvers that made it possible for President Nixon and his protean assistant for national security affairs, within days of the Haiphong decision, to be exchanging champagne toasts with Brezhnev and the Politburo in the Kremlin.

The Moscow summit of May 22–29 more than lived up to its advance billing. The two delegations managed to keep agree-

---

[67] *Pravda*, May 12, 1972, quoted in Kulski, *The Soviet Union in World Affairs*, pp. 439–440.
[68] *RN: The Memoirs of Richard Nixon* (New York: 1978), p. 602. See also Kissinger, *White House Years*, pp. 1176–1182.
[69] *New York Times*, May 12, 1972.

ments flowing roughly at the rate of one a day, on issues ranging from the avoidance of naval incidents at sea to health and
environmental cooperation and plans for a joint Soviet-American space mission.[70] No specific decisions were reached on economic issues, but a joint trade commission was established to
facilitate future discussions on this point. The SALT I accords,
limiting ABM and ICBM deployments, required hard bargaining and last-minute compromises, but the first major bilateral
arms control agreement of modern times was finally signed late
on the evening of May 26. Three days later, the conference
wound up with a solemn declaration of "Basic Principles"
jointly affirming the doctrine of "peaceful coexistence," undertaking to prevent the development "of situations capable of
causing a dangerous exacerbation" of Soviet-American relations, and recognizing that "efforts to obtain unilateral advantage at the expense of the other, directly or indirectly, are inconsistent with these objectives."[71]

No amount of adroit diplomacy could have produced the results achieved between 1969 and 1972 had not the circumstances been right—had not the Nixon administration had the
good fortune to come to power at a time when the internal situations in the United States, the Soviet Union, and the People's
Republic of China simultaneously favored detente. But auspicious circumstances are no guarantee of success in and of themselves; clumsy diplomacy has snatched failure from the jaws of
triumph more than once. There was undeniably skill, as well as
luck, in a foreign policy that expanded American freedom of action in the world at a time when American strategic power, relative to that of the Soviet Union, was declining. There was wisdom, as well as expediency, in a course of action that reverted
to the original concept of containment: the conviction that only
Soviet expansionism, not international communism, possessed
the capacity to threaten American security, and that the United
States could effectively weaken the former phenomenon by exploiting strains that existed within the latter. The future of detente would, of course, be at the mercy of both men and circumstances; its prospects for survival, however, would depend

---

[70]The joint Apollo-Soyuz mission, involving the link-up of manned American and Soviet satellites in earth orbit, took place in July, 1975.
[71]*Department of State Bulletin*, LXVI(June 26, 1972), 898–899.

in large measure on the extent to which the agreements reached at Moscow matched the interests of the states whose statesmen signed them.

IV

Curiously, few careful efforts were made, in either official or academic circles in the United States, to define "detente" until after that policy had been mutually endorsed by Nixon and Brezhnev at the 1972 Moscow summit. This lapse stemmed partly from the hope that there would be no substantive differences in the way Soviet and American leaders understood the term; partly too, one suspects, from fear that too close an investigation might expose just such contradictions. Once the belated exercise was carried out, it was discovered that while areas of congruence did exist, there were also important discrepancies in the behavior each side expected of the other. Clarification of these by no means destroyed "detente," but it did lead to a gradual scaling-down of expectations—to a realization that despite progress made, much remained to be done before the word could accurately be regarded as a synonym for "rapprochement."

In one sense, Brezhnev's concept of detente paralleled that of Nixon and Kissinger. Like the Americans, the Soviet leader saw contradictory tendencies shaping the other side's foreign policy and sought to reinforce those he considered desirable. "We are realists," Brezhnev proclaimed in December, 1972,

and are well aware that influential circles in the imperialist world have not yet abandoned attempts to conduct policy "from positions of strength." . . . The Soviet Union will continue to work for detente and for consolidation of peace, persevering in its efforts to untie the knots of international tension, and working for stable good relations with countries with a differing social system. And if our policy evokes the appropriate response from them, then we shall say confidently that detente will become stable, and peaceful coexistence a universally accepted standard of inter-state relations.

But then Brezhnev added an important qualification:

The CPSU [Communist Party of the Soviet Union] has always held, and now holds, that the class struggle between the two systems—the capitalist and the socialist—in the economic and political, and also, of course, the ideological domains, will continue. That is to be expected since the world outlook and the class aims of socialism and capitalism are opposite and irreconcilable. But we shall strive to shift this historically inevitable struggle onto a path free from the perils of war, of dangerous conflicts, and an uncontrolled arms race. This will be a tremendous gain for world peace, for the interests of all peoples, of all states.[72]

This distinction between diplomatic and ideological goals was, of course, no new phenomenon in Soviet foreign policy, but it did call into question Brezhnev's acknowledgment, in the Moscow statement on "Basic Principles" six months earlier, of a "special responsibility" to ensure "that conflicts or situations will not arise which would serve to increase international tensions."[73]

It would, perhaps, have been too much to expect the general secretary of the Soviet Communist Party to disavow the class struggle, even in an era of detente, but there did exist in Washington the expectation that the Kremlin would continue to cooperate in "managing" crises generated by third parties in order to prevent escalation that might involve the superpowers. "The leaders of the Soviet Union are serious men," Nixon noted in May, 1973: "Their willingness to commit themselves to certain principles for the future must be taken as a solemn obligation."[74] Within five months, that assumption would be called into serious question.

There is no evidence that the Soviet Union instigated the October 6, 1973, attack on Israel by Egypt and Syria or the oil embargo against Israel's supporters in the West that the Arab members of the Organization of Petroleum Exporting Countries (OPEC) imposed several days later. But Soviet behavior during this crisis did seem difficult to reconcile with the "code of conduct" Nixon and Brezhnev had agreed upon the previous year. Despite advance knowledge of the attack by at least 48 hours, the Russians made no explicit effort to warn Washington. Nor did they seek to restrain the Egyptians and Syrians from initiating hostilities or make any moves to encourage a cease-fire

---

[72]Brezhnev, *On the Policy of the Soviet Union*, pp. 230–231. See also Garthoff, *Detente and Coexistence*, pp. 40–44.

[73]*Department of State Bulletin*, LXVI(June 26, 1972), 899.

[74]Richard M. Nixon, *U.S. Foreign Policy for the 1970's: Shaping a Durable Peace: Report to the Congress, May 3, 1973* (Washington: 1973), pp. 37–38.

until is had become clear that the Israelis were going to win. Moscow welcomed the OPEC embargo, a tactic it had been advocating in broadcasts to the Arab world for some time. And, on October 24, angered by Israeli violations of a cease-fire that Kissinger and the Russians had now arranged, Brezhnev in a harsh note to Nixon proposed dispatching a Soviet-American peacekeeping force to the Middle East. "I will say it straight," he added: "If you find it impossible to act jointly with us in this matter, we should be faced with the necessity urgently to consider the question of taking appropriate steps unilaterally."[75]

Alarmed by this development—but also preoccupied to the point of almost total distraction by the rapidly intensifying Watergate crisis[76]—Nixon authorized Kissinger late that evening to order a worldwide Defense Condition 3 military alert (DefCon 1 is war), news of which became public the following morning. The White House coupled this with a note to Brezhnev warning that unilateral action in the Middle East could threaten detente and suggesting instead the dispatch of a United Nations peacekeeping force from which the big powers would be excluded. Brezhnev denied plans for unilateral intervention and accused Nixon of fabricating the crisis, but as the Egyptian-Israeli cease-fire began to take hold, tensions eased and both sides reiterated their commitment to detente.[77] The episode had shown clearly, though, that Moscow's cooperation in managing third-party crises would extend only to preventing escalation to nuclear war, not to forgoing opportunities to exploit such developments at the expense of the West.[78]

This pattern of behavior showed up in other areas as well. Detente proved to be of little value in extricating the United States gracefully from the Vietnam War: although the Russians may have helped arrange the January, 1973, cease-fire, they

---

[75]Brezhnev to Nixon, October 24, 1973, quoted in Henry A. Kissinger, *Years of Upheaval* (Boston: 1982), p. 583. Kissinger's memoir (pp. 450–583) is the fullest account of the events leading up to this crisis, but see also, for a more charitable assessment of Soviet intentions, Garthoff, *Detente and Confrontation*, pp. 360–378.

[76]See Kissinger, *Years of Upheaval*, pp. 581–582.

[77]Kalb and Kalb, *Kissinger*, pp. 492–493; Garthoff, *Detente and Confrontation*, pp. 379–385.

[78]Ibid, pp. 385–393; see also Theodore Draper, "Detente," *Commentary*, LVII(June, 1974), 38–40.

were either unwilling or unable to prevent the North Vietnamese from launching the series of offensives that finally over-
whelmed South Vietnam and Cambodia two years later, thereby inflicting a humiliating defeat upon the United States. Nor
could the Russians resist passing up opportunities created by
the April, 1974, revolution in Portugal: they not only funneled
aid to Portuguese communists in their unsuccessful bid for
power but also sought to fill the vacuum created by the resulting collapse of Portugal's African empire by supporting Marxist
factions in Mozambique and Angola. The latter enterprise even
involved the dispatch of Cuban mercenaries, a move Secretary
of State Kissinger denounced in January, 1976, as "counter to
the crucial principles of avoidance of unilateral advantage and
scrupulous concern for the interests of others which we have
jointly enunciated."[79]

But Soviet officials, too, had reason to complain that detente
had not met their expectations. To a greater extent than had
been apparent in the West, they had looked to imports of food
and technology from the United States to relieve their own
overburdened economy, confronted as it was with the simultaneous necessities of improving living standards in a backward
society while providing military security against two potential
adversaries. As good Marxists, Kremlin leaders expected economic self-interest to ensure American cooperation; and indeed
had such decisions been left to the business community alone,
this might well have happened. But Soviet analysts have shown
a persistent tendency to underestimate the influence of
noneconomic considerations on American foreign policy; they
therefore failed to anticipate the extent to which the price of
American economic assistance would come to hinge on considerations other than profit and loss.

Nixon had regarded Soviet willingness to repay World War II
Lend-Lease debts as sufficient compensation for extending
Export-Import Bank credits and "most-favored nation" tariff
treatment (MFN), but Congress had to approve these moves
and quickly made it clear that it considered the price too low. In
October, 1972, Senator Henry M. Jackson of Washington introduced an amendment to the Trade Reform Act denying credits

---

[79]Kissinger press conference, January 14, 1976, *Department of State Bulletin*,
LXXIV(February 2, 1976), 125. See also Garthoff, *Detente and Coexistence*, pp.
256–261, 485–489, 502–537.

and MFN to "nonmarket economies" that taxed or restricted the emigration of their citizens; Congressman Charles Vanik of Ohio had earlier proposed similar legislation in the House of Representatives.[80] It required little imagination to realize that this obliquely worded measure was aimed at Soviet practices regarding Jewish emigration, or to conclude from its list of seventy-two Senate cosponsors that it had excellent chances of passage. Administration officials spent much of the next two years in parallel negotiations, with the Russians to get them to raise emigration levels and with Jackson to get him to modify his amendment on the grounds that the trade bill was an inappropriate instrument with which to try to reform Soviet society. Jackson was able to claim a major victory on October 18, 1974, when he announced that the Russians had agreed to allow at least 60,000 Jewish emigrants to leave the Soviet Union each year in return for Eximbank credits and MFN.[81]

The Senator spoke too soon, though, for on January 10, 1975, shortly after final Congressional passage of the trade bill, the Russians abruptly rejected the entire economic package that had been under discussion since 1972—tariffs, credits, and Lend-Lease debts. Soviet leaders took this action, one suspects, not so much from fear of relaxing emigration requirements as from reluctance to yield to external pressure on a sensitive internal matter. The dangers of establishing such a precedent apparently outweighed the relatively marginal benefits promised by MFN and Eximbank credits, especially after Congress in December (in a further amendment offered by Senator Adlai E. Stevenson III of Illinois) cut the latter back to $300 million, a figure most experts regarded as unreasonably low.[82] The legislators' effort to tie increased trade to increased emigration raised the price of the first commodity beyond what the Russians were willing to grant in terms of the second, with the result that neither side achieved either.

Oddly, no comparable efforts were made to use food as an instrument of reform, despite the Soviet Union's obvious need for it to meet agricultural shortfalls and despite the fact that the

---

[80]*Congressional Record*, October 4, 1972, pp. 33658–33659. See also Funigiello, *American-Soviet Trade in the Cold War*, p. 185.

[81]*New York Times*, October 19, 1974.

[82]Garthoff, *Detente and Confrontation*, pp. 453–462; Funigiello, *American-Soviet Trade in the Cold War*, pp. 186–188.

Russians had few sources other than the United States to which to turn for it, something that was not the case in most other items of trade. Soviet purchasers had been allowed to buy wheat in 1972 at prices so low that they failed to match resulting costs to American taxpayers in export subsidies and inflated prices for bread and flour; no political concessions were demanded in exchange. Three years later, Russian buyers again entered the American market on a large scale; this time the only demand made on them was that they sign a long-term purchasing agreement designed to cushion the impact of massive wheat sales on American consumers.[83] The most plausible explanation for this striking disparity in trading tactics is also, unfortunately, the least charitable one: Congress's solicitude regarding the plight of Soviet Jews did not exceed its unwillingness to alienate American farmers by restricting grain exports. It was an illuminating commentary on the priorities of those who had sought to enlist detente in the cause of human rights.

The temptation to use economics as an instrument with which to reform the internal structure of the Russian state was, of course, an old one: as early as 1911, it had brought about abrogation of the Russian-American commercial treaty; similar considerations had entered into Roosevelt's negotiations with Litvinov over recognition in 1933 and discussions on the extension of credits after World War II. In each of those cases, Russian officials had refused to relax internal controls to obtain external benefits; domestic order, and the means to maintain it, occupied a higher priority in their minds than did the advantages to be derived from expanding trade with the West. Whether this was still the case in the 1970s was open to question: certainly internal prosperity in the Soviet Union had come to depend, to a greater extent than in the past, on economic contacts with the capitalist world; on the other hand it seems unlikely that the Kremlin would have been willing at any stage to risk Western intervention in Soviet domestic affairs to secure that assistance.[84] What is clear is that Congress blunted American bargaining potential by looking more to its own po-

---

[83]Ibid., p. 185; Marshall I. Goldman, *Detente and Dollars: Doing Business with the Soviets* (New York: 1975), pp. 193–224.

[84]Ibid., pp. 69–70, 279–280. See also John Lewis Gaddis, "The Evolution of U.S. Policy Goals toward the USSR in the Postwar Era," in Seweryn Bialer and Michael Mandelbaum, eds., *Gorbachev's Russia and American Foreign Policy* (Boulder, Colorado: 1988), pp. 319–325.

litical priorities than to those of the Russians in deciding what price to place on the economic component of detente.

Congress also intervened—again with Senator Jackson taking the lead—to shape the future course of arms control negotiations. The 1972 SALT I agreements had allowed the Russians a numerical superiority of 564 ICBMs and 84 SLBMs over what would be available to the United States: this imbalance had reflected the number of launchers deployed on each side at that time, together with the assumption that American missiles—many of which now carried multiple warheads—were more accurate than their Soviet counterparts. Jackson perceived, quite correctly as it turned out, that the Russians would soon catch up in both guidance and MIRV technology, and late in 1972 secured passage of a Congressional resolution demanding that future SALT agreements would provide for numerical equality in weapons systems on both sides. This requirement for across-the-board parity created problems in discussions with Moscow because of the quite different characteristics of the two nations' strategic arsenals: neither military establishment was eager to configure its forces according to the other's pattern. Nor was it at all clear how such compliance with such a rule might be verified, since some weapons could be more easily detected from satellites than others. But the domestic political appeal of parity was unquestionable, and it became clear as a consequence that any future SALT II treaty would have to incorporate that principle.[85]

With this constraint in mind, President Gerald R. Ford met with Brezhnev outside Vladivostok in November, 1974, three months after Nixon's resignation: there they agreed on a general set of guidelines for SALT II that imposed an overall mutual limitation of 2,400 strategic delivery systems, including ICBMs, SLBMs, and heavy bombers; within that limit, no more than 1,320 ICBMs and SLBMs could carry multiple warheads.[86] But because this accord provided numerical parity only in aggregate terms, not in individual categories of weapons, it went only part of the way toward meeting Jackson's requirement; moreover, Ford and Brezhnev failed to agree on whether the aggregates would cover such new systems as the American cruise missile, a subsonic but cheap and highly-accurate weapon, or

---

[85]See, on these points, Strobe Talbott, *Endgame: The Inside Story of SALT II* (New York: 1979), pp. 23–24.

[86]Ibid., pp. 31–37; Garthoff, *Detente and Coexistence*, pp. 442–453.

the Soviet Backfire bomber, which Western analysts claimed might have the range to fly intercontinental missions. No further progress would be made on these issues through the remainder of Ford's term.[87]

If detente is looked upon solely as a bargaining process, then evidence from the years 1972–1976 would tend to sustain the argument that the Russians handled themselves more shrewdly than did their American rivals. Detente imposed no significant limitations on the Soviet Union's ability to intervene by proxy in Third World areas, nor did rejection of the 1972 trade package deny them access to American agriculture or to Western technology. Internally, the Soviet regime became less tolerant of dissent than before, with the result that such figures as Alexander Solzhenitsyn and Andrei Sakharov emerged as vigorous critics of detente. That policy produced no reduction in Soviet military expenditures, which continued to rise relative to gross national product while by the same standard American military spending declined.[88] And, at the Conference on Security and Cooperation in Europe, held in Helsinki on July 30–August 1, 1975, the Russians in return for an unenforceable promise to respect human rights successfully capped a twenty-year campaign by securing the signatures of the United States and its NATO allies on a document affirming the "inviolability" of—and thereby appearing to legitimize—all existing boundaries in Europe.[89]

Meanwhile, American policy seemed paralyzed by indecision and self-doubt, products of the twin traumas of Vietnam and Watergate. Despite Israel's victory in the Middle East war, the United States found itself deferring respectfully to oil-rich sheiks and potentates suddenly possessed of the capacity to wreck havoc with its economy, not to mention those of its European and Japanese allies. Proliferating scandals eroded the Nixon administration's credibility to the point that the October, 1973, DefCon 3 military alert was widely regarded as an artifi-

---

[87]Gaddis, *Strategies of Containment*, p. 327.

[88]John M. Collins, *U.S.–Soviet Military Balance: Concepts and Capabilities, 1960–1980* (New York: 1980), pp. 83–85.

[89]*Department of State Bulletin*, LXXIII(September 1, 1975), 324–325. See also John J. Maresca, "Helsinki Accord, 1975," in George, Farley, and Dallin, eds., *U.S.–Soviet Security Cooperation*, pp. 106–122.

cially generated crisis, intended to distract attention from Watergate.[90] Nixon came to rely on his personal relationship with Brezhnev as a major justification for remaining in office, but the Russians uncharitably dropped the word "personal" from their translation of one of his speeches on the subject during the June, 1974, Moscow summit and then further added to the president's discomfiture by holding several of the sessions at a place called Yalta.[91]

Continuing Congressional distrust kept the new Ford administration from taking steps to save American clients in Southeast Asia or from opposing Soviet and Cuban efforts in Angola; Ford himself inadvertently projected an image of appeasement by refusing to receive the now-exiled Solzhenitsyn at the White House in July, 1975 (for fear of upsetting talks with Brezhnev at the Helsinki Conference later that month), and by abruptly firing Secretary of Defense James R. Schlesinger, a staunch critic of the Russians, at the end of October. The image became stronger when news leaked in April, 1976, of an off-the-record talk State Department Counselor Helmut Sonnenfeldt had given some months before that could be read—with some stretching—as appearing to acknowledge Eastern Europe's subordination to the Soviet Union.[92]

These developments, to be sure, lay more in the realm of symbolism than of substance, but in political campaigns symbolism can have substantive effects. The perception that the Nixon and Ford administrations—and Kissinger in particular—

---

[90]Kalb and Kalb, *Kissinger*, pp. 494–495; Kissinger, *Years of Upheaval*, p. 596.
[91]Ibid., pp. 1162, 1170.
[92]*A Time to Heal: The Autobiography of Gerald R. Ford* (New York: 1979), pp. 297–298, 320–330; see also Garthoff, *Detente and Confrontation*, pp. 495–496. What Sonnenfeldt actually said, according to the State Department's subsequently-released summary of his remarks, was that "[w]ith regard to Eastern Europe, it must be in our long-term interest to influence events in this area—because of the present unnatural relationship with the Soviet Union—so that they will not sooner or later explode, causing World War III. This inorganic, unnatural relationship is a far greater danger to world peace than the conflict between East and West.... So it must be our policy to strive for an evolution that makes the relationship between the Eastern Europeans and the Soviet Union an organic one.... [O]ur policy must be a policy of responding to the clearly visible aspirations in Eastern Europe for a more autonomous existence within the context of a strong Soviet geopolitical influence." [*New York Times*, April 6, 1976.]

had been too accommodating toward the Soviet Union led California governor Ronald Reagan to challenge Ford for the 1976 Republican presidential nomination. The president, now very much on the defensive, at first defended "detente," but then in March announced his intention to drop the use of the term altogether.[93] At the Republican convention later that summer, Reagan came remarkably close to denying Ford renomination; his forces did succeed in inserting into the party platform language that pointedly praised Solzhenitsyn, condemned "secret agreements," and described the Helsinki agreements as "taking from those who do not have freedom the hope of one day getting it." Ford himself inadvertently sharpened his image of gullibility by claiming, during a televised debate with Democratic presidential candidate Jimmy Carter, in October, that "there is no Soviet domination of Eastern Europe": the gaffe may well have cost Ford the election.[94]

For Carter—with a shrewdness that would not reappear once he had entered the White House—had managed to use the human rights issue to portray Ford as naive and cynical at the same time: naive in his alleged "appeasement" of the Russians by not having protested more vigorously their violations of the Helsinki agreements on human rights; cynical in having allowed Kissinger's alleged "amorality" to dominate his administration's foreign policy. It was a potent combination of arguments, well-calculated to appeal to critics of detente on both the Right and the Left.[95]

V

It was often noted in the United States during the mid-1970s that detente had no domestic constituency of its own. Special interest groups, whether military contractors hungry for bigger defense budgets, ethnic minorities determined to distrust whatever the Russians did, or humanitarians eager to use what leverage the United States had to reform the Soviet system, all had the advantage of organization: despite their small numbers,

---

[93]Garthoff, *Detente and Coexistence*, pp. 547–548.
[94]Ford, *A Time to Heal*, pp. 398, 422–425.
[95]Gaddis Smith, *Morality, Reason and Power: American Diplomacy in the Carter Years* (New York: 1986), pp. 30–31.

the views of these "lobbies" carried weight in a national political system that was increasingly susceptible to such influences. Few organized groups were available outside the professional diplomatic and academic communities to make the case that detente was in fact paying dividends consistent with the national interest.

Because of the bias in American politics that tends to lend greater credibility to those who "view with alarm" than to those who take the position that "all is well," that case would not have been easy to make even in the best of circumstances. Alarmists generally appear to be vigilant and patriotic; their critics too often come across as complacent, passive, and naive. In the context of 1976, a year in which American power and influence in the world did seem to be crumbling, it was difficult not to be alarmed at what was happening, even if it was not always easy to demonstrate that the Russians had caused it to happen. When combined with the hothouse atmosphere that normally builds up in an election year, this combination of circumstances had served to place supporters of detente, at the time the Ford administration left office, very much on the defensive.

But things are not always what they seem to be in diplomacy. Thanks to Kissinger's efforts, it turned out to have been Soviet and not American influence that declined in the Middle East following the 1973 Arab-Israeli War; similar trends would, in time, emerge in southern Africa and in Southeast Asia as well. Vietnam and Watergate would come to be seen as less than total losses for the United States: the first because it brought an end to indiscriminate globalism in American foreign policy; the second because it demonstrated, in a way few other countries could have managed, the supremacy of constitutional processes over individual leaders, however powerful.[96] The Helsinki declaration came to be remembered less for its implied recognition of Russian hegemony in Eastern Europe than for the standard its human rights provisions established against which to measure the Soviet Union's treatment of its own citizens and those of its satellites. In short, the phenomenon of "unintended consequence," which has shaped so many aspects

---

[96]See International Institute for Strategic Studies, *Strategic Survey, 1975* (London: 1976), pp. 1–4.

of Soviet-American relations, should have been enough to give responsible analysts pause before jumping to the conclusion that the Russians had surged far ahead in the great "game" of detente.

For the fact was that detente was not a game from which one side or the other had to emerge victorious: it was rather a process by which the superpowers agreed to *refrain* from competition in certain areas, while continuing it in others. Its durability would depend on the extent to which agreements not to compete could be reconciled with perceived interests on each side and on the ability of the competitors, in areas where competition still persisted, to keep it limited. It was not likely, in and of itself, to alter decisively existing world power relationships: by its very nature it ruled out dramatic coups by one side at the expense of the other. Moreover, to an increasing degree, influence in international affairs was coming to be the product of circumstances only partly within the control of the superpowers. What detente could do was to lessen the danger of war by preventing competition in one area from producing escalation in another, while functioning simultaneously to identify and expand such congruities of interest as existed. As such, it represented progress toward the goal of "graduated reciprocation in tension reduction"; but beyond that it would not have been wise to claim too much.

CHAPTER X

# The Rise and Fall of the Second Cold War: 1976–1988

IN HIS CLASSIC STUDY OF THE POST-NAPOLEONIC CONCERT OF EUROPE, written before he himself abandoned the world of scholarship for that of the statesman, Henry Kissinger had invoked the myth of Nemesis, known for frustrating human ambitions by granting the opposite of what was desired: "Those ages which in retrospect seem most peaceful were least in search of peace. Those whose quest for it seems unending appear least able to achieve tranquillity."[1] The future architect of detente could hardly have known, when he so characterized the age of Metternich and Castlereagh, how precisely his words would also fit the post-detente era in Soviet-American relations presided over by Jimmy Carter, Ronald Reagan, Leonid Brezhnev, and, in time, Mikhail Gorbachev. For when both sides devoted their efforts consciously to terminating the Cold War, they only wound up reviving it. But, in Nemesis-like fashion, once they had resigned themselves to its perpetuation, they managed to stumble into a situation that, by the end of the 1980s, had brought the Cold War closer to a conclusion than at any point in its history.

I

Jimmy Carter took office in January, 1977, determined, as no previous American president had been, to end the Cold War. "I believed," he later recalled, "that too many of our international concerns were being defined almost exclusively by the chronic United States–Soviet confrontation mentality, which seemed to me shortsighted and counterproductive." In his first major for-

---

[1] Henry A. Kissinger, *A World Restored* (New York: 1957), p. 1.

eign policy address, the new chief executive complained that "for too many years, we've been willing to adopt the flawed and erroneous principles of our adversaries." Vietnam had demonstrated the "intellectual and moral poverty" of that approach, but failure there had led the nation back to first principles: "Being confident of our own future, we are now free of that inordinate fear of communism which once led us to embrace any dictator who joined us in that fear."[2]

But where Nixon and Kissinger had sought to end the Cold War within the framework of containment, Carter appeared to reject that strategy altogether: however appropriate it might have been for countering Soviet expansionism immediately after World War II, the president seemed to be saying, times had changed, but the strategy had not. Containment had evolved into a knee-jerk reaction against revolutions everywhere, revolutions that might well be Marxist but that might also reflect legitimate aspirations for political self-determination, economic progress, and human rights. The chief threat to American interests was no longer the Soviet Union, therefore, but rather the misguided policies Washington itself had chosen to follow in its outdated efforts to make containment work.[3] "It is a new world," Carter insisted, "that calls for a new American foreign policy—a policy based on constant decency in its values and on optimism in our historical vision."[4]

The new president moved quickly to dismantle remaining vestiges of Cold War diplomacy. Shortly after taking office, he announced his intention to establish normal relations, not just with the People's Republic of China—Nixon's breakthrough had paved the way for that—but with two more recent adversaries as well, Cuba and Vietnam. He promised to honor a campaign pledge to withdraw United States troops from South Korea, where they had remained since the 1953 armistice. He

---

[2] Jimmy Carter, *Keeping Faith: Memoirs of a President* (New York: 1982), p. 188; Speech at Notre Dame University, May 22, 1977, *Public Papers of the Presidents: Jimmy Carter, 1977* (Washington: 1978), p. 956.
[3] For a useful distinction between "externalist" and "internalist" perceptions of threat, see Smith, *Morality, Reason and Power*, pp. 13–14.
[4] Carter Notre Dame address, May 22, 1977, *Carter Public Papers, 1977*, p. 957. For a useful overview of Carter administration foreign policy priorities in 1977, see Jerel A. Rosati, *The Carter Administration's Quest for Global Community: Beliefs and Their Impact on Behavior* (Columbia, South Carolina: 1987), pp. 39–51.

decided unilaterally, and without seeking reciprocal concessions from the Russians, to suspend production of the new B-1
strategic bomber and the neutron bomb, a battlefield weapon
that would have inflicted casualties more through radiation
than through blast effects. And Carter even speculated openly
about the possibility of eliminating nuclear weapons altogether:
the goal was impracticable in the foreseeable future, he admitted, but it might well be possible to reduce nuclear arsenals dramatically on each side, perhaps even to the point at which deterrence could work with as few as 200 warheads apiece.[5]

At the same time, the president sought to define more positive objectives for a post–Cold War foreign policy. These included, most conspicuously, the promotion of human rights
throughout the world, a cause to which Carter had become
committed through a combination of religious conviction, personal experience, and political expediency.[6] The new administration also worked to improve what it saw as a neglected relationship with the industrialized democracies of Western Europe
and Japan, and to address long-deferred "North-South" concerns,
generally understood to involve the unequal relationship between
the so-called "developed" and "nondeveloped" parts of the
world. All of these, Carter and his advisers believed, were interests the Nixon and Ford administrations had overlooked in their
preoccupation with the "East-West" issues of detente.[7]

The Carter strategy by no means rejected detente: the new
administration was particularly eager to build upon—and, indeed, improve upon—the limited progress in arms control

---

[5]Smith, *Morality, Reason and Power*, pp. 66, 74, 79–81, 103–104, 115–117. See
also Carter, *Keeping Faith*, p. 215; Talbott, *Endgame*, p. 43; and Zbigniew
Brzezinski, *Power and Principle: Memoirs of the National Security Adviser, 1977–1981*
(New York: 1983), p. 157.

[6]For the origins of Carter's human rights policy, see Carter, *Keeping Faith*,
pp. 141–144; also Brzezinski, *Power and Principle*, p. 49; Joshua Muravchik, *The
Uncertain Crusade: Jimmy Carter and the Dilemmas of Human Rights Policy* (Lanham,
Maryland: 1986), pp. 1–7; and A. Glenn Mower, Jr., *Human Rights and American
Foreign Policy: The Carter and Reagan Experiences* (Westport, Connecticut: 1987),
pp. 12–21.

[7]Brzezinski, *Power and Principle*, pp. 7, 53–54; Cyrus Vance, *Hard Choices:
Critical Years in America's Foreign Policy* (New York: 1983), pp. 23–25. For the role
of the Trilateral Commission in shaping administration thinking on these
points, see Smith, *Morality, Reason and Power*, pp. 37–38; and Hamilton Jordan,
*Crisis: The Last Year of the Carter Presidency* (New York: 1982), p. 45.

SALT had produced. With that objective in mind, it quickly put forward a plan for deep cuts in land-based strategic missiles that went well beyond what Ford and Brezhnev had agreed to at Vladivostok in 1974: Carter had resolved, as he put it, "to evolve proposals that would push the *limitation* talks into *reduction* talks."[8] He also called for negotiations with the Russians on a wide range of other issues, including a comprehensive nuclear test ban treaty, a prohibition on the development of anti-satellite, chemical, and radiological weapons, demilitarization of the Indian Ocean, limitations on conventional arms transfers to Third World countries, and nuclear nonproliferation.[9]

The administration was determined, though, not to let Soviet-American issues dominate the foreign policy horizon to the extent that they had in the past. Its principal briefing book on international affairs, prepared in the spring of 1977, listed ten priorities for the next four years; among these, the construction of "a more stable U.S.–Soviet relationship" came fourth, after closer political cooperation with the advanced industrial democracies, weaving a "web" of bilateral contacts with newly-emerging "regional influentials," and the development of "more accommodating North-South relations." Maintenance of "a defense posture capable of deterring the Soviet Union...from hostile acts and from political pressure" was tenth and last.[10]

As this list suggests, Carter's strategy for ending the Cold War suffered from a number of contradictions that made implementation difficult. The most important of these involved disputes among his own advisers as to Moscow's intentions. The new secretary of state, Cyrus Vance, saw threats as more likely to arise from blunders than from malevolence: danger lay in the

---

[8]Carter, *Keeping Faith*, p. 216. The Carter proposal would have reduced the Vladivostok ceiling on all strategic delivery systems from 2,400 to between 1,800 and 2,000, and would have cut MIRVed ICBMs from 1,320 to between 1,100 and 1,200; but because of the existing configuration of forces, these cuts would have disproportionately affected the Soviet side. See Garthoff, *Detente and Coexistence*, pp. 801–808; Talbott, *Endgame*, pp. 38–67; and Brzezinski, *Power and Principle*, pp. 156–161.

[9]Garthoff, *Detente and Coexistence*, pp. 755–756. For further details on the course of these negotiations, see George, Farley, and Dallin, eds., *U.S.–Soviet Security Cooperation*, passim.

[10]Brzezinski, *Power and Principle*, pp. 54–57. See also Rosati, *The Carter Administration's Quest for Global Community*, p. 41.

superpowers' *common* insensitivity to conditions that might lead to overcommitment. The Soviets themselves, Vance thought, were unlikely to challenge international stability, and for that reason need not dominate Washington's priorities.[11] Carter's national security adviser, Zbigniew Brzezinski, took a less benign view. A Polish emigre and a long-time critic of Soviet policies, Brzezinski insisted that the Russians were pursuing detente "not only as a means of preserving peace but also as a way of creating favorable conditions for the acquisition of power by Communist parties." The United States should respond, he argued, by placing Moscow on the defensive through increased American contacts with Eastern Europe and the People's Republic of China and by strongly condemning violations of human rights inside the USSR, while at the same time avoiding an "excessive preoccupation" with Soviet-American relations that might risk either euphoria or hysteria.[12]

Disagreements between Vance and Brzezinski made it particularly difficult to know what to do about "linkage." The secretary of state tended to see Third World crises as arising from circumstances internal to those parts of the world: his was the classic "regionalist" position, predicated on the assumption that the superpowers had little to do with most of what happened beyond their borders, and that to attempt to "link" disconnected events for the purpose of bargaining with the Russians would only be to revert to Kissinger's now discredited "Sovietocentrism." Brzezinski, no fan of Kissinger either, nonetheless shared his predecessor's "globalist" view with its emphasis on interconnections between events across regions; when combined with his suspicions regarding Soviet intentions, it was as easy for Brzezinski to assume the need to "link" as it was for Vance not to.[13]

---

[11]Vance, *Hard Choices*, especially pp. 441–462. See also Smith, *Morality, Reason and Power*, pp. 40–41; and David S. McLellan, *Cyrus Vance* (Totowa, New Jersey: 1985), pp. 25–27, 32–36.

[12]Brzezinski and Richard Gardner to Carter, February 16, 1976, quoted in Brzezinski, *Power and Principle*, pp. 149–150. See also Smith, *Morality, Reason and Power*, pp. 35–36; and Rosati, *The Carter Administration's Quest for Global Community*, pp. 52–57.

[13]Vance, *Hard Choices*, pp. 84–85, 91–92, 116; Brzezinski, *Power and Principle*, pp. 185–186. On the regional versus globalist dichotomy, see Gerald J. Bender, "Angola, the Cubans, and American Anxieties," *Foreign Policy*, #31(Summer, 1978), 3–30.

Because the president refused or was unable to choose between these approaches during his first years in office, policy toward the USSR was more often in a state of confusion than of clarity. Carter's indecisiveness reached an extreme in June, 1978, when he gave an address on Soviet-American relations at the U.S. Naval Academy, one half of which appeared to reflect Vance's views, the other half Brzezinski's. As a *New York Times* editorial commented, Carter had "told the Lions to keep on roaring about Soviet behavior [and]... the Beavers to keep on building a structure of arms control agreements. And he told the Russian leaders that he must govern a nation of both lions and beavers."[14]

Another difficulty was hyperactivity, and the loss of coherence that normally follows from it. Carter later described his approach as one of "inventorying the country's major problems and determining what should be done about as many of them as possible. At least for me, it was natural to move on many fronts at once."[15] What this meant in practice, though, was that the White House failed to define a clear set of foreign policy priorities. "[W]e attempted to do too much all at once," Brzezinski later acknowledged, with the result that "some of our goals in the global issues area contradicted our strategic objectives."[16] The Carter strategy sought to remove the "Sovietocentric" focus in American foreign policy at the same time that it was seeking to reform the Soviet Union through its human rights campaign, to negotiate with Moscow on a wide spectrum of arms control issues, and to discourage the Russians from exploiting opportunities in the Third World.[17] It was a lot to expect to accomplish all at once.

There followed, as a result, an inability to see how actions taken in one sphere might affect those contemplated in others. The President's highly-publicized February, 1977, letter to the Soviet dissident scientist, Andrei Sakharov, for example, was not well-calculated to win approval for "deep cuts" in strategic

---

[14]"From Linkage to Sausage," *New York Times*, June 8, 1978. See also Garthoff, *Detente and Confrontation*, pp. 601–604. The speech, given on June 7, 1978, is in the *Public Papers of the Presidents: Jimmy Carter: 1978* (Washington: 1979). pp. 1052–1058.

[15]Carter, *Keeping Faith*, p. 66.

[16]Brzezinski, *Power and Principle*, p. 145.

[17]See Gaddis, *Strategies of Containment*, p. 350.

weapons when Secretary of State Vance carried that proposal to Moscow the following month. Despite warnings from Brezhnev, Carter refused to see how one line of policy might undermine the other and years later was still expressing incredulity over the abruptness with which the Russians rejected the Vance proposals: "they seemed to have doubted my motives."[18] Nor did the administration anticipate the extent of Moscow's irritation at having been invited to participate, later that year, in a Geneva conference on Middle Eastern affairs, only to have Washington abruptly abandon the idea when Egyptian president Anwar Sadat surprised everyone by beginning direct talks with the Israelis.[19] Certainly both Carter and Brzezinski underestimated the suspicion with which the Russians would view the normalization of relations with China when that event finally took place at the beginning of 1979 on the eve of critical negotiations with respect to SALT II.[20]

This tendency to compartmentalize issues arose largely from Carter's own inability to perceive interrelationships: he had "an enormous capacity to store and retain masses of facts," one observer has written. "He had great difficulty, however, connecting, relating, and interpreting these facts. He could not see patterns and trends, and had little sense of history."[21] Carter failed to anticipate, in 1978, how his negotiation of treaties turning the Panama Canal over to the Panamanians by the end of the century would burden the administration with an image of insensitivity to national security concerns that would leave it with few friends on Capitol Hill when the SALT II treaty came before Congress the following year.[22] Similarly, the president person-

---

[18]Carter, *Keeping Faith*, p. 217. See also Brzezinski, *Power and Principle*, pp. 155–156; Vance, *Hard Choices*, pp. 45–55; and Garthoff, *Detente and Confrontation*, pp. 568–574.

[19]Smith, *Morality, Reason and Power*, pp. 160–162; Garthoff, *Detente and Confrontation*, p. 582. The reasons for the shift in American policy are discussed in William B. Quandt, *Camp David: Peacemaking and Politics* (Washington: 1986), pp. 148–151.

[20]Garthoff, *Detente and Confrontation*, pp. 709–710.

[21]James A. Bill, *The Eagle and the Lion: The Tragedy of American-Iranian Relations* (New Haven: 1988), p. 257. See also Smith, *Morality, Reason and Power*, p. 245.

[22]Ibid., pp. 114–115. See also Walter LaFeber, *The Panama Canal: The Crisis in Historical Perspective* (New York: 1978); and J. Michael Hogan, *The Panama Canal in American Politics: Domestic Advocacy and the Evolution of Policy* (Carbondale, Illinois: 1986).

ally devoted weeks of his time to mediating the laboriously-negotiated Camp David agreement between Egypt and Israel during the summer and fall of 1978; but as a consequence neither he nor other top administration officials were able to pay much attention to events taking place at the same time in Iran, Nicaragua, and Afghanistan—events that would obscure Carter's genuine accomplishments in Central America and the Middle East, and ultimately make it impossible to proceed with his objective of ending the Cold War.[23]

There is no reason to question President Carter's sincerity in pursuing that goal: in his willingness to contemplate the possibility that the Cold War might end, he went well beyond what any of his predecessors had done. But great accomplishments require more than just good intentions: they demand a clear understanding of how to get from where one is to where one wants to go, and this Carter did not possess. As one contemporary comment put it, "the Administration often seemed more intent on making a point than on shaping a policy."[24] Nor was Carter willing to entrust any of his subordinates with sufficient authority to provide strong foreign policy direction in his place.

Even if he had been able to do this, though, success in getting to the desired objective would have required luck as well as skill: not only would the Russians have had to cooperate, but circumstances in the world at large and at home would have had to favor such a development. It quickly became evident that none of these prerequisites for concluding the Cold War were in place at the time Carter chose to move in that direction.

## II

The possibility that the Soviet Union might cooperate in ending the Cold War was by no means implausible at the beginning of Carter's term. Although his sudden political emergence clearly surprised them, Kremlin leaders did go out of their way follow-

---

[23]On the distractions of Camp David, see Smith, *Morality, Reason and Power*, pp. 219–220; also Bill, *The Eagle and the Lion*, pp. 244–245; and Gary Sick, *All Fall Down: America's Tragic Encounter with Iran* (New York: 1985), pp. 60, 65. The Camp David negotiations are covered in Quandt, *Camp David*, pp. 206–319.

[24]International Institute for Strategic Studies, *Strategic Survey, 1977* (London: 1978), p. 9.

ing the new president's election to express their hope that progress toward detente would continue. In an important public address, given at the Russian city of Tula two days before Carter's inauguration, Brezhnev defined "detente" more explicitly than ever before as "the overcoming of the cold war and a transition to normal, equable relations between states." It was, he continued, a way of resolving differences through negotiation rather than force; it also meant "a certain trust and the ability to take one another's legitimate interests into account."[25]

Brezhnev was probably as sincere as Carter in stating these principles, but he and his subordinates were as subject to the gap between intentions and accomplishments as were their American counterparts. For despite the Soviet leader's protestations that he had no desire to perpetuate the Cold War, Soviet actions over the next three years would do just that; respect for the "legitimate interests" of other states would be precisely the quality lacking in Moscow's foreign policy. The result, when combined with the Carter administration's own ineptitude, would be a revival rather than a disappearance of Cold War tensions.

Allegations that the Soviet Union was seeking military superiority over the West or even a "first-strike" capability against it were "absurd and utterly unfounded," Brezhnev told his audience at Tula; "our country will never embark on the path of aggression and will never lift its sword against other peoples."[26] But Soviet military spending had not declined in the five years since the SALT I agreements: indeed by some calculations the Russians were spending more on their military forces under detente than they had at the height of the Cold War.[27] Certainly they had taken full advantage of the fact that SALT I had imposed only quantitative limitations on strategic missiles by im-

---

[25]Brezhnev speech at Tula, January 18, 1977, *Current Digest of the Soviet Press,* XXIX(February 16, 1977), 3–4.

[26]Ibid., p. 3. See also Holloway, *The Soviet Union and the Arms Race,* pp. 48–49.

[27]See Walter Laqueur, "U.S.–Soviet Relations," *Foreign Affairs,* LXII(America and the World, 1983), 565. For the difficulties of estimating Soviet defense expenditures, see International Institute for Strategic Studies, *The Military Balance: 1979–1980* (London: 1979), pp. 11–12.

proving accuracy and installing multiple warheads; they also implemented a large-scale civil defense program and continued, in their military doctrine, to stress the importance of *offensive* operations, an emphasis that appeared to contradict what Brezhnev had said about not seeking a "first-strike capability."[28]

This ambiguity in Soviet strategy had been quite enough to provide American critics of detente with the opportunity to sound loud alarms even before Carter had taken office. They had done so most effectively through the formation, late in 1976, of a bipartisan private organization, the Committee on the Present Danger, that sought to rebuild an American consensus in favor of increased defense expenditures and against further concessions to the Russians on arms control; significantly, its founders included Paul Nitze, who had been the principal author of NSC-68 in 1950 and a strong supporter of the Gaither Committee report in 1957. Nitze had also participated in a highly-critical external review of the Central Intelligence Agency's estimates on Soviet capabilities which its director, George Bush, had arranged earlier that year. The conclusions Nitze and his "Team B" colleagues reached—quickly leaked to the press—were that the agency for years had been underestimating Soviet strategic capabilities, and that the United States now had no choice but to catch up.[29]

Carter firmly rejected these alarmist recommendations, and pointedly excluded most members of the Committee on the Present Danger from his administration.[30] But Soviet behavior in the years that followed did little to sustain his sanguine attitude as the Russians continued development of the Backfire bomber and began an extensive program of modernizing their intermediate-range nuclear forces in Europe by replacing aging SS-4 and SS-5 missiles with a new, solid-fueled, mobile missile,

---

[28]Ibid., pp. 49–55. Recent estimates show Soviet military spending as increasing at a rate of 4 to 5 percent a year up to 1976, with an increase of only about 2 percent a year after that. But the post-1976 cutback did not become apparent in CIA estimates until 1983. See Garthoff, *Detente and Confrontation*, pp. 795–796.

[29]Ibid., p. 539. See also Rearden, *The Evolution of American Strategic Doctrine*, pp. 19–26, 41–46; Talbott, *The Master of the Game*, pp. 144–147; and Jerry W. Sanders, *Peddlers of Crisis: The Committee on the Present Danger and Containment* (Boston: 1983), pp. 149–160.

[30]Talbott, *The Master of the Game*, pp. 147–150.

the SS-20.[31] By 1979, even Carter had come to the conclusion that the United States and its allies could not ignore these developments: realizing that the administration would never get a SALT II treaty through the Senate without some response to this trend, Carter reluctantly endorsed several new weapons systems for the United States, including the MX missile and the "Stealth" (radar-invisible) bomber. And, responding to concerns expressed most strongly by West German Chancellor Helmut Schmidt, the United States, with the uneasy support of its NATO allies, agreed late in 1979 to counter the Soviet SS-20 deployment by stationing American cruise missiles and Pershing II intermediate-range missiles in Western Europe within four years.[32]

The Carter administration had admittedly complicated the SALT II negotiations in 1977 by raising the issue of human rights just as it was seeking "deep cuts" in strategic missiles. The negotiations did get back on track, though, and after another delay occasioned by the administration's decision to establish diplomatic relations with China, Carter and a now visibly-aged Brezhnev finally met at Vienna in June, 1979, to sign a complex, lengthy, and delicately-worded SALT II treaty.[33] But by this time, Moscow's rapid development of new and more accurate ICBMs—allowed under SALT I—had convinced critics that SALT II would be a bad bargain for the United States: on these grounds alone, the treaty would have had difficulty gaining the Senate's approval. The Soviet Union had failed to show the restraint in military spending that would have been necessary if the American consensus in favor of arms

---

[31]Holloway, *The Soviet Union and the Arms Race*, pp. 69–70.

[32]Smith, *Morality, Reason, and Power*, pp. 81–84, 216–218, 237.

[33]The SALT II treaty limited the total number of strategic nuclear delivery vehicles—including ICBMs, SLBMs, bombers, and air-launched ballistic missiles, to 2,400 apiece, to be reduced to 2,250 by the end of 1981. Within that total, each side was allowed a subtotal of 1,320 MIRVed ICBMs and bombers equipped with long-range cruise missiles. Limitations were also placed on the number of warheads each type of missile could carry, and on the number of cruise missiles per bomber that would be allowed. For further details, see United States Arms Control and Disarmament Agency, *Arms Control and Disarmament Agreements: Texts and Histories of Negotiations* (Washington: 1982), pp. 242–277. The SALT II negotiations are best covered in Talbott, *Endgame*, *passim*.

control—already shaky at the time Carter took office—was to be sustained.

But SALT could hardly be isolated from what was going on elsewhere in the world, and here Soviet behavior had even more damaging consequences. Brezhnev had not stressed, in his 1977 Tula speech, his previous insistence that the class struggle in the Third World would continue despite detente, and that the Soviet Union had an obligation to help it along; nor had he invoked the 1968 "Brezhnev Doctrine." His failure to do so appeared to accord well with Carter's determination to avoid seeing Marxist movements everywhere as instruments of the Kremlin. The Russians were now finding themselves surprised, though, by the actions of Third World Marxists largely beyond their control, actions they felt they could neither ignore nor disavow without compromising their claim to ideological leadership. Accordingly—but, from the standpoint of Soviet-American relations, disastrously—Brezhnev chose this moment to begin to match actual policies to his earlier promises.

The pattern had begun with the North Vietnamese conquest of South Vietnam in 1975, an event the Russians had not instigated, but which they were obviously in no position to condemn, despite its problematic implications for a still reasonably cordial relationship with the United States. Then, late in 1978, the communist government of a now-unified Vietnam invaded and ultimately occupied Cambodia. Because the Vietnamese had imprudently insisted that Washington pay war reparations, Carter had already backed away from his expressed intention to normalize relations with Hanoi; this new development brought about still closer contacts between the Americans and the Chinese, an outcome Moscow could hardly have welcome despite the Soviet Navy's new access to former American base facilities at Danang and Cam Ranh Bay. Nor was anything more heard about Carter's plan to withdraw U.S. forces from South Korea.[34]

A similar trend developed in southern Africa, where—partly as a result of Congressionally-imposed restrictions on the Ford administration's ability to extend covert assistance to pro-

---

[34]Garthoff, *Detente and Confrontation*, pp. 440, 663–664, 674–675; Smith, *Morality, Reason and Power*, pp. 95–99, 105. See also, on the question of Soviet aid to the North Vietnamese after 1973, Arnold R. Isaacs, *Without Honor: Defeat in Vietnam and Cambodia* (New York: 1983), pp. 334–335.

Western groups there—a Soviet-supported regime had seized power in Angola in 1976 with the assistance of Cuban combat troops flown in by the Russians.[35] And in East Africa in July, 1977, Somalia, which had received arms from the Russians and even granted them a naval base on the Gulf of Aden, nonetheless went against Moscow's advice and attacked Ethiopia, where a Marxist government had been in place since 1974. Despite their ties to the Somalis, the Russians responded favorably to an Ethiopian request to help counter the Somali offensive in the bleak Ogaden desert: they did this by providing arms, and by sending in still more Cuban troops. These developments ended whatever prospect there might have been that the Carter administration would recognize Castro's government in Havana;[36] they also revived old questions in the minds of American officials about Soviet intentions.

For if the Russians were going to take advantage of American restraint in Third World areas—the United States had, after all, refrained from intervening to prevent the Angolan and Ethiopian revolutions—how could such actions be made consistent with the spirit of detente? Regionalists within the Carter administration like Secretary of State Vance thought the question irrelevant: these were all disconnected incidents, they argued; what was important was for the United States to stay out of them. The Russians, if unwise enough to intervene, would discover the costs of doing so soon enough. But for globalists like Brzezinski, these developments were all part of a pattern. Indulging his fondness for geopolitical metaphor, the national security adviser began speaking ominously of an "arc of crisis" extending from Southeast Asia around through the Middle East to southern Africa, throughout which the Soviet Union was exploiting local unrest to advance its own interests. Such actions could only harm Soviet-American relations in other areas like arms control: "SALT," Brzezinski insisted dramatically, "lies buried in the sands of the Ogaden."[37]

President Carter, characteristically, sought to have it both

---

[35]Garthoff, *Detente and Confrontation*, pp. 502–537, 576–577; Smith, *Morality, Reason and Power*, pp. 117–118, 147–148.

[36]Garthoff, *Detente and Confrontation*, pp. 630–653.

[37]Brzezinski, *Power and Principle*, pp. 187–189. See also Vance, *Hard Choices*, p. 91; Smith, *Morality, Reason and Power*, pp. 153–156; and Garthoff, *Detente and Confrontation*, pp. 646–653.

ways. He did not link progress on arms control to Soviet restraint in the Third World: the SALT II treaty was signed accompanied by no such promises from Moscow. But at the same time, and under the influence of Brzezinski, Carter fell into a tendency to hold the Russians responsible for Third World crises; he even began attributing to them actions with which they had had nothing to do. In May, 1978, for example, the Angolans, for the second time in as many years, attacked neighboring Shaba province in Zaire. Carter had responded to the first attack by stressing the local origins of the conflict, but on the second occasion, in a conversation with a surprised Soviet Foreign Minister Gromyko, he bluntly accused the Soviet Union and Cuba of having instigated it. Subsequent evaluations revealed this not to have been the case.[38]

Even more damaging was the administration's response to intelligence reports, during the summer of 1979, that the Soviet Union had secretly deployed a combat brigade in Cuba. Coming shortly before the Senate was to consider the SALT II treaty and when it was becoming clear that Carter himself would face a difficult fight for reelection, the administration thought it preferable to make this information public and to take a tough stand on it, rather than to have it leak out. Secretary of State Vance announced that he would not be satisfied "with the maintenance of the status quo," while Carter proclaimed the situation in Cuba "not acceptable." Only at this point, though, did the president's advisers begin researching the background of the controversy, only to find, embarrassingly, that the "combat brigade" had been in place since 1962, and that its presence had been part of the Kennedy-Khrushchev agreement that had ended the Cuban missile crisis. By this time, though, the Senate had further delayed the SALT II treaty and the administration's wavering reputation for competence had been severely shaken.[39] "Sovietocentrism," in a president who had initially spurned it, had now grown to the point of seeing Moscow's sinister intent where it did not even exist.

Curiously, one Third World crisis to which the administra-

---

[38]Smith, *Morality, Reason and Power*, pp. 148–149.

[39]For this affair, see Garthoff, *Detente and Coexistence*, pp. 828–848; and David D. Newsom, *The Soviet Combat Brigade in Cuba: A Study in Political Diplomacy* (Bloomington, Indiana: 1987).

tion did not pay sufficient attention took place in Afghanistan in April, 1978, when a Marxist coup overthrew the pro-Western government of Mohammed Daoud and quickly sought support from the USSR. Washington's reaction was curiously muted—at least when compared with its responses to events in the Ogaden, Shaba, and Cuba—even after the American ambassador to Kabul, Adolf Dubs, was kidnapped and murdered in February, 1979, an event Soviet officials on the scene made no apparent effort to prevent.[40] The administration's restraint in this case probably reflected its determination to avoid situations that would require propping up reactionary regimes, a policy that had become clear when Islamic fundamentalists forced the Shah of Iran, a long-time American ally, to flee his country a month earlier. Unlike certain of his predecessors, Carter did not authorize covert or even overt intervention to save the Shah; instead the United States reluctantly accepted the Ayatollah Khomeini's new government and sought—albeit with considerable misgivings—to cooperate with it.[41] Nor did Washington attempt to rescue its old Nicaraguan client Anastasio Somoza when the Sandinistas overthrew that unsavory dictator later that year.[42]

The administration's imperturbability in the face of these crises caused grumbling among its critics but no irreparable damage until the end of 1979, when two disconnected but striking developments abruptly pulled together a growing sense within the country that what the president and his advisers had been demonstrating was not so much coolness under pressure as weakness and gullibility. One was the seizure by Iranian radicals, on November 4, of American diplomats in Teheran: most would remain there as hostages until the Carter administration left office 444 days later. The other shock was the Soviet Union's abrupt military invasion of Afghanistan during the final week of December, in an effort to prop up its own now-sagging client regime there. Despite the fact that there was no

---

[40] Thomas T. Hammond, *Red Flag over Afghanistan: The Communist Coup, the Soviet Invasion, and the Consequences* (Boulder, Colorado: 1984), especially pp. 64–65.

[41] Sick, *All Fall Down*, especially p. 138; Bill, *The Eagle and the Lion*, pp. 278–284.

[42] Smith, *Morality, Reason and Power*, pp. 118–122.

immediate connection between these two incidents, their abrupt juxtaposition put an end once and for all to Carter's hopes for ending the Cold War. With greater candor than he had intended, the president revealed that the invasion of Afghanistan had "made a more dramatic change in my own opinion of what the Soviets' ultimate goals are than anything they've done in the previous time I've been in office."[43]

Which left Carter's critics to ask, uncharitably but with some point, where he himself had been during the past three years. The administration's tolerance toward Third World revolutions, they charged, had only resulted in the losses of Iran, Nicaragua, and now Afghanistan: that latter event in particular raised questions as to whether the Russians had not sought something like this outcome all along. Certainly these developments made it appear that Brzezinski had been right in maintaining a wary view of Soviet intentions: Afghanistan, from his perspective, could serve as an altogether convincing keystone in a crumbling "arc of crisis."

Carter's response was to embrace precisely the "Sovietocentrism" he had earlier condemned: he withdrew the still-unratified SALT II treaty from the Senate, ordered embargoes on shipments of grain and technology to the USSR, endorsed a new program of draft registration, asked for an increase in American defense spending including the creation of a "rapid-deployment" force capable of reacting quickly to Third World crises, and in an ultimate act of linkage even demanded a boycott of the 1980 Moscow Olympics. In an address to Congress on January 23, he invoked the spirit of containment as practiced by a succession of American presidents since the 1940s, denounced the Soviet invasion of Afghanistan as "the most serious threat to the peace since the Second World War," and in the best tradition of the Cold War went on to proclaim his own doctrine: "Any attempt by any outside force to gain control of the Persian Gulf region will be regarded as an assault on the vital interests of the United States of America, and such an as-

---

[43]*New York Times*, January 1, 1980. This somewhat embarrassing comment was not included in the normal published compilation of presidential documents. See, on this point, Garthoff, *Detente and Confrontation*, p. 950n.

sault will be repelled by any means necessary, including military force."[44]

The Carter Doctrine reflected widespread concern that the Soviet occupation of Afghanistan and the outbreak of strident anti-Americanism in Iran might somehow combine to deny the West access to Persian Gulf oil at a time when the energy crisis had once again become a serious problem. What had seemed, at first, a disconnected series of events now took on an ominous pattern, in a way statesmen of the early Cold War would have found entirely familiar. Nor did the administration's response to these setbacks differ all that much from that of its predecessors in similar circumstances: the chief priority was to demonstrate toughness in order to recapture the credibility that the crisis seemed to demand. With that objective in mind, Carter even went so far as to approve, in the summer of 1980, a new strategy that appeared to envisage the possibility of fighting and winning—as opposed to simply deterring—a nuclear war: he quickly arranged to have the substance of this document, known as PD-59, leaked to the press.[45]

The Carter administration must bear some of the responsibility for the revival of the Cold War that the Carter Doctrine and PD-59 symbolized. No postwar administration had greater difficulty deciding what its foreign policy priorities were to be or how to implement them; as a result, no postwar president exerted weaker leadership when it came to Soviet-American relations. But these deficiencies were, to a considerable degree, the result of an unprecedented effort to liberate American foreign policy from the Cold War fixations that had burdened it since 1945: Carter and his advisers were moving into uncharted territory, and a certain amount of confusion was unavoidable as a result. Where the administration failed was not so much in its

---

[44]Speech to Congress, January 23, 1980, *Public Papers of the Presidents: Jimmy Carter, 1980–81* (Washington: 1982), p. 197. The initial Carter defense budget had projected an annual increase of 3% when adjusted for inflation. Carter raised this to 4% in the wake of the Afghanistan invasion, and to 5% in his final budget before leaving office. [Samuel P. Huntington, "The Defense Policy of the Reagan Administration, 1981–1982," in Fred I. Greenstein, *The Reagan Presidency: An Early Assessment* (Baltimore: 1983), p. 87.]

[45]On PD-59, see Garthoff, *Detente and Coexistence*, pp. 789–790; also Brzezinski, *Power and Principle*, pp. 456–459.

objectives as in its timing: 1977 was closer to the worst than to the best of all possible moments to attempt so sweeping a redefinition of foreign policy goals. At a time when defeat in Vietnam had severely shaken American self-confidence, when the energy crisis appeared to be demonstrating American impotence, when the military balance seemed to be shifting in the Russians' favor, and when the domestic consensus in favor of detente was rapidly dissolving, the atmosphere simply was not right for a shift to a foreign policy based more on principles than on power: determined to forge ahead regardless of the circumstances, the president was one of the last to see how inauspicious those circumstances were for what he was trying to do.

But the primary responsibility for what happened must rest with the Soviet Union and its increasingly senescent leader, Leonid Brezhnev. For, given the long-term economic and social problems that confronted it, the Soviet Union needed an end to the Cold War more than did the United States. Brezhnev had even recognized this fact—without acknowledging the reasons for it—in his 1977 Tula speech. And yet, the Soviet leader was unable to see that he had, in Jimmy Carter, an American counterpart who shared that goal: instead, he chose to view the administration's fumbling earnestness as a sinister plot directed against Soviet interests. From Carter's first months in the White House, Brezhnev was apparently determined not to trust the first postwar American president who was prepared, in his own admittedly naive way, to trust the USSR.

Brezhnev also erred by allowing Soviet foreign policy to get caught up in the same pattern of imperial overextension that had afflicted the United States in the 1950s and 1960s. It was Soviet credibility more than a sober view of Soviet interests that dictated involvement in so diverse and unpromising an array of outposts as Angola, Ethiopia, Vietnam, and Afghanistan: just as the Americans had felt obliged, in the initial decades of the Cold War, to prevent the coming to power of Third World Marxist governments, so the Russians now believed it necessary to sustain such governments, whatever the effect on the Soviet economy, on relations with Washington, or on Moscow's overall reputation in world affairs. There was indeed, as Brzezinski insisted, a common thread that linked these crises, but it was not the farsighted *offensive* drive for world power he detected; rather, it was a shortsighted *defensive* effort to maintain Soviet influence through indiscriminate involvement. "It is often only with the best and most defensive of intentions," the British historian Michael Howard pointed out in an early evaluation of the Afghanistan invasion, "that empires extend their sway."[46]

That, though, was precisely the difficulty. For by equating expansionism with defense, Brezhnev made the same mistake Stalin had made in the late 1940s: he brought about what he must have most feared.[47] It could not have been reassuring to know, as he approached death in 1982, that Afghanistan had brought about a precipitous loss of Soviet influence in the Third World; that a new American military buildup was underway with widespread domestic support; that an unusually determined NATO alliance had decided to deploy a new generation of missiles capable of striking Moscow itself; that detente was dead; and that Ronald Reagan had become president of the United States.

## III

Soviet behavior was by no means the sole reason for Reagan's landslide victory in the 1980 election. Carter and his advisers had provoked the ire of voters on a score of issues, including the failure to control inflation, soaring interest rates, the energy crisis, the Panama Canal treaties, and, most of all, their inability to resolve the lingering Iranian hostage crisis: an ill-conceived effort to rescue the hostages had failed miserably in April of that year, thereby reinforcing the administration's already sizable reputation for ineffectiveness.[48] But taken together, these inadequacies conveyed an unmistakable impression of weakness and irresolution: when viewed in the light of what had appeared to be Soviet purposefulness—whether on such matters as military spending, support for Third World Marxist movements, or the invasion of Afghanistan—the effect could only be

---

[46]Michael Howard, "Return to the Cold War?" *Foreign Affairs*, LIX(America and the World: 1980), 463.

[47]See, on the Soviet failure to anticipate the effects of the Afghanistan invasion, Garthoff, *Detente and Confrontation*, pp. 991, 996–997; also Robert Legvold, "War, Weapons, and Soviet Foreign Policy," in Bialer and Mandelbaum, eds., *Gorbachev's Russia and American Foreign Policy*, pp. 111–112.

[48]Sick, *All Fall Down*, pp. 280–302. For an assessment of Reagan's 1980 victory, see Ole R. Holsti and James N. Rosenau, *American Leadership in World Affairs: Vietnam and the Breakdown of Consensus* (Boston: 1984), pp. 240–241.

to place Carter at an even greater disadvantage than Ford had been four years earlier as voters assessed his record in dealing with Moscow.

Reagan had come close to denying Ford the 1976 Republican nomination with charges that detente had failed to prevent Soviet expansionism. Carter's abortive effort to end the Cold War and his belated rediscovery of containment made him an even more credible target for such accusations, and Reagan easily won nomination in 1980 on a platform calling for rejection of the SALT II treaty, a rapid increase in defense spending that would produce "military superiority" over the Soviet Union, and a return to containment in its most militant form. During the fall campaign, the Republican candidate softened his rhetoric somewhat to avoid coming across as trigger-happy: he even spoke at one point, unexpectedly, of the need "to have a reduction of these nuclear weapons to the point that neither of us represents a threat to the other."[49] But there was little visible evidence, at the time he took office, that the new president expected anything other than a renewed Cold War; in his first White House press conference he asserted that the Soviet Union had used detente as "a one-way street...to pursue its own its own aims," that those aims included "the promotion of world revolution and a one-world Socialist or Communist state," and that "they reserve unto themselves the right to commit any crime, to lie, to cheat, in order attain that."[50]

Key foreign policy appointments appeared to reflect this hard line. Reagan named, as secretary of state, the hyperbolic former general Alexander M. Haig, Jr., who had been White House chief of staff under Nixon and NATO supreme commander under Ford: contemptuous of what he would later characterize as "the Carter experiment in obsequiousness," Haig warned that the Soviet Union's "tremendous accumulation of armed might has produced perhaps the most complete reversal

---

[49]Elizabeth Drew, *Portrait of an Election: The 1980 Presidential Campaign* (New York: 1981), pp. 202, 323–325. For evidence that the idea of *reducing*—as opposed to limiting—strategic weapons was in Reagan's mind as early as 1976, see Martin Anderson, *Revolution* (New York: 1988), pp. 63–73.

[50]News conference, January 29, 1981, *Public Papers of the Presidents: Ronald Reagan, 1981* (Washington: 1982), p. 57.

of global power relationships ever seen in a period of relative peace."[51] Where Carter and Vance had tried not to see Third World instability as the product of Kremlin machinations, the new secretary of state pointedly described Moscow as "the greatest single source of international insecurity today."[52] Even more than had been the case with Brzezinski, Haig literally saw the hand of the Russians at work, whether directly or by proxy, in locations ranging from Central America through southern Africa, the Middle East, southwest and southeast Asia: American attitudes toward Third World regimes, he implied, would be shaped less by their performance on human rights than by their cooperation in containing the Soviet Union's push for world domination.[53]

Reagan entrusted the Defense Department to former Nixon administration budget director Caspar Weinberger, who took an equally jaundiced view of detente. Pointing out that Soviet military spending had grown "more rapidly and more steadily" during that period than in "the so-called 'cold war'," he insisted that Kremlin leaders had not shared the West's hope "that the nuclear balance could be stabilized through arms control agreements."[54] Weinberger quickly raised Carter's projected increase in defense expenditures from 5 to 7% annually, authorized significant improvements in ground combat readiness, reinstituted the B-1 bomber program that Carter had cancelled, and approved construction of a 600-ship Navy which would now have the task, if war came, not simply of protecting

---

[51]Haig statement to Senate Foreign Relations Committee, January 9, 1981, U.S. Department of State, *American Foreign Policy: Current Documents, 1981* [hereafter *AFP*] (Washington: 1984), p. 3. The comment about Carter is in Alexander M. Haig, Jr., *Caveat: Realism, Reagan, and Foreign Policy* (New York: 1984), p. 29.

[52]Haig speech to American Society of Newspaper Editors, Washington, April 24, 1981, *AFP: 1981*, p. 36.

[53]See Haig's speech to the Trilateral Commission, Washington, March 31, 1981, ibid., pp. 369–370; also Mower, *Human Rights and American Foreign Policy*, pp. 32–37; and, for an article that strongly influenced administration thinking on this point, Jeane J. Kirkpatrick, "Dictatorships and Double Standards," *Commentary*, LXVIII(November, 1979), 34–45.

[54]Weinberger address, American Newspaper Publishers Association, Chicago, May 5, 1981, *AFP: 1981*, p. 39.

sea lanes but of actually attacking the Soviet Navy in its own home ports.[55]

Arms control was not one of the new administration's highest priorities: indeed the president appeared to have gone out of his way to entrust that responsibility to some of its most fervent critics. Eugene V. Rostow, one of the founders of the Committee on the Present Danger, became head of the Arms Control and Disarmament Agency; Paul Nitze, another pillar of that organization and a vociferous opponent of SALT II, took on the task of negotiating reductions in intermediate-range nuclear forces (INF) in Europe, a condition the NATO allies had insisted on before agreeing to deploy American Pershing II and cruise missiles on their territory. Equally striking were the appointments of Harvard historian Richard Pipes as chief Soviet specialist on the National Security Council—Pipes had headed the 1976 "Team B" exercise that had castigated the Central Intelligence Agency for underestimating Soviet strategic capabilities—and, as assistant secretary of defense for international security policy, of Richard Perle, a long-time staff aide to Senator Henry Jackson and an ardent foe of arms control in all its forms: characteristically Perle worried that Nitze might be too *soft* in dealing with the Russians and actually agree to something.[56]

The administration's proposals on arms control seemed designed to subvert rather than advance that process. Perle himself proposed the elimination of *all* Soviet SS-20s—whether in Europe or Asia—in return for NATO's agreement not to deploy Pershing II and cruise missiles: despite complaints that the Russians would never agree to trade actual missiles for nonexistent ones (the NATO deployment was not to take place until 1983), President Reagan endorsed this "zero option" late in 1981, thereby confirming his critics' suspicion that he was not really interested in reaching an INF agreement.[57] At the same time, Rostow and other advisers had recommended shifting the

---

[55]Huntington, "The Defense Policy of the Reagan Administration, 1981–1982," pp. 87, 98–99. For the Navy's "maritime" strategy, see Robert W. Komer, *Maritime Strategy or Coalition Defense?* (Cambridge, Massachusetts: 1984), especially pp. 55–63.

[56]Talbott, *The Master of the Game*, pp. 113–114, 146, 163, 167–171; Sanders, *Peddlers of Crisis*, pp. 281–289. See also Strobe Talbott, *Deadly Gambits: The Reagan Administration and the Stalemate in Nuclear Arms Control* (New York: 1984), pp. 15–18.

[57]Ibid., pp. 169–170.

focus of strategic arms talks from "limitation" to "reduction"—
the new acronym would be START instead of SALT—and in
May, 1982, Reagan accepted this proposal as well, calling publicly for a reduction by one-third of ballistic missile warheads on
each side, with no more than half of those that remained to be
land-based.[58] Reagan's START proposal appeared to echo one
George F. Kennan had made a year earlier for an immediate
50% across-the-board reduction in nuclear arsenals; but because
START would have required disproportionate cuts in Soviet
warheads—seven out of every ten of which were on land-based
ICBMs, as opposed to two out of ten for the United States—
most observers regarded it, along with the "zero option," as an
effort to stalemate arms control negotiations rather than as a
sincere effort to achieve the real reductions the two proposals
professed to seek.[59]

Despite the fact that he was at least negotiating with the
Russians—and that, despite his criticisms of the unratified
SALT II treaty, he had agreed to adhere to its numerical limits
on strategic weapons deployments—President Reagan and his
advisers quickly gained a reputation for irresponsibility, even
recklessness, on nuclear issues. The administration's obvious
preference for rearmament over arms control contributed to
this; so too had a series of injudicious remarks by key officials
about the development of nuclear "war-fighting strategies," the
firing of nuclear "warning shots," and, in one case, the possibility of surviving a nuclear attack provided everyone had
"enough shovels" to build backyard bomb shelters: "It's the
dirt that does it."[60] By the end of 1982 there had developed, as

---

[58]Reagan speech at Eureka College, Eureka, Illinois, May 9, 1982, *Public Papers of Presidents: Ronald Reagan, 1982* (Washington 1983). p. 585. For the origins
of START, see Talbott, *Deadly Gambits*, pp. 222–223.

[59]See Stephen S. Rosenfeld, "Testing the Hard Line," *Foreign Affairs*,
LXI(America and the World, 1982), 492, 504. The Kennan proposal, made on
the occasion of receiving the Albert Einstein Peace Prize, is in George F.
Kennan, *The Nuclear Delusion: Soviet-American Relations in the Atomic Age* (New
York: 1982), pp. 174–182. For warhead figures, see George E. Hudson and
Joseph Kruzel, eds., *American Defense Annual: 1985–1986* (Lexington,
Massachusetts: 1985), p. 93. Reagan himself later admitted that he had not re-
alized at the time of the May, 1982, speech that the Russians relied primarily on
land-based ICBMs. [Talbott, *Deadly Gambits*, p. 263.]

[60]Ibid., pp. 224–226, 287. See also Rosenfeld, "Testing the Hard Line," pp.
504–508; and, for a catalog of such statements, Robert Scheer, *With Enough Shovels: Reagan, Bush and Nuclear War* (New York: 1983).

a consequence, the strongest upsurge in public concern over the danger of nuclear war since the Cuban missile crisis: in Europe this took the form of demonstrations against the planned 1983 deployment of Pershing II and cruise missiles; in the United States it produced a widespread movement calling for an immediate "freeze" on the production, testing, and deployment of both Soviet and American nuclear weapons—a proposal popular enough to win in eight out of nine states where it was placed on the ballot in the November elections.[61]

It was with advocates of the "freeze" very much in mind that President Reagan in March, 1983, made his most memorable pronouncement on the Soviet Union. "If history teaches anything," he told a receptive audience of evangelical ministers, "it teaches that simple-minded appeasement or wishful thinking about our adversaries is folly."

I urge you to speak out against those who would place the United States in a position of military and moral inferiority...I urge you to beware the temptation of pride—the temptation of blithely declaring yourselves above it all and label[ing] both sides equally at fault, to ignore the facts of history and the aggressive impulses of an evil empire, to simply call the arms race a giant misunderstanding and thereby remove yourself from the struggle between right and wrong and good and evil.

It was important to remember that "there is sin and evil in the world....We are enjoined by scripture and the Lord Jesus to oppose it with all our might." And the simple fact was that the Soviet Union was "the focus of evil in the modern world."[62]

---

[61]Spencer R. Weart, *Nuclear Fear: A History of Images* (Cambridge, Massachusetts: 1988), pp. 375–388; William Schneider, "Rambo and Reality: Having It Both Ways," in Kenneth A. Oye, Robert J. Lieber, and Donald Rothchild, eds., *Eagle Resurgent? The Reagan Era in American Foreign Policy* (Boston: 1987), pp. 42–44. See also Jonathan Schell, *The Fate of the Earth* (New York: 1982), a book that contributed powerfully to fueling this concern; and the 1983 American Catholic bishops' pastoral letter, *The Challenge of Peace: God's Promise and Our Response* (Washington: 1983), which attempted to address the moral dimensions of the issue.

[62]Speech to the National Association of Evangelicals, Orlando, Florida, March 8, 1983, *Public Papers of the Presidents: Ronald Reagan, 1983* (Washington: 1984). pp. 363–364. For an attempt to place this speech in a broader philosophical context, see William K. Muir, Jr., "Ronald Reagan: The Primacy of Rhetoric," in Fred I. Greenstein, ed., *Leadership in the Modern Presidency* (Cambridge, Massachusetts, 1988), pp. 271–278.

Two weeks later, the president surprised even his closest advisers with a proposal that questioned the whole basis of mutual vulnerability—and mutual assured destruction—upon which nuclear deterrence, since the early 1960s, had been based:

What if free people could live secure in the knowledge that their security did not rest upon the threat of instant U.S. retaliation to deter a Soviet attack, that we could intercept and destroy strategic ballistic missiles before they reached our own soil or that of our allies?

Calling upon "the scientific community in our country, those who gave us nuclear weapons, to turn their great talents now to the cause of mankind and world peace," Reagan announced the beginning of a long-term research and development program to create defenses against attacks by strategic missiles, with a view ultimately to "rendering these nuclear weapons impotent and obsolete."[63]

The Strategic Defense Initiative (which, inspired by the film and by Reagan's "evil empire" rhetoric, immediately became known as "Star Wars") was the most fundamental challenge to existing orthodoxies on arms control since negotiations with the Russians on that subject had begun almost three decades earlier. By implicitly undermining the 1972 ABM treaty's ban on strategic defenses, the administration now appeared to have added the dismantling of SALT I to its list of priorities. By proposing the introduction of weapons into space, Reagan appeared to be challenging the Russians to a new and costly arms race in which they would be ill-equipped to compete; they were quick to denounce the plan not only as a diversion from arms control but as an effort to regain American strategic superiority, possibly even a first-strike capability against the USSR. By proposing a technological "fix" to the problem of mutual vulnerability in the nuclear age, the White House in the view of its critics appeared to be projecting political objectives well beyond what the constraints of physics, mathematics, and a national economy already burdened by growing budget deficits could possibly allow.[64]

---

[63]Radio-television address, March 23, 1983, *Reagan Public Papers: 1983*, pp. 442–443.

[64]Criticisms of SDI, together with arguments in its favor, can be sampled in Franklin A. Long, Donald Hafner, and Jeffrey Boutwell, eds., *Weapons in Space* (New York: 1986). For the Soviet reaction, see David Holloway, "The Strategic Defense Initiative and the Soviet Union," ibid., pp. 265–268.

Anyone who listened to the "evil empire" speech—or who considered the implications of "Star Wars"—might well have concluded that President Reagan saw the Soviet-American relationship as a elemental confrontation between virtue and wickedness that would allow neither negotiation nor conciliation in any form: his tone seemed more appropriate to a medieval crusade than to a revival of containment. Certainly there were those within his administration who held such views, and their influence, for a time, was considerable. But Reagan himself seems to have understood—or to have quickly learned—the dangers of basing foreign policy solely on ideology:[65] the president combined his militancy with a surprising degree of operational pragmatism and a shrewd sense of timing. To the astonishment of his own hard-line supporters,[66] what appeared to be an enthusiastic return to the Cold War in fact turned out to be a more solidly-based approach to detente than anything the Nixon, Ford, or Carter administrations had been able to accomplish.

## IV

There had always been a certain ambivalence in the Reagan administration's image of the Soviet Union. On the one hand, dire warnings about Moscow's growing military strength suggested an almost Spenglerian gloom about the future: time, it appeared, was again on the Russians' side, much as it had seemed to be at such earlier points in Cold War as the drafting of NSC-68, or the launching of Sputnik, or the Vietnam War. But mixed with this pessimism was a strong sense of self-confidence, growing out of the ascendancy of conservatism within the United States and an increasing enthusiasm for capitalism overseas, that assumed the unworkability of Marxism as a form of political, social, and economic organization: "The West won't contain communism, it will transcend communism," the president predicted in May, 1981. "It won't bother to . . . denounce it, it will dismiss it as some bizarre chapter in human history

---

[65]See Arthur M. Schlesinger, Jr., *The Cycles of American History* (Boston: 1986), pp. 56–58.

[66]See, for example, Norman Podhoretz, "The Reagan Road to Detente," *Foreign Affairs*, LXIII(America and the World, 1984), 447–464.

whose last pages are even now being written."[67] By this logic the Soviet Union had already reached the apex of its strength as a world power, and time in fact was on the side of the West.

Events proved the optimism to have been more justified than the pessimism, for over the next four years, the Soviet Union would undergo one of the most rapid erosions both of internal self-confidence and external influence in modern history: that this happened just as Moscow's long and costly military buildup should have begun to pay political dividends made the situation all the more frustrating for the Russians. It may have been luck for President Reagan to have come into office at a peak in the fortunes of the Soviet Union and at a trough in those of the United States: things would almost certainly have improved regardless of who entered the White House in 1981. But it took more than luck to recognize what was happening, and to capitalize on it to the extent that the Reagan administration did.

Indications of Soviet decline took several forms. The occupation of Afghanistan had produced only a bloody Vietnam-like stalemate, with Soviet troops unable to suppress the rebellion, or to protect themselves or their clients, or to withdraw. In Poland a long history of economic mismanagement had produced, in the form of the Solidarity trade union, a rare phenomenon within the Soviet bloc: a true workers' movement. The Warsaw government's surprise arrest of Solidarity leaders at the end of 1981 defused the immediate crisis without direct Soviet intervention, but what the experience revealed about the failures of communism could hardly have provided more credible confirmation for the obituary Reagan had pronounced over that ideology earlier in the year. Soviet ineffectiveness became apparent in the Middle East as well in 1982 when the Russians were unable to provide any significant help to the Palestinian Liberation Organization during the Israeli invasion of Lebanon; even more embarrassingly, Israeli pilots using American-built fighters shot down some 80 Soviet-supplied Syrian jets without

---

[67]Speech at Notre Dame University, May 17, 1981, *Reagan Public Papers, 1981*, p. 434. See also Reagan's speech to the British Parliament, London, June 8, 1982, *AFP: 1982*, pp. 14–20; Michel Tatu, "U.S.–Soviet Relations: A Turning Point?" *Foreign Affairs*, LXI(America and the World, 1982), 592–595; and Anderson, *Revolution*, pp. 17–32.

a single loss of their own.[68] Meanwhile, the Soviet domestic economy, which Khrushchev had once predicted would overtake that of the United States, had in fact stagnated: after growing rapidly in the 1950s and 1960s, the Soviet gross national product relative to that of the United States leveled off at about 50% after 1975. During the early 1980s, Japan actually overtook the USSR as the world's second largest producer of goods and services, and even China, a nation with four times the population of the Soviet Union, now became an agricultural exporter at a time when Moscow still required food imports from the West to feed its own people.[69]

What all of this meant was that the Soviet Union's appeal as a model for Third World political and economic development—once formidable—had virtually disappeared; indeed as Moscow's military presence in those regions grew during the late 1970s, the Russians increasingly came to be seen, not as liberators, but as latter-day imperialists themselves.[70] The Reagan administration moved swiftly to take advantage of this situation by funneling military assistance—sometimes openly, sometimes covertly—to rebel groups (or "freedom fighters," as the president insisted on calling them) seeking to overturn Soviet-backed regimes in Afghanistan, Angola, Ethiopia, Cambodia, and Nicaragua; in November, 1983, to huge domestic acclaim but with dubious legality, Reagan even ordered the direct use of American military forces to overthrow an unpopular Marxist government on the tiny Caribbean island of Grenada. The Reagan Doctrine, as this strategy became known, sought to ex-

---

[68]Karen Dawisha, "The U.S.S.R. in the Middle East: Superpower in Eclipse?" *Foreign Affairs*, LXI(Winter, 1982/83), 438–452. See also Joseph J. Sisco, "Middle East: Progress or Lost Opportunity?" ibid., LXI(America and the World, 1982), 621. For events in Poland, see Charles Gati, "Polish Futures, Western Options," ibid., LXI(Winter, 1982/83), 292–308; and Seweryn Bialer, *The Soviet Paradox: External Expansion, Internal Decline* (New York: 1986), pp. 213–231.

[69]For overviews of Soviet economic problems, see ibid., pp. 47–50, 165; also Robert W. Campbell, "The Economy," in Robert F. Byrnes, ed., *After Brezhnev: The Sources of Soviet Conduct in the 1980s* (Bloomington: 1983), pp. 68–124. For the growing gap between Soviet and Chinese agricultural production, see Kennedy, *The Rise and Fall of the Great Powers*, p. 492.

[70]Francis Fukuyama, "Gorbachev and the Third World," *Foreign Affairs*, LXIV(Spring, 1986), especially pp. 720–721. For the efforts of Soviet analysts to come to grips with this phenomenon, see Jerry F. Hough, *The Struggle for the Third World: Soviet Debates and American Options* (Washington: 1986).

THE RISE AND FALL OF THE SECOND COLD WAR  323

ploit vulnerabilities the Russians had created for themselves in the Third World: with the single exception of Nicaragua— where memories of an American "imperial" legacy still per- sisted—this latter-day effort to "roll back" Soviet influence would, in time, produce impressive results at minimum cost and risk to the United States.[71]

Compounding the Soviet Union's external difficulties was a long vacuum in internal leadership occasioned by Brezhnev's slow enfeeblement and eventual death in November, 1982, by the installation as his successor of an already-ill Yuri Andropov, who himself died in February, 1984, and by the death in turn of his equally geriatric successor, Konstantin Chernenko, in March, 1985. At a time when a group of strong Western leaders had emerged—including not just President Reagan but Prime Minister Margaret Thatcher in Great Britain, President François Mitterand in France, and Chancellor Helmut Kohl in West Germany—this apparent inability to entrust leadership to any- one other than party stalwarts on their deathbeds was a severe commentary on what the sclerotic Soviet system had become. "We could go no further without hitting the end," one Russian later recalled of Chernenko's brief reign. "Here was the General Secretary of the party, who is also the Chairman of the Presid- ium of the Supreme Soviet, the embodiment of our country, the personification of the party, and he could barely stand up."[72]

There was no disagreement within the Reagan administra- tion about the desirability, under these circumstances, of press- ing the Russians hard: the president and his advisers did not, like several of their predecessors, see containment as requiring

---

[71]For the Reagan Doctrine, see Stephen S. Rosenfeld, "The Guns of July." *Foreign Affairs*, LXIV(Spring, 1986), 698–714; and Alexander Dallin and Gail W. Lapidus, "Reagan and the Russians: American Policy toward the Soviet Union," in Oye, Lieber, and Rothchild, eds., *Eagle Resurgent?* pp. 223–226. Un- like the Truman, Eisenhower, and Carter Doctrines, the Reagan Doctrine for- malized a strategy that was already underway. The closest thing to a definitive statement of it would not come until President Reagan's 1985 State of the Union address: "Our mission is to nourish and defend freedom and democracy and to communicate these ideals everywhere we can.... We must stand by our demo- cratic allies. And we must not break faith with those who are risking their lives—on every continent, from Afghanistan to Nicaragua—to defy Soviet- supported aggression and secure rights which have been ours from birth." [Ad- dress to Congress, February 6, 1985, *Public Papers of the Presidents: Ronald Reagan, 1985* (Washington: 1987), p. 135.]

[72]*New York Times*, January 22, 1989.

the application of sticks and carrots in roughly equal propor-
tions; wielders of sticks definitely predominated among them.[73]
But there were important differences over what the purpose of
wielding the sticks was to be. Some advisers, like Weinberger,
Perle, and Pipes, saw the situation as a historic opportunity to
exhaust the Soviet system: noting that the Soviet economy was
already stretched to the limit, they advocated taking advantage
of American technological superiority to engage the Russians in
an arms race of indefinite duration and indeterminate cost. Others, including Nitze, the Joint Chiefs of Staff, career Foreign
Service officer Jack Matlock, who succeeded Pipes as chief Soviet expert at the NSC, and—most important—Haig's replace-
ment as secretary of state after June, 1982, the unflamboyant
but steady George Shultz, endorsed the principle of "negotiation from strength": the purpose of accumulating military
hardware was not to debilitate the other side, but to convince it
to negotiate.[74]

The key question, of course, was what President Reagan's
position would be. Despite his rhetoric, he had been careful not
to rule out talks with the Russians once the proper conditions
were met: even while complaining, in his first press conference,
about the Soviet propensity to lie, cheat, and steal, he had also
noted that "when we can, . . . we should start negotiations on
the basis of trying to effect an actual reduction in the numbers
of nuclear weapons. That would then be real strategic arms
limitation."[75] But most observers—and probably many of his
own advisers—assumed that when the president endorsed negotiations leading toward the "reduction," as opposed to the
"limitation," of strategic arms, or the "zero option" in the INF
talks, or the Strategic Defense Initiative, he was really seeking
to avoid negotiations by setting minimal demands well above
the maximum concessions the Russians could afford to make:
he was looking for a way, they believed, to gain credit for co-
operativeness with both domestic and allied constituencies
without actually having to give up anything.

---

[73]Tatu, "U.S.–Soviet Relations," pp. 592–593; Seweryn Bialer and Joan
Afferica, "Reagan and Russia," Foreign Affairs, LXI(Winter, 1982/83), 252.

[74]For a sophisticated attempt to analyze differences among the president's
advisers, see Dallin and Lapidus, "Reagan and the Russians: American Policy
toward the Soviet Union," pp. 199–202.

[75]Reagan press conference, January 29, 1981, Reagan Public Papers, 1981, p. 57.

This would turn out to be a gross misjudgment of President Reagan, who may have had cynical advisers but was not cynical himself. It would become apparent with the passage of time that when the chief executive talked about "reducing" strategic missiles he meant precisely that; the appeal of the "zero option" was that it really would get rid of intermediate-range nuclear forces; the Strategic Defense Initiative might in fact, just as the president had said, make nuclear weapons "impotent and obsolete." A simple and straightforward man, Reagan took the principle of "negotiation from strength" literally: once one had built strength, one negotiated.[76]

The first indications that the president might actually be interested in something other than an indefinite arms race began to appear in the spring and summer of 1983. Widespread criticism of his "evil empire" speech apparently shook him: although his view of the Soviet system itself did not change, Reagan was careful, after that point, to use more restrained language in characterizing it.[77] In April of that year, by accepting the report of a presidential commission on strategic forces headed by former national security adviser Brent Scowcroft, Reagan quietly acknowledged the improbability that a "window of vulnerability" might tempt the Russians into launching a surprise attack on the United States: he thereby undercut an argument the Committee on the Present Danger had been loudly advancing since its formation in 1976.[78] By August the president was acknowledging—before a convention of the American Legion, no less—that there had been "encouraging movement" in negotiations with the Russians about arms

---

[76]See, on this point, John Lewis Gaddis, "Arms Control: Hanging Tough Paid Off," *Bulletin of the Atomic Scientists,* XLV(January/February, 1989), 11–14; also, for a perceptive early comment on the importance of simplicity in Reagan's strategy, Robert E. Osgood, "The Revitalization of Containment," *Foreign Affairs,* LX(America and the World, 1981), 471.

[77]Except on one occasion in August, 1984, when the president, while testing what turned out to be an open microphone, jocularly announced: "My fellow Americans. I am pleased to tell you I just signed legislation which outlaws Russia forever. The bombing begins in five minutes." [*New York Times,* August 13, 1984.]

[78]White House press release, April 19, 1983, *AFP: 1983,* pp. 68–70. For the Scowcroft Commission report, see the *Report of the President's Commission on Strategic Forces* (Washington: 1983).

control.[79] And when, on September 1, 1983, Soviet fighters mistakenly shot down a South Korean airliner that had strayed over Sakhalin with 269 passengers aboard (including 63 Americans, one a member of the House of Representatives), an outraged president nonetheless limited the American response to demands for an apology and compensation for the victims, the suspension of a few bilateral negotiations, and an insistence that the Russians cooperate to ensure the future safety of civilian aviation. Arms control, he pointedly noted, would not be affected: "we must not give up our effort to reduce the arsenals of destructive weapons threatening the world."[80]

The Korean airliner incident was a particularly vivid illustration of Moscow's ineptitude, with regard to both air defense and public relations. The plane had been over Soviet territory for several hours before it was intercepted; even then Soviet pilots apparently thought they were shooting down an American spy plane and not an airliner. After acknowledging what had happened, Kremlin leaders nevertheless petulantly refused to apologize and even accused the Americans—without credible evidence—of having somehow staged the incident for intelligence purposes. It had all been a "sophisticated provocation, organized by the US special services," Soviet General Secretary Andropov insisted late in September: "If anyone had any illusions concerning the possibility of an evolution for the better in the policy of the current American administration, events of recent times have thoroughly dispelled them."[81] And in Novem-

---

[79]Reagan speech to American Legion convention, Seattle, August 23, 1983, *Reagan Public Papers: 1983*, p. 1192.

[80]Reagan television address, September 5, 1983, ibid., p. 1230. For the Korean airliner incident, see Alexander Dallin, *Black Box: KAL 007 and the Superpowers* (Berkeley: 1985); and Seymour M. Hersch, *"The Target Is Destroyed": What Really Happened to Flight 007 and What America Knew about It* (New York: 1987).

[81]Andropov statement, September 28, 1983, *Current Digest of the Soviet Press*, XXXV(October 26, 1983), 1. The most recent and thorough assessment of this incident concludes that the airliner was not in fact on an intelligence mission, but that the Reagan administration did withhold evidence that would have shown that the Soviet pilots had not realized they were shooting at a civilian airliner. [Hersch, *"The Target Is Destroyed,"* especially pp. 354–355.] It is an indication of President Reagan's luck—but also of a much better approach to public relations than the Russians showed in 1983—that when an American naval vessel accidentally shot down an Iranian airliner in the Persian Gulf in July, 1988, with the loss of 291 lives, the international repercussions from the incident were minimal.

ber, after the West German Bundestag had voted to go ahead with the long-planned deployment of Pershing II and cruise missiles, Soviet negotiators on orders from Moscow broke off talks on arms control altogether.[82]

Significantly, the president did not respond to these developments—as one might have expected him to—by reviving his "evil empire" rhetoric: instead he announced, in a remarkably conciliatory television address early in January, 1984, that the United States was "in its strongest position in years to establish a constructive and realistic working relationship with the Soviet Union."[83] It was possible to construct self-serving motives for this startling shift in tone. With a presidential campaign under-way, the White House was sensitive to Democratic charges that Reagan was the only postwar president not to have met with a Soviet leader while in office. Certainly it was to the advantage of the United States in its relations with Western Europe to look as reasonable as possible in the face of Soviet intransigence. But events would show that the president's interest in an improved relationship was based on more than just electoral politics or the needs of the alliance: it was only the unfortunate tendency of Soviet leaders to die upon taking office that was depriving the American chief executive—himself a spry septuagenarian—of a partner with whom to negotiate.[84]

In the months that followed Andropov's death in February, 1984, the Russians appear to have realized two things: that their tough line had failed to produce American or West European concessions, and that Reagan's chances for reelection were excellent. In June, Moscow offered to begin a new series of negotiations on banning weapons in space; the White House agreed on the condition that talks on strategic and intermediate-range nuclear forces take place as well. By the end of September—and to the dismay of Democratic partisans who saw Republicans snatching the "peace" issue from them—a contrite Soviet Foreign Minister Andrei Gromyko had come to Washington to dis-

---

[82]Talbott, *Deadly Gambits*, pp. 193–206.

[83]Reagan television address, January 16, 1984, *Reagan Public Papers: 1984*, pp. 40–44. The president concluded this address by speculating on how a typical Soviet couple—Ivan and Anya—might find they had much in common with a typical American couple—Jim and Sally: "They might even have decided that they were all going to get together for dinner some evening soon."

[84]See Reagan's comments to a meeting of regional editors and broadcasters, March 11, 1984, ibid., p. 270.

cuss these possibilities with the president himself. Shortly after Reagan's landslide reelection victory over Democratic candidate Walter Mondale in November, the United States and the Soviet Union announced that a new set of arms control negotiations would begin early the following year, linking together discussions on START, INF, and weapons in space.[85] And in December, a hitherto obscure member of the Soviet Politburo, Mikhail Gorbachev, announced while visiting Great Britain that the USSR was prepared to seek "radical solutions" looking toward a ban on nuclear missiles altogether.[86] Three months later, Andropov's feeble and unimaginative successor Chernenko himself expired, and Gorbachev—a man who was in no way feeble or unimaginative—became the General Secretary of the Communist Party of the Soviet Union. Nothing would ever be quite the same again.

## V

Several years after Gorbachev had come to power a still-vigorous George F. Kennan was asked in a television interview how so unconventional a Soviet leader could have risen to the top in a system that placed such a premium on conformity. Kennan's candid reply reflected the perplexity American experts on Soviet affairs have felt in seeking to account for the Gorbachev phenomenon: "I really cannot explain it."[87] It seemed most improbable that a regime so lacking in the capacity for innovation, self-evaluation, or even minimally-effective public relations should suddenly produce a leader who excelled in all of these qualities; even more remarkable was the fact that Gorbachev saw himself as a revolutionary—a breed not seen in Russia for decades—determined, as he put it, "to get out of the quagmire of conservatism, and to break the inertia of stagnation."[88] Whatever the circumstances that led to it, the accession of Gorbachev reversed almost overnight the pattern of

---

[85]For these developments, see Talbott, *Deadly Gambits*, pp. 350–356.

[86]*London Times*, December 18, 1984.

[87]Kennan television interview, MacNeil-Lehrer News Hour, December 21, 1988, Public Broadcasting Network.

[88]Mikhail Gorbachev, *Perestroika: New Thinking for Our Country and the World* (New York: 1987), p. 51.

the preceding four years: after March, 1985, it was the Soviet Union that seized the initiative in relations with the West. It did so in a way that was both reassuring and unnerving at the same time: by becoming so determinedly cooperative as to convince some supporters of containment in the United States and Western Europe—uneasy in the absence of the intransigence to which they had become accustomed—that the Russians were now seeking to defeat that strategy by depriving it, with sinister cleverness, of an object to be contained.[89]

The new Soviet attitude of cooperation began to appear as early as April, 1985, when Gorbachev announced a unilateral freeze on the further deployment of intermediate-range missiles in Europe and proposed a moratorium on all nuclear weapons tests; despite the American failure to reciprocate (on the grounds that it would not be possible to verify such a ban), Gorbachev maintained his own halt in Soviet testing through early 1987.[90] The Russians began to look more favorably on the possibility of "deep cuts" in strategic missile forces: when Nitze, never an SDI enthusiast, began quietly pushing for a deal that would trade limits on strategic defenses for a 50% reduction in nuclear arsenals over a ten-year period, Soviet negotiators responded with interest and publicly endorsed the idea late in September. In November, Gorbachev added yet another proposal to what was already on the table: an offer to allow the mutual on-site inspection of nuclear test facilities as a way to verify a comprehensive test ban.[91]

Meanwhile, President Reagan had moved quickly to establish a personal relationship with the new Soviet leader. The

---

[89]See Caspar A. Weinberger, "Arms Reductions and Deterrence," *Foreign Affairs*, LXVI(Spring, 1988), 701–719; also Lynn E. Davis, "Lessons of the INF Treaty," ibid., p. 723.

[89]Alan Neidle, "Nuclear Test Bans: History and Prospects," in George, Farley, and Dallin, eds., *U.S.–Soviet Security Cooperation*, pp. 200–201.

[91]Talbot, *The Master of the Game*, pp. 260–273; "Chronology 1985," *Foreign Affairs*, LXIV(America and the World 1985), 656–658. As SDI research progressed, the idea of a "shield" against incoming missiles began to look less and less feasible from both a technological and budgetary point of view. The Russians nonetheless continued to offer substantial cuts in existing land-based ICBMs in return for Washington's agreement not to deploy this nonexistent system; this led presidential assistant for national security affairs Robert MacFarlane to characterize SDI as "the greatest sting operation in history." [Talbott, *The Master of the Game*, p. 204.]

chief executive's attitude toward Moscow had softened considerably in the two years since the "evil empire" speech; moreover, British Prime Minister Thatcher—not known herself for mincing words when it came to the Russians—had described Gorbachev, after meeting him late in 1984, as someone with whom "we can do business together."[92] Within four days of Gorbachev's taking power, the president was characterizing the Russians as "in a different frame of mind than they've been in the past...[T]hey, I believe, are really going to try and, with us, negotiate a reduction of armaments." And within four months the White House was announcing that Reagan would meet Gorbachev at Geneva in November for the first Soviet-American summit since 1979.[93]

The Geneva summit, like so many before it, was long on symbolism and short on substance. The two leaders appeared to get along well with each other: they behaved, as one Reagan adviser later put it, "like a couple of fellows who had run into each other at the club and discovered that they had a lot in common."[94] They also surprised the press by holding unexpectedly lengthy personal conversations, some of them with only interpreters present. Reagan agreed to discuss deep cuts in strategic weapons systems and improved verification, but he made it clear that he was not prepared to forgo development of the Strategic Defense Initiative in order to get them. His reason—which Gorbachev may not have taken seriously until this point—had to do with his determination to retain SDI as a means ultimately of rendering nuclear weapons obsolete. The president's stubbornness on this point precluded progress, at least for the moment, on what was coming to be called the "grand compromise": Nitze's idea of accepting limits on SDI in return for sweeping reductions in strategic missiles.[95] But it did leave the way open for an alert Gorbachev, detecting the president's personal enthusiasm for nuclear abolition, to surprise

---

[92]*London Times*, December 18, 1984.

[93]White House announcement, July 2, 1985, *AFP: 1985*, p. 402n. For Reagan's comment, see his reply to questions from members of the Magazine Publishing Association, March 14, 1985, *Reagan Public Papers: 1985*, p. 285.

[94]Donald T. Regan, *For the Record: From Wall Street to Washington* (New York: 1988), p. 351.

[95]For the Geneva summit, see ibid., pp. 327–355; also Talbott, *The Master of the Game*, pp. 285–288.

the world in January, 1986, with his own plan for accomplishing that objective: a Soviet-American agreement to rid the world of nuclear weapons altogether by the year 2000.[96]

It was easy to question Gorbachev's motives in making so radical a proposal in so public a manner with no advance warning: he appeared to be attempting to scuttle SDI by substituting a nuclear-free world based on diplomatic, not technological, safeguards. Certainly any discussion of even reducing—much less abolishing—nuclear arsenals would raise difficult questions with American allies, where an abhorrence of nuclear weapons continued to coexist uneasily alongside the conviction that only their presence could deter superior Soviet conventional forces. Nor was the Gorbachev proposal clear on how Russians and Americans could ever impose abolition, even if they themselves agreed to it, on other nuclear and near-nuclear powers. And, for those who believed that nuclear deterrence had helped make possible four decades of superpower competition without superpower war, Gorbachev was noticeably silent on what might replace it as an equivalent stabilizing mechanism. Still, the line between rhetoric and conviction is a thin one: the first Reagan-Gorbachev summit may not only have created a personal bond between the two leaders; it may also have sharpened a vague but growing sense in the minds of both men that, despite all the difficulties in constructing an alternative, an indefinite continuation of life under nuclear threat was not a tolerable condition for either of their countries, and that their own energies might very well be directed toward overcoming that situation.

That both Reagan and Gorbachev were thinking along these lines became clear at their second meeting, the most extraordinary Soviet-American summit of the postwar era, held on very short notice at Reykjavik, Iceland, in October, 1986. The months that preceded Reykjavik had seen little tangible progress toward arms control; there had also developed, in August, an unpleasant skirmish between intelligence agencies as the KGB, in apparent retaliation for the FBI's highly publicized arrest of a Soviet United Nations official in New York on espionage charges, set up, seized, and held *US News* Moscow correspondent Nicholas Daniloff on trumped-up accusations for

---

[96]Ibid., pp. 289–290.

just under a month.[97] It was a sobering reminder that the Soviet-American relationship existed at several levels, and that cordiality in one did not rule out the possibility of confrontation in others. The Daniloff affair also brought opportunity, though, for in the course of negotiations to settle it Gorbachev proposed a quick "preliminary" summit, to be held within two weeks, to try to break the stalemate in negotiations over intermediate-range nuclear forces in Europe, the aspect of arms control negotiations where progress at a more formal summit seemed most likely. Reagan immediately agreed.[98]

But when the president and his advisers arrived at Hofdi House, the bleak, windswept setting outside Reykjavik where the meeting was to take place, they found that Gorbachev had much more grandiose proposals in mind. These included not only an endorsement of 50% cuts in Soviet and American strategic weapons across the board, but also agreement not to demand the inclusion of British and French nuclear weapons in these calculations—a concession that removed a major stumbling block to START—and acceptance in principle of President Reagan's 1981 "zero option" for intermediate-range nuclear forces, all in return for an American commitment not to undermine SALT I's ban on strategic defenses for the next ten years. Impressed by the scope of these concessions, the American side, with—remarkably—Richard Perle taking the lead, quickly put together a compromise that would have cut ballistic missiles to zero within a decade in return for the right, after that time, to deploy strategic defenses against the bomber and cruise-missile forces that would be left. (President Reagan had, the previous July, proposed such a phasing out of ballistic missiles, although with no specific timetable.) Gorbachev quickly countered by proposing the abolition of *all* nuclear weapons within ten years, thus moving his original deadline from the year 2000 up to 1996. According to the account of at least one participant, Reagan quickly replied: *"All* nuclear weapons? Well, Mikhail, that's exactly what I've been talking about all along....That's always been my goal."[99]

[97]See Nicholas Daniloff, *Two Lives, One Russia* (Boston: 1988).
[98]Regan, *For the Record,* pp. 376–381.
[99]Quoted in ibid., p. 390. See also Talbott, *The Master of the Game,* pp. 315–325.

A series of events set in motion by a Soviet diplomat's arrest on a New York subway platform and by the reciprocal framing of an American journalist on a Moscow street had wound up with the two most powerful men in the world agreeing—for the moment, and to the astonishment of their aides[100]—on the abolition of all nuclear weapons within ten years. But the moment did not last. Gorbachev went on to insist, as a condition for nuclear abolition, upon a ban on the laboratory testing of SDI, which Reagan immediately interpreted as an effort to kill strategic defense altogether. Because the ABM treaty does allow for some laboratory testing, the differences between the two positions were not all that great. But in the hothouse atmosphere of this cold-climate summit no one explored such details, and the meeting broke up in disarray, acrimony, and mutual disappointment.[101]

It was probably just as well. The sweeping agreements contemplated at Reykjavik grew out of hasty improvisation and high-level posturing, not careful thought. They suffered from all the deficiencies of Gorbachev's unilateral proposal for nuclear abolition earlier in the year; they also revealed how susceptible the leaders of the United States and the Soviet Union were to each other's amplitudinous rhetoric. It was as if Reagan and Gorbachev had been trying desperately to outbid the other in a gigantic but surrealistic auction, with the diaphanous prospect of a nuclear-free world somehow on the block.[102]

---

[100]The White House later tried to deny that Reagan had agreed to this: "You couldn't have," national security assistant John M. Poindexter is said to have insisted. "John," the president replied, "I was there, and I did." [John Newhouse, "The Abolitionist," New Yorker, LXIV(January 9, 1989), 62.]

[101]Ibid., p. 64. See also Regan, For the Record, pp. 391–396.

[102]As an illustration of what can happen when a summit conference gets out of control, Reykjavik resembled as nothing else the 1905 meeting between Tsar Nicholas II and Kaiser William II in which, in a single memorable evening, they personally negotiated and signed a treaty settling long-standing Russo-German differences, only to have their horrified governments—and allies—immediately repudiate it. "One should never forget," one of the Kaiser's advisers later commented, "that a discussion between two princes is propitious only when it confines itself to the weather." [Quoted in Michael Balfour, The Kaiser and His Times (Boston: 1964), p. 257.] For post-mortems on Reykjavik, see Stanley Hoffmann, "An Icelandic Saga," New York Review of Books, XXXIII(November 20, 1986), 15–17; and James Schlesinger, "Reykjavik and Revelations: A Turn of the Tide?" Foreign Affairs, LXV(America and the World, 1986), 426–446.

Reykjavik did, however, produce substantive—if not cosmic—results. The two sides managed to establish the framework for agreements looking toward the elimination of all intermediate-range nuclear missiles, toward cuts in strategic missiles arsenals that would go well beyond what President Carter had so unsuccessfully proposed to the Russians in 1977, and toward an understanding that there would be no immediate withdrawal from the ABM treaty to deploy strategic defenses. Improvisation under pressure—at least on these matters—did pay off. And despite its abrupt end, the summit appears not to have damaged the personal relationship between Reagan and Gorbachev—as unlikely a pair, in their own way, as Kennedy and Khrushchev had been a quarter of a century earlier: indeed, Reykjavik may have reinforced it as each discovered the intensity of the other's desire somehow to break the nuclear stalemate.

Meanwhile, the Gorbachev "revolution" inside the Soviet Union was paralleling these striking developments in arms control. The new Soviet leader's determination to bring about fundamental "restructuring" (*perestroika*) within the USSR had produced something not seen since the days of Khrushchev: an official willingness to acknowledge error. Gorbachev's comments on his predecessors were scathing: they had been too much inclined, he complained, to making "ambitious and unfounded promises and predictions," to indulging in "grandiloquent twaddle,...red tape, unwarranted splendor, abstract slogans, and recurrences of pompous ostentation."[103] Efforts to construct a centrally-planned modern industrial economy had produced only stagnation: socialism could be made to work, Gorbachev seemed to be saying, only by making room for individual initiative and personal gain. The regime now candidly acknowledged past human rights abuses and sought to make amends by releasing dissidents, lifting most restrictions on emigration, and stressing the need for the rule of law at home. Openness (*glasnost'*) became the order of the day as the Soviet media suddenly and luxuriantly blossomed with unorthodox viewpoints, citizen complaints, and even Western-style investi-

---

[103]Gorbachev, *Perestroika*, pp. 43, 105.

gative reporting. Once taboo historical topics were now openly debated. And when a Soviet nuclear reactor at Chernobyl exploded in April, 1986, spreading radioactive material throughout the Northern Hemisphere, the Russians after an initial hesitation admitted Western journalists, scientists, and medical personnel to the site; the Kremlin's public report on the disaster was fully comparable, in its candor and self-criticism, to the American investigation of a similar but far less destructive nuclear accident at Three-Mile Island in 1979.[104]

Soviet foreign and military policy, too, had begun to show the effects of Gorbachev's leadership. One of his first actions after taking power had been to replace the dour but durable Andrei Gromyko as foreign minister—Gromyko had held the post for twenty-eight years—with an engaging Georgian, Eduard Shevardnadze. There soon followed an apparent effort to eliminate as many sources of friction with the West as possible: the Russians made it clear that they would provide only limited assistance to the Sandinistas in Nicaragua; in Angola, negotiations looking toward the removal of Soviet-supplied Cuban troops began to show promise; the Vietnamese, presumably with Moscow's encouragement, announced their intention to withdraw their forces from Cambodia; and, most important, in April, 1988, the Russians committed themselves to evacuating all of their troops from Afghanistan within nine months, thereby acknowledging an ignominious military defeat comparable only to that suffered by the United States in Vietnam a decade and a half earlier.[105] Meanwhile—and in line with Gorbachev's emphasis on "new thinking"—Soviet military doctrine was shifting from an emphasis on offensive operations to one that stressed the importance of defense; the general secretary himself began talking about the need for "mutual" as opposed to unilateral security. And in a striking advance over Brezhnev's position, Gorbachev in 1987 acknowledged that in an era

---

[104]For accounts of Soviet internal developments under Gorbachev, see Bialer and Mandelbaum, eds., *Gorbachev's Russia and American Foreign Policy*, especially pp. 3–299; also Seweryn Bialer, ed., *Politics, Society and Nationality: Inside Gorbachev's Russia* (Boulder, Colorado: 1989).

[105]Rosanne Klass, "Afghanistan: The Accords," *Foreign Affairs*, LXVI (Summer, 1988), 922–945.

of nuclear weapons the concept of "peaceful coexistence" was no longer consistent with that of "class struggle": just as cooperation between the Soviet Union and its Western allies had been possible to defeat fascism, "today, too, in the face of a still worse danger, states belonging to different social systems can and must cooperate with one another in the name of peace."[106]

As if to reflect this principle, negotiations on arms control continued in the year that followed Reykjavik, with both sides edging toward the long-awaited "grand compromise" that would defer SDI in return for progress toward a START agreement. Reagan and Gorbachev did sign an intermediate-range nuclear forces treaty in Washington in December, 1987, which, for the first time, provided that Russians and Americans would actually dismantle and destroy—literally before each other's eyes—an entire category of nuclear missiles.[107] There followed a triumphal Reagan visit to Moscow in May, 1988, featuring the unusual sight of a Soviet general secretary and an American president strolling amiably through Red Square, greeting tourists and bouncing babies in front of Lenin's tomb, while their respective military aides—each carrying the codes needed to launch nuclear missiles at each other's territory—stood discreetly in the background. Gorbachev made an equally triumphal visit to New York in December, 1988, to address the United Nations General Assembly: there he announced a *unilateral* Soviet cut of some 500,000 ground troops, a major step toward moving arms control into the realm of conventional forces.[108]

When, on the same day Gorbachev spoke in New York, a disastrous earthquake killed some 25,000 Soviet Armenians, the

---

[106]Gorbachev, *Perestroika*, pp. 146–147. See also Jack Snyder, "The Gorbachev Revolution: A Waning of Soviet Expansionism?" *International Security*, XII(Winter, 1987/88), 93–131; and Stephen M. Meyer, "The Sources and Prospects of Gorbachev's New Political Thinking on Security," ibid., XIII(Fall, 1988), 124–163.

[107]Michael Mandelbaum, "The Reagan Administration and the Nature of Arms Control," in Joseph Kruzel, ed., *American Defense Annual: 1988–1989* (Lexington, Massachusetts: 1988), pp. 204–208. Well-connected Russians were given to presenting American friends, during this period, with small pocket-sized pieces of cut-up SS-20 rockets as souvenirs.

[108]*New York Times*, December 6, 1989.

outpouring of aid from the United States and other Western countries was unprecedented since the days of Lend-Lease. One had the eerie feeling, watching anguished television reports from the rubble that had been the cities of Leninakan and Stipak—the breakdown of emergency services, the coffins stacked like logs in city parks, the mass burials—that one had glimpsed, on a small scale, something of what a nuclear war might actually be like. The images suggested just how vulnerable both superpowers remained after almost a half-century of trying to minimize vulnerabilities. They thereby reinforced what had become almost a ritual incantation pronounced by both Reagan and Gorbachev at each of their now-frequent summits: "A nuclear war cannot be won and must never be fought."[109]

But as the Reagan administration prepared to leave office the following month, in an elegaic mood very different from the grim militancy with which it had assumed its responsibilities eight years earlier, the actual prospect of a nuclear holocaust seemed more remote than at any point since the Soviet-American nuclear rivalry had begun. Accidents, to be sure, could always happen. Irrationality, though blessedly rare since 1945, could never be ruled out. There was reason for optimism, though, in the fact that as George Bush prepared to enter the White House early in 1989, the point at issue no longer seemed to be "how to fight the Cold War" at all, but rather "is the Cold War over?"[110]

Only future historians could settle that question with any assurance, but one thing did seem clear as the 1980s came to an end: containment had finally and belatedly worked, much in

---

[109]See Bundy, *Danger and Survival*, p. 583.

[110]Prime Minister Margaret Thatcher noted, accurately enough, in December, 1988: "If anyone else had said the cold war was over, you might be much more alarmed. With me, you need not be alarmed, because you know I will always keep up defense." *U.S. News*, CV(December 19, 1988), 18. See also the transcript of President Bush's first press conference, January 27, 1989, *New York Times*, January 28, 1989; and George F. Kennan, "After the Cold War," *New York Times Magazine*, February 5, 1989. For the preliminaries to this discussion, see W. W. Rostow, "On Ending the Cold War," *Foreign Affairs*, LXV(Spring, 1987), 831–851; John Lewis Gaddis, "How the Cold War Might End," *Atlantic*, CCLX(November, 1987), 88–100; and Richard H. Ullman, "Ending the Cold War," *Foreign Policy*, #72(Fall, 1988), 130–151.

the way that Kennan had predicted it would in 1946. For what were Gorbachev's reforms if not the long-delayed "mellowing" of Soviet society that Kennan had said would take place with the passage of time? The Stalinist system that had required outside adversaries to justify its own existence now seemed to be passing from the scene; Gorbachev appeared to have concluded that the Soviet Union could continue to be a great power in world affairs only through the introduction of a market economy, democratic political institutions, official accountability, and respect for the rule of law at home.[111] But if that was true, it suggested an even more astonishing conclusion: that the very survival of the ideology Lenin had imposed on Russia in 1917 now required infiltration—perhaps even subversion—by precisely the ideology the great revolutionary had sworn to overthrow.

For this reason, it would have been most unwise, in 1989, to assume that Gorbachev could remain in power indefinitely, or to speculate on who—or what—might replace him. What one could say with confidence was that the changes he had wrought in both the internal character and external behavior of the Soviet state had gone far beyond what even the most adventurous foreign expert on the Soviet Union would have predicted in 1985; even if Gorbachev should be overthrown, it would be very difficult now to revert to the way things had been before he appeared on the scene. And that meant that the future of Soviet-American relations, whether for good or ill, was unlikely to resemble what Soviet-American relations had been during what the world had once known as the Cold War.

---

[111]Bialer, ed., *Politics, Society and Nationality, passim.*

# CHAPTER XI

# *Epilogue*

S ECURITY IS, OF COURSE, A RELATIVE AND NOT AN ABSOLUTE CONCEPT; much in international affairs depends on how statesmen define it. The history of relations between the United States and Russia can be written largely in terms of variations, within both countries, between what might be called "universalist" and "particularist" approaches to the problem of achieving security in the world.[1] The "universalist," equating security with homogeneity, discounts the possibility of achieving that condition until the international environment has been modified to resemble the nation; only then can there be assurance that nothing in that environment can pose a threat. The "particularist" seeks to ensure that nothing in the international environment can harm the nation, whether the environment resembles the nation or not; security, from this perspective, requires diversity. The "universalist" sees harmony as a distant but attainable prospect in world affairs, and thinks that security ultimately depends on achieving it. The "particularist" regards harmony as unlikely, but thinks that security can be obtained nonetheless, through a careful balancing of power, interests, and antagonisms.

Not surprisingly, periods of relative cordiality in Russian-American relations have coincided with those points at which particularism has prevailed in both countries. Thus the long history of amicable contacts during the nineteenth century grew

---

[1] I have employed here, in a slightly different context, terminology used by George F. Kennan in a 1948 Policy Planning Staff paper, PPS 23, "Review of Current Trends, U.S. Foreign Policy," February 24, 1948, *FR: 1948*, I, 526–527. See also Kennan, *The Realities of American Foreign Policy* (Princeton: 1954), pp. 15–16; and Charles Burton Marshall, *The Limits of Foreign Policy* (Baltimore: 1968), pp. 38–39.

out of the American government's restraint regarding European issues, and out of the fact that the Russians, while hardly particularist in dealing with their immediate neighbors, were so when it came to the affairs of the New World. This pattern of mutual forbearance broke down during the late nineteenth and early twentieth centuries, first as a result of a broadened American perception of vital interests, then from the advent within Russia of an ideology possessed of global pretensions. Despite the competing universalist legacies of Wilson and Lenin, cooperation remained possible where interests coincided, as in the area of economic relations during the 1920s or military collaboration against the Axis in World War II. Even after that latter event had catapulted both powers into a contest for world leadership, reason dictated respect for certain "rules of the game," most notably an inclination to avoid risks that might lead to nuclear war. All too often, though, relations between Russia and the United States in the twentieth century reflected the conviction, on each side, that its rival would not rest until it had altered fundamentally the environment the other considered necessary for its security.

Neither Russians nor Americans are likely explicitly to abandon their respective ideological positions anytime soon. But as the careers of Ronald Reagan and Mikhail Gorbachev amply demonstrate, ideologies do have a way of bending to accommodate circumstances. And what has been striking about the Cold War is the extent to which the passage of time—time purchased, one suspects, largely through nuclear stalemate—has allowed common interests to emerge that neither Washington nor Moscow could have anticipated in 1945. It is as if the very condition of being global rivals transforms interests and moderates ideologies: however different their starting points, however contradictory their avowed objectives, even bitter antagonists can develop a joint stake in perpetuating the international system within which they are obliged to compete, if the alternative is the unknown. From this perspective, particularism and universalism are not as contradictory as they might seem.

But international systems themselves rise and fall: nothing guarantees that the postwar order Russians and Americans have carved out for themselves will last forever, or even that the indices by which power is measured will remain what they have been. One circumstance future Soviet and American leaders will almost certainly have to take into account is their declining ability to shape events in the world at large.[2] The two countries are approaching the point at which they will be able to project military power safely only by proxy: force may soon be a luxury allowed only to small, "unsophisticated" states—not because their "sophisticated" counterparts have any monopoly on wisdom, or even peaceful intent, but because the costs and risks of direct involvement, as the experiences of Vietnam and Afghanistan so painfully revealed, have soared far beyond possible gains.[3] And "influence," short of force, has proven to be a decidedly fragile commodity in what is now, more than ever, the "age of nationalism." Logic, it would appear, leaves Washington and Moscow little choice but to embrace particularism: to learn to live with a diverse world.

Unfortunately, international relations do not always proceed in a logical manner. Foreign policy ultimately reflects the internal structure of the states it serves; accommodation to diversity requires not just a rational assessment of the international situation but a favorable domestic climate as well. At the beginning of 1989, that climate, in both the United States and the Soviet Union, was as auspicious as it had been at any time since the end of World War II: Gorbachev was well on the way toward dismantling a Soviet structure of power that had required outside enemies, while Reagan had unexpectedly rebuilt the American domestic consensus in support of detente. But these changes, dramatic though they are, remain at the mercy of internal forces in both countries that do not always proceed from a concern above all else to sustain international systemic stability. Prospects for an amicable Soviet-American relationship will continue to depend, as they have in the past, on the extent to which a particularist view of the world can be reconciled with the requirements and exigencies of wielding power at home.

Still, it is worth noting that on November 8, 1988, the day George Bush was elected president of the United States, the nations of Europe surpassed the previous record, set in 1871–1914, for their longest period without war in modern history. That

---

[2] See, on this point, Kennedy, *The Rise and Fall of the Great Powers*, especially pp. 395–413.

[3] See John Mueller, *Retreat from Doomsday: The Obsolescence of Major War* (New York: 1989).

was an achievement in itself, but the even greater achievement—one for which Russians and Americans, as well as Europeans, deserve credit—was that hardly anyone noticed. For in a manner so imperceptible as to be evident only in retrospect, the Cold War has somehow evolved into a Long Peace: it has not been universal peace, or a wholly just peace, or even a coherently-designed peace. But it has not been World War III either, and that simple fact—after four and a half decades—ought to provide grounds for quiet satisfaction on the part of Americans and Russians over the relative wisdom with which they have managed their long, at times acrimonious, but so far not disastrous relationship.

# Bibliographical Essay

FOR A BOOK BURDENED WITH THE NUMBER OF FOOTNOTES THIS ONE HAS, an extended bibliographical essay would only be an exercise in redundancy. What follows, rather, is an attempt to identify and evaluate the basic body of literature with which students of Russian-American relations should be familiar. I have also ventured some suggestions as to where more work needs to be done.

First, a word about primary sources. From the American side, the most important single source is the Department of State's documentary series, *Foreign Relations of the United States*, which begins in 1861 and has, as of this writing, reached 1957 for relations with the Soviet Union. Published documentary sources for the pre-1861 period exist, but the most reliable approach is to work through the documents themselves, which are conveniently available on microfilm from the National Archives for the period 1781–1954. Because *Foreign Relations* is selective, especially for the pre-World War I period, these microfilmed records provide a valuable supplement even for the years covered by that series. For the period since 1954, the *Declassified Documents Quarterly* (Carrollton, Virginia, 1975– ) is a convenient but by no means complete guide to documents that have become available through systematic review or Freedom of Information Act requests. Public documents can be followed through several Department of State publications, including: *A Decade of American Foreign Policy: Basic Documents, 1941–1949* Revised Edition (Washington: 1985); *American Foreign Policy, 1950–1955: Basic Documents* (Washington: 1957), 2 volumes; *American Foreign Policy: Current Documents, 1956–1967, 1977–* (Washington: 1959–1969, 1983– ). For presidential documents, the standard source is the *Public Papers of the Presidents of the United States* (Washington: 1960– ).

Russian documents, as one might expect, are much less accessible. A pioneering effort to document the early history of the Russian-American relationship from archival sources on both sides is the volume *The United States and Russia: The Beginnings of Relations, 1765–1815* (Washington: 1980), prepared by a joint Soviet-American editorial board under the direction of Sergei L. Tikhvinskii and David F. Trask. But Russian archives for most twentieth century topics are not open to Western historians, and for the postwar period, even Soviet historians have only minimal access to them. Students with a knowledge of Russian can derive some benefit, however, from several series published by the Soviet Ministry of Foreign Affairs, including: *Vneshnaia politika Rossii XIX i nachala XX veka [Russian Foreign Policy in the 19th and the Beginning of the 20th Centuries]* (Moscow: 1960–    ); *Dokumenty vneshnei politiki SSSR [Documents on the Foreign Policy of the U.S.S.R]* (Moscow: 1957–    ); and *Sovetsko-amerikanskie otnosheniia vo vremiia velikoi otechestvennoi voiny, 1941–1945 [Soviet-American Relations during the Period of the Great Patriotic War, 1941–1945]* (Moscow: 1984), 2 volumes. A collection of reports from Russian ministers in Washington between 1818 and 1823 was published in the *American Historical Review*, XVIII(1913), 309–345, 537–562; also useful is Frank A. Golder, *Guide to Materials for American History in Russian Archives* (Washington: 1917, 1937). For Soviet public documents on foreign policy up to World War II, the standard source is Jane Degras, ed., *Soviet Documents on Foreign Policy, 1917–41* (London: 1951–1953), 3 volumes; for later periods the series *Documents on International Affairs* (London: 1929–    ) is helpful.

There are three general surveys of Russian-American relations from the American side, all now badly out of date. Foster Rhea Dulles's *The Road to Teheran: The Story of Russia and America, 1781–1943* (Princeton: 1944) is a competent discussion, but reflects the period of wartime cooperation during which it was written. Thomas A. Bailey's *America Faces Russia: Russian-American Relations from Early Times to Our Own Day* (Ithaca: 1950) is vigorous and anecdotal, but also much influenced by the atmosphere within which it was composed. The most complete survey is William A. Williams, *American-Russian Relations, 1781–1947* (New York: 1952), a pioneering work in its anticipation of New Left revisionism but not always persuasive in its conclusions. For a Soviet perspective on the overall history of Russian-American relations, a good place to start is Nikolai V. Sivachev and Nikolai N. Yakovlev, *Russia and the United States,* translated by Olga Adler Titelbaum (Chicago: 1979).

Among surveys of Soviet-American relations since the Bolshevik Revolution the most eloquent account (although heavily weighted toward the 1917–1921 period) is George F. Kennan's *Russia and the West under Lenin and Stalin* (Boston: 1961). Two works covering the entire history of Soviet-American relations but with emphasis on the Cold War are Andre Fontaine, *History of the Cold War* (New York: 1968–1969), 2 volumes, and D. F. Fleming, *The Cold War and Its Origins, 1917–1960* (Garden City, New York: 1961), 2 volumes, an early revisionist account. Adam B. Ulam's authoritative *Expansion and Coexistence: The History of Soviet Foreign Policy, 1917–73,* Second Edition (New York: 1974), shows where policy toward the United States fit within the overall priorities of Soviet foreign policy. Two important memoirs covering much of the history of Soviet-American relations are George F. Kennan, *Memoirs* (Boston: 1967, 1972), 2 volumes, and Charles E. Bohlen, *Witness to History: 1929–1969* (New York: 1973). For a revealing Soviet perspective on these events, see A. A. Gromyko and B. N. Ponomarev, eds., *Soviet Foreign Policy, 1917–1980* (Moscow: 1981), 2 volumes.

Soviet scholars have been active in studying the early history of Russian-American relations, most notably N. N. Bolkhovitinov, whose *The Beginnings of Russian-American Relations, 1775–1815,* translated by Elena Levin (Cambridge, Massachusetts: 1975), is now the definitive account. Bolkhovitinov can be supplemented with two much older studies: John C. Hildt, *Early Relations of the United States with Russia* (Baltimore: 1906); and Benjamin Platt Thomas, *Russo-American Relations, 1815–1867* (Baltimore: 1930). Also valuable for the particular topics with which they deal are Alfred W. Crosby, Jr., *America, Russia, Hemp and Napoleon: American Trade with Russia and the Baltic, 1783–1812* (Columbus: 1965), Alan Dowty, *The Limits of American Isolationism: The United States and the Crimean War* (New York: 1971), and Max Laserson, *The American Impact on Russia—Diplomatic and Ideological—1874–1917.* Norman Saul is now completing what will become the standard history of Russian-American relations up to 1917.

One topic from this period that has been well covered is the Alaska Purchase and the events leading up to it. Among the best accounts are Howard I. Kushner, *Conflict on the Northwest*

*Coast: American-Russian Rivalry in the Pacific Northwest, 1790–1867* (Westport, Connecticut: 1975), Ronald J. Jensen, *The Alaska Purchase and Russian American Relations* (Seattle: 1975), and Paul S. Holbo, *Tarnished Expansion: The Alaska Scandal, the Press, and Congress, 1867–1871* (Knoxville: 1983). See also Victor J. Farrar, *The Annexation of Russian-America to the United States* (Washington: 1937), and Hector Chevigny, *Russian-America: The Great Alaskan Venture, 1741–1867* (New York: 1965).

The only comprehensive history of Russian-American relations during the period immediately after the Alaska Purchase is by a Soviet scholar, G. P. Kuropiatnik, *Rossiia i SShA: ekonomicheskie, kul'turnye i diplomaticheskie sviazi, 1867–1881* [*Russia and the USA: Economic, Cultural and Diplomatic Relations, 1867–1881*] (Moscow: 1981). There is still no completely satisfactory account of American concern regarding Russian persecution of Jews and dissidents in the late nineteenth and early twentieth centuries, although Stephen M. Berk, *Year of Crisis, Year of Hope: Russian Jewry and the Pogroms of 1881–1882* (Westport, Connecticut: 1985), does deal briefly with the issue, and there are good articles on this subject by Naomi Cohen, Clifford Egan, Ann E. Healy, Ronald J. Jensen, Philip Schoenberg, Allan Spetter, and Taylor Stults, all cited in the text. Some attention is also paid to the problem in David Hecht, *Russian Radicals Look to America, 1825–1894* (Cambridge, Massachusetts: 1947), and in Arthur W. Thompson and Robert W. Hart, *The Uncertain Crusade: America and the Russian Revolution of 1905* (Amherst, Massachusetts: 1970), but neither is a satisfactory account. The only full biography of the first George Kennan is Frederick F. Travis, *George Kennan and the American-Russian Relationship, 1865–1924* (Athens, Ohio: 1989); but see also E. I. Melamed, *Dzhordzh Kennan protiv tsarisma* [*George Kennan against Tsarism*] (Moscow: 1981). For an interesting collection of accounts by Russian travelers in the United States, see Olga Peters Hasty and Suzanne Fusso, eds., *America through Russian Eyes, 1874–1926* (New Haven: 1988).

Russian-American antagonism in East Asia during this period has been thoroughly covered. The most satisfactory single account is still Edward H. Zabriskie, *American-Russian Rivalry in the Far East: A Study in Diplomacy and Power Politics, 1895–1914* (Philadelphia: 1946). Pauline Tompkins, *American-Russian Relations in the Far East* (New York: 1949), treats the subject within a broader chronological framework. Other works which address this topic in varying degrees of detail are: Howard K. Beale,

*Theodore Roosevelt and the Rise of America to World Power* (Baltimore: 1956); Tyler Dennett, *Roosevelt and the Russo-Japanese War* (Garden City, New York: 1925); Raymond A. Esthus, *Theodore Roosevelt and Japan* (Seattle: 1966) and *Double Eagle and Rising Sun: The Russians and Japanese at Portsmouth in 1905* (Durham, North Carolina, 1988); Michael H. Hunt, *Frontier Defense and the Open Door: Manchuria in Chinese-American Relations, 1895–1911* (New Haven: 1973); Frederick W. Marks III, *Velvet on Iron: The Diplomacy of Theodore Roosevelt* (Lincoln, Nebraska: 1979); Charles Neu, *An Uncertain Friendship: Theodore Roosevelt and Japan, 1906–1909* (Cambridge, Massachusetts: 1967); Walter V. and Marie V. Scholes, *The Foreign Policies of the Taft Administration* (Columbia, Missouri: 1970); Eugene P. Trani, *The Treaty of Portsmouth: An Adventure in American Diplomacy* (Lexington: 1969); John A. White, *The Diplomacy of the Russo-Japanese War* (Princeton: 1964); Marilyn Blatt Young, *The Rhetoric of Empire: American China Policy, 1895–1901* (Cambridge, Massachusetts: 1968); and a Soviet account, L. I. Zubok, *Ekspansionistskaia politika SShA v nachale XX veka* [*Expansionist Policies of the USA at the Beginning of the 20th Century*] (Moscow: 1969).

Secondary sources are still thin for Russian-American economic relations prior to World War I. Two dated but still valuable unpublished dissertations are George S. Queen, "The United States and the Material Advance in Russia, 1887–1906" (University of Illinois, 1942), and Gilbert C. Kohlenberg, "Russian-American Economic Relations, 1906–1917" (University of Illinois, 1951). Fred V. Carstensen, *American Enterprise in Foreign Markets: Studies of Singer and International Harvester in Imperial Russia* (Chapel Hill: 1984), documents the activity of two large American corporations in Russia during the late Tsarist period. For Russian-American relations immediately prior to American entry into World War I, see R. Sh. Ganelin, *Rossiia i SShA, 1914–1917* [*Russia and the USA, 1914–1917*] (Leningrad: 1969), and Benson Lee Grayson, *Russian-American Relations in World War I* (New York: 1979).

The definitive work on the United States and the Bolshevik Revolution is, of course, George F. Kennan's magisterial *Soviet-American Relations, 1917–1920* (Princeton: 1956, 1958) 2 volumes. Kennan's account should be supplemented, however, with Arno Mayer's *Wilson vs. Lenin: Political Origins of the New Diplomacy, 1917–1918* (New Haven: 1958) and *The Politics and Diplomacy of Peacemaking: Containment and Counterrevolution at*

*Versailles, 1918–1919* (New York: 1967), as well as N. Gordon Levin, *Woodrow Wilson and World Politics* (New York: 1968). For a comprehensive Soviet account, see L. A. Gvishiani, *Sovetskaia Rossiia i SShA, 1917–1920* [*Soviet Russia and the USA, 1917–1920*] (Moscow: 1970).

There is no complete account of American relations with the Provisional Government, but two helpful dissertations are Harry H. Savage, "Official Policies and Relations of the United States with the Provisional Government of Russia, March–November, 1917" (University of Minnesota, 1971), and Alton Earl Ingrams, "The Root Mission to Russia, 1917" (Louisiana State University, 1970). There is an extensive literature on the decision to intervene in Russia and its aftermath: see especially William S. Graves, *America's Siberian Adventure: 1918–1920* (New York: 1931), an absorbing account by the commander of United States forces in Siberia; three books by Leonid I. Strakhovsky, *American Opinion about Russia: 1917–1920* (Toronto: 1961), *The Origins of American Intervention in North Russia, 1918* (Princeton: 1937), and *Intervention at Archangel* (Princeton: 1944); John A. White, *The Siberian Intervention* (Princeton: 1950); Betty M. Unterberger, *America's Siberian Expedition, 1918–1920* (Durham, North Carolina: 1956) and *The United States, Revolutionary Russia, and the Rise of Czechoslovakia* (Chapel Hill: 1989); Robert D. Warth, *The Allies and the Russian Revolution from the Fall of the Monarchy to the Peace of Brest-Litovsk* (Durham, North Carolina, 1954); John M. Thompson, *Russia, Bolshevism, and the Versailles Peace* (Princeton: 1966); Robert J. Maddox, *The Unknown War with Russia: Wilson's Siberian Intervention* (San Rafael, California: 1977); and Benjamin D. Rhodes, *The Anglo-American Winter War with Russia, 1918–1919: A Diplomatic and Military Tragicomedy* (Westport, Connecticut: 1988).

Other useful treatments of special topics relating to Russian-American relations during the Revolution include: Beatrice Farnsworth, *William C. Bullitt and the Soviet Union* (Bloomington: 1967); David F. Trask, *The United States in the Supreme War Council: American War Aims and Inter-Allied Strategy, 1917–1918* (Middletown, Connecticut: 1961); W. B. Fowler, *British-American Relations, 1917–1918: The Role of Sir William Wiseman* (Princeton: 1969), good on the role of coalition diplomacy in the decision to intervene; Christopher Lasch, *American Liberals and the Russian Revolution* (New York: 1962), and Robert K. Murray,

*Red Scare: A Study in National Hysteria, 1919–1920* (Minneapolis: 1955), both helpful on the ideological impact of the Revolution in the United States; Linda Killen, *The Russian Bureau: A Case Study in Wilsonian Diplomacy* (Lexington: 1983), on the role of a special wartime agency established to provide economic assistance to Russia; Lloyd C. Gardner, *Safe for Democracy: The Anglo-American Response to Revolution, 1913–1921* (New York: 1984), on the coincidence of Wilson's and Lloyd George's policies; and Frederick S. Calhoun, *Power and Principle: Armed Intervention in Wilsonian Foreign Policy* (Kent, Ohio: 1986), on the Wilson administration's overall attitude toward intervention.

Soviet-American relations during the years of nonrecognition have been surprisingly well covered. Two persuasive and methodologically sophisticated treatments are Peter G. Filene, *Americans and the Soviet Experiment: 1917–1933* (Cambridge, Massachusetts: 1967), and Joan Hoff Wilson, *Ideology and Economics: United States Relations with the Soviet Union, 1918–1933* (Columbia, Missouri: 1974). Frederick L. Schuman, *American Policy toward Russia Since 1917* (New York: 1928), is an early but still useful account, while Edward M. Bennett, *Recognition of Russia: An American Foreign Policy Dilemma* (Waltham, Massachusetts: 1970), covers the period from the perspective of the recognition issue.

Valuable treatments of particular topics include: Daniel M. Smith, *Aftermath of War: Bainbridge Colby and Wilsonian Diplomacy, 1920–1921* (Philadelphia: 1970); Benjamin M. Weissman, *Herbert Hoover and Famine Relief to Soviet Russia, 1921–1923* (Stanford: 1974); Theodore Draper, *American Communism and Soviet Russia: The Formative Years* (New York: 1960); Floyd J. Fithian, "Soviet-American Economic Relations, 1918–1933: American Business in Russia during the Period of Non-Recognition" (Ph.D. Dissertation, University of Nebraska, 1964); Anthony C. Sutton, *Western Technology and Soviet Economic Development, 1917 to 1930* (Stanford: 1968); Meno Lovenstein, *American Opinion of Soviet Russia* (Washington: 1941); Sylvia R. Margulies, *The Pilgrimage to Russia: The Soviet Union and the Treatment of Foreigners, 1924–1937* (Madison: 1968); James K. Libbey, *Alexander Gumberg and Soviet-American Relations, 1917–1933* (Lexington: 1977); and, on the reporting of American journalists in the Soviet Union, Whitman Bassow, *The Moscow Correspondents: Reporting on Russia from the Revolution to Glasnost* (New York: 1988).

On the decision to recognize the Soviet Union, in addition to works on the subject already mentioned, see Robert Paul Browder, *The Origins of Soviet-American Diplomacy* (Princeton: 1953), and Donald G. Bishop, *The Roosevelt-Litvinov Agreements: The American View* (Syracuse: 1965), which concentrates on implementation of the recognition agreement. Soviet-American relations during the 1930s are now well-covered in Thomas R. Maddux, *Years of Estrangement: American Relations with the Soviet Union, 1933–1941* (Tallahassee: 1981), and Edward M. Bennett, *Franklin D. Roosevelt and the Search for Security: American-Soviet Relations, 1933–1939* (Wilmington: 1985). See also Orville H. Bullitt, ed., *For the President: Personal and Secret: Correspondence between Franklin D. Roosevelt and William C. Bullitt* (Boston: 1972), and George W. Baer, ed., *A Question of Trust: The Origins of U.S.–Soviet Diplomatic Relations: The Memoirs of Loy W. Henderson* (Stanford: 1986), both of which should be balanced against the breathless and deliberately selective account of Bullitt's successor as ambassador to the Soviet Union, Joseph E. Davies, *Mission to Moscow* (New York: 1941). Jonathan Haslam, *Soviet Foreign Policy, 1930–33: The Impact of the Depression* (New York: 1983), and *The Soviet Union and the Struggle for Collective Security in Europe, 1933–39* (New York: 1984), provide good background on Soviet foreign policy, as does Jiri Hochman, *The Soviet Union and the Failure of Collective Security, 1934–1938* (Ithaca: 1984).

On the series of events leading up to World War II, the most comprehensive account is still William L. Langer and S. Everett Gleason, *The Challenge to Isolation: The World Crisis of 1937–1940 and American Foreign Policy* (New York: 1952), and *The Undeclared War, 1940–1941* (New York: 1953), but these volumes should be supplemented with Robert Dallek, *Franklin D. Roosevelt and American Foreign Policy, 1932–1945* (New York: 1979), Wayne S. Cole, *Roosevelt and the Isolationists, 1932–45* (Lincoln, Nebraska: 1983), Waldo Heinrichs, *Threshold of War: Franklin D. Roosevelt and American Entry into World War II* (New York: 1988), Donald Cameron Watt, *How War Came: The Immediate Origins of the Second World War, 1938–1939* (New York: 1989) and, for a critical view of Roosevelt's policies, Frederick W. Marks III, *Wind over Sand: The Diplomacy of Franklin Roosevelt* (Athens, Georgia: 1988). Pavel Sevostyanov, *Before the Nazi Invasion: Soviet Diplomacy in September 1939–June 1941*, translated by David Skirvsky (Moscow: 1984), provides a Soviet perspective on the period of collaboration between Hitler and Stalin; see also, for a German view, Franz Knipping, *Die Amerikanische Russland-politik in der Zeit des Hitler-Stalin-Pakts, 1939–1941* (Tübingen: 1974). The Russo-Finnish War is covered in Andrew J. Schwartz, *American and the Russo-Finnish War* (Washington: 1960), and Robert Sobel, *The Origins of Interventionism: The United States and the Russo-Finnish War* (New York: 1960). On Lend-Lease, the definitive work is still Raymond H. Dawson's excellent *The Decision to Aid Russia: 1941* (Chapel Hill: 1959).

For World War II, in addition to the studies of Roosevelt's diplomacy cited above, see William H. McNeill, *America, Britain and Russia: Their Cooperation and Conflict, 1941–1946* (New York: 1953), which remains, despite its age, an extraordinarily perceptive account. Herbert Feis, *Churchill, Roosevelt, Stalin: The War They Waged and the Peace They Sought* (Princeton: 1957), is long on detail, short on analysis. Two briefer but perceptive surveys are Gaddis Smith, *American Diplomacy During the Second World War, 1941–1945*, Second Edition (New York: 1985), and William L. Neumann, *After Victory: Churchill, Roosevelt, Stalin and the Making of the Peace* (New York: 1965). My own book, *The United States and the Origins of the Cold War, 1941–1947* (New York: 1972), examines tensions within the wartime alliance and the events that led to its breakup. For a relentlessly New Left analysis, see Gabriel Kolko, *The Politics of War: The World and United States Foreign Policy, 1943–1945* (New York: 1968).

Views of well-placed observers can be traced in William H. Standley and Arthur H. Ageton, *Admiral Ambassador to Russia* (Chicago: 1955), John R. Deane, *The Strange Alliance: The Story of Our Efforts at Wartime Cooperation with Russia* (New York: 1947), W. Averell Harriman and Elie Abel, *Special Envoy to Churchill and Stalin, 1941–1945* (New York: 1975), and Dwight William Tuttle, *Harry L. Hopkins and Anglo-American-Soviet Relations, 1941–1945* (New York: 1983). These accounts should be balanced with the extraordinary diary of Henry A. Wallace, accessible in John Morton Blum, ed., *The Price of Vision: The Diary of Henry A. Wallace, 1942–1946* (Boston: 1973).

Accounts of special topics include: Robert Beitzell, *The Uneasy Alliance: America, Britain and Russia, 1941–1943* (New York: 1972); Richard W. Steele, *The First Offensive, 1942: Roosevelt, Marshall and the Making of American Strategy* (Bloomington: 1973); and Mark A. Stoler, *The Politics of the Second Front: American Mil-*

*itary Planning in Diplomacy and Coalition Warfare, 1941–1943* (Westport, Connecticut: 1977), all of which address the second front question; Lynn Etheridge Davis, *The Cold War Begins: Soviet-American Conflict over Eastern Europe* (Princeton: 1974), Geir Lundestad, *The American Non-Policy Towards Eastern Europe, 1943–1947* (New York: 1975), Richard C. Lukas, *The Strange Allies: The United States and Poland, 1941–1945* (Knoxville: 1978), Thomas T. Hammond, ed., *Witnesses to the Origins of the Cold War* (Seattle, 1982), and Michael M. Boll, *Cold War in the Balkans: American Foreign Policy and the Emergence of Communist Bulgaria, 1943–1947* (Lexington: 1984), for Eastern Europe; George C. Herring, Jr., *Aid to Russia, 1941–1946: Strategy, Politics, the Origins of the Cold War* (New York: 1973), Robert Huhn Jones, *The Roads to Russia: United States Lend Lease to the Soviet Union* (Norman: 1969), and Leon Martel, *Lend-Lease, Loans, and the Coming of the Cold War: A Study of the Implementation of Foreign Policy* (Boulder, Colorado: 1979), for Lend-Lease; Bruce Kuklick, *American Policy and the Division of Germany* (Ithaca: 1972), and John H. Backer, *The Decision to Divide Germany: American Foreign Policy in Transition* (Durham, North Carolina: 1978), on Germany; Marc S. Gallicchio, *The Cold War Begins in Asia: American East Asian Policy and the Fall of the Japanese Empire* (New York: 1988), for East Asia; Ralph B. Levering, *American Opinion and the Russian Alliance, 1939–1945* (Chapel Hill: 1976), a sophisticated study of public opinion; and Lisle A. Rose, *Dubious Victory: The United States and the End of World War II* (Kent, Ohio: 1973), for the events of 1945.

The Teheran Conference is covered in Keith Eubank, *Summit at Teheran: The Untold Story* (New York: 1985), and Keith Sainsbury, *The Turning Point: Roosevelt, Stalin, Churchill, and Chiang Kai-shek: The Moscow, Cairo, and Teheran Conferences* (New York: 1985). For the Yalta conference, see Diane Clemens, *Yalta* (New York: 1970), and Russell D. Buhite, *Decisions at Yalta: An Appraisal of Summit Diplomacy* (Wilmington, Delaware: 1986). The Potsdam conference is discussed in Herbert Feis, *Between War and Peace: The Potsdam Conference* (Princeton: 1960), and Charles L. Mee, Jr., *Meeting at Potsdam* (New York: 1975), an oversimplified account. For a Soviet diplomat's account of the wartime conferences, see Valentin Berezhkov, *History in the Making: Memoirs of World War II Diplomacy* (Moscow: 1983).

The best overall account of Soviet diplomacy during World

War II is Vojtech Mastny, *Russia's Road to the Cold War: Diplomacy, Warfare, and the Politics of Communism, 1941–1945* (New York: 1979); but see also William Taubman, *Stalin's American Policy: From Entente to Detente to Cold War* (New York: 1982), and Steven Merritt Miner, *Between Churchill and Stalin: The Soviet Union, Great Britain, and the Origins of the Grand Alliance* (Chapel Hill: 1988), which is based in part on new Soviet documentary sources. Soviet atomic espionage is covered in Ronald Radosh and Joyce Milton, *The Rosenberg File: A Search for the Truth* (New York: 1983), and in Robert Chadwell Williams, *Klaus Fuchs, Atom Spy* (Cambridge, Massachusetts: 1987). For a Soviet historian's account, see Vilnis Sipols, *The Road to Great Victory: Soviet Diplomacy, 1941–1945* (Moscow: 1984).

Gar Alperovitz, *Atomic Diplomacy: Hiroshima and Potsdam*, expanded and updated edition (New York: 1985), is a misleading account of the decision to use the atomic bomb, first published in 1965; more reliable are Herbert Feis, *The Atomic Bomb and the End of World War II* (Princeton: 1966), Walter Smith Schoenberger, *Decision of Destiny* (Athens, Ohio, 1969), Martin J. Sherwin, *A World Destroyed: Hiroshima and the Origins of the Arms Race* (New York: 1987), Robert S. Messer, *The End of an Alliance: James F. Byrnes, Roosevelt, Truman, and the Origins of the Cold War* (Chapel Hill: 1982), Richard Rhodes, *The Making of the Atomic Bomb* (New York: 1986), and McGeorge Bundy, *Danger and Survival: Choices about the Bomb in the First Fifty Years* (New York: 1988). For the impact of the atomic bomb on American attitudes, see Paul Boyer, *By the Bomb's Early Light: American Thought and Culture at the Dawn of the Atomic Age* (New York: 1985), and Spencer Weart, *Nuclear Fear: A History of Ideas* (Cambridge, Massachusetts: 1988). John Newhouse, *War and Peace in the Nuclear Age* (New York: 1989), is written as an accompaniment to an excellent Public Broadcasting System television documentary series on the subject.

The most comprehensive survey of postwar Soviet-American relations is Walter LaFeber, *America, Russia and the Cold War: 1945–1984*, Fifth Edition (New York: 1985). Other accounts focusing on particular themes in that relationship are Richard J. Barnet, *The Giants: Russia and America* (New York: 1977); Thomas B. Larson, *Soviet-American Rivalry* (New York: 1978); Seweryn Bialer and Michael Mandelbaum, *The Global Rivals* (New York: 1988); Linda R. Killen, *The Soviet Union and the United States: A*

*New Look at the Cold War* (Boston: 1989); and Karl W. Ryavec, *United States–Soviet Relations* (New York: 1989). For a useful overall history of the Soviet-American strategic arms race, see Charles S. Morris, *Iron Destinies, Lost Opportunities: The Arms Race between the U.S.A. and the U.S.S.R., 1945–1987* (New York: 1988); also, for an overview of postwar arms control efforts, Colt D. Blacker, *Reluctant Warriors: The United States, the Soviet Union, and Arms Control* (New York: 1987). United States nuclear strategy is discussed in Lawrence Freedman, *The Evolution of Nuclear Strategy* (New York: 1981), Fred Kaplan, *The Wizards of Armageddon* (New York: 1983), and Gregg Herken, *Counsels of War* (New York: 1985); for the Soviet side, see David Holloway, *The Soviet Union and the Arms Race* (New Haven: 1983). American attitudes toward international communism are covered in Bernard S. Morris, *Communism, Revolution, and American Policy* (Durham: 1987); and Thomas G. Paterson, *Meeting the Communist Threat: Truman to Reagan* (New York: 1988). Joseph S. Nye, Jr., ed., *The Making of America's Soviet Policy* (New Haven: 1984), examines policy-making processes during the Cold War years. For a pioneering effort to address the social dimensions of the Cold War, see Elaine Tyler May, *Homeward Bound: American Families in the Cold War Era* (New York: 1988).

The debate over the origins of the Cold War has been both protracted and bitter. The most satisfactory introduction to it is Thomas G. Paterson, ed., *The Origins of the Cold War*, Second Edition (Lexington, Massachusetts: 1974). The orthodox point of view can be traced in W. W. Rostow, *The United States in the World Arena: An Essay in Recent History* (New York: 1960), Herbert Feis, *From Trust to Terror: The Onset of the Cold War, 1945–1950* (New York: 1970), John W. Spanier, *American Foreign Policy Since World War II*, Eleventh Revised Edition (Washington: 1988), John Wheeler-Bennett and Anthony Nicolls, *The Semblance of Peace: The Political Settlement After the Second World War* (New York: 1974), Lisle A. Rose, *After Yalta: America and the Origins of the Cold War* (New York: 1973); and in the most satisfactory orthodox accounts, Louis J. Halle, *The Cold War as History* (New York: 1967), and Adam B. Ulam, *The Rivals: American and Russia Since World War II* (New York: 1971).

Representative revisionist accounts include Lloyd C. Gardner, *Architects of Illusion: Men and Ideas in American Foreign Policy, 1941–1949* (Chicago: 1970), Thomas G. Paterson, *Soviet-*

*American Confrontation: Postwar Reconstruction and the Origins of the Cold War* (Baltimore: 1973), Stephen E. Ambrose, *Rise to Globalism: American Foreign Policy since 1938*, Fourth Revised Edition (New York: 1985), and, most thoroughly, Joyce and Gabriel Kolko, *The Limits of Power: The World and United States Foreign Policy, 1945–1954* (New York: 1972). The only revisionist account written with emphasis on Soviet policy is Alexander Werth, *Russia: The Power Years* (New York: 1971).

During the past decade and a half, the "post-revisionist" viewpoint—a synthesis of the strongest elements of orthodoxy and revisionism—has come to dominate the field of Cold War historiography. For examples, see: Daniel Yergin, *Shattered Peace: The Origins of the Cold War and the National Security State* (Boston: 1977); Thomas G. Paterson: *On Every Front: The Making of the Cold War* (New York: 1979); Bruce R. Kuniholm, *The Origins of the Cold War in the Near East: Great Power Conflict and Diplomacy in Iran, Turkey, and Greece* (Princeton: 1980); Geir Lundestad, *America, Scandinavia, and the Cold War, 1945–1949* (New York: (1980); Robert J. Pollard, *Economic Security and the Origins of the Cold War, 1945–1950* (New York: 1985); John Lewis Gaddis, *The Long Peace: Inquiries into the History of the Cold War* (New York: 1987); and my book on the origins of the Cold War, cited above. Several recent studies have given particular weight to the role of British policy in the coming of the Cold War, among them: Terry H. Anderson, *The United States, Great Britain, and the Cold War, 1944–1947* (Columbia, Missouri: 1981); Robert A. Hathaway, *Ambiguous Partnership: Britain and America, 1944–1947* (New York: 1981); Alan Bullock, *Ernest Bevin: Foreign Secretary* (New York: 1983); Fraser J. Harbutt, *The Iron Curtain: Churchill, America, and the Origins of the Cold War* (New York: 1986); Hugh Thomas, *Armed Truce: The Beginnings of the Cold War, 1945–46* (London: 1986); Robin Edmonds, *Setting the Mould: The United States and Britain, 1945–1950* (Oxford: 1986); and James L. Gormly, *The Collapse of the Grand Alliance, 1945–1948* (Baton Rouge: 1987). Lawrence Aronsen and Martin Kitchen, *The Origins of the Cold War in Comparative Perspective: American, British and Canadian Relations with the Soviet Union, 1941–1948* (New York: 1988) incorporates a Canadian viewpoint as well.

The evolution of containment can be traced in John Lewis Gaddis, *Strategies of Containment: A Critical Appraisal of Postwar*

*American National Security Policy* (New York: 1982), and Seyom Brown, *The Faces of Power: Constancy and Change in United States Foreign Policy from Truman to Reagan* (New York: 1983). See also Thomas H. Etzold and John Lewis Gaddis, eds., *Containment: Documents on American Policy and Strategy, 1945–1950* (New York: 1978). Deborah Welch Larson, *Origins of Containment: A Psychological Explanation* (Princeton: 1985), provides a new interpretation based on psychological perspectives. Military and strategic issues are covered in Warner R. Schilling, Paul Y. Hammond, and Glenn H. Snyder, *Strategy, Politics and Defense Budgets* (New York: 1962), Harry R. Borowski, *A Hollow Threat: Strategic Air Power and Containment before Korea* (Westport, Connecticut: 1982), Gregg Herken, *The Winning Weapon: The Atomic Bomb in the Cold War, 1945–1950* (New York: 1980), and a series of important articles by David Alan Rosenberg, cited in the text.

Joseph M. Jones, *The Fifteen Weeks (February 21–June 5, 1947)* (New York: 1955), is still valuable for the origins of the Truman Doctrine and the Marshall Plan; but more recent treatments include Howard Jones, *"A New Kind of War": America's Global Strategy and the Truman Doctrine in Greece* (New York: 1989); Alan S. Milward, *The Reconstruction of Western Europe, 1945–51* (Berkeley: 1984); and Michael J. Hogan, *The Marshall Plan: America, Britain, and the Reconstruction of Western Europe, 1947–1952* (Cambridge: 1987). The Berlin crisis is covered in Avl Shlaim, *The United States and the Berlin Blockade, 1948–1949: A Study in Crisis Decision-Making* (Berkeley: 1983). For the origins of NATO, see Timothy P. Ireland, *Creating the Entangling Alliance: The Origins of the North Atlantic Treaty Organization* (Westport, Connecticut: 1981), Lawrence S. Kaplan, *The United States and NATO: The Formative Years* (Lexington: 1984), and Olav Riste, ed., *Western Security: The Formative Years: European and Atlantic Defence, 1947–1953* (Oslo: 1985). On the issue of negotiations with the Soviet Union, see Coral Bell, *Negotiation from Strength: A Study in the Politics of Power* (New York: 1963).

For Soviet policy during the early Cold War years, see, in addition to books by Mastny, Taubman, and Holloway, cited above: Marshall Shulman, *Stalin's Foreign Policy Reappraised* (Cambridge, Massachusetts: 1963); Roy A. Medvedev, *Let History Judge: The Origins and Consequences of Stalinism*, Revised and Expanded Edition, edited and translated by George Shriver (New York: 1989); Adam B. Ulam, *Stalin: The Man and His Era*

(New York: 1973); William O. McCagg, Jr., *Stalin Embattled: 1943–1948* (Detroit: 1978); Werner G. Hahn, *Postwar Soviet Politics: The Fall of Zhdanov and the Defeat of Moderation, 1946–53* (Ithaca: 1982); and Hannes Adomeit, *Soviet Risk-Taking and Crisis Behavior: A Theoretical and Empirical Analysis* (London: 1982).

East Asian issues are covered in: Russell D. Buhite, *Soviet-American Relations in Asia, 1945–1954* (Norman: 1981); William Whitney Stueck, Jr., *The Road to Confrontation: American Policy toward China and Korea, 1947–1950* (Chapel Hill: 1981); Michael Schaller, *The American Occupation of Japan: The Origins of the Cold War in Asia* (New York: 1985); Charles M. Dobbs, *The Unwanted Symbol: American Foreign Policy, the Cold War, and Korea, 1945–1950* (Kent, Ohio: 1981); and James Irving Matray, *The Reluctant Crusade: American Foreign Policy in Korea, 1941–1950* (Honolulu: 1950). The best overall account of the Korean War from the American side is now Burton I. Kaufman, *The Korean War: Challenges in Crisis, Credibility, and Command* (New York: 1986); see also John W. Spanier, *The Truman-MacArthur Controversy and the Korean War* (New York: 1965), and Rosemary Foot, *The Wrong War: American Policy and the Dimensions of the Korean Conflict, 1950–1953* (Ithaca: 1985). Robert R. Simmons, *The Strained Alliance: Peking, Pyongyang, Moscow and the Politics of the Korean Civil War* (New York: 1975), provides the best explanation we have of the war's origins.

For internal security issues and McCarthyism, see, in addition to works by Williams, Radosh, and Milton, cited above: Alan D. Harper, *The Politics of Loyalty: The White House and the Communist Issue, 1946–1952* (Westport, Connecticut: 1969); Allen Weinstein, *Perjury: The Hiss-Chambers Case* (New York: 1978); Robert G. Lamphere, *The FBI-KGB War: A Special Agent's Story* (New York: 1986); Earl Latham, *The Communist Controversy in Washington* (Cambridge, Massachusetts: 1966); Richard M. Fried, *Men Against McCarthy* (New York: 1976); Thomas C. Reeves, *The Life and Times of Joe McCarthy: A Biography* (New York: 1982); David M. Oshinsky, *A Conspiracy So Immense: the World of Joe McCarthy* (New York: 1983); and, on the role of British spies for the Soviet Union, Anthony Glees, *The Secrets of the Service: A Story of Soviet Subversion of Western Intelligence* (New York: 1987).

Important memoirs and biographies from the period include: Harry S. Truman, *Memoirs* (Garden City, New York: 1955,

1956), 2 volumes; Robert J. Donovan, *Conflict and Crisis: The Presidency of Harry S. Truman, 1945–1948* (New York: 1977) and *Tumultuous Years: The Presidency of Harry S. Truman, 1949–1953* (New York: 1982); Walter Millis, ed., *The Forrestal Diaries* (New York: 1951); Walter Bedell Smith, *My Three Years in Moscow* (Philadelphia: 1950); Forrest C. Pogue, *George C. Marshall: Statesman, 1945–1959* (New York: 1987); Gaddis Smith, *Dean Acheson* (New York: 1972); David S. McLellan, *Dean Acheson: The State Department Years* (New York: 1976); Ronald W. Pruessen, *John Foster Dulles: The Road to Power* (New York: 1982); J. Samuel Walker, *Henry A. Wallace and American Foreign Policy* (New York: 1976); T. Michael Ruddy, *The Cautious Diplomat: Charles E. Bohlen and the Soviet Union, 1929–1969* (Kent, Ohio: 1986); David Mayers, *George Kennan and the Dilemmas of US Foreign Policy* (New York: 1988); Anders Stephanson, *Kennan and the Art of Foreign Policy* (Cambridge, Massachusetts: 1989); and a remarkable collective biography, Walter Isaacson and Evan Thomas, *The Wise Men: Six Friends and the World They Made: Acheson, Bohlen, Harriman, Kennan, Lovett, McCloy* (New York: 1986).

For the Eisenhower period, the most useful general account is Stephen E. Ambrose, *Eisenhower: The President* (New York: 1984), but see also: Fred I. Greenstein, *The Hidden-Hand Presidency: Eisenhower as Leader* (New York: 1982); Herbert Parmet, *Eisenhower and the American Crusades* (New York: 1972); Peter Lyons, *Eisenhower: Portrait of the Hero* (Boston: 1974); Blanche Wiesen Cook, *The Declassified Eisenhower: A Divided Legacy of Peace and Political Warfare* (New York: 1981); Stephen E. Ambrose, *Nixon: The Education of a Politician, 1913–1962* (New York: 1987); Townsend Hoopes, *The Devil and John Foster Dulles* (Boston: 1973); Michael A. Guhin, *John Foster Dulles: A Statesman and His Time* (New York: 1972); Charles C. Alexander, *Holding the Line: The Eisenhower Era, 1952–61* (Bloomington: 1975); and H. W. Brands, Jr., *Cold Warriors: Eisenhower's Generation and American Foreign Policy* (New York: 1988). For Eisenhower's own views, see Dwight D. Eisenhower, *The White House Years* (Garden City, New York: 1963, 1965), 2 volumes; and Robert H. Ferrell, ed., *The Eisenhower Diaries* (New York: 1981). Shifting historiography on the Eisenhower era can be traced in Richard A. Melanson and David Mayers, eds., *Reevaluating Eisenhower: American Foreign Policy in the Fifties* (Urbana: 1987), and Richard

H. Immerman, ed., *John Foster Dulles and the Diplomacy of the Cold War* (Princeton: 1989).

Nuclear strategy during the Eisenhower years is most fully covered in Bundy, *Danger and Survival*, cited above, but see also: Richard K. Betts, *Nuclear Blackmail and Nuclear Balance* (Washington: 1987); Alexander George and Richard L. Smoke, *Deterrence in American Foreign Policy: Theory and Practice* (New York: 1974); Robert A. Divine, *Blowing on the Wind: The Nuclear Test Ban Debate, 1954–1960* (New York: 1978); and, for Sputnik and the "missile gap" controversy, Richard A. Aliano, *American Defense Policy from Eisenhower to Kennedy* (Athens, Ohio: 1975); Paul B. Stares, *The Militarization of Space: U.S. Policy, 1945–1984* (Ithaca: 1985); and Walter A. McDougall, *The Heavens and the Earth: A Political History of the Space Age* (New York: 1985). John Prados, *The Soviet Estimate: U.S. Intelligence Analysis and Russian Military Strength* (New York: 1982), and Lawrence Freedman, *U.S. Intelligence and the Soviet Strategic Threat*, Second Edition (Princeton: 1986), deal with the general problem of estimating Soviet military capabilities.

For regional issues during the Eisenhower years, see: Audrey Keith Cronin, *Great Power Politics and the Struggle over Austria, 1945–1955* (Ithaca: 1986); Jack M. Schick, *The Berlin Crisis, 1958–1962* (Philadelphia: 1971); Ronald H. Spector, *Advice and Support: The Early Years of the United States Army in Vietnam* (New York: 1985); Melanie Billings-Yun, *Decision against War: Eisenhower and Dien Bien Phu, 1954* (New York: 1988); David Mayers, *Cracking the Monolith: U.S. Policy against the Sino-Soviet Alliance, 1949–1955* (Baton Rouge: 1986); Donald Neff, *Warriors at Suez: Eisenhower Takes America into the Middle East* (New York: 1981); and Stephen G. Rabe, *Eisenhower and Latin America: The Foreign Policy of Anticommunism* (Chapel Hill: 1988).

The role of the Central Intelligence Agency and covert operations are covered in John Ranelagh, *The Agency: The Rise and Decline of the CIA* (New York: 1986), Rhodri Jeffreys-Jones, *The CIA and American Democracy* (New Haven: 1989), Kuross A. Samii, *Involvement by Invitation: American Strategies of Containment in Iran* (University Park, Pennsylvania: 1987), Richard H. Immerman, *The CIA in Guatemala: The Foreign Policy of Intervention* (Austin: 1982); Robin W. Winks, *Cloak and Gown: Scholars in the Secret War, 1939–1961* (New York: 1987); and, on the development and use of the U-2, W. W. Rostow, *Open Skies: Eisenhower's Proposal of July 21, 1955* (Austin: 1982), William E. Burrows, *Deep Black: Space Espionage and National Security* (New York: 1986), and Michael R. Beschloss, *Mayday: Eisenhower, Khrushchev, and the U-2 Affair* (New York: 1986).

The most important source on Soviet foreign policy during this period, now that its authenticity has been confirmed, is Nikita S. Khrushchev, *Khrushchev Remembers* (Boston: 1970), and *Khrushchev Remembers: The Last Testament* (Boston: 1974), translated and edited by Strobe Talbott, an account as revealing about decision-making within the Soviet Union as about its colorful author. See also Roy Medvedev, *Khrushchev,* translated by Brian Pearce (Garden City, New York: 1983), and the recently-published but not very revealing memoirs of Andrei Gromyko, *Pamiatnoe* (Moscow: 1988). Scholarly studies of importance include: Thomas W. Wolfe, *Soviet Power and Europe: 1945–1970* (Baltimore: 1970), a book of broader scope than its title indicates; Arnold L. Horelick and Myron C. Rush, *Strategic Power and Soviet Foreign Policy* (Chicago: 1966), a cogent account of the Soviet practice of "strategic deception"; Michel Tatu, *Power in the Kremlin: From Khrushchev to Kosygin* (New York: 1969), good on Khrushchev's later years in power; and William Zimmermann, *Soviet Perspectives on International Relations, 1956–1967* (Princeton: 1969), a study of the changing view of international relations within the Soviet Union. A somewhat comparable study from the American side is William Welch, *American Images of Soviet Foreign Policy* (New Haven: 1970).

The Cuban missile crisis has generated a vast body of literature, portions of which can be sampled in Robert A. Divine, ed., *The Cuban Missile Crisis*, Second Edition (New York: 1988). The best account of the origins of the crisis is Herbert S. Dinerstein, *The Making of a Missile Crisis: October, 1962* (Baltimore: 1976). Graham T. Allison, *Essence of Decision: Explaining the Cuban Missile Crisis* (Boston: 1971), is important for its methodological insights into the nature of bureaucracies, but outdated now as an account of the crisis itself. A popular but sound account is Elie Abel, *The Missile Crisis* (New York: 1966). A strong defense of Kennedy's handling of the crisis can be found in Theodore C. Sorensen, *Kennedy* (New York: 1965); and in Robert F. Kennedy, *Thirteen Days: A Memoir of the Cuban Missile Crisis* (New York: 1969). Less favorable assessments include

Richard J. Walton, *Cold War and Counterrevolution: The Foreign Policy of John F. Kennedy* (New York: 1972), Louise FitzSimons, *The Kennedy Doctrine* (New York: 1972), and Bruce Miroff, *Pragmatic Illusions: The Presidential Politics of John F. Kennedy* (New York: 1976). There is important new information on the crisis in Bundy, *Danger and Survival*, cited above, Raymond Garthoff, *Reflections on the Cuban Missile Crisis* (Washington: 1987), and James G. Blight and David A. Welch, *On the Brink: Americans and Soviets Reexamine the Missile Crisis* (New York: 1989).

Studies of other aspects of Soviet-American relations during the Kennedy-Johnson years are still surprisingly few, but see Norman Gelb, *The Berlin Wall: Kennedy, Khrushchev, and a Showdown in the Heart of Europe* (New York: 1986); two volumes by Glenn T. Seaborg and Benjamin S. Loeb, *Kennedy, Khrushchev, and the Test Ban* (Berkeley: 1981) and *Stemming the Tide: Arms Control and the Johnson Years* (Berkeley: 1987); and, for the perspective of individual statesmen, Thomas J. Schoenbaum, *Waging Peace and War: Dean Rusk in the Truman, Kennedy and Johnson Years* (New York: 1988); Lyndon Baines Johnson, *The Vantage Point: Perspectives on the Presidency, 1963–1968* (New York: 1971); W. W. Rostow, *The Diffusion of Power: An Essay in Recent History* (New York: 1972). Almost nothing has been written on the impact of the Vietnam war on Soviet-American relations, but an important study of the war's domestic political effect and its foreign policy implications is Ole R. Holsti and James N. Rosenau, *American Leadership in World Affairs: Vietnam and the Breakdown of Consensus* (Boston: 1984). Soviet policy during this period is best traced in Robin Edmonds, *Soviet Foreign Policy, 1962–1973: The Paradox of Super Power* (London: 1975); but see also W. W. Kulski, *The Soviet Union in World Affairs: A Documented Analysis, 1964–1972* (Syracuse, 1973).

The Nixon-Ford years are better covered. The best place to start is Raymond Garthoff's massive *Detente and Confrontation: American-Soviet Relations from Nixon to Reagan* (Washington: 1985). Henry Kissinger's memoirs, *White House Years* (Boston: 1979) and *Years of Upheaval* (Boston: 1982), are detailed and important; less detailed but very revealing is Richard M. Nixon, *RN: The Memoirs of Richard Nixon* (New York: 1978). William G. Hyland's *Mortal Rivals: Understanding the Pattern of Soviet-American Conflict* (New York: 1987), provides the perspective of a key Kissinger adviser during this period. Gerald R. Ford, *A*

*Time to Heal: The Autobiography of Gerald R. Ford* (New York: 1979), is still one of the few accounts available for the Ford administration. Alexander L. George, Philip J. Farley, and Alexander Dallin, eds., *U.S.–Soviet Security Cooperation: Achievements, Failures, Lessons* (New York: 1988), contains a series of valuable case studies on Soviet-American relations, drawn chiefly from the 1970s; see also, on the Nixon Doctrine, Robert S. Litwak, *Detente and the Nixon Doctrine: American Foreign Policy and the Pursuit of Stability, 1969–1976* (Cambridge: 1984).

Carter administration policies toward the Soviet Union are succinctly analyzed in Gaddis Smith, *Morality, Reason and Power: American Diplomacy in the Carter Years* (New York: 1986). Carter's own memoirs, *Keeping Faith: Memoirs of a President* (New York: 1982), are disappointing; more useful are Zbigniew Brzezinski, *Power and Principle: Memoirs of the National Security Adviser, 1977–1981* (New York: 1983), and Cyrus Vance, *Hard Choices: Critical Years in America's Foreign Policy* (New York: 1983). Other significant memoirs covering shorter periods include Hamilton Jordan, *Crisis: The Last Year of the Carter Presidency* (New York: 1982), and Gary Sick, *All Fall Down: America's Tragic Encounter with Iran* (New York: 1985).

Issues of trade and human rights are discussed in Philip J. Funigiello, *American-Soviet Trade in the Cold War* (Chapel Hill: 1988), Joshua Muravchik, *The Uncertain Crusade: Jimmy Carter and the Dilemmas of Human Rights* (Lanham, Maryland: 1986), A. Glenn Mower, Jr., *Human Rights and American Foreign Policy: The Carter and Reagan Experiences* (New York: 1987), and Jerel A. Rosati, *The Carter Administration's Quest for Global Community: Beliefs and Their Impact on Behavior* (Columbia, South Carolina: 1987). For other special topics, see: William Quandt, *Camp David: Politics and Peacemaking* (Washington: 1986); J. Michael Hogan, *The Panama Canal in American Politics: Domestic Advocacy and the Evolution of Policy* (Carbondale, Illinois: 1986); Jerry W. Sanders, *Peddlers of Crisis: The Committee on the Present Danger and Containment* (Boston: 1983); David D. Newsome, *The Soviet Combat Brigade in Cuba: A Study in Political Diplomacy* (Bloomington: 1987); and Thomas T. Hammond, *Red Flag over Afghanistan: The Communist Coup, the Soviet Invasion, and the Consequences* (Boulder: 1984).

It is, of course, too early for there to be many studies of Reagan administration foreign policy, but there is interesting information in Richard A. Melanson, ed., *Neither Cold War nor Detente? Soviet-American Relations in the 1980s* (Charlottesville: 1982), Fred I. Greenstein, ed., *The Reagan Presidency: An Early Assessment* (Baltimore: 1983), and Kenneth A. Oye, Robert J. Lieber and Donald Rothchild, eds., *Eagle Resurgent? The Reagan Era in American Foreign Policy* (Boston: 1987). Relevant memoirs include Alexander M. Haig, Jr., *Caveat: Realism, Reagan, and Foreign Policy* (New York: 1984), Donald T. Regan, *For the Record: From Wall Street to Washington* (New York: 1988), and Martin Anderson, *Revolution* (New York: 1988); see also, on Reagan himself, Garry Wills, *Reagan's America: Innocents at Home* (Garden City, New York: 1987).

For the strategic arms race and arms control efforts in the early 1970s, see Harland B. Moulton, *From Superiority to Parity: The United States and the Strategic Arms Race, 1961–1971* (Westport, Connecticut: 1973), John Newhouse, *Cold Dawn: The Story of SALT* (New York: 1973), Gerard Smith, *Doubletalk: The Story of SALT I* (New York: 1980). Strobe Talbott has written a valuable series of books that chronicle the process of arms control from the mid-1970s to the present. They include *Endgame: The Inside Story of Salt II* (New York: 1979), *Deadly Gambits: The Reagan Administration and the Stalemate in Nuclear Arms Control* (New York: 1984), and *The Master of the Game: Paul Nitze and the Nuclear Peace* (New York: 1988). Issues of strategic defense are covered in Ernest J. Yanarella, *The Missile Defense Controversy: Strategy, Technology, and Politics, 1955–1972* (Lexington: 1977) and, for the revival of this issue during the Reagan administration, Franklin A. Long, Donald Hafner and Jeffrey Boutwell, eds., *Weapons in Space* (New York: 1986), and Alvin M. Weinberg and Jack N. Barkenbus, eds., *Strategic Defenses and Arms Control* (New York: 1988). For two contradictory assessments of the role of nuclear weapons in maintaining the postwar international system, see Michael Mandelbaum, *The Nuclear Revolution: International Politics Before and After Hiroshima* (Cambridge: 1981), and John Mueller, *Retreat from Doomsday: The Obsolescence of Major War* (New York: 1989).

Soviet foreign policy during the late 1970s and early 1980s can be traced in: Adam B. Ulam, *Dangerous Relations: The Soviet Union in World Politics, 1970–1982* (New York: 1983); Robert F. Byrnes, ed., *After Brezhnev: The Sources of Soviet Conduct in the 1980s* (Bloomington: 1983); Seweryn Bialer, *The Soviet Paradox:*

*External Expansion, Internal Decline* (New York: 1986); and Jerry F. Hough, *The Struggle for the Third World: Soviet Debates and American Options* (Washington: 1986). The Korean airliner incident is best covered in Alexander Dallin, *Black Box: KAL 007 and the Superpowers* (Berkeley: 1985), and Seymour Hersch, *"The Target Is Destroyed": What Really Happened to Flight 007 and What America Knew about It* (New York: 1987).

The best place to start in evaluating the Gorbachev reforms is Gorbachev's own book, *Perestroika: New Thinking for Our Country and the World* (New York: 1987). Also valuable are Seweryn Bialer and Michael Mandelbaum, eds., *Gorbachev's Russia and American Foreign Policy* (Boulder: 1988); and Seweryn Bialer, ed., *Politics, Society, and Nationality inside Gorbachev's Russia* (Boulder: 1989). William and Jane Taubman, *Moscow Spring* (New York: 1989), provides a vivid personal account of changes taking place inside the Soviet Union, while Zbigniew Brzezinski, *The Grand Failure: The Birth and Death of Communism in the Twentieth Century* (New York: 1989), argues that these changes are part of a larger worldwide pattern that reflects the growing irrelevance of traditional Marxism-Leninism to contemporary and future problems.

A series of recent books have sought to place the history of postwar Soviet-American relations within a larger international systemic framework. They include, in addition to my own *The Long Peace,* cited above: Kenneth N. Waltz, *Theory of International Politics* (New York: 1979); Robert Gilpin, *War and Change in World Politics* (Cambridge: 1981); Robert Axelrod, *The Evolution of Cooperation* (New York: 1984); Richard Rosecrance, *The Rise of the Trading State: Commerce and Conquest in the Modern World* (New York: 1986); and Paul Kennedy, *The Rise and Fall of the Great Powers: Economic Change and Military Conflict from 1500 to 2000* (New York: 1987).

# Index